COMPENDIUM OF LANDSHELLS

BOOKS BY R. TUCKER ABBOTT

Seashells of the World (Golden Guide, 1962 and 1986)
American Seashells (Van Nostrand Reinhold, 1954 and 1974)
Seashells of North America (Golden Press, 1968 and 1986)
Kingdom of the Seashell (Crown Publ. Co., 1972)
The Shell (with Hugh and Marguerite Stix) (Harry Abrams, Co., 1968)
How to Know the American Marine Shells (New World Library, 1961)
Introducing Sea Shells (Van Nostrand, 1955)
Standard Catalog of Shells (with R.J.L. Wagner) (American Malacologists, Inc., 1978)
Seashells (Bantam Books, 1978)
Register of American Malacologists (editor, American Malacologists, Inc., 1987)
The Best of the Nautilus (editor, American Malacologists, Inc., 1976)
Caribbean Seashells (with G.L. Warmke) (Dover Pub., 1976)
Compendium of Seashells (with S. Peter Dance) (American Malacologists, Inc., 1986)
Collectible Florida Shells (American Malacologists, Inc., 1984)

Photos of Cuban *Polymita picta* (Born, 1778) by José R. Martinez F.

Compendium
of Landshells

A Color Guide to More than 2,000 of the World's Terrestrial Shells

by
R. Tucker Abbott, Ph. D.

AMERICAN MALACOLOGISTS, INC.
Melbourne, Florida

Library of Congress Catalog Card Number : 89-84434

Designed by Cecelia and R. Tucker Abbott

Produced by Madison Publishing Associates, Inc., New York

Published by
American Malacologists, Inc.
Melbourne, FL and Burlington, MA
(P.O. Box 1192, Burlington, MA 01803)

ISBN 0-915826-23-2

FIRST EDITION

Printed and bound in Hong Kong by VCM Graphics

CONTENTS

*This book is dedicated
to my collecting companion,
my wife, Cecelia*

Cuban Tree Snails abound on low bushes in the eastern provinces of Cuba.

PREFACE

Although marine mollusks have been capturing the attention and admiration of the general public for many years, the equally diverse and fascinating world of air-breathing, terrestrial shells has largely been ignored by amateur naturalists and private shell collectors. There are over 30,000 species of landshells, representing about 85 families. There is scarcely a place on the dry surface of the world, outside of the polar regions, where one cannot find at least a few examples of land snails.

Since Aristotle's time and the days of the ancient Romans, land mollusks have been a focus of man's attention. They have served as food, are major agricultural pests, are hosts to parasitic diseases of humans and domestic animals, offer clues in the studies of archaeology, evolution and geologic history, and often have been the treasured objects of shell collectors.

Their lack of popularity among today's amateur conchologists is perhaps due to the absence of a modern, understandable guide to the large and more colorful species. It is also true that many smaller species cannot be identified without special internal anatomical studies. Yet, today, one third of the mollusk research literature deals with terrestrial snails. Today's more advanced research on the classification, ecology and evolution of mollusks deals with land, not marine, mollusks.

One of the purposes of this book is to awaken people to the wonders of our natural world and to encourage amateur conchologists to protect our disappearing land fauna from the inroads of pollution and habitat destruction. In fact, many as yet undescribed species will probably be driven to extinction before they can be discovered and described as new.

This book, with illustrations of about 2,000 species, is only a bridge to more complete and much more useful monographs and scholarly revisions. American collectors may turn to Henry A. Pilsbry's four-volume *Land Mollusca of North America* or to his monumental 28-volume *Manual of Conchology* (series 2) to identify the myriads of species not included here. Europeans have the excellent *Field Guide to the Land Snails of Britain and Northwest Europe* by Kerney and Cameron (1979) and its later improved German edition to assist them. Our bibliography, uniquely illustrated with examples of shells, contains 750 additional useful references, half of them arranged by families, the others by countries and states.

Some terrestrial ground snails, such as these small, emerald-green *Helicina* from the Island of Hispaniola, have a shelly operculum, and climb up into bushes.

WHO ARE THE LANDSHELLS?

Who has not heard of or perhaps even seen a garden snail, an edible "escargot" or a slug? They belong to the large gastropod class of mollusks found in all parts of the world and in many diverse habitats. Of the estimated 60,000 kinds of snails, about 25,000 live in the ocean, 5,000 in freshwater lakes and rivers, and the remaining 30,000 species on dry land.

The ancestors of the air-breathing terrestrial snails undoubtedly arose from families originally living in the ocean. Their invasion of the land resulted in two great, unrelated subclasses, one being the common, so-called pulmonate snails which have a lung for breathing air, four tentacles on the head, have no operculum or trapdoor, and possess a set of male and female sex organs in each individual. The smaller group known as the prosobranchs, arose from two marine stocks, the neritoids and littorinoid periwinkles and as a result lack a lung, have only two tentacles, possess a hard or soft opercular trapdoor, and usually have separate sexes.

This great division in the landshells is not unlike the similar subclasses in the marine shells—the operculated prosobranch families, such as the periwinkles, helmet shells and buccinid whelks—and the nonoperculate, opisthobranch families, such as the hermaphrodite nudibranchs, the Aplysiidae seahares and the Bullidae bubble shells.

Best known of the green tree snails is *Papuina (Papustyla) pulcherrima* Rensch, 1931. It is an abundant species living very high in the tall trees in certain parts of Manus Island, northeast of New Guinea. The 1-inch long shell was put on the U.S. endangered list, although only the destruction of their habitat is endangering their existence.

The major classification of the terrestrials may be summarized in the following catagories:

Phylum MOLLUSCA (mollusks)

Class GASTROPODA (snails, whelks)

Subclass PROSOBRANCHIA (gill-bearers)

Order Archaeogastropoda (helicinids)

Order Caenogastropoda
(pomatiasids; annularids; truncatellids)

Subclass PULMONATA (lung-bearers)

Order Archaeopulmonata
(ellobiids; melampids)

Order Basommatophora
(siphonariid limpets; freshwater pond snails)

Order Stylommatophora
(4-tentacled, pulmonate snails)
(most land snails)

Order Systellommatophora

(onchidiums and veronicellid slugs)
(not treated in this book)

Names - scientific and common

Below these major divisions there is a standard hierarchy of an arbitrary nature in which the phylogeny or "genealogy" of every species can be arranged. Here is an example (the author and date of naming follows the italized scientific Latin names of genera, subgenera and species):

Superfamily *Helicoidea* Rafinesque, 1815
(*Helicacea* or -*acea* ending used by some).

Family *Helicidae* Rafinesque, 1815
(-idae endings)

Subfamily *Helicinae* Rafinesque, 1815
(-inae endings)

Genus *Helix* Linnaeus, 1758

Subgenus *Helix* Linnaeus, 1758

species *pomatia* Linnaeus, 1758

A species may be defined as a series of populations having common genetic qualities which enable the individuals to interbreed and produce similar, viable offspring. Members of the species are usually isolated from other species geographically, physiologically, genetically or in behavioral patterns. Semi-isolated populations, having slight differences, are termed geographical races or subspecies.

A form or variety or *forma* is merely an individual variation, sometimes due to the environment or to a single gene. Examples are dwarfs, albinos, heavily ribbed shells, unique color patterns or sinistrally coiling specimens. Sometimes, outstanding or well-known forms are given scientific names, such as forma *rubra* (red form) or forma *alba* (white). Form names are not legally acceptable on the same level as species or subspecies (trivial) names, but they are useful in identifying and naming various color forms in, for instance, Florida tree snails.

For centuries common names have been used for the better known species, and recently they have served a purpose for agriculturists identifying garden pests and for beginning hobbyists. Although we have used these common names, and created many new ones, serious students and many beginners will find the scientific names more reliable and universally understood.

In our brief account of each illustrated species we sometimes have listed synonyms. These are names of an unnecessary nature that have been given to the same species. Space has not permitted us to list but one or two in each case although some common and particularly the spectacular and variable ones, may have as many as a dozen synonyms.

THE PROSOBRANCHS
How they live, grow and reproduce

Most prosobranch snails live in the ocean or in freshwater although several thousand species have adapted to a life on land. The aquatic ones have a row of short gills within the open-fronted mantle cavity. In the land species the gills are reduced or replaced by mantle tissue capable of absorbing oxygen.

Like most of the ocean-dwelling groups, the terrestrial prosobranchs bear a circular trapdoor or operculum on the top of the rear part of the fleshy foot. When the snail withdraws into its shell the operculum seals the aperture of the shell, thus keeping out beetles and ants, as well as preventing the loss of vital internal moisture. The helicinid land snails have a hard, calcareous operculum; the cyclophorids have a horny, flexible, multi-spiral operculum similar to those found in the marine trochids; and the pomatiasid snails have a horny and calcareous, paucispiral operculum not unlike those found in the littorinid periwinkles.

The shelly trapdoor, or operculum, of the prosobranch land shells is similar to those of their marine cousins. The Beautiful Annularid from Jamaica has a distinct pattern to its operculum. Photo: Richard Goldberg.

Land prosobranchs differ from garden snails in having only one set of tentacles with the eyes at the bases. An operculum, shown here on top of the rear of the foot, is absent in most pulmonate snails. (*Tudora humphreysiana* (Pfeiffer, 1846)) from Jamaica. Photo: Richard Goldberg.

Feeding and the Radular Teeth

The eating organ, or odontophore, consists of microscopic teeth, or radulae, attached to a tongue-like membrane. The teeth rasp or lick off particles of food. In the prosobranchs the central teeth are few in number and in many families there may be only seven teeth in each of the 100-or-so rows (taenioglossate), although in the helicinids there are up to several dozen or more fine, marginal teeth (rhipidoglossate). This is in contrast to the pulmonate radulae of the helicid snails which may have 170 rows with about 160 teeth per row (27,000 teeth in one individual). In carnivorous pulmonates the teeth maybe reduced to a simple awl-shape without a cutting edge. In herbivorous pulmonates there is a single large banana-shaped jaw in the roof of the mouth, a feature absent in the terrestrial prosobranchs.

There are almost as many kinds of food for snails as there are different families and genera of mollusks. Each group of gastropods specializes in its choice of menu. Most popular among the pulmonates are the leafy vegetables, the fungal-rich detritus of the forest floor and the tender roots of plants. The true tree snails avoid eating the protective leaves of the branches and concentrate on the lichen and fungal growths on the trunks and bark.

Some pulmonates are carnivorous, an outstanding example being the Rosy Glandina of southeast United States, a two-inch long, active ground snail that snaps up and devours other small snails. In New Zealand, the fragile-shelled paraphantids feed almost

The radular teeth, borne on a movable base within the snail's mouth, are microscopic and numerous in the prosobranchs, as seen in this set from the Brittle Snowflake Snail, *Meganipha*, from the Dominican Republic.
Photo: Fred G. Thompson.

The Giant African Snail can demolish a ripe papaya fruit overnight.

A week-old Provisor Zachrysia follow its inch-long parent. This Cuban pulmonate was introduced to Florida and the Bahamas. Photo: George Raeihle.

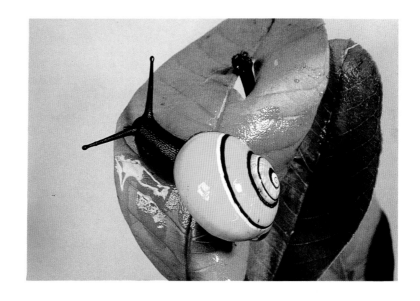

The common striped form of the Painted Polymita snail lives on low bushes in eastern Cuba. It is one of several color forms. Photo: José R. Martinez F.

The two-inch Florida Orthalicus is threatened by the deforestation of southern Florida and the keys. The gray mantle rim of flesh produces the shell.

Sexual differences are shown in the shells of some operculate proso-branchs. The male shell of the Cuban Royal Viana, on the right, shows a notch in the lip to accommodate the soft penis.

exclusively on large, black earthworms. The curious *Testacella* slug of Europe which carries a small shell at its posterior end is capable of following earthworms into their burrow holes. Almost like a starfish attacking an oyster the *Testacella* slug can completely evert and protrude its radula and buccal mass far out in front of its mouth into the earthworm. Other carnivorous snails, like the African streptaxids grow a curiously lopsided shell, which has the appearance of having been "squashed". This permits these small carnivores to enter the large aperture of a vegetarian snail, like the *Achatina*, and to devour its prey within the shell.

Sex and Reproduction in Prosobranchs

The sexes are separate in the prosobranchs, in contrast to the hermaphroditic pulmonate snails, and in some instances the shells may differ to a slight degree. The shell of the male is usually smaller. In the Cuban operculate genus *Viana*, (family Helicinidae) the edge of the outer lip of the male shell has a deep, V-shaped notch. In most families of prosobranchs the males have a single pronglike penis, usually situated on the side of the head, just behind the right tentacle. The helicinid males do not have a penis, but the sperm are transferred by means of motile spermatophore packets.

Birth of a Snail

Shelly eggs, less than 3 mm, were laid by the Rosy Glandina snail of Florida. Photos: Patricia Armes.

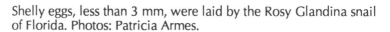

"I see daylight, and my heart is beating!"   "Foot and eyes first, then I'll be out."   "I came from that!?"

The females usually have an internal receptacle in which they store live sperm for several weeks or months. The fertilized eggs are passed down the oviduct past an egg gland where a protective jellylike covering is added before the egg is laid in the earth or to the surface of a piece of moist wood. Mating and egglaying usually take place after a protracted period of aestivation due to very cold months or long droughts. The number of eggs laid varies greatly with the species and local conditions, but ranges from only a single to a few hundred. Hatching occurs after warm rains and the young snails immediately crawl away in search of food.

THE PULMONATES

Sex and Reproduction in the Pulmonates

The lung-bearing pulmonate snails differ from their distant cousins, the terrestrial prosobranchs, in several respects. They have no operculum or trapdoor; they have two pairs of tentacles on the head, with one pair bearing an eye at the very distal end of each tentacle. More importantly, they are functional hermaphrodites—that is, each individual has two sets of sex organs, one with testes, sperm and penis, the other with ovaries, eggs, an oviduct and a pouch or receptacle for holding in reserve the sperm of another individual. Self-fertilization is possible in rare instances, but normally mating takes place between two individuals with a mutual exchange of sperm. Egg-laying follows later, usually at nearby suitable locations.

The manufacture of sperm and eggs takes place simultaneously in special halves of the ovotestis, a gland located beside the brown liverlike digestive gland in the spire of the snail. A duct for each product winds forward, one to the penis which is usually

Hermaphroditic pulmonates make a mutual and simultaneous exchange of sperm. A "pair" of *Satsuma mercatoria* (Pfeiffer, 1845) from Japan. Photo: Masao Azuma.

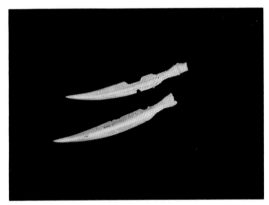

Almost a quarter of an inch in length, these calcareous "love darts" are thrust into the genitals of *Helix* mates as a sexual stimulus.

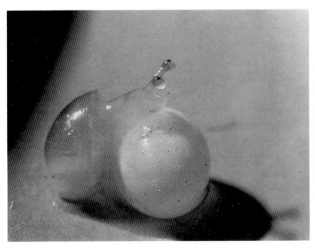

"What a wondrous world!"

"At three weeks, I'm off for more food."

Not until grown to maturity do the annularid snails of the West Indies produce this frilly outer lip. The stepped, shelly operculum grows from birth.

Resembling a coil of rope, the soft operculum of Itier's Cyclophorus seals the aperture of this Sri Lanka ground snail. Photo: Richard Goldberg.

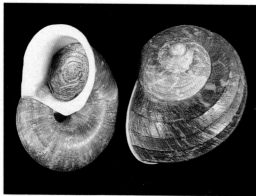

The ground-dwelling Cyclophore Snails are represented in southeast Asia and the East Indies by over 100 species. Note the horny, brown operculum in the aperture. *Cyclophorus fulguratus* (Pfeiffer, 1852) from Thailand.

usually located at the base of the right tentacle. It is usually closely associated with and joins the vagina, so that there is a common opening or so-called gonophore.

Reciprocal copulation takes place sometimes after an hour of exchanging caresses with the tentacles and oral lappets. In the *Helix* snails each partner may eject a small, 3mm-long calcareous dart into its mate. The dart evokes heightened sexual excitement, and after considerable maneuvering the animals put their gonopores close to each other in order to permit the entrance of the penis. The sperm are packaged in transferable spermatophores. Mating may last for two or three hours. The dart is lost and eventually a new one is secreted by the dart sac in a few days.

The structural details of the anatomy of these complicated sex organs have been used to unravel the mysteries of the relationships between families whose shells otherwise look the same. For instance, the shells of a camaenid snail from the Philippines or a helminthoglyptid snail from Central America resemble those of some members of the European helicid family. These distant cousins have grown to resemble each other outwardly over generations of response to their environment and their genetics. Their internal anatomy tells the story of their great differences and different origins. This is known to students of biogeography as "convergent evolution."

Development and Longevity

The eggs of pulmonates are rather large, have yolk within, are laid singly in sticky masses usually in moist crevices or self-made holes in the soil or among leaves. An average clutch of eggs for shelled snails varies from a dozen to a hundred, but slugs are known to produce three or four hundred at one sitting. Several clutches may be produced in one season if conditions are satisfactory. *Amphidromus* and *Helicostyla* tree snails of the Philippines form nests by plastering leaves together. The megasnails of South America lay large, white shelly eggs resembling half-inch-long pigeon eggs.

The eggs of most pulmonates hatch as anatomically complete young snails, except for the reproductive system which may require another 8 to 14 months to mature. Temperature, food, moisture and the availability of calcium carbonate are factors which influence the growth and longevity of snails. Many months, even years, may be spent in rest periods of summer aestivation or sometimes in winter hibernation. There are several records of *Helix* living for 5 to 10 years, *Cepaea* 5 to 9 years and *Limax* slugs from 3 to 5 years.

Sinistral Landshells

Gastropod shells are basically tubes that grow in size by the addition of more shell material at the edge of the large apertural opening. Most snail shells coil around an axis or columella, and the coiling may, as in most cases, be in a clockwise direction. We popularly refer to them as "right-handed" or dextrally coiling shells. Of the many thousands of species only a few hundred customarily coil the opposite way, that is, in a "left-handed" or sinistral direction.

There appears to be no evolutionary survival factor in this coiling feature, except perhaps that mating is apt to be more readily accomplished among snails that coil in the same direction. Some *Partula* snails from Polynesian islands may coil either way. So also may some species of *Amphidromus* from the East Indies. There are some species and a few genera that coil only in a sinistral direction.

Occasionally, through some embryological accident in a normally dextral species, a sinistral specimen will be born and grow to adulthood. These freaks are greatly sought after by some collectors. Sinistral specimens were reported and illustrated as early as the 1700's of the Haitian Tree Snail, *Liguus virgineus*, and the edible escargot, *Helix pomatia*. Nearly every large common species has produced a freak "left-handed" specimen, including the genera *Achatina* and *Strophocheilus*.

Where Landshells Live

Unlike the aquatic mollusks that are comfortably surrounded by water, the land mollusks have had to adapt themselves to dry conditions by choosing moist conditions or by modifying their anatomy and food habits to obtain and retain sufficient water. Most landshells can suspend activities and prevent loss of moisture for many months, even years in some recorded cases, by sealing the aperture of the shell, either with an operculum or an agglutinized hardened seal of mucus, called the epiphragm. This form of rest or sleep is called aestivation.

Other protective measures against long dry spells include burying in secluded places, frequent production of the drought-proof eggs, and the retention of the young in the parent's oviduct. The finding of the opposite sex is made easier because of the hermaphroditic condition of each individual, mutual intercourse and the production of fertilized eggs by both individuals. In the camaenid snails a wartlike gland on the head exudes an attrative fluid that stimulates copulation.

So-called "left-handed" shells are coiled sinistrally, that is, built so the aperture appears on the left. These Culion Amphidromus from the Philippines are always sinistral.

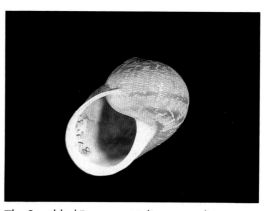

The Speckled Escargot, *Helix aspersa* (Linnaeus, 1756) is normally "right-handed" but this rare specimen coils in a left or sinistral direction.

On the left is the only recorded sinistral example of the Three-toothed Polygyra. To the right is *Triodopsis tridentata* subspecies *juxtidens* (Pilsbry, 1894) from Virginia coiling in a normal "dextral" direction. 10 mm. Photo: John Slapcinsky.

Color Patterns

One kind of banded Polymitas selected from a multi-colored herd of Cuban snails.

After periods of rain, snails may gather to mate. Trochoid Asperitas from Komodo Island, Indonesia. Photo: Jean-Claude Cailliez.

These 1/2-inch-long Reticulate Annularids from Cuba live on limestone cliffs, and come in many bright colors.

Habitats for Landshells

From the steaming jungles of the tropics to the barren rocks of Arizona and to the sandy deserts of Africa, landshells are adapted to all kinds of weather.

AUSTRALIAN BUSH
Sometimes dry, sometimes flooded, the woodlands of coastal Queensland are the home of *Varohadra* and *Thersites* snails lurking under rotting logs and leaves.

FLORIDA EVERGLADES
High up in the lyseloma trees of the elevated "hammocks" in south central Florida the colorful Liguus Tree Snails feed on lichens on trunks and limbs. Eggs are laid in the ground each spring and early summer. The living Liguus are now protected by law. There are about 54 Florida color forms.

BAHAMA ISLANDS
Along the seacoast of the Bahama Islands and usually associated with seagrape trees, the abundant Cerion or "peanut" shells occur in isolated, distinct colonies. A great deal of hybridization exists among various populations. Over 600 forms have been described, but there are less than a dozen true species.

NEW GUINEA JUNGLES
The highest trees in the tropical thickets of islands in the South Pacific harbor a dazzling collection of Papuina Snails. Here the author's wife explores Manus Island in the Admiralty Islands for the Green Papuina Snail, seen at the right. Only when a tall tree is felled will these colorful snails be scattered about on low bushes and hibiscus plants.

Land snails are worldwide in distribution but certain families seem to have adapted themselves to the colder termpperate regions and can withstand freezing conditions. These species are found in wooded areas, in grassy fields, among protective boulders or under fallen logs. They are more abundant where there are limestone outcrops or areas lacking acid soil. Many species bury into the soil and can survive very cold winters or high mountainous conditions.

In contrast, some families are strictly tropical in distribution and cannot survive frosts or freezing weather. A few tropical and subtropical families have species that live high in trees. Best known are the Florida and Cuban *Liguus* and Philippine *Helicostyla* tree snails. Some families, such as the *Cerion* peanut shells, are abundant only along the seacoasts of such tropical islands as the Bahamas. In Cuba, where there are many cliffs and mogotes of limestone, there are many hundreds of species of abundant prosobranch landshells.

Curiously, there are quite a few genera of pulmonate snails that prefer to live in dry desert conditions. Some live in dry rocky areas, usually deep under protective slabs of rocks away from the heat of the sun's rays. The snails' activities during the entire year may be limited to short periods of rain showers. Feeding and reproducing must be accomplished in a few days. The few eggs that are laid must be capable of surviving long droughts. But even in the great deserts of the world there are small patches of plants, as well as the dew of cool evenings to sustain these snails. Their white shells and thick epiphragms over the shell apertures help them survive in these sun-beaten, dry habitats.

The Geography of Landshells

Every form of modern plant or animal life has a natural distribution in some part or other of the world. This has come about through the consequences of geological and ecological changes over millions of years and millions of generations of genetic activities. While the average person is ready to accept the fact that polar bears are limited to the north polar regions and the Bengal Tiger only to southeast Asia, few realize that the same principles and biogeographical reasons apply to the distribution of the land-dwelling gastropods.

There are historical biological reasons why the giant African *Achatina* genus is endemic to Africa, or why the *Achatinella* Agate Snails are limited to the Hawaiian Island chain or why the polygyra snails have been dominant in eastern North America since Cretaceous times. This is not the place to give a discourse on the existence of that ancient continent, Pangea, nor to recount the geologic history of drifting continents. I refer the reader to John Peake's 1978 scholarly, but necessarily unfinished account on the distribution of the pulmonates. If the history of the distribution of landshells is hazy to the scientist it certainly has not been helped by modern man's accidental or purposeful spreading of various species of snails to all parts of the world.

Introduced Species

As soon as man built and launched his first sea-going crafts, aestivating land snails, amid the clutter of firewood, shade branches and ship's rigging, began their journeys around the world. Edible snails, such as *Helix aspersa*, served as fresh meat on long voyages. This prolific species was a natural candidate for colonization in foreign parts visited by European sailors. Today, several dozen introduced land species have an almost worldwide distribution, among them being *Bradybaena similaris*, *Theba pisana*, *Otala lactea*, *Cepaea nemoralis*, *Subulina octona* and several slugs of the genera *Deroceras* and *Limax* (see our geographical bibliography, under "United States"). Other early man-made distributions were doubtlessly made by wandering, sea-going Polynesians and the Carib Indians in the West Indies. The modern saga of the Giant East African Snail, *Achatina fulica*, has been related by A.R. Mead (1961) and R.T. Abbott (1949).

Many of these introduced species became serious pests in grain fields, gardens and fruit groves. Because some carnivorous snails were thought to be a practical way of controlling these herbivores, snail-eating *Gonaxis* and *Euglandina* were unwisely introduced to the Marianas, Hawaii and Bermuda. Instead of attacking the giant African snail or the *Otala* edible Morocco snail, these carnivores turned upon the local harmless snails. In Hawaii the native Agate Snails have almost been eliminated.

The greatest disturbances to natural distributions have been the major ecologic changes wrought by man. Woodland species have particularly suffered as man has cleared vast areas of forests, not only in Europe prior to the sixteenth century, but also in North America two hundred years ago, and to an unbelievable extent in recent years in the Philippines, southeastern Asia and Brazil.

Early European colonists accidentally introduced the inch-long Decollate Snail, *Rumina decollata* on several independent occasions. Bishop Elliott found it in Charleston, South Carolina, in the early 1800's, and a century before that it was found near Spanish missions in Texas and around French houses in New Orleans. The snail is a voracious attacker of local snails, but will also feed on decaying vegetation.

Landshell Regions

It has been known since the early days of great explorations that certain major parts of the world had their own families of mammals, birds, plants and snails. In some cases the endemics were localized, such as the paraphanta snails only found in New Zealand or the helicostylid tree snails located only in the Philippines. Other families have a divided distribution, with some of their genera living in Australia and others in South Africa. These "disjunct" distributions were brought about, long before man's appearance, by the massive splitting and gradual shifting of some of the major continents.

For convenience sake, most biogeographers recognize five land snail regions. Their peculiar climates and isolation by the major oceans have kept them fairly distinct.

Holarctic Region - (viewed best from a satellite hovering over the North Pole). This is the cold-to-temperate region of North America as far south as Northern Mexico, the European area and northern Africa, as well as the Asian lands north of the Himalayan range of mountains. This region is sometimes divided into the Palearctic Region (Europe and Asia) and the Nearctic Region (North America). Over millions of years and many climatic changes, this region has had a common exchange of genera and species within the families Cochlicopidae, Valloniidae and Helicidae.

The Spanish Edible Snail, *Otala lactea* (Müller, 1774) has been introduced to southeast United States, Bermuda and Cuba. It is commonly found in European and New York fish markets.

Native to cool northwest Europe, the Banded Grove Snail, *Cepaea nemoralis* (Linnaeus, 1758) was brought to Massachusetts, New Jersey and Virginia by English colonists in the 18th century.

The Nearctic subregion changes as one goes southward into warmer, temperate zones. In eastern United States families like the Polygyridae and Haplotrematidae are common, while in the western part the unique subfamilies are the Oreohelicinae, Sonorellinae and Humboldtianinae.

The Palearctic subregion likewise changes its dominant groups in the warmer Mediterranean area where the Clausiliidae and Hygrominae thrive.

Neotropical Region - the New World tropical and subtropical parts of Mexico, Central America, the West Indies and South America. Terrestrial prosobranchs abound here, as well as the large Strophocheilidae and colorful *Polymita* and *Liguus*.

Oriental Region - India, Sri Lanka, southern China and Japan, southeastern Asia and eastern Indonesia. The Camaenidae, Acavidae, Helicostylinae and Bradybaeninae are a few of the dominant groups in this tropical area.

Ethiopian Region - Africa south of the Sahara and the adjacent Indian Ocean islands such as the Seychelles and Madagascar.

Australian Region - Australia, western Indonesia, New Guinea, Melanesia and New Zealand. A region long isolated and having many unique genera, such as *Papuina* and *Placostylus*.

Other unique, smaller regions include the isolated Atlantic Islands of the Canaries, Madeira and Cape Verdes. Their families are allied to those of northern Africa but many endemic species have developed there. Equally unique are the numerous but isolated Polynesian islands which were colonized from Malaysia and South America, but which have exploded with their own particular species over the last few million years. Tiny species are readily carried by birds, high altitude winds and floating debris.

Land Snails as Disease Carriers

In addition to the obvious risk of the spread of parasite eggs and *Salmonella* infection by slugs and snails associated with fresh vegetables, there are major adverse effects from the spread of plant diseases among crops. Domestic animals are also seriously affected by parasites carried by land snails. Fortunately, the very serious trematode worm diseases of man, such as schistosomiasis, are restricted to a few species of freshwater gastropods in the tropics.

The trematodes that cause diseases in mammals and birds must pass part of their life cycle within a molluscan intermediate host. A typical example is the extraordinary *Leucochloridium* parasite of song birds. This small adult worm lives in the anal cloaca of the

The so-called Nearctic subregion includes lower Canada and the United States where the family Polygyridae is very prominent in woodland areas. The Thyroid Polygyra, *Mesodon*, is common in eastern United States.

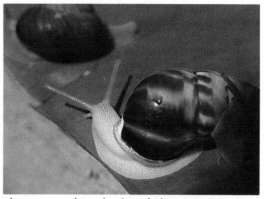
The snow-white body of the Perverse Amphidromus of Indonesia is characteristic of this sinistrally coiled species.

Never before illustrated alive, this inch-long Egg-shaped Helicostyla was found in trees on Palawan Island by the photographer, Margaret K. Langworthy.

14

bird. The worms are attached to and gain their substance from the cloacal wall. As the adult worms reproduce, its eggs are passed out with the bird's droppings on to the leaves of nearby plants. Leaf-eating Amber Snails (*Succinea*) then ingest the worm eggs. As soon as they reach the intestine of the snail they hatch into microscopic, ciliated larvae which bore through the intestinal wall and migrate to the "liver" or so-called hepatopancreas of the host snail. Here tiny larvae are transformed into one or two huge irregular sporocysts. These invade the tentacles of the snail causing them to swell into brightly colored "balloons". The tentacles are now loaded with tiny infectious metacercariae—a larval form of the parasite, ripe and ready for some hungry bird. Each "ballooned" tentacle, loaded with about 300 metacercariae, throbs and quivers in such a fashion that the bird is enticed to peck at and eat the tentacle—cercariae and all. Once ingested by the bird, the cercariae enter the blood system of its new warm-blooded host and within a month transform into adult worms that lodge in the bird's cloaca. Thus the life cycle is completed—from bird to plant to snail to bird.

A similar parasite, the Small Liver Fluke (*Dicrocoelium dendriticum*) of cattle and sheep is spread by its molluscan intermediate hosts, *Helicella itala* and *Zebrina detrita*. Other parasite worms, such as the cestode fatal to chickens and the nematode lung worms of sheep have as intermediate hosts the Arionidae slugs, *Helicella*, *Monacha* and *Cepaea*. In Thailand the Giant African Snail, *Achatina fulica*, is a major intermediate host of the human lungworm, *Angiostrongylus cantonensis*. A lungworm parasite in the Virginia Deer is carried by the common glossy *Zonitoides arboreus*.

Land Snails as Agricultural Pests

There is a much wider and economically more serious impact by terrestrial snails on man's agricultural and horticultural activities. What gardner has not been aware of the damage done to plants and roots by slugs and snails? Many millions of dollars of damage are annually caused by snails to seedlings, celery, beans, commercially grown edible mushrooms, citrus trees, and a myriad kinds of ornamentals and flowers. Various kinds of sprays and baits have been developed to counter these molluscan foragers. An excellent and modern account of the snail pest problem and the use of molluscicides was written by Dora Godan in her "Pest Slugs and Snails" (Springer - Verlag, Berlin and N.Y., 1983).

Various governments have done careful and extensive research on the effects of molluscicides on the

Barney's Thersite (*Thersites (Hadra) barneyi* (Cox, 1873)) from northern Queensland is one of numerous, localized species of Australian landshells. Photo: Queensland Museum.

Most Papuinas live in Melanesia, but MacGillivray's *Rynchotrochus* is one of the few species in northeast Australia, close to New Guinea. Photo: Queensland Museum.

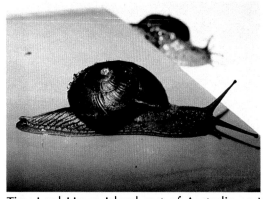

Tiny Lord Howe Island east of Australia and with ancient connections with Melanesia to the north, has strange endemic plants and animals. Here is 2-inch-long *Gudeoconcha sophiae* Iredale, 1944. Photo: Berniece Beechey.

15

Carnivorous Snails

Most land snails are herbivorous, but several families have become carnivorous, some eating other snails and others feeding on earth worms and dead flesh. In the Glandina Snails the body has become more elongate in order to enter other shells, and the radular teeth have become fewer and longer. At left is the snail-eating Rosy Glandina from Florida.

environment, on humans and on the mollusks themselves. DDT and the insecticide, pyrethrum, have no effect on mollusks. The most popular poisons today are metaldehyde and the carbamates. The latter are more effective and less harmful to the environment. The U.S. Department of Agriculture has available Farmers' Bulletin No. 1895 (revised 1959), on "Land Slugs and Snails and Their Control."

Landshells in Archaeology

In the history of man the past explains the present and may foretell the future. Archaeologists have used many tools to unravel past mysteries. The nature of the climate, the kinds of vegetation, the domestic animals and local environmental conditions can be deduced by the examination of subfossil tree pollens, vertebrate bone and the shells of mollusks.

Burial sites and kitchen middens of prehistoric peoples are rich with molluscan clues. Even excavated columns of earth, if properly sampled and sorted, can reveal what and how early people farmed or hunted.

The Rosy Glandina buries a dozen or so shell-covered eggs each year. They hatch in a few weeks. Photo: Patricia Armes.

Other carnivorous families include the streptaxids, the *Testacella* European slugs, the American haplotrema snails and even calcium-starved helicid herbivores. Here is the 3-inch Giant Glandina, *Euglandina gigantea* (Pilsbry, 1926), from Costa Rica. Photo: Robert W. Trevor.

From the evidence of remaining shells archeologists have shown that the famous Stonehenge structures in England were built during the Bronze Age, about 1500 B.C. A census of land snail species and their relative abundance indicate that farming began in the British Isles about 4,000 B.C.

In Neolithic mortuary houses carnivorous *Oxycheilus* snails found in skulls and among bones indicate that the bodies were exposed long enough for these snails to enter the burial sites. One can deduce the nature of the terrain by the presence or absence of *Succinea*, *Vertigo* and *Helicella* shells.

The study of numerous archeological sites has shown that in all liklihood *Helix aspersa* was introduced during the first century A.D. and that the common escargot, *Helix pomatia* was deliberately introduced for food purposes by the Romans. A dozen other species were evidently introduced at later times, including *Helicella elegans* which must have arrived in Britain after the French revolution.

Not only can weather conditions be worked out, but by studying the proportion of banded and non-banded *Cepaea nemoralis* one can deduce the presence or absence of the snail-eating thrushes. Part of this is associated with climatic conditions, the existence of certain trees and hence the effect on bird populations.

All of the two dozen species of New Zealand Paryphanta feed on earth worms. The shells explode when kept in collections under dry conditions. Some species have been driven to extinction.

Land Slugs

Pulmonate snails with reduced or absent shells are called slugs. World-wide there are a dozen unrelated families that have independently lost their shells through evolution. Best known is the Giant European Slug, *Limax maximus* (Linnaeus, 1758), sometimes 8 inches long.

In the same family, Limacidae, is the Reticulated Slug, *Deroceras reticulatum* (Müller, 1774), also a major agricultural pest and also introduced to America.

The Red-triangle Slug of the rainforests of Queensland has a tracheal lung and vestigial shell bits under the red triangle. Sometimes entirely colored red. *Triboniophorus graeffei* Humbert, 1863 (family Athoracophoridae). Photo: Queensland Museum.

Color Patterns

Color and patterns in landshells are inherited through genes that control these factors, but diet and environmental conditions, such as the lack of moisture or lime in the soil may have a major influence.

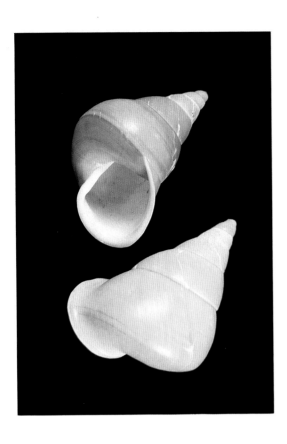

Usually solid green, this Manus Island Papuina may be finely streaked with green, solid yellow or ashen white depending upon climatic conditions. Contrary to belief, they are not artificially treated.

The fragile-shelled Varicolored Amphidromus of Sumba and Flores Islands, Indonesia, sports a variety of colors. *Amphidromus floresianus* Fulton, 1897.

The many subspecies and color forms of the Hawaiian Agate Snails of the genera *Achatinella* and *Partulina* are well-known for their beauty. These *Partulina mighlesiana* (Pfeiffer, 1847) are the color form *bella* (Reeve, 1850) from Molokai Island. X 1.

Sculpture and Form

Outdoing even some of the most bizarre marine shells, many terrestrial shells have developed intricate sculpturing, sometimes perhaps for camouflage, protection against insect predators or to ward off the heat of the sun's rays. These three species demonstrate the extremes that some Cuban forms have developed in the limestone valleys of Pinar del Rio Province.

Resembling some marine *Astraea* Star Trochus, these quarter-inch jewels from the Isle of Pines are common on rocky cliffs. Constellate Star Snail, *Priotrochatella constellata* (Pfeiffer, 1850).

The amazing Cuban Porcupine Snail, no larger than a sunflower seed, is found only on one high mountain in Viñales Valley, western Cuba. *Blaesospira echinus* (Pfeiffer, 1864).

Paddle-shaped ribs adorn the whorls of Bishop Elliott's Urocop from the Sierra de Guane, western Cuba. One inch. *Gongylostoma elliotti* (Poey, 1858).

Surface Texture

Under a strong handlens or microscope many ordinary-looking landshells burst into intriguing works of nature's art. Ribs, pimples, beads, hairs and glossy surfaces serve some protective purpose.

Finely ribbed to ward off the incessant heat of the Western Australian back country, this camaenid, inch-long shell also has a thick white lip. *Turgenitubulus pagodulus* Solem, 1986. Photo: Richard Goldberg.

With hairs, sometimes 1 mm in length, the Hairy Trichia helicid snail lives in the high Alps of France and Bavaria. *Trichia villosa* (Studer, 1789). Photo: Richard Goldberg.

The tiny Golden Pupina of Luzon Island is the miniature Golden Cowrie of the land world. *Moulinsia aurantia* (Grateloup, 1840), 8 mm, has a horny operculum and lives on the forest floor.

Apertures

Once a non-operculate snail has withdrawn into its shell, it must protect itself from beetles, small mammals and other carnivorous snails. Shelly teeth serve this purpose.

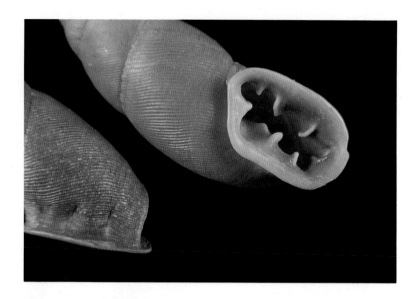

The mouth of the shell of the Brazilian Tooth-mouthed Snail is well-endowed with protective teeth. *Odontostomus odontostomus* (Sowerby, 1824) from Bahia, Brazil. 4 cm

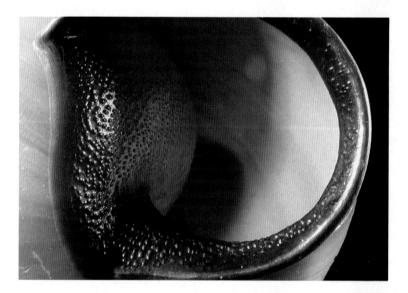

The aperture and outer lip of the north Australian landshell bear microscopic beads that hold the mantle in place. *Xanthomelon spheroideum* (Le-Guillou, 1845). 4 cm. Photo: Richard Goldberg.

The gross folds or teeth in the aperture of Florida's Eared Polygyra ward off intruders. *Polygyra auriculata* (Say, 1818). 1.5 cm.

Gems on Land

Here are a few examples of the color and architectural wonders of the landshell world from the bejeweled Diadema Snail from Malay (right) to the Wentletrap Cyclotus (below).

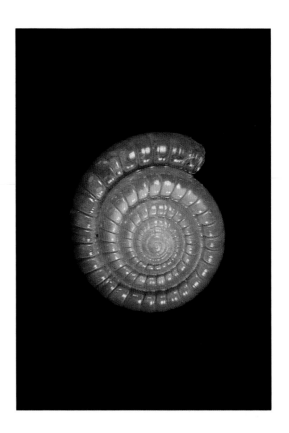

Apical or top view of Dall's Diadema Snail, *Syama diadema* (Dall, 1897) a half-inch shell from Malaya.

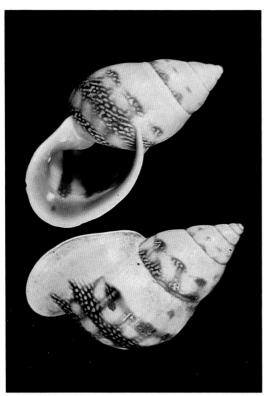

Glaucus Drymaeus from Venezuela is noted for its lavendar aperture and white-dotted spots. *Drymaeus glaucostomus* (Albers, 1852). Natural size.

Madagascar was blessed with many strange landshells before over-population by man destroyed them. This is the extinct Wentletrap Cyclotus, *Acroptychia metableta* Crosse and Fisher, 1877.

Shells without Color

White shells are not uncommon among landshells, especially those in hot, arid localities. Sculpturing is commonly pronounced to aid cooling.

Allan's Urocop from Pinar del Rio, Cuba, is only 5 mm and look like lizard feces. *Tetrentodon alleni* (Torre, 1929).

Equally white, but sporting tiny spines and a sugary operculum is the Prickly Xenopoma, *Xenopoma hystrix* (Pfeiffer, 1861) from Oriente Province, eastern Cuba.

Among the whitest and smallest of the peanut shells of the Bahamas is Turner's Cerion, *Cerion turnerae* Clench and Aguayo, 1952 from Great Inagua. 15 mm. Named after Dr. Ruth D. Turner.

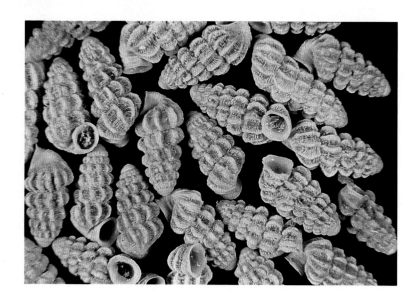

Strange Shapes

Through random mutations and the selection of the best fitted to survive, many odd shapes have developed in mollusks.

Brooks' Urocop from Guantanamo, Cuba, gives up coiling when mature, and produces an un-coiled tube at the end. *Brachypodella brooksiana* (Pfeiffer, 1859). 1.8 mm. Photo: Richard Goldberg.

Resembling the beautiful geometric coiling of some fossil ammonite, penny-sized Buckley's Snail from Ecuador is a flat, spiral, operculate prosobranch in the family Poteriidae. *Buckleyia martinezi* (Hidalgo, 1866).

Why should so many species of Bahia Province snails in Brazil have triangular mouths? Only an ecologic study of *Cochlorina navicula* (Wagner, 1827) and other bulimulids would solve this riddle.

Collecting Landshells

Although terrestrial mollusks are found in nearly every part of the world—in sunlit meadows or deep, shaded woods; in the highest tropical trees or deep under rock slides in arid regions—the best places to look for them are not always obvious to the beginning collector. An elementary knowledge of the wants and dislikes of land mollusks is helpful.

All land mollusks are moisture lovers. Some may haunt the damp hillsides of ravines; but do not expect to find many in the bordering plains of rivers where rushing waters drown them out during flood times. There are some genera that prefer a salty atmosphere, such as the halophilic peanut shells (*Cerion*) of the Bahama Islands. Seldom are these abundant snails found more than a thousand yards from the seagrape trees of the seacoast. If you are seeking Arizona or New Mexico desert snails of the genera *Micrarionta* or *Sonorella*, you will have to dig away at the stones and flat rocks of a hillside rockslide. During rare wet spells these snails may emerge at night or early morning to feed, but normally when the sun is bright and the ground dry they will have crawled deep down among the subterranean recesses.

Terrestrial snails also thrive in areas of limestone. Acid conditions, such as those found under oak or pine trees are not kindly for mollusks which build calcareous shells. The granite hills of New England have few species and few specimens compared to the abundance of landshells in the limestone cliffs of Cuba or the calcareous soils of Polynesian Islands.

Colorful tropical tree snails are found high above ground. In some Philippine species eggs are laid and enwrapped in the leaves of the tree, but in other groups, such as the now protected *Liguus* tree snails of Florida, the adults descend to the ground in the spring season to lay their eggs in the soil on the ground.

While larger shells may be easily spotted and hand-picked, the many kinds of minute species are best gathered with a pair of tweezers. The collector may work on his knees and scratch among the leaves while wearing a pair of protective cotton gloves. Some collectors gather up dry forest debris and shake it through seives or take it home for leisurely examination under a hand lens or dissecting microscope. Porous soil under rotting logs, at the base of limestone ledges, amid the tangle of moss coverings or under loose bark are all good hiding places for landshells.

Debris along the banks of rivers is often well-supplied with dead land shells, some still in good condition. Many of these were drowned out from hillsides further up-stream. The locality data is not as accurate as one would wish. Some collectors have successfully trapped living minute snails, such as *Cochlicopa*, by placing on the ground a wet burlap bag, folded several times and weighted by boards or flat rocks. Overnight, several dozen specimens will take refuge under the moist bags.

Identifying these minute species is beyond the scope of this book, but several good references on the land species of Europe, New Zealand and North America

Farming and a cottage industry of snail-raising is a multi-million dollar industry in edible snails in Europe. Here in Seville, Spain, a vendor sells live *Helix*. Photo: Jean-Claude Cailliez.

From the drier parts of northwest Africa and Spain the Spanish Edible Snail, sometimes marketed in New York as the Morocco Milk Snail, is used extensively in "escargot" recipes. Photo: David Mulliner.

From the Florida backyard of an amateur conchologist, Dr. Harry Lee, came these tiny landshells, including a species new to science in 1986. He used a seive, tweezers and a binocular dissecting microscope. Photo: Harry G. Lee.

From the hills of Florida Island, Solomons, came this one-day catch of edible *Placostylus palmarum* (Mousson, 1869). Millions more will reproduce unless the forests are cut down for firewood and lumber.

are available to help in these identifications (consult our geographical bibliography). Further details on collecting may be found in the booklet "How to Study and Collect Shells" issued by the American Malacological Union.

Collecting Equipment

Sensible clothing and normal protection against too much sun, poisonous plants and insects will help the collector avoid unpleasant surprises. Cotton gloves, tweezers, plastic vials, cotton collecting bags, pencil and a supply of labels are the bare essentials.

Specimens that you personally collect but are kept without accurate locality data are worthless for future identification or scientific study. Since land mollusks are able to eat paper labels, it is best to write a field number on a small piece of plastic garden label. The number should signify your collecting station as outlined in a field book. Record the date of collection, exact locality, relative abundance, and any ecologic information such as the type of vegetation and soil. Waterproof notebooks are on the market for surveyors and biologists.

Cleaning and Preserving

Large shells, exceeding a half-inch or 2 cm in size may be briefly boiled and the meat contents removed with a bent safety pin. Alternate preferred methods include freezing for 24 hours, then thawing; or placing in a plastic bag and cooking in a microwave oven for three minutes on high (the animal will pop out); or drowning in a jar full of water for about 10 hours. If

anatomical work is to be done later, drowned specimens may be preserved in 60 to 70 percent grain alcohol (or 50 percent wood or isopropyl alcohol). Formaldehyde should be avoided because its acidity will etch and discolor the shells. Minute specimens may be soaked in strong alcohol for several days and then set out to dry. In warm or damp climates all portions of dead flesh should be flushed out with a tiny jet of water—a bulb syringe used in a pan of water will do. Colorful shells particularly those with greens and purples should be cleaned by drowning or freezing, as boiling will destroy the colors. It is best to dry shells in the shade. Be sure to save the operculum, or trapdoor, of the prosobranch specimens. They are essential for identifying.

The Landshell Collection

Unlike seashell collections, land mollusk collections usually take up much less space but are not as adaptable for display purposes because of their comparatively small sizes. Larger, colorful tropical species, especially those with little data, may be displayed in wooden, compartmentalized printer's type trays hung on the wall. A black background is best. Single or a small group of shells may be displayed on a circular board or marble slab with a clear glass protective dome. So-called "riker mount"—inch-deep, cotton-layered, glass-topped, square cardboard boxes—may be used to align small interesting specimens in neat rows.

However, the museum-type study collection is the most practical way of organizing your landshell collection. The shells may be arranged in systematic order (the same standard sequence of families used in this book) and will serve as a handy identification and reference collection. It also permits the collector to locate any specimen quickly and add new material with a minimum of rearranging. Proper housing and the keeping of accurate locality data is most essential, for data-less specimens arranged haphazardly are useless. By maintaining a catalog kept in a simple numerical order, you may assign numbers to your shells and thus prevent mixing or loss of data. The accompanying drawing suggests a practical system. The ideal cabinet has outside measurements of about 40 (or 80) inches in height, 22 inches in width and 32 inches in depth.

Number large specimens within the aperture with fine-lined India ink numbers. Minute specimens, sorted to species, may be placed with a numbered slip, in glass vials loosely plugged with clean cotton (not corks or snap lids). Small zip-lock plastic bags may be used. Keep a small part open or make small holes in the bag so that some air circulation will prevent mildewing and fungus growth. Labels, kept in the vials so that the identification shows, or placed in the bottom of a small open, cardboard tray, should bear the genus, species, author and date (when known) but especially the collecting locality, date, and name of the collector.

Exchanging and Purchasing Shells

Building up a self-collected shell collection is a rewarding experience. Today, collectors practice sensible conservation, avoid over-collecting and unnecessarily disturbing the environment. The adverse effects of taking samples from nature are very slight compared to the natural pruning done by birds, mammals and carnivorous insects, or by the occasional disasters of forest fires, floods or violent wind storms.

The names and addresses of fellow landshell collectors may be found in shell club newsletters or such directories as the *Register of American Malacologists*. There are many more landshell enthusiasts in Europe, Japan and inland America than elsewhere, and many of them are willing to exchange specimens with detailed locality data. It is unlawful in most countries to mail or import live snails because of their potential threat to agriculture, but cleaned or preserved snail shells have no restrictions or custom's duty. Consult your postoffice or custom's officials if you are in doubt about certain endangered species.

Many excellent and honest dealers now handle terrestrial shells. Many of the specimens they sell are from old collections and some species, now extinct,

are occasionally re-circulated from collection to collection. Insist upon as detailed locality data as the dealer can supply.

Brief History of Landshell Collecting

The earliest recorded student of land snails was Aristotle who at the age of about 40 wrote a considerable account in his *Historia Animalium*. He wrote briefly about the mating habits, the radula, and the various forms of shells. True works on land snails did not come into being until after the invention of the printing press and the use of woodblocks to reproduce drawings. In the 1600's James Petiver, a London apothecary, the Dutch druggist, Albert Seba (1665-1736), and the Governor of Jamaica, Sir Hans Sloane (1660-1753) either wrote about or collected many exotic landshells. Martin Lister, physician to Queen Anne of England, and prolific writer about shells was publishing learned accounts of landshells as early as 1669. Baron Ignatius von Born illustrated in full color the handsome Cuban *Polymita picta* in 1780.

Landshells reached their zenith of popularity during two separate periods in Europe, the first being from about 1750 to 1790 when large colorful snail shells from early exploratory voyages brought enormous sums at the public auctions of great collections, including that of the Peruvian, Don Pedro Davila, in 1767, and that of the Duchess of Portland in 1786 in England.

A hundred years later, as great shell collectors, such as Hugh Cuming, returned from the Philippines and East Indies laden down with exotic tree snails, there was a resurgence of scientific interest in terrestrials. Humboldt and Bonpland explored South America, Alcide d'Orbigny filled volumes on Cuban landshells, and Louis Pfeiffer (1815-1877) of Germany described many thousands of species. In America Thomas Say (1787-1834) and Dr. John Jay (1808-1891) accumulated and studied local landshells. The craze for landshells blossomed and reached its zenith until World War I devastated Europe from 1914 to 1918. Kobelt, Quadras, Moellendorff, Albers, the Sarasin brothers, Sowerby and Fulton, and the American dealer, Walter F. Webb were some of the famous names associated with that active period of landshells.

After the 1930's there continued major research in the scientific field of landshell malacology. The leading workers included Henry A. Pilsbry and H. Burrington Baker of Philadelphia, Dr. and Mrs. Bernard Rensch and the Boettgers of Germany, Tom Iredale of Australia, W.J. Clench and J.C. Bequaert of Boston to mention but a few of the prodigious workers. The upsurge of interest in marine mollusks after World War II and the invention of Scuba gear eclipsed interest in landshells.

Resembling a submarine snorkel, this shelly tube permits air to enter the shell when the aperture is sealed off by the shelly operculum. An inch-long prosobranch from Burma hills *Rhiostoma housei* (Haines, 1855).

Today there is a reawakening of interest in this field, and perhaps not too soon considering the rapid deterioration of our terrestrial environment.

There are many large and active scientific land collections in museums today. Among these are the Senckenberg Museum in Frankfurt-am-Main, Germany, the U.S. Natural History Museum (Smithsonian) in Washington, D.C., the Academy of Natural Sciences of Philadelphia, Chicago Field Museum of Natural History, the Museum of Comparative Zoology at Harvard, the Florida Museum of Natural History in Gainesville, the Australian Museum in Sydney, and the National Museum of Japan in Tokyo. Other fine but less active centers exist in Holland, London, Vienna, South Africa, India, Honolulu and Auckland, New Zealand. A more detailed and complete account of early malacology may be found in S. Peter Dance's *A History of Shell Collecting* (1986) and the anthology, *The Best of the Nautilus* (American Malacologist, Inc., 1976) which reprinted interesting tales of landshell collecting.

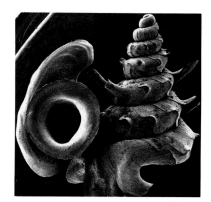

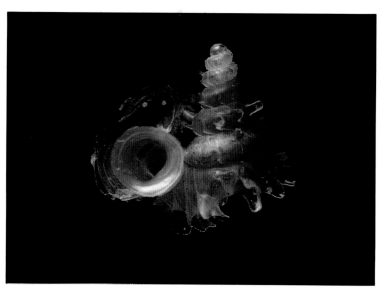

The Miraculous Diplomat Snail, only 5 mm, lives in limestone caves in Sabah, Malayasia. Family Diplommatinidae. Above is an electron scanning microscope enlargement. Photo on right by Robert Robertson.

Shell Cabinets

A well-organized and fully documented collection of land shells serves as a useful reference and identification tool. Although large shells may be displayed in glass-fronted cabinets or housed in flat cardboard boxes, ideally your collection should be cataloged, the specimens numbered, and placed in shell cabinets. The steel cabinet at the right, designed by the author, is now used in major museums.

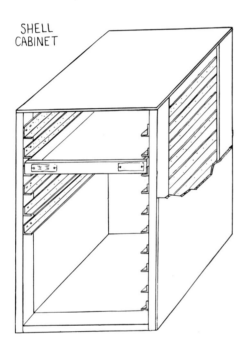

SHELL
CABINET

Drawing of cabinet and catalog samples

PERSONAL CATALOG NUMBER	STANDARD CATALOG NUMBER	IDENTIFICATION (Genus, species and author)	LOCALITY DATA				
		DATE OF COLLECTING	COLLECTOR OR SOURCE	NUMBER OF SPECIMENS	PRICE PAID OR VALUE	DATE CATALOGED	HABITAT; REMARKS

Form

Some landshells bear a strong likeness in shape to those of marine shells. To the right is the heavy, ribbed Double-lipped Auris from Bahia, Brazil *(Auris bilabiata* (Broderip and Sowerby, 1829)). It resembles some *Buccinum* marine whelks. In some forms the lip is black.

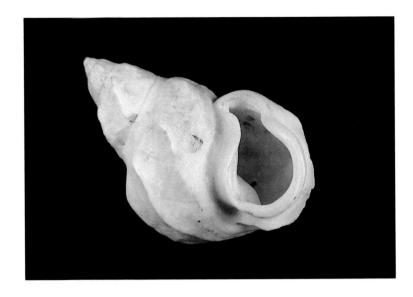

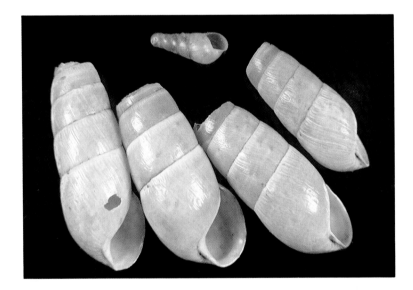

Adults of the Decollate Snail from the Mediterranean area and introduced to Texas lose their early whorls and seal off the exposed apex. *Rumina decollata* (Linnaeus, 1758): family Subulinidae.

Not a marine shell at all! The two-inch Giant False Limpet, living on intertidal ocean rocks in West Central America, is a pulmonate land snail. If submerged too long, it will drown. *Siphonaria gigas* Sowerby, 1825.

Transparent Shells—Green Bodies

Blues and greens are rare shell colors in landshells, despite the fact that such colors would be useful as camouflage in green foliage. But several kinds of tropical snails deposit chlorophyll pigment in their mantle bodies and display green through translucent shells.

The green body of Woodford's Crystal Snail from the Solomon Islands shows through its translucent shell. *Crystallopsis woodfordi* Sowerby, 1889. 12 mm (1/2 inch).

The Puerto Rican Green Ear Snail, only an inch in length, carries a fragile, transparent shell buried in its green and yellow soft parts. Photo: Charlotte M. Lloyd.

Phylum **MOLLUSCA**

Class **GASTROPODA**
Subclass
PROSOBRANCHIA

The Gilled Snails

Mostly marine shells but several families are entirely freshwater or solely terrestrial. Head with a single pair of tentacles; mantle cavity with one or two gills. Sexes separate in most groups. Operculum, either horny or calacareous, usually present. Only a few families have developed a life on land—the Helicinidae, Cyclophoridae Poteriidae; Pomatiasidae, Chondropomidae and Truncatellidae.

Order **Archaegastropoda**

Superfamily **NERITOIDEA**
(Neritacea)

Family **HELICINIDAE**
Small, squat, solid shells, usually with a callus pad over the umbilicus. Operculum horny and with a strong calcareous outer layer. Mantle cavity has vascularized lung. Radular teeth has many transverse and vertical rows (rhipidoglossate).

Females lays single eggs in ground. Males lack a penis. Six subfamilies, most grounddwellers, a few are arboreal or live on limestone cliffs. Many species in West Indies and tropical Asia.

Glutinous Carrier Snail
(0.3") 1 cm
Geophorus agglutinans (Sowerby, 1842). Masbate Id., Philippines. Operculum hard. Mud clods rub off. Type of the genus.

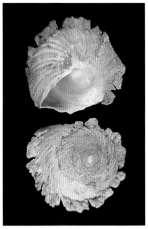

Mud Carrier Snail (0.3") 1 cm
Geophorus agglutinans (Sowerby, 1842). forma *pachychilus* (Moellendorff, 1901). Guimaras, off Iloilo, Philippines.

Romblon Carrier Snail
(0.5") 1.2 cm
Geophorus romblonensis Bartsch, 1918. Romblon Id., Philippines. Edge sharp. Paratypes.

Frilled Carrier Snail
(0.5") 1.2 cm
Geophorus nogieri Dautzenberg and Bouge, 1901. Than Mai, Viet Nam.

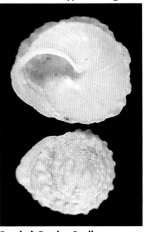

Beaded Carrier Snail
(0.5") 1.2 cm
Calybium (*Geotrochatella*) *mouhoti* (Pfeiffer, 1862). Long Fou, Viet Nam. Ground dweller. Type of subgenus.

Beautiful Trochatella
(0.3") 1 cm
Eutrochatella pulchella (Gray, 1824). Central and western Jamaica. Type of genus. Common. Operculum shelly.

Tankerville's Trochatella
(0.5") 1.2 cm
Eutrochatella tankervillii (Gray, 1824). Cockpit country of Jamaica. Uncommon.

Cutthroat Trochatella
(0.3") 1 cm
Eutrochatella jugulata (Poey, 1858). Sierra de Guane, Pinar del Rio Prov., Cuba.

Constellate Star Snail
(0.3") 1 cm
Priotrochatella constellata (Pfeiffer, 1850). Sierra de Casas, Isle of Pines, Cuba. Common. Type of genus.

Torre's Star Snail
(0.5") 1.3 mm
Priotrochatella torrei W.F. Clapp, 1918. Sierra de Casas, Isle of Pines, Cuba. Base smooth.

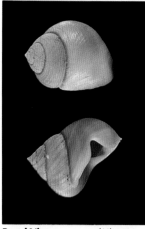

Royal Viana   (1") 2.5 cm
Viana regina (Morelet, 1849). Pinar del Rio Prov., Cuba. Upper: female shell; lower: male with notched lip.

Striate Royal Viana   (1") 2.5 cm
Viana regina (Morelet, 1848), forma *multistriata* ("Velasquez," Pfeiffer, 1852). yellow and striate. Pinar del Rio, Cuba.

Smooth Royal Viana   (1") 2.5 cm
Viana regina (Morelet, 1849), forma *laevigata* (Pfeiffer, 1865). Vinales Valley, Pinar del Rio Prov., Cuba.

Marmorate Viana   (1") 2.5 cm
Viana regina forma *marmorata* Torre, 1950. Mogote del Indio, Pinar del Rio, Cuba. Paratypes.

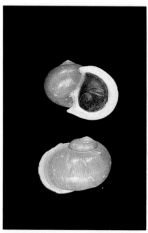

False Helicina   (0.6") 1.4 cm
Pseudohelicina helicinaeformis (Pfeiffer, 1851). Ecuador. Syn.: *Bourciera*. Type of the genus.

Concealed Helicina   (0.2") 7 mm
Hendersonia occulta (Say, 1831). Wisconsin to Maryland and Tennessee. Whorls angular.

Glowing Helicina   (0.2") 6 mm
Hendersonia calida (Weinland, 1862) subsp. *barbouri* (Clench, 1933). Miraguana Id., Bahamas.

Little Orb Helicina   (0.3") 7 mm
Helicina (*Oligyra*) *orbiculata* (Say, 1818). Texas to Florida; Illinois to Kentucky. Type of subgenus.

Clapp's Helicina   (0.3") 8 mm
Helicina (*Helicina*) *clappi* Pilsbry, 1909. Southern Florida. Introduced (?) to Cedar Key.

Major Alcadia   (0.9") 2 cm
Alcadia major Gray (1824) Jamaica. Type of the genus.

Japanese Helicina   (O.4") 8 mm
Waldemaria japonica (A. Adams, 1861). Shikoku Id., Japan. Yellow operculum shelly.

Nerite Helicina   (0.3") 6 mm
Helicina neritella Lamarck, 1801. Widespread in Jamaica. Common. Type of the genus.

Gold-mouthed Helicina
(0.3") 9 cm
Helicina aurantia Gray, 1824.
Jamaica.

Sprinkled Helicina (1") 2.5 cm
Helicina adspersa Pfeiffer, 1839.
Vinales Valley, Pinar del Rio
Prov., Cuba.

Gabb's Emerald Helicina
(0.6") 1.5 cm
Helicina gabbi Crosse, 1873.
Loma Rucilla, Santo Domingo,
West Indies. Rare.

Green Emerald Helicina
(0.3") 1.1 cm
Helicina prasinata Jacobson and
Clench, 1971. Monteado Nuevo,
Dominican Republic.

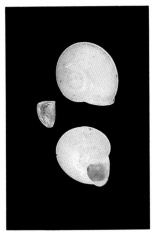

Amalia's Helicina (0.5") 1.3 cm
Sulfurina (*Kosmetopoma*)
amaliae Kobelt, 1886). Surigao
Prov., Mindanao Id., Philippines.
Type of subgenus.

Mauger's Helicina (0.3") 9 mm
Orobophana maugeriae (Gray,
1824). Raiatea Id., Society Ids.
(Polynesia). Common.

Pacific Island Helicina
(0.1") 4 mm
Orobophana pacifica (Pease,
1865). Mangaia, Cook Ids., Polynesia. Syn.: *flavescens* Pease,
1868.

Ochraceous Emoda (1") 2.5 cm
Emoda silacea (Morelet, 1849).
Baracoa, Oriente Prov., Cuba.
Type of the genus.

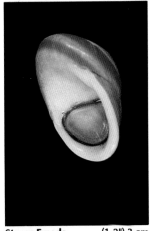

Strong Emoda (1.2") 3 cm
Emoda briarea (Poey, 1852).
Trinidad, Cuba.

Sagra's Emoda (1") 2.5 cm
Emoda sagraiana (Orbigny,
1842). La Mina Peak, Pinar del
Rio Prov., Cuba.

de la Torre's Emoda (1.3") 3 cm
Emoda torrei (Henderson, 1909).
Los Negros, Bayamo, Oriente
Prov., Cuba. Topotypes.

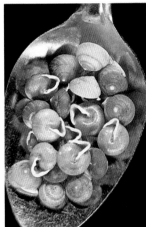

Golden Lucidella (0.2") 4 mm
Lucidella aureola (Férussac,
1822). Hollymont, Jamaica. Type
of the genus. Aperture triangular.

Order
CAENOGASTROPODA
(Modern Gastropod Snails)

Few radular teeth; most operculate; sexes separate. Includes old Meso-and Neo-
gastropod divisions.

Superfamily
CYCLOPHOROIDEA
(Cyclophoracea)
Family CYCLOPHORIDAE

Medium-sized shells, usually
discoidal or turbinate; operculum horny, many-whorled.
Mostly ground dwellers living in tropical and warm
temperate areas of Asia, Africa, Australia and Melanesia.

Silky Leptopoma (0.5") 1.2 cm
Leptopoma sericatum (Pfeiffer,
1851). Daat Id., Borneo. Operculum circular, horny.

Coron Leptopoma (0.5") 1.2 cm
Leptopoma coronensis Quadras
& Moellendorff, 1895. Coron
Calamianes Ids., Philippines.
Syntypes.

Translucent Leptopoma
(0.3") 1 cm
Leptopoma perlucidum (Grateloup, 1840). Philippines and
Papua New Guinea.

Muswar Leptopoma
(0.5") 1.2 cm
Leptopoma muswarense Fulton,
1910. Mios Waar Id., western
New Guinea. Probable syntypes
from Fulton.

Dohrn's Leptopoma
(0.7") 2 cm
Leptopoma dohrni Adams &
Angas, 1864. Guadacanal Id.,
Solomon Ids. Probable syntypes
from Fulton.

Lamellate Leptopoma
(0.7") 2 cm
*Leptopoma (Leucoptychia)
lamellatum* Sykes, 1903. Waigeu
Id., West New Guinea. Probable
syntypes from Fulton.

Trochiform Leptopoma
(1") 2.5 cm
Leptopoma geotrochiforme E.A.
Smith, 1895. Rabong Mt. Sarawak, Borneo.

Trochiform Leptopoma
(1") 2.5 cm
Leptopoma geotrochiforme E.A.
Smith, 1895. Borneo.

Shining Leptopoma (0.5") 1.2 cm
Leptopoma vitreum (Lesson,
1830). Masahet Id., Lihir Group,
Bismarck Ids. Syn.: *nitidum*
Sowerby, 1843.

Woodford's Leptopoma
(0.5") 1.2 cm
Leptopoma woodfordi Sowerby,
1889. Guadacanal Id., Solomon
Ids.

Helicoid Leptopoma
(0.5") 1.2 cm
*Leptopoma (Trocholeptopoma)
helicoides* (Grateloup, 1840).
Luzon Id., Philippines.

Polillo Leptopoma (0.9") 2.1 cm
Leptopoma polillanum (Moellendorff, 1894). Polillo Id; east of Luzon Id., Philippines.

Stainforth's Leptopoma
(0.4") 8 mm
Leptopoma stainforthi (Sowerby, 1842). Ticao Id., Philippines.

Roepstorff's Leptopoma
(0.3") 1 cm
Leptopoma roepstorffianum Nevill, 1878. Andaman Ids., Bay of Bengal.

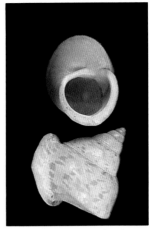

Fibula Leptopoma (0.8") 2 cm
Leptopoma fibula (Sowerby, 1843). Borneo, Indonesia.

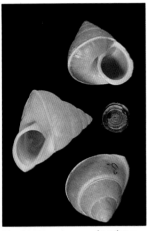

Cap Leptopoma (0.4") 8 mm
Leptopoma pileus (Sowerby, 1843). Sinait, Ilocos Prov., Luzon Id., Philippines.. Syntypes from H. Cuming.

Busuanga Leptopoma
(0.5") 2.2 cm
Leptopoma sericinum Quadras & Moellendorff, 1894. Busuanga Id., Philippines. Syntypes.

Sado Leptopoma (0.4") 6 mm
Japonia sadoensis Pilsbry & Hirase, 1903. Niibomura, Sado, Japan. Photo by Masao Azuma.

Hairy-edged Snail 4 mm
Craspedotropis cuspidata (Benson, 1851). India. Type of the genus.

Planorb Two-edge Snail 6 mm
Ditropis planorbis (Blanford, 1869). Tinnwalley, Madura Hills, India. Type of the genus.

Marie's Cow-horn Snail
(0.5") 1.2 cm
Cyclosurus mariei Morelet, 1881. Mayotte Id., Comores Ids., Indian Ocean. Type and sole species of genus.

Mesager's Cyclophorus
(1") 2.5 cm
Ptychopoma mesageri (Bavay & Dautzenberg, 1900). Tonkin, S.E. Asia.

Hensan Cyclophorus
(1") 2.5 cm
Ptychopoma hensanense (Gredler, 1887). Hunan Province, China.

Giant Planorb Cyclophorus
(1.5") 4 cm
Crossopoma cornuvenatorium (Gmelin, 1791). Sumatra Id. Syn. and type of genus: *planorbulum* (Lamarck, 1822).

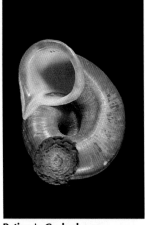

Petiver's Cyclophorus
(1.3") 3 cm
Myxostoma petiverianum (Wood, 1828). Pulo Condor Id., off south China. Type and sole species in genus.

Theobald's Cyclophorus
(1.5") 4 cm
Theobaldius annulatus (Troschel, 1847). Koondah Mountains, India.

Snaky Cyclophorus   (1.2") 3 cm
Theobaldius anguis Hanley & Theobald, 1875. Nilgiris, India.

Hirsute Hairy-edge Snail
(0.4") 6 mm
Scabrina hirsuta Moellendorff, 1884. Hainan Island, south China.

Denuded Hairy-edge Snail
(0.5") 1.2 cm
Scabrina denudata Bavay & Dautzenberg, 1899. Lao Kay, Vietnam. Syntypes from Dautzenberg.

Locard's Hairy Cyclophorus
(0.5") 1.2 cm
Scabrina locardi (Mabille, 1887). Haiphong, north Vietnam.

Intricate Cyclophorus
(1.3") 3.1 cm
Cyclophorus involutus (Müller, 1774). Common, operculate snail with two tentacles. Ground dwellers.

Intricate Cyclophorus
(1.3") 3.1 cm
Cyclophorus involutus (Müller, 1774). Throughout Sri Lanka Id. (Ceylon). Common.

Wandering Cyclophorus
(1.3") 3.1 cm
Cyclophorus altivagus Benson, 1854. India.

Arthritic Cyclophorus   (2") 5 cm
Cyclophorus arthriticus Theobald, 1864. Tonghoo, Burma. (with operculum).

Beddome's Cyclophorus
(2.5") 6 cm
Cyclophorus beddomeanus Preston, 1914. Naga Hills, Assam.

Exceptional Cyclophorus
(2") 5 cm
Cyclophorus eximius Mousson,
1848. Rangoon area, Burma.

Himalayan Cyclophorus
(2") 5 cm
Cyclophorus himalayanus (Pfeiffer, 1851). Himalayan Mountains,
north India.

Indian Cyclophorus
(1.5") 3.6 cm
Cyclophorus indicus Deshayes,
1832. Poona and east of Bombay, India.

Pearson's Cyclophorus
(1.5") 3.6 cm
Cyclophorus pearsoni Benson,
1851. Khasi Hills, Shillong, Assam.

Siam Cyclophorus (2.5") 6 cm
Cyclophorus siamensis (Sowerby,
1850). Khasi Hills, Assam.

Narrow Cyclophorus
(1.5") 3.5 cm
Cyclophorus stenomphalus
(Pfeiffer, 1846). Near Bombay,
India. Extinct?

Zebra Cyclophorus (2") 5 cm
Cyclophorus zebrinus (Benson,
1836). Khasi Hills, Assam, India.

Zebra Cyclophorus (2") 5 cm
Cyclophorus zebrinus (Benson,
1836). Shillong, Assam. Showing variations.

Sharp-edged Cyclophorus
(1") 2.5 cm
Cyclophorus acutimarginatus
(Sowerby, 1842). Near Borongan, Samar Id., Philippines. Extinct?

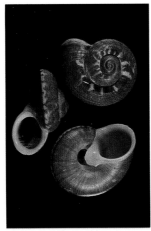

Appended Cyclophorus
(1.2") 3 cm
Cyclophorus appendiculatus
(Pfeiffer, 1851). Lubang Id., Philippines.

Appended Cyclophorus
(1.2") 3 cm
Cyclophorus appendiculatus
(Pfeiffer, 1851) forma *residiva*
Moellendorff, 1898. Naujan,
Mindoro Id., Philippines.

Appended Cyclophorus
(1.2") 3 cm
Cyclophorus appendiculatus
(Pfeiffer, 1851). Boac, Marinduque Id., Philippines.

Golden-mouthed Cyclophorus
(3") 7 cm
Cyclophorus aurantiacus (Schumacher, 1817). Burma.

Golden-mouthed Cyclophorus
(3") 7 cm
Cyclophorus aurantiacus (Schumacher, 1817). Burma.

Malayan Cyclophorus
(2.5") 6 cm
Cyclophorus malayanus (Benson, 1852). Samui, Thailand.

Excellent Cyclophorus
(1.5") 6 cm
Cyclophorus excellens (Pfeiffer, 1854). Pegu, Burma.

Pfeiffer's Cyclophorus
(2") 5 cm
Cyclophorus pfeifferi (Reeve, 1861). Prang, Malaya.

Swarthy Cyclophorus
(1.7") 4 cm
Cyclophorus aquilus Sowerby, 1840. Singapore. Extinct?

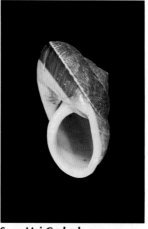

Song Mai Cyclophorus
(2") 5 cm
Cyclophorus songmaensis Morelet, 1891. Song Mai, Vietnam.

Borneo Cyclophorus
(1.5") 4 cm
Cyclophorus borneense (Metcalfe, 1851). Labuan Id., Borneo.

Kinabalu Cyclophorus
(1.7") 4.5 cm
Cyclophorus kinabaluensis E.A. Smith, 1895. Mt. Kinabalu, north Borneo.

Flame Cyclophorus (3") 7 cm
Cyclophorus fulguratus (Pfeiffer, 1852). Pegu; Burma; Thailand.

Tuba Cyclophorus (2.2") 5 cm
Cyclophorus tuba (Sowerby, 1942). Malakka, Sumatra Id., Indonesia.

Darangan Cyclophorus
(1.5") 4 cm
Cyclophorus daranganicus Hidalgo, 1888. Polillo Id., east of Luzon Id., Philippines.

Prieto's Cyclophorus
(1.5") 3.5 cm
Cyclophorus prietoi Hidalgo,
1888. Paac, Catanduanes Id.,
Philippines.

Sturdy Cyclophorus (2") 5 cm
Cyclophorus validus (Sowerby,
1842). Leyte and Samar Ids.,
Philippines. Type of subgenus
Glossostylus.

Tricolored Cyclophorus
(2") 5 cm
Cyclophorus (G.) fusicolor Godwin-Austen, 1876. Chellah, Assam.

Kibler's Cyclophorus
(1.5") 4 cm
Cyclophorus (Otopoma) kibleri
Fulton, 1903. Nias Id., Sumatra.

Fernandez's Cyclophorus
(0.6") 2 cm
Cyclophorus fernandezi Hidalgo,
1890. Baco, Mindoro Id., Philippines

Saffron Cyclophorus (1") 2.5 cm
*Cyclophorus (Otopoma) croca-
tus* (Born, 1778). Nicobar Ids.,
Indian Ocean. Type of the subgenus.

Itier's Cyclophorus (1") 2.5 cm
Aulopoma itieri Guérin, 1847.
Sri Lanka. Type of the genus.
Operculum sculptured.

Grand Cyclophorus (1") 2.5 cm
Aulopoma grande (Pfeiffer,
1855). Sri Lanka.

Kenya Cyclophorus (1") 2.5 cm
Maizania magilensis (Craven,
1880). Diani Beach, Kenya. R.T.
Abbott, coll. 1950. In family
Maizaniidae.

Elevated Cyclophorus (1") 2.5 cm
Maizania elatior (von Martens,
1892). Uganda and Nyassland,
East Africa.

Japanese Peg Cyclophorus
(0.3") 9 mm
Spirostoma japonicum (A.
Adams, 1867). Shikoku Id., Japan. Type of the genus. Operculum peglike.

Rocky Cyclophorus
(0.9") 2.2 cm
Pterocyclos rupestris Benson,
1832. Bengal.

Two-horned Cyclophorus
(1") 2.5 cm
Pterocyclos birostris (Pfeiffer, 1854). Borneo.

Wide-mouthed Cyclophorus
(1.4") 3 cm
Pterocyclos latilabrum E.A. Smith, 1895. Banguey Id., Borneo.

Enganio Cyclophorus
(1.3") 3 cm
Pterocyclos enganoensis (Aldrich, 1898). Enganio Id., S.W. Sumatra Id., Indonesia.

Angulate Cyclophorus
(1.3") 3 cm
Pterocyclos anguliferus (Souleyet, 1841). Viet Nam. Mature specimen.

Angulate Cyclophorus
(1.3") 3 cm
Pterocyclos anguliferus (Souleyet, 1841). Viet Nam Immature specimen.

Short-lip Cyclophorus
(1.3") 3 cm
Pterocyclos tenuilabiatus (Metcalfe, 1851). Borneo.

Cuming's Cyclophorus
(0.8") 2.1 cm
Pterocyclos cumingi Pfeiffer, 1851. Sri Lanka (Ceylon).

Variegated Cyclophorus
(1") 2.5 cm
Cyclotus variegatus Swainson, 1840. Basilan Id., Philippines. Type of the genus.

Palawan Cyclophorus
(1") 2.5 cm
Cyclotus palawanicus E.A. Smith, 1895. Palawan Id., Philippines.

Pearson's Snorkel Cyclophorus
(1.2") 3 cm
Pearsonia hispida (Pearson, 1833). Khasi Hills, Assam, India.

House's Snorkel Cyclophorus
(1") 2.5 cm
Rhiostoma housei (Haines, 1855). Koh-Samui Id., Gulf of Siam. Syn.: *haughtoni* Benson, 1860 from Burma. Type of genus.

Snorkel Cyclophorus
(1") 2.5 cm
Rhiostoma from Thailand. When withdrawn behind operculum, breathing done by "snorkel." *R. haughtoni* is type of the genus.

Smith's Snorkel Cyclophorus
(2") 5 cm
Rhiostoma smithi Bartsch, 1932.
Kao Sabah, Thailand. Paratype.

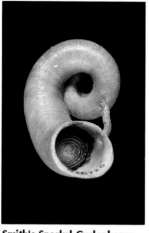

Smith's Snorkel Cyclophorus
(2") 5 cm
Rhiostoma smithi Bartsch, 1932.
Kao Sabah, Thailand. Paratype.

Feathery Cyclophorus 9 mm
Mychopoma pennatum Jutting,
1958. In trees, Fakal, Misool Id.,
West New Guinea. Paratype.

Family POTERIIDAE

This is the New World equivalent of the Asian cyclophorid snails but in most cases the multispiral operculum is calcareous. The males have a thin penis on the dorsal midline of the head. Main genera *Poteria, Neocyclotus, Crocidopoma* and *Mexcylotus* are in tropical Americas, but small *Ostodes* and *Gassiesia* are on South Pacific islands. All are ground-dwellers.

Streaked Ostodes (0.6") 1 cm
Ostodes strigatus (Gould, 1847).
Tutuila Id., Samoa. Common.
Type of genus. R.T. Abbott, coll.
1939.

Jamaica Poteria (1.3") 3.2 cm
Poteria jamaicensis (Wood,
1828). Jamaica. Type of the genus. Common among limestone rocks.

Corrugate Poteria (1") 2.3 cm
Ptychocochlis corrugata (Menke,
1830). St. Ann's Parish, Jamaica.
Syn.: *portlandensis* (Chitty, 1857).

Marten's Poteria (1.2") 3 cm
Ptychocochlis martensi (Kobelt,
1912). Northern Jamaica.

Pale Poteria (1.2") 3 cm
Poteria pallescens (C.B. Adams,
1852). Northeastern Jamaica.

Ribbon Poteria (1.2") 3 cm
Neocyclotus cingulatus (Sowerby, 1843). Pereiza, Cauca, Colombia.

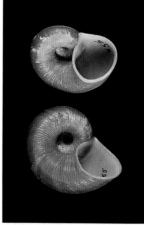

Quito Poteria (1.5") 3.5 cm
Neocyclotus quitensis (Pfeiffer,
1852). Quito, Ecuador.

Buckley's Cyclotus (0.8") 2.2 cm
Buckleyia martinezi (Hidalgo,
1866). Ecuador. Syn.: *montezumi*
Higgins, 1872. Type of the genus.

Sutured Cyclotus (0.5") 1.2 cm *Cyclojamaicia suturalis* (Sowerby, 1843). St. Elizabeth Parish, Jamaica. Type of the genus.

Mexican Cyclotus (1.1") 2.7 cm *Aperostoma mexicanum* (Menke, 1830). Vera Cruz, Mexico. Type of the genus.

Half-nude Cyclotus (1") 2.5 cm *Neocyclotus seminudus* (C.B. Adams, 1852). Jamaica. Type of subgenus *Cyclodamsia*.

Ruber Cyclotus (1") 2.5 cm *Neocyclotus (Cycloadamsia) ruber* (Chitty, 1857). St. Elizabeth Parish, Jamaica.

Striate Cyclotus (0.5") 1.2 cm *Cyclopilsbrya striosa* (Chitty, 1857). Ipswich, St. Elizabeth, Jamaica.

Translucent Cyclotus (1") 2.5 cm *Neocyclotus translucidus* (Sowerby, 1843) subsp. *trinitensis*, Crosse, 1890. Trinidad, West Indies.

Perez's Cyclotus (1") 2.5 cm *Neocyclotus perezi* (Hidalgo, 1866). El Oriente Prov., Ecuador.

Twirling Farcimen (1") 2.5 cm *Farcimen tortum* (Wood, 1828). Havana Prov., Cuba. Type of genus. Subfamily Megalomastomatinae.

Bi-tubercle Farcimen (1.4") 3 cm *Farcimen bituberculatum* (Sowerby, 1843) subspecies *giganteum* Torre & Bartsch, 1942. Trinidad, Cuba.

Henderson's Farcimen (1") 2.5 cm *Farcimen hendersoni* Torre & Bartsch, 1942. La Cantera, Pinar del Rio, Cuba.

Man's Farcimen (1.3") 3 cm *Farcimen mani* (Poey, 1851). Near Rangel, Pinar del Rio, Cuba.

High Farcimen (1.3") 3 cm *Farcimen procer* (Poey, 1854). Sierra Casas, Isle of Pines (Youth), Cuba. See also p. 47.

Brown Megalomouth (0.7") 2 cm
Megalomastoma brunneum
Swainson, 1840. Virgin Islands,
Lesser Antilles. Common on
ground.

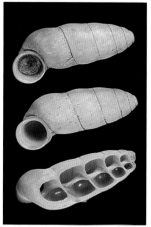

Saffron Megalomouth (1.2") 3 cm
Megalomastoma croceum
(Gmelin, 1791). Puerto Rico.
Common on ground in woods.

Geale's Cyclotus (2") 6 cm
Tomocyclus gealei Crosse & Fischer, 1872. Guatemala. Surface
with riblets.

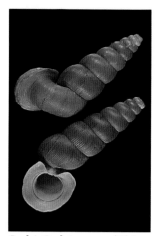

Geale's Cyclotus (2") 6 cm
Tomocyclus gealei Crosse & Fischer, 1872. Guatemala. Embay-
ment in lip-collar.

Similar Cyclotus (1.4") 3 cm
Tomocyclus simulacrum
(Morelet, 1849). Vera Paz, Gua-
temala. Type of the genus.

Wentletrap Cyclotus (1.5") 4 cm
Acroptychia metableta Crosse &
Fischer, 1877. Madagascar. May
be in Pomatiasidae.

Family
DIPLOMMATINIDAE

A large family of small,
ground-dwelling, operculate
snails. Whorls often irregu-
larly coiled. Radulae with
seven rows of teeth (taenioglossate). Contains Asian *Nicida* and *Opisthostoma*, as
well as the small European
Cochlostomatinae with a two-
layered operculum.

Roebelen's Mustard Snail 6mm
Alycaeus roebeleni Moellendorff,
1894. Koh-Samui, Thailand.
Topotypes. Subfamily Aly-
caeinae.

Belted Nicida Snail 2 mm
Nicida liricincta (Blanford, 1868).
Poona, India. One spiral cord on
convex whorls.

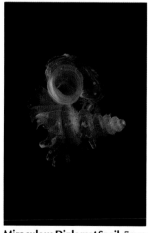

Miraculous Diplomat Snail 5mm
Opisthostoma mirabile E.A.
Smith, 1893. Gomantong Caves,
Sandakan, Sabah. Photo by R.
Robertson.

Miraculous Diplomat Snail 5 mm
Opisthostoma mirabile E.A.
Smith, 1893. Sandakan, Sabah.
Photo by Fred Thompson.

Large-spined Diplomat Snail
2.4 mm
Opisthostoma (*Geothauma*) *gran-
dispinosum* Godwin-Austen,
1889. Niah Hills, Sarawak. Photo
by Fred Thompson.

Beddome's Diplomat Snail 2mm
Opisthostoma (Plectostoma) beddomei E.A. Smith, 1904. Sarawak, North Borneo. Photo by Fred Thompson.

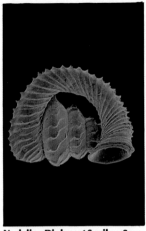

Yodeling Diplomat Snail 2mm
Opisthostoma (Plectostoma) species. Sarawak, North Borneo. Photo by Fred Thompson.

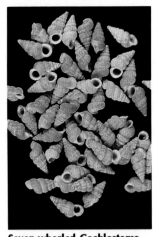

Seven-whorled Cochlostome 8mm
Cochlostoma septemspirale (Razoumowsky, 1789). Southern France to Austria. Woodland floor. Common.

Ear-mouth Cochlostome 9mm
Cochlostoma (Auritus) auritum (Rossmässler, 1837). Dalmatia, Hungary.

Family PUPINIDAE

Small, ovoid-conical, shells, many with a bright, polished surface. Aperture circular, thick-edged with an accessory breathing canal. Operculum corneous, multispiral. Males usually without a penis. Live and feed on damp moss. Genera *Pupina*, *Moulinsia* and *Tortulosa* are from southeast Asia, Australia and Melanesia. *Realia* (subfamily Realiinae) is from New Zealand.

Elephant Pupina (1") 2.5 cm
Pollicaria elephas (de Morgan, 1885). Malacca and Perak, Borneo.

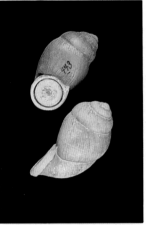

Rochebrun's Pupina (1.5") 3.6 cm
Pollicaria rochebruni (Mabille, 1887) form *crossei* Dautzenberg & Hamonville, 1887. Cho-Ra, Vietnam.

Forbes' Pupina (1") 2.5 cm
Scaeopupina forbesi (Pfeiffer, 1853). Louisiade Ids., Bismarcks. Syn.: *grandis* Forbes, 1852, non Gray, 1841.

Southern Pupina (0.5") 1.3 cm
Pupina (Signepupina) meridionalis (Pfeiffer, 1864). North Queensland.

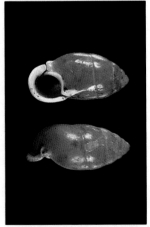

Two-canal Pupina 6mm
Pupina (Tyloechus) bicanaliculata (Sowerby, 1841). Cebu Id., Philippines.

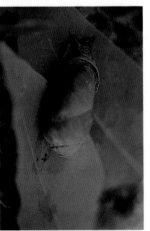

Pollicaria Pupina (1.5") 3.6 cm
Pollicaria from Thailand. Operculum corneous, circular. Note leopard pattern on head. Photo by Fred Thompson.

Swinhoe's Pupina 6mm
Pupinella (Pupinopsis) swinhoei (H. Adams, 1866). Hotawa, Taiwan Id. Type of the subgenus.

Golden Pupina (0.3") 8 mm
Moulinsia aurantia (Grateloup, 1840). Luzon Id., Philippines. Orange to yellow in color. Syn: *grandis* Gray, 1840.

Dusky Pupina (0.3") 8 mm
Moulinsia fusca (Gray, 1840). Southern Luzon Id., Philippines.

Chrysalis Pupina (0.8") 2 cm
Rhaphaulus chrysalis (Pfeiffer, 1852). Maulmein, Burma. R. *chrysallis* is a misspelling.

Blanford's Pupina (0.2") 6 mm
Streptaulus blanfordi (Benson, 1857). Darjiling, India.

Tall Schistolome (1.2") 3 cm
Schistoloma alta (Sowerby, 1842). Negros Id., Philippines. Common ground snail.

Funiculate Schistolome
(1") 2.5 cm
Schistoloma funiculata (Sowerby, 1850). Darjiling, India.

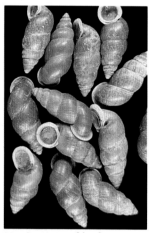

MacGregor's Schistolome
(1") 2.5 cm
Schistoloma macgregori Bartsch, 1909. Mindoro and Tablas Ids., Philippines. Paratypes.

Recurved Tortulose Snail
(1") 2.5 cm
Tortulosa recurvata (Pfeiffer, 1862). Anamullay Mountains, India.

Austen's Tortulose Snail
(1") 2.5 cm
Tortulosa austeniana (Benson, 1853). Heneratgodde, Sri Lanka (Ceylon).

Layard's Tortulose Snail
(1") 2.5 cm
Tortulosa layardi (Pfeiffer, 1852). Rambodde, Sri Lanka (Ceylon).

Miranda Farcimen (1.5") 3 cm
Farcimen ungula Poey, 1856 forma *miranda* Pilsbry, 1940. Oriente Prov., Cuba. Paratypes.

Ventricose Farcimen (1") 2.5 cm
Farcimen ventricosum (Orbigny, 1842). Pan de Guajaibon, Cuba. Abundant on ground. See p. 44.

Superfamily
LITTORINOIDEA

Family **POMATIASIDAE**
(Pomatiidae)

A large family of operculate snails with turbinate to turret-shaped shells. Operculum chitinous within, calcareous on the outside. Males with a penis behind the right tentacle. Most ground-dwellers, preferring lime stone areas. Many species in Europe (*Pomatias*), Madagascar (*Tropidophora*) and Indian Ocean islands.

Half-threaded Cyclotope
(0.4") 1 cm
Cyclotopsis semistriata (Sowerby, 1843). Poona, India. Type of the genus.

Land Natica (2") 5 cm
Socotora naticoides (Récluz, 1843). Socotra Island, mouth of Red Sea. Syn.: *Georgia* Bourguignat, 1882, non Thompson, 1857.

Insular Tropid Snail (0.4") 7 mm
Tropidophora (Ligatella) insularis (Pfeiffer, 1851). Kowie, South Africa. (and Mauritius?).

Cuvier's Tropid Snail
(3") 7.5 cm
Tropidophora cuvieriana (Petit, 1841). Northeastern Madagascar. Extinct. Type of the genus.

Carinate Tropid Snail
(1.5") 4 cm
Tropidophora tricarinata (Müller, 1774) forma *carinata* (Born, 1778). Madagascar. Extinct.

Rough Tropid Snail (1.2") 3 cm
Tropidophora aspera (Potiez & Michaud, 1838). Madagascar.

Articulate Tropid Snail
(1") 2.5 cm
Tropidophora articulata (Gray, 1834). Rodriquez and Mauritius Ids., Indian Ocean.

Sir David's Tropid Snail
(1") 2.5 cm
Tropidophora barclayana (Pfeiffer, 1851). Mauritius.

Betsilo Tropid Snail (1") 2.5 cm
Tropidophora betsiloensis (E.A. Smith, 1882). Matilavu, Madagascar. Alt. 600 meters.

Bi-carinate Tropid Snail
(1.5") 4 cm
Tropidophora tricarinata forma *bicarinata* (Sowerby, 1843). Madagascar. Extinct.

Kindred Tropid Snail
(1.3") 3 cm
Tropidophora tricarinata forma *consanguinea* (Sowerby, 1874). Fort Dauphin, Madagascar.

Mrs. de Burgh's Tropid Snail
(2.5") 6 cm
Tropidophora deburghiae (Reeve, 1861). Mananara, Madagascar. Very rare.

Mrs. de Burgh's Tropid Snail
(1.5") 6 cm
Tropidophora deburghiae (Reeve, 1861). Madagascar. Dorsal view.

Delicious Tropid Snail
(1") 2.5 cm
Tropidophora deliciosa (Férussac, in Sowerby, 1850). Madagascar.

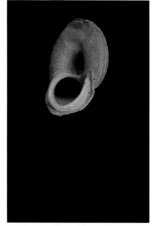

Deshayes' Tropid Snail
(0.8") 2.2 cm
Tropidophora deshayesiana (Petit, 1844). Southern Madagascar.

Beautiful Tropid Snail
(2") 5 cm
Tropidophora formosa (Sowerby, 1849). East coast of Madagascar. Extinct?

Michaud's Tropid Snail
(1.2") 3 cm
Tropidophora michaudi (Grateloup, 1840). Madagascar.

Moulins' Tropid Snail
(1.5") 3.5 cm
Tropidophora moulinsii (Grateloup, 1840). Madagascar. Syn.: *carinifera* (Sowerby, 1843).

Many-striped Tropid Snail
(1.5") 3.5 cm
Tropidophora multifasciata (Grateloup, 1840). Maromandia, Madagascar. Syn.: *belairi* Petit, 1853.

Tri-carinate Tropid Snail
(1") 2.5 cm
Tropidophora tricarinata (Müller, 1774). Mauritius (and Madagascar). Many forms named.

One-carinate Tropid Snail
(1.5") 4 cm
Tropidophora tricarinata forma *unicarinata* (Lamarck, 1822). Madagascar. Syn.: *fulvifrons* (Sowerby).

Ribboned Tropid Snail
(1.3") 3 cm
Tropidophora vittata (Sowerby, 1843). Nossi Bé, Madagascar.

Purple-mouth Tropid Snail
(1") 2.5 cm
Tropidophora xanthocheilus (Sowerby, 1850). Mayotte Island.

Zoned Tropid Snail (1.5") 3 cm
Tropidophora zonata (Petit, 1850). Madagascar.

Elegant Pomatias (0.6") 1.6 cm
Pomatias elegans (Müller, 1774). South England, France, Belgium, West Germany. Type of the genus.

Sulcate Pomatias (0.5") 1.3 cm
Pomatias sulcata (Draparnaud, 1805). Around the Mediterranean area and Malta.

Family ANNULARIIDAE
(Chondropomatidae; Licinidae)

Similar to the Old World Pomatiasidae but separated on radula and anatomical grounds (see F. Thompson, 1978). Penis behind right tentacle. All prefer limestone habitat; most less than one inch (2.5 cm). Apertural lip flaring, sometimes with tube or pore. Operculum corneous or calcified. Foot ditaxic (shuffles one side at a time). Numerous genera and species, especially in Cuba.

Vignales Annularid (0.6") 1.8 cm
Chondropometes (C.) vignalense (Pfeiffer, 1863). Near San Vicente, Pinar del Rio, Cuba. Type of genus.

Clapp's Annularid (0.9") 2.2 cm
Chondropometes vignalense subsp. *clappi* Torre & Bartsch, 1938. N. end of Sierra de la Chorrera, Pinar del Rio, Cuba. Paratypes.

de la Torre's Annularid
(1") 2.4 cm
Chondropometes (C.) torrei Torre & Bartsch, 1938. Mogote Canalete, P. de R., Cuba. Paratype.

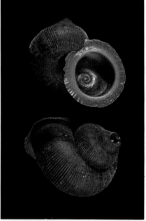

Mina Annularid (1") 2.3 cm
Chondropometes (C.) torrei subsp. *minaense* Torre & Bartsch, 1938. Mogote Mina, P. del R., Cuba. Paratypes.

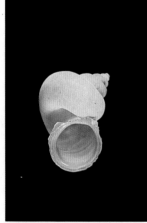

Wide-lipped Annularid
(0.6") 1.8 cm
Chondropometes (C.) latilabre (Orbigny, 1842). San Juan de Sagua, P. del R., Cuba.

Exquisite Annularid (0.6") 1.9 cm
Chondropometes (Chondrothyroma) exquisitum Torre & Bartsch, 1938. Sierra la Guira, P. del R., Cuba. Paratypes.

Prettiest Annularid (1") 2.5 cm
Chondropometes (Chondrothyroma) bellisimum Torre & Bartsch, 1938. Mogote del Bosque de Galalon, Cuba.

Henderson's Annularid
(1.3") 3.1 cm
Hendersonina hendersoni (Torre, 1909). Costanera del Abra, P. del R., Cuba. Type of the genus.

Sinuate Annularid (1") 2.5 cm
Turrithyra (Turrithyretes) sinuosa(Pfeiffer, 1862), forma *vicinia* Torre & Bartsch, 1938. Sierra Vinales, Cuba. Paratypes.

Deceptive Annularid
(1") 2.3 cm
Turrithyra (Turrithyra) deceptor (Arango, 1882). West end of Sierra San Andrés, Cuba.

Distinguished Annularid
(1.1") 2.7 cm
Chondrothyra (C.) egregia (Pfeiffer, 1856). Vinales Valley, Cuba. Type of genus.

Red Annularid (1.1") 2.7 cm
Chondrothyra (C.) egregia form *rutila* Torre & Bartsch, 1938. El Queque, Pinar del Rio, Cuba. Animal rose-red. Paratypes.

Black-mouth Annularid
(1.1") 2.7 cm
Chondrothyra (C.) atristoma Torre & Bartsch, 1938. Abra de Bejarano, Vinales, Cuba. Paratypes.

Discolored Annularid
(0.7") 2 cm
Chondrothyra discolorans(Pfeiffer, 1863). Mogotes in Vinales Valley, Cuba.

Uniplicate Annularid
(1") 2.4 cm
Chondrothyra (Plicathyra) uniplicata Torre & Bartsch, 1938. Cayo San Felipe, P. del R., Cuba.

Crass Annularid (1.3") 3 cm
Chondrothyra (Plicathyra) crassa Torre & Bartsch, 1938. Luiz Lazo, Sierra San Carlos, P. del R., Cuba.

Large Impressed Annularid
(1") 2.5 cm
Chondrothyretes impressa T.& B., 1938, forma *gigantea* Torre & Bartsch, 1938. Vinales Valley, Cuba.

Rosario Annularid
(0.7") 1.7 cm
Chondrothyretes impressa forma *rosariensis* Torre & Bartsch, 1938. Sierra El Rosario, P. del R., Cuba.

Reticulated Annularid
(1.1") 2.6 cm
*Chondrothyretes reticulata*Torre & Bartsch, 1938. Banos San Vincente, P. del R., Cuba.

Thickened Annularid
(1.1") 2.6 cm
Chondrothyretes incrassata (Pfeiffer, 1862). Sierra Vinales, Pinar del Rio, Cuba

Thickened Annularid
(1.1") 2.6 cm
Chondrothyretes incrassata (Pfeiffer, 1862), forma *aurantiaca* Torre & Bartsch, 1938. Vinales Valley, Pinar del Rio, Cuba.

Barbour's Annularid
(1.4") 3.4 cm
Chondrothyretes barbouri Torre & Bartsch, 1938. San Carlos Magote, P. del R., Cuba. Paratypes.

Gundlach's Annularid
(1") 2.3 cm
Chondrothyretes gundlachi (Arango, 1862). Sierra de Paso Real, P. del R., Cuba. Paratypes.

Related Annularid   (1.2") 3 cm
Chondrothyretes affinis Torre & Bartsch, 1938. Vinales Valley, P. del R., Cuba.

Equal Annularid   (1") 2.4 cm
Chondrothyretes parilis Torre & Bartsch, 1938. Mogote de la Jagua, Vinales, Cuba.

Modest Annularid   (0.6") 1.5 cm
Chondrothyrella (C.) pudica (Orbigny, 1842). Mt. Guajaibon, P. del R., Cuba. Type of the genus.

Painted Annularid   (0.7") 2 cm
Chondropoma (C.) pictum (Pfeiffer, 1839). Pinar del Rio and Matanzas Prov., Cuba.

Gould's Annularid   (1") 2.5 cm
Chondropoma pictum subsp. *gouldianum* (Poey, 1854). Yumari Valley, Cuba.

Cape Comet Annularid
(0.4") 1 cm
Chondropoma (Chondrops) cometense Bartsch, 1946. Cape Comete, East Caicos Id., Bahamas.

Augusta's Annularid
(0.5") 1.2 cm
Parachondria augustae (C.B. Adams, 1849), forma *rufilabra* C.B. Adams, 1851. Port Antonio, Jamaica.

Columnar Annularid (0.4") 1 cm
Parachondria columna (Wood, 1828). Mt. Diablo, Jamaica.

Candé's Annularid (0.5") 2.1 cm
Annularia (Trochelvindex) candeana (Orbigny, 1842). Matanzas Prov., Cuba. Common.

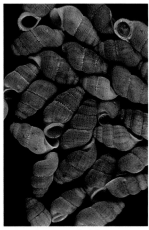

Bahamian Annularid
(0.5") 1.2 cm
Opisthosiphon bahamiense (Shuttleworth, 1865). New Providence Id., Bahamas. Minute tube at upper end of aperture.

Prickly Xenopoma (0.6") 1.4 cm
Xenopoma hystris (Pfeiffer, 1861). Cayo del Rey, Oriente Prov., Cuba. Type of the genus.

Most Spiny Xenopoma
(0.5") 1.2 cm
Xenopoma spinosissimum Torre & Bartsch, 1941. Cayo del Rey, Oriente Prov., Cuba.

Wonderful Adamsnail
(0.5") 2.1 cm
Adamsiella miranda (C.B. Adams, 1848). Hollymount, Jamaica.

Mrs. Pearman's Adamsnail
(0.3") 1 cm
Adamsiella pearmanaeana (Chitty, 1853). Trelawny Parish, Jamaica.

Monstrous Adamsnail
(0.3") 1 cm
Adamsiella monstrosa (C.B. Adams, 1849). Williamsfield, Jamaica.

Lacy Annularid (0.6") 1.6 cm
Annularia lincina (Linnaeus, 1758). Bogwalk, southern Jamaica. Type of the genus.

Beautiful Annularid (1.2") 3 cm
Annularia pulchra (Wood, 1828). Dry Harbour Mountain, Jamaica.

Fimbriated Annularid
(0.6") 1.6 cm
Annularia fimbriatula (Sowerby, 1825). Mandeville, Jamaica.

Victor's Annularid (0.6") 1.6 cm
Annularia (Annularella) victoris Torre & Bartsch, 1941. Cape Maisi, Oriente Prov., Cuba.

Brittle Snowflake Snail 8mm
Meganipha rhecta Thompson, 1978. Puerto Plata Prov., Dominican Republic, 700 m. alt. Paratypes.

Morelet's Abbottsnail
(0.5") 1.2 cm
Abbottella moreletiana (Crosse, 1873). Samana Peninsula, Dominican Republic. Type of the genus.

Edged Annularid (0.5") 1.2 cm *Annularia (Eutudora) limbifera* (Pfeiffer, 1846). Matanzas and Santa Clara Prov., Cuba. Common.

Camoa Annularid (0.6") 1.5 cm *Annularia (Eutudorisca) camoensis* Torre & Bartsch, 1941. Loma de Camoa, Habana Prov., Cuba.

Cuban Porcupine Snail (0.4") 1 cm *Blaesospira echinus* (Pfeiffer, 1864). El Queque, Palmarito, Vinales, Ciba.

Roca's Porcupine Snail (0.3") 9 mm *Blaesospira rocai* Torre & Bartsch, 1941. North side of Sierra de San Andreas, W. Cuba.

Family ASSIMINEIDAE

A worldwide family of small amphibious to terrestrial snails. Gills greatly reduced; eyes at the base of short, stubby tentacles. Operculum corneous, few-whorled. Sexes separate. Several genera and many Southeast Asian and Philippine species, usually found in estuarine conditions. Includes such genera as *Assiminea* (formerly *Syncera*), *Paludinella* and *Omphalotropis*.

 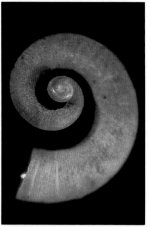 

Coultas False Cyclotus (0.3") 1 cm *Pseudocyclotus coultasi* Clench, 1959. Tavi Village, Manus Id., Admiralty Ids. Paratypes.

Balamban Snail 4 mm *Balambania aries* (Moellendorff, 1890). Philippines. Type of the genus.

Cooke's Land Periwinkle 5mm *Omphalotropis cookei* Abbott, 1949. Flores Point, Saipan Id., Mariannas. Paratypes.

Superfamily RISSOACEA

Family TRUNCATELLIDAE

Very small, cylindrical, operculate shells. Gills degenerated. Sexes separate, the males with a simple penis. *Truncatella* is worldwide, smooth or ribbed, and lives under debris near the seashore. *Geomelania* is entirely terrestrial and common in Jamaica. They occur in large colonies.

  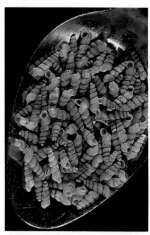

Beautiful Truncatella 4mm *Truncatella pulchella* Pfeiffer, 1839. S. Florida; West Indies. 17 to 40 riblets per whorl. Common.

Ladder Truncatella 5mm *Truncatella scalaris* (Michaud, 1830). Florida Keys; West Indies. 8 to 12 riblets per whorl.

Poor Geomelania (0.4") 1 cm *Geomelania pauperata* C.B. Adams, 1850. Jamaica hills. Common.

Subclass PULMONATA

Order ARCHAEOPULMONATA

Small, airbreathing snails with a pulmonary cavity, one pair of tentacles with eyes at the base. Usually no operculum. Hermaphrodites which lay eggs in jelly masses. Two families, the Ellobiidae represented by 21 genera, and the monotypic. Otinidae with its very small (2.5 mm) *Otina ovalis* from Europe.

Superfamily ELLOBIOIDEA
(syn.: Ellobiacca)

Family ELLOBIIDAE

Worldwide estuarine and land snails, varying from minute Pedipes (3 mm) to the 4-inch Ellobium of the tropics. Aperture usually has folds or teeth. Operculum absent. Some live in high mountains, or in caves, but most found on tidal mudflats or near mangroves. Planktonic veliger larvae may have operculum.

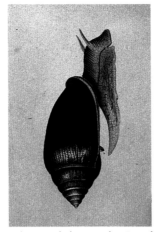

The 3-inch long Midas Ear of the East Indies has only one pair of tentacles and no operculum. This air-breathing ground snail lives on sandy mud flats near the sea.

Coffee Melampus (0.8") 2 cm *Melampus coffeus* (L., 1758). South Florida and Bermuda to Brazil. Common on mud near mangroves. Type of the genus. Syn.: *coniformis* (Brug., 1789).

Eastern American Melampus (0.6") 1.5 cm *Melampus bidentatus* Say, 1822. Southern Quebec to Texas; Bermuda; West Indies. Abundant in salt marshes.

Californian Melampus (0.6") 1.5 cm *Melampus olivaceus* Carpenter, 1857. California and Baja. Abundant in shady, salty debris. Syn.: *californianus* S.S. Berry, 1964.

Banded Melampus (0.5") 1.3 cm *Melampus fasciatus* Deshayes, 1830. Central Pacific. Shady, wooded shores; common.

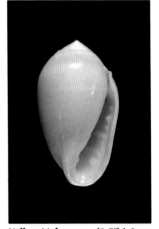

Yellow Melampus (0.5") 1.2 cm *Melampus luteus* Quoy & Gaimard, 1832. Indo-Pacific. In debris in shade near seashore. Abundant on soft earth.

Costate Tralia (0.2") 4 mm *Tralia costata* Quoy and Gaimard, 1832. Southwest Pacific. Uncommon in shoreline debris on muddy earth. Type of the subgenus *Persa* H. & A. Adams, 1855.

Louse Pedipes (0.2") 4 mm *Pedipes pedipes* (Bruguière, 1789). West Africa. On shoreline rocks above high tide mark in shade. Common.

Angular Pedipes (0.2") 6 mm *Pedipes angulatus* C.B. Adams, 1852. Southern California to Panama. Outer lip with one tooth. Locally common.

Miraculous Pedipes (0.2") 5 mm *Pedipes mirabilis* (Mühlfeld, 1816). Bermuda, South Florida to Texas and to Brazil. Under rocks above tide line. Locally common.

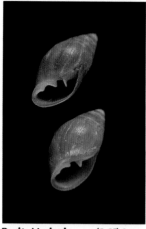

Pepita Marinula   (0.2") 6 mm
Marinula pepita King & Broderip, 1832. Seashore line of Chile. Type of the genus. Similar *M. succinea* (Pfeiffer, 1854) is from S.E. U.S., Cuba.

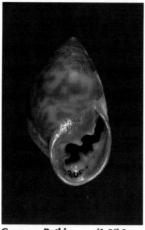

Common Pythia   (1.2") 3 cm
Pythia scarabaeus (L., 1758). S.W. Pacific. Woodland snail; common. Many forms. Type of the genus.

Reeve's Pythia   (1.2") 3 cm
Pythia reeveana Pfeiffer, 1853. Philippine Islands; locally common under leaves on ground.

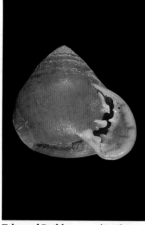

Trigonal Pythia   (0.8") 2 cm
Pythia trigonus Troschel, 1840. Philippines. Locally uncommon. Type of subgenus *Trigonopythia* Kobelt, 1898.

Cat's Ear Cassidula   (1") 2.5 cm
Cassidula aurisfelis (Bruguière, 1789). West Australia; mangroves. Common. Type of the genus.

Angulate Cassidula   (1") 2.5 cm
Cassidula angulifera Petit, 1841. Northwest Territory, Australia. Mud near mangroves. Locally common.

Nucleus Cassidula (0.6") 1.5 cm
Cassidula nucleus (Gmelin, 1791). Indo-Pacific; mangrove areas. Common. Syn.: *mustelina* Deshayes.

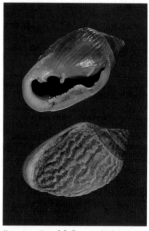

Rugose Cassidula   (1") 2.5 cm
Cassidula rugata Menke, 1853. South Australia. Mud shores. Locally common.

Bat Cassidula   (0.4") 1 cm
Cassidula vespertilionis (Lesson, 1831). Philippines. Mangroves; locally common.

Midas Ear Cassidula (3") 7.5 cm
Ellobium aurismidae (L. 1758). S.W. Pacific. Near mangroves; locally abundant. Shell white underneath periostracum.

Panama Swamp Cassidula
            (1.3") 3 cm
Ellobium stagnalis Orbigny, 1853. El Salvador to Ecuador. Mangrove swamps; common.

Judas Ear Cassidula   (2") 5 cm
Ellobium aurisjudae (L., 1758). S.W. Pacific. Mangrove swamps. Common.

Order BASOMMATOPHORA

Shells limpet like or coiled, usually without operculum, except in Amphibolidae. One pair of tentacles with eyes at base. Gills absent.

Superfamily AMPHIBULOIDEA (Amphibolacea)

Family AMPHIBOLIDAE

Only airbreathing pulmonate that retains operculum in the adult. Two genera found in Australasia and South Africa: Mainly intertidal brackish water species, locally common.

Superfamily SIPHONARIIODEA (Siphonariacea)

Family TRIMUSCULIDAE

White, cap-shaped shells. Operculum absent. Pulmonary furrow oblique and on right. 7 species, intertidal or in tropical marine caves.

Family SIPHONARIIDAE

Shells limpetlike, colored. Pulmonary interior furrow runs from apex to right margin. About 70 species in warm seas. Nocturnal, on rocks. Lay jelly egg masses.

New Zealand Amphibola (1") 2.5 cm *Amphibola avellana* (Bruguière, 1789). New Zealand. Type of the genus. Syn.: *crenata* Gmelin, 1791.

The New Zealand Amphibola has an operculum. It feeds on mudflat detritus and leaves a continuous sand string of feces. Jelly egg mass contains thousands of eggs.

Fragile Salinator (1/2") 1.5 cm *Salinator fragilis* (Lamarck, 1822). South Australia to Tasmania to south Queensland, Australia. Common on intertidal mudflats.

Reticulated Gadinia (1.2") 3 cm *Trimusculus reticulata* (Sowerby, 1835). S. California to Gulf of California. Uncommon in intertidal rocks. Syn.: *Gadinia*.

Stellate Gadinia (1/2") 15 mm *Trimusculus stellatus* (Sowerby, 1835). Gulf of California to Nicaragua. Intertidal on rocks; uncommon.

Fringed False Limpet (1") 2.5 cm *Siphonaria laciniosa* (L., 1758). Indo-Pacific. Common on shore rocks. Type of the genus. Syn.: *luzonica* Röding.

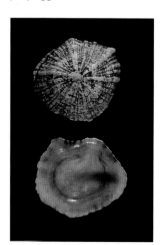

Say's False Limpet (0.7") 1.8 cm *Siphonaria alternata* Say, 1826. S.E. United States; Bahamas. Intertidal rock shore; common.

Antarctic False Limpet (1") 2.5 cm *Siphonaria antarctica* Gould, 1852. Orange Harbor, Argentina; S. Chile. Intertidal high rocks. Common.

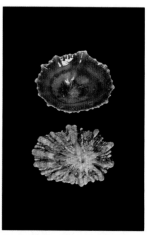

Austral False Limpet (1") 2.5 cm *Siphonaria australis* Quoy & Gaimard, 1833. Southern New Zealand on holdfasts of giant kelp. Common.

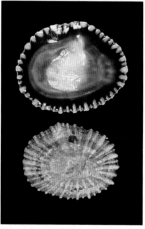

Van Diemen False Limpet (1") *Siphonaria diemenensis* Quoy & Gaimard, 1833. South Australia to Tasmania. Type of subgenus *Hubendickula* McAlpine, 1952. Common on rocks.

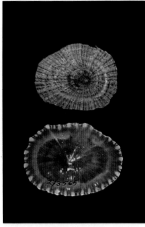

Japanese False Limpet
(1") 2.5 cm
Siphonaria japonica (Donovan, 1834). Southern Japan to south China. Common on shore rocks. 20 riblets.

Javanese False Limpet
(1") 2.5 cm
Siphonaria javanica (Lamarck, 1819). Indo-Pacific. Shore rocks. Common.

Lesson's False Limpet   2.5 cm
Siphonaria lessoni (Blainville, 1824). Peru to Uruguay; Falkland Ids. Type of subgenus *Pachysiphonaria* Hubendick, 1945. Common.

Striped False Limpet (1") 2.5 cm
Siphonaria pectinata (L., 1758). Florida to Texas, Caribbean, South Europe. Intertidal rocks; locally common. Type of subgenus *Patellopsis* Nobre, 1886.

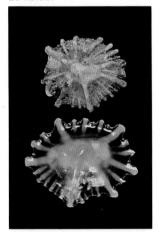

Sirius False Limpet (0.6") 1.3 cm
Siphonaria sirius Pilsbry, 1894. S.W. Pacific; Japan. Intertidal high rocks; common. Syn.: *subatra* Pilsbry, 1904.

Giant False Limpet   (2") 5 cm
Siphonaria gigas Sowerby, 1825. West Mexico to northern Peru. Intertidal rocks: common. Type of subgenus *Heterosiphonaria* Hubendick, 1945.

Oblique False Limpet   (2") 5 cm
Benhamina obliquata (Sowerby, 1825). Cook Strait, New Zealand southward. Common on shaded, upper tidal rocks. Type of the genus.

Order
STYLOMMATOPHORA

The majority of the pulmonate land snails and slugs belong to this order. Two pairs of tentacles, the top two bearing the eyes at the tips. Operculum absent. All are hermaphroditic. Lay eggs or incubate them in oviduct. Larval veliger stage absent. About 25,000 species worldwide. Four suborders.

Suborder ORTHURETHRA

Three primitive superfamilies with simple undivided foot; includes Hawaiian achatinellids, minute pupillid snails and Cochlicopoidea.

Superfamily
ACHATINELLOIDEA

Family ACHATINELLIDAE
A large family of primitive Pacific Island snails, some ground dwellers (Tornatellininae), others brightly colored and living in trees in Hawaii. Some give birth to 5 to 20 live snails, others lay single eggs. Species have limited distribution in valleys. Many have become extinct because of habitat destruction.

Splendid Partulina   (1") 2.5 cm
Partulina splendida (Newcomb, 1853). In the high valleys of west Maui. Photo by Mike Severns.

Tawny-tipped Achatinella
(0.7") 2 cm
Achatinella apexfulva (Dixon, 1789). Waialua, central Koolan Range, Oahu, Hawaii. 12 subspecies recognized

Bright-colored Achatinella
(0.7") 2 cm
A. a. chromatacme Pilsbry & Cooke, 1914. Manana-Waiawa Ridge, Koolau Range, Oahu. Tip pinkish buff. Holotype below.

Turgid Achatinella (0.7") 2 cm
Achatinella apexfulva subsp. *turgida* Newcomb, 1853. Waimano, south Central Oahu, Hawaii.

Swift's Achatinella (0.7") 2 cm
A.a. subsp. *turgida* forma *swifti* Newcomb, 1853. Wahiawa, S.W. Oahu, Hawaii. Yellowish blotched with brown.

Cooke's Achatinella (0.7") 2 cm
A.a. subsp. *cookei* Baldwin, 1895. Waimano-Manana Ridge, Oahu Id. Paratypes.

Concave Achatinella (0.7") 2 cm
Achatinella concavospira Pfeiffer, 1859. Palihua, south end of Waianae Range, Oahu Id., Hawaii. Syn.: *turbiniformis* Gulick, 1873. See *mustelina*.

Abbreviated Achatinella
(0.7") 2 cm
Achatinella abbreviata Reeve, 1850. Dextral. Crater of Palolo Valley, Oahu, in axils of ieie trees (*Freycinetia*). Base vivid green.

Bryon's Achatinella (0.7") 2 cm
Achatinella bryonii (Wood, 1828). Ahonui, Wahiawa District, Oahu. Name for Lord Byron who collected it in 1824. Several subspecies and rugose forms.

Budd's Achatinella (0.7") 2 cm
Achatinella buddii Newcomb, 1853. Formerly in Palolo Valley and Makiki, Oahu Id. Sinistral. In kukkui trees. Now extinct? Syn.: *fuscozona* E.A. Smith.

Bulimoid Achatinella (0.7") 2 cm
Achatinella bulimoides Swainson, 1828. Valleys Kawailoa, Waimea, Waialee, Oahu Id. Dextral. 6 subsp., many forma. Once common.

Decorated Achatinella
(0.8") 2.1 cm
Achatinella decora (Férussac, 1821). Kawailoa; Opaeulu; on kukui trees. Formerly abundant. Syn,: *perversa* Swainson, 1828.

Short Achatinella (0.6") 2 cm
Achatinella curta Newcomb, 1853. Ahonui to Kawailoa, and across the range in Laie, Oahu. Syn.: *delta* Gulick; *undulata* Newcomb.

Double-form Achatinella 1.8 cm
Achatinella dimorpha Gulick, 1858. Northwest ridges; Paumalu; Waialee, Oahu. Syn.: *albescens, zonata, contracta* all Gulick, 1858.

Flashy Achatinella (0.7") 2 cm
Achatinella fulgens Newcomb, 1853. Many-colored, sinistral; formerly common, northern Oahu. These from Kailua. Many synonyms.

Strapped Achatinella (0.7") 2 cm
Achatinella lorata (Férussac, 1824). Manoa to Moanalua, Koolau Range, Oahu Id. Many variations. Syn,: *pulchella* Pfeiffer, 1855.

Weasel Achatinella (0.7") 2 cm
Achatinella mustelina Mighels, 1845. Waianae Range, S.W. Oahu. Several races present. This from Pukuloa.

Lyman's Achatinella (0.7") 2 cm
A.m. lymaniana Baldwin, 1895. Waianae Range and Lihue, Oahu. Mostly sinistral. Subsutural white line absent. Syntypes.

Makaha Achatinella (0.7") 2 cm
Achatinella makahaensis Pilsbry & Cooke, 1914. Makaha Valley, S.W. Oahu. Paratypes.

More Beautiful Achatinella
(0.8") 2 cm
Achatinella pulcherrima Swainson, 1828. Koolau Range; Waialua; Kawaihalona, Oahu Id. Once common.

Rosy Achatinella (0.7") 2 cm
Achatinella rosea Swainson, 1833. Helemano to Kaukinehua, Oahu. Lip rose. Shell rarely green or white. Extinct?

Stewart's Achatinella (0.7") 2 cm
Achatinella stewartii (Green, 1827). Left row from Manoa-Palolo Ridge; right row: Tantalus, Oahu. Syn.: *producta* Reeve, 1850.

Banded Achatinella (0.7") 2 cm
Achatinella taeniolata Pfeiffer, 1846. Crater Ridge, Palolo, Oahu. Several color forms.

Reddish Banded Achatinella
(0.7") 2 cm
Achatinella taeniolata forma *rubiginosa* Newcomb, 1853. Between Waialae and Wailupe, Oahu.

Greenish Achatinella (0.7") 2 cm
Achatinella viridans Mighels, 1845. Manoa and Palolo Valleys, Oahu. Once common. Syn.: *radiata* Pfeiffer, 1845.

Auburn Achatinella (0.7") 2 cm
Achatinella viridans forma *rutila* Newcomb, 1853. East of Palolo, Oahu. These topotypes from Niu.

Subgreen Achatinella (0.7") 2 cm
A. viridans forma *subvirens* Newcomb, 1853. Waialae Valley, Oahu. From Newcomb collection.

Foxy Achatinella   (0.7") 2 cm
Achatinella vulpina (Férussac, 1824). Makiki to Manana Valleys, Oahu. Very variable patterns. Once common.

Ribbon Achatinella   (0.7") 2 cm
Achatinella vittata Reeve, 1850. Eastern ridge of Nuuanu Valley and west Oahu. Syn.: *simulans* Reeve, 1850. Once common.

Dole's Partulina   (1") 2.5 cm
Partulina dolei (Baldwin, 1895). 7000 ft., east Maui. Paratypes. Named after S.B. Dole, President Republic of Hawaii.

Nearest Partulina   (1") 2.5 cm
Partulina proxima (Pease, 1862). Kahanui, Molokai Id., Hawaii. Sinistral. Lip rosy.

Splendid Partulina   (1") 2.5 cm
Partulina splendida (Newcomb, 1853). West Maui, Hawaii. On tutui trees. 50% are sinistral.

Rev. Thwing's Partulina
    (0.6") 1.7 cm
Partulina thwingi Pilsbry & Cooke, 1914. Auwahi, Maui Id., Hawaii. Paratypes. In subgenus *Perdicella* Pease.

Stripped Partulina   (1") 2.5 cm
Partulina virgulata (Mighels, 1845). Eastern third of Molokai Id., Hawaii. 90% are sinistral. Very variable. At 1,700 ft., on ieie.

Plicate Newcombia   (0.8") 2 cm
Newcombia plicata (Pfeiffer, 1848). Molokai Id., Hawaii. Syn.: *gemma* Pfeiffer, *sulcata* Pfr., and *costata* Borcherding 1901.

Channeled Newcombia
    (1/2") 1.4 cm
Newcombia canaliculata (Baldwin, 1905). Halawa, Molokai Id. Syntypes. Ribs acute.

Pfeiffer's Newcombia
    (1/2") 1.3 cm
Newcombia pfeifferi (Newcomb, 1853). Kaluaaha Valley, Molokai Id., on bark in a fork.

Cinnamon Newcombia   1.9 cm
Newcombia cinnamomea (Pfeiffer, 1857). Molokai Id., Hawaii. This is forma *honomuniensis* Pilsbry & Cooke, 1912, with purplish spire. Paratypes.

Cuming's Newcombia
    (0.7") 2 cm
Newcombia cumingi (Newcomb, 1853). Throughout high parts of Maui. These from Wailuku, West Maui.

Superfamily
COCHLICOPOIDEA
(Cionellacea)

Family AMASTRIDAE

A primitive ground-dwelling group limited to the Hawaiian Islands. Mostly ovoviviparous. Columella usually with a lamella. They have developed numerous, small, isolated subspecies or closely related species. Those on the central islands of Molokai, Lanai and Maui are inter-related. There are 10 genera, some now being extinct on Kauai. About 250 species in family.

Girdle Dwarf Amastra
(1/2") 1.4 cm
Leptachatina cingula (Mighels, 1845). Palolo; Mt. Tantalus, Oahu Id. Syn.: *vitrea* and *fumosa* Newcomb, 1853. Egg-layers.

Labiate Dwarf Amastra
(1/2") 1.4 cm
Leptachatina labiata (Newcomb, 1853). Waianae Mts., Oahu Id. Type of subgenus *Labiella* Pfr., 1854. Outer lip toothed.

Great Amastra   (1.3") 3 cm
Amastra magna (C.B. Adams, 1850). Lanai Id., Hawaii. Animal inky black, veined in white. Columella lamella long. Periostracum deciduous.

Spiral-zoned Amastra   2 cm
Amastra spirizona (Férussac, 1824). Waianae Range, west Oahu. On ground and bushes. Type of subgenus *Paramastra* Hyatt & Pils.

Kauai Amastra   (1") 2.5 cm
Kauaia kauaiensis (Newcomb, 1860). 2,000-4,500 ft. alt. on Kauai Id., Hawaii. Type of the genus

Knudsen's Amastra (1.4") 3.5 cm
Kauaia knudseni (Baldwin, 1895). Very rare on high mountain, near Halemanu, Kauai Id. Type of subgenus *Armiella* Pils., 1911.

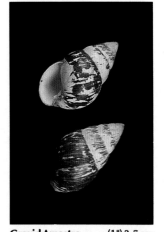

Gravid Amastra   (1") 2.5 cm
Laminella gravida (Férussac, 1824). Central Oahu; Palolo Valley, in trees; lays eggs. Type of the genus. Sinistral.

Bloody Amastra   (0.7") 2 cm
Laminella sanguinea (Newcomb, 1853). Waianae and south side of Koolau Ranges, Oahu Id. Bottom of foot light-green.

Painted Amastra   (0.7") 2 cm
Laminella picta (Mighels, 1848). Lahaina, western Maui Id., Hawaii.

King Winged-discus (0.6") 1.4 cm
Tropidoptera rex (Sykes, 1904). Summit of Konahuanui, Oahu. Under moss. Periostracum forms peripheral keel. Rare. Syn.: *Pterodiscus.*

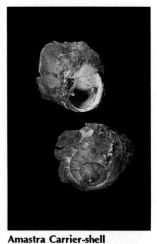

Amastra Carrier-shell
(0.3") 1 cm
Cyclamastra agglutinans (Newcomb, 1853). West Maui, Keel daubed with mud pads. Oblique columellar fold. Rare.

Bi-colored Carelia (1.3") 3.6 cm
Carelia bicolor (Jay, 1839). Hanekapiai, Kauai Id. Under *Dracaena* leaves on ground. Type of the genus. Extinct?

Shelly Carelia (1.5") 4 cm
Carelia cochlea (Reeve, 1849). Kauai Id., Hawaii. Spiral cords. Rare; probably made extinct.

Hugh Cuming's Carelia (1.8") 4.6 cm
Carelia cumingiana (Pfeiffer, 1855). Kauai Id., Hawaii. Probably made extinct. Faint spiral cords.

Kalau Carelia (1.3") 3.6 cm
Carelia kalauensis Cooke, 1931. Kalalau, Kauai Id., Hawaii. Paratype.

Towered Carelia (3") 8 cm
Carelia turricula (Mighels, 1845). Hanalei, Kauai Id. Largest Hawaiian land shell. Probably made extinct.

Family COCHLICOPIDAE
(Cionellidae)

Small (less than 10 mm), glossy, elongate, ground-dwelling snails, mainly in the north temperate areas around the world. Four genera, the best know species being the Teardrop Snail, *Cochlicopa lubrica* which lives in damp, shaded areas near water. Synonyms of *Cochlicopa* include *Cionella* Jeffreys, 1829 and *Zua* Turton, 1831. It is a nuisance to sprouting garden seeds.

Slippery Teardrop Snail 6 mm
Cochlicopa lubrica (Müller, 1774). Widespread (by man) in Europe, North America and northern Asia. Many minor forms named.

Superfamily PUPILLOIDEA

Mainly very small insignificant ground-dwelling snails, some less than 5 mm. Includes families Pupillidae, Vertiginidae, Pleurodiscidae (Pyramidulidae), Valloniidae, Enidae and Strobilopsidae.

Family PUPILLIDAE

Shells minute, less than 5 mm, cylindrical; aperture usually with 3 to 5 teeth or lamellae. Subfamilies: Vertigininae, Orculininae and Chondrininae.

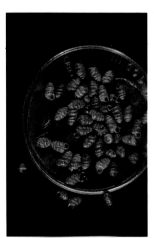

Toothless Columella Snail 2.5 mm
Columella edentula (Draparnaud, 1805). Throughout western Europe. 5 to 6 convex whorls. Common; moist woodlands. Subfamily Vertigininae.

Moderate Vertigo 2.5 mm
Vertigo modesta (Say, 1824). North America, northern Europe and Asia. Numerous forms and subspecies. Common.

Ovate Vertigo 2.3 mm
Vertigo ovata Say, 1822. Canada and U.S., most widely spread *Vertigo*. Common. Photo by Harry G. Lee.

Cask Orcula 8 mm
Orcula dolium (Draparnaud, 1801). S.E. France to Rumania. Common. Type of genus. Subfamily Orculinae.

Rye-seed Abida 7mm
Abida secale(Draparnaud,1801).
Western Europe. Rocky, dry high
areas. Common. Subfamily
Chondrininae.

Oat-seed Chondrina 7 mm
Chondrina avenacea (Bruguière,
1792). Eastern France to Czecho-
slovakia. Chalky dolomite in high
areas to 2,000 meters.

Similar Chondrina 12 mm
Solatopupa similis (Bruguière,
1792). Southern France, Spain
and Italy. Limestone, rocky, high
areas. Common. Chondrininae.

Armed Gastrocopta 4.5 mm
Gastrocopta armifera (Say, 1821).
Quebec to Georgia, Alberta and
to New Mexico. Common. Subfamily Gastrocoptinae.

Little Louse Gastrocopta 3 mm
Gastrocopta pediculus (Shuttle-
worth, 1852). Islands of S.W.
Pacific to Guam, Polynesia and
N.E. Australia.

Fly-speck Pupilla 3.5mm
Pupilla muscorum (L., 1758).
Throughout western Europe.
Chalky rock areas in high areas.
Common. Subfamily Pupillinae
s.s.

Shiny Pupilla 4 mm
Pupoides nitidulus (Pfeiffer,
1839). North America; West
Indies; Bermuda. Common. Syn.:
*albilabris*C.B. Adams; *marginata*
Say.

Family **PLEURODISCIDAE**
(Pyramidulidae)

Small, discoidal shells with
a simple aperture, and widely
umbilicate. Ground dwellers
of southern Europe to Japan.
Only two genera,
Pleurodiscus and *Pyramidula*,
and there are few species.

Rock Pyramidula 3mm
Pyramidula rupestris (Draparnaud, 1801). British Isles and
southern Europe. Limestone rock
areas. Common. Type of the
genus.

Family **VALLONIIDAE**

Small, discoidal shells, usually less than 3 mm in diame-
ter, some having axial niblets,
others being smooth. All from
northern Eurasia or North
America. The apertural lip is
reflected, the shells umbilicate. True Valloninae have
about 25 species, and the subfamily Acanthinulinae has
four genera, including *Zoogenetes.*

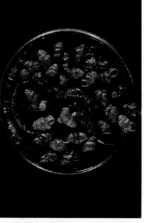

Beautiful Vallonia 2.5 mm
Vallonia pulchella (Müller,
1774). Widespread throughout
Europe, north of Italy and Greece.
Type of the genus.

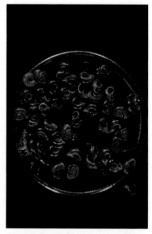

Evezard's Pupisoma 2 mm
Pupisoma evezardi (Blanford,
1880). Poona and Bombay region, India. Bark of trees.

Asterisk Planogyra 1.9 mm
Planogyra asteriscus (Morse, 1857). Quebec to Mass. and to Michigan. Prominent cuticular riblets. Smallest U.S. land shell. Rarely smoothish.

Family STROBILOPSIDAE

Only one genus, the trochiform, minute *Strobilops* with internal shell teeth. About 30 species, most in North America, others in West Indies, Galapagos and east Asia. Found in moist decaying logs and leaves.

Labyrinth Strobilops 2.3 mm
Strobilops labyrinthica (Say, 1817). Quebec to Manitoba to Georgia and to Kansas. Under loose bark of logs. Type of genus.

Family ENIDAE

Worldwide family of elongate-ovoid shells with a short aperture which rarely has teeth. Contains numerous genera and species, the best know being the European *Zebrina, Chondrula, Ena* and *Buliminus*. They can carry the parasitic liver fluke, *Dicrocoelium*, that affects grazing animals.

Three-toothed Ena (0.3") 1 cm
Chondrula tridens (Müller, 1774). South half of Europe, north of Italy. Type of the genus.

Four-toothed Ena (0.4") 1 cm
Jaminia quadridens (Müller, 1774). Southeastern France and Austria. Type of the genus.

Boreal Ena (0.3") 9 mm
Jaminia borealis (Morelet, 1858). Asia Minor.

Mountain Ena (0.6") 1.5 cm
Ena montana (Draparnaud, 1801). Western Europe, especially eastern. Type of the genus.

Extended Pupa (0.4") 1 cm
Pupinidius porrectus (Mlldff., 1901). Lu-Ding-Chiar, Szechuan Prov., China.

Distorted Pupa (0.4") 1 cm
Pupinidius streptaxis (Mlldff., 1901). Siku, Kansu, China.

Detritus Ena (0.8") 2 cm
Zebrina detrita (Müller, 1774). S.E. Europe, north of the Alps. Common. Type of the genus.

Zebra Ena (0.6") 1.4 cm
Chondrus zebra (Olivier, 1801). Greece and Asia Minor. Common in dry areas. Type of the genus.

Hasty Ena (1.3") 3 cm *Buliminus labrosus* (Olivier, 1801). Asia Minor. Common in dry grassy areas. Type of the genus.

Ornate Pachnodus (1.3") 3 cm *Pachnodus ornatus* (Dufo, 1840). Endemic to Vallée de Mai, Praslin Id., Seychelles.

Bequaert's Cerastua (1") 2.5 cm *Mabilliella* (*Paracerastus*) *bequaerti* (Pilsbry, 1919). Masisi, East Zaire, Africa.

Order MESURETHRA

Superfamily CLAUSILOIDEA
(Clausilacea)

A group of three families, the relict group of elongate Megaspiridae, the delicate, numerous Clausiliidae and the prolific, tubby *Cerion* of the West Indies.

Family MEGASPIRIDAE

Only 3 genera and less than a dozen species, all narrow and elongate. *Megaspira* is from Brazil, the others from Australia and New Guinea.

Ruschenberg's Megaspire (2.4") 6 cm *Megaspira ruschenbergiana* Jay, 1836. Rio Province, Brazil. Known only from old collections, perhaps by 30 specimens.

Family CLAUSILIIDAE
(Door Snails)

Small, elongate, narrow shells, most having a peculiar shelly plate, called the clausilium which is used to close the aperture.

Over 200 genera, with several hundreds of species, mostly European, Asian and South American. Most species are ovoviviparous, giving birth to live young. The subfamily Neniinae is mainly from western South America, but there are two West Indies species.

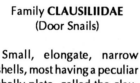

Tryon's Door Snail 12mm *Stereophaedusa tryoni* (Pilsbry, 1901). Central Japan. The genus is widespread in China and Japan. Photo by M. Azuma.

Yokohama Door Snail (1.5") 4 cm *Megalophaedusa yokohamensis* (Crosse, 1876). Area of Yokohama, Japan. Now wiped out by city?

Leading Door Snail (2") 5 cm *Mundiphaedusa ducalis* (Kobelt, 1876), forma *dorcas* (Pilsbry, 1901). Kiyomi-mura, Hida, Japan. Holotype.

Hirase's Door Snail (1.5") 4 cm *Mesophaedusa hiraseana* (Pilsbry, 1901). Okinoshima, Tosa, Japan. Syntypes.

Marten's Door Snail (2.2") 5.5 cm *Mesophaedusa martensi* (von Martens, 1860). Mikawa, Japan. Type of genus.

Mikado Door Snail (1.2") 3 cm *Tryannophaedusa mikado* (Pilsbry, 1900). Ibuki, Omi, Japan. Syntypes. Type of genus.

Rainy Door Snail (1.5") 4 cm
Hemiphaedusa pluviatilis (Benson, 1876). Ningpo, China. Type of the genus.

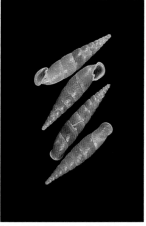

Very Oily Door Snail (1") 2.5 cm
Hemiphaedusa hyperobia (von Martens, 1880). Hakone, Sagami, Japan.

Gorgeous-lip Door Snail
(1.5") 4 cm
Luchuphaedusa callistochila (Pilsbry, 1901). Kuchan, Okinawa Id. Paratypes.

Japanese Door Snail (1.5") 4 cm
Stereophaedusa japonica (Crosse, 1871). Japan. Five subspecies recognized.

Rear-end Door Snail (1") 2.5 cm
Phaedusa proctostoma (Mabille, 1887). Chi Ne, Viet Nam.

Chariot Door Snail (1") 2.5 cm
Phaedusa aurigani Bavay & Dautzenberg, 1909. That Khé, Viet Nam.

Pointed Door Snail (0.3") 1 cm
Euphaedusa aculus (Benson, 1842). Kiangsu Prov., China.

Tridens Door Snail (1.3") 3 cm
Nenia tridens (Schweigger, 1820). Puerto Rico. On tree trunks and vines at high altitudes.

Earthy Door Snail (1") 2.5 cm
Nenia terrestris Weyrauch, 1957. Santa Rosa, Peru at altitude 1,400 meters.

Vasquez's Door Snail (2") 5 cm
Columbinia vasquezi Thompson, 1985. Villa Tunari, Bolivia. 440 m. alt. Holotype.

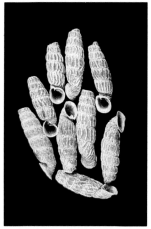

Andean Door Snail (0.5") 1.3 cm
Andinia taczanowskii (Lubomerski, 1879). Peru. Paratypes.

Malleated Door Snail 1.3 cm
Steeriana malleolata (Philippi, 1867). Cajamarca plains, Peru. Type of genus. Syn.: *steeriana* (Sykes).

Syracuse Door Snail
(0.6") 1.5 cm
Isabellaria syracusana (Philippi, 1836). Asia Minor. Dry rock and grass areas.

Papillate Door Snail (0.6") 5 cm
Papillifera papillaris (Müller, 1774). Northern coasts of the Mediterranean. Syn.: *bidens* Gmelin, not Linné.

Peru Door Snail (1.1") 3 cm
Peruinia flachi Boettger, 1930. Rio Chanchamayo, Peru. 1,200 meters alt.

Big-mouth Door Snail
(1") 2.5 cm
Zilchiella grandiportus Weyrauch, 1957. Peña Rota, Peru. Type of the genus.

Peruvian Door Snail (1.2") 3 cm
Peruinia peruana (Troschel, 1847). Huancabamba, Peru. Syn.: *bradina* Pilsbry, holotype shown here.

Rugose Door Snail (0.5") 1.3 cm
Clausilia rugosa (Draparnaud, 1801). Coast of Mediterranean France. Common. Type of the genus.

Macaran Door Snail (1.2") 3 cm
Medora macarana (Rossmässler, 1835). Makaska, Dalmatia. Type of the genus.

Bluish Door Snail (0.5") 1.3 cm
Albinaria coerulea (Rossmässler, 1835). Greek Islands. Type of the genus.

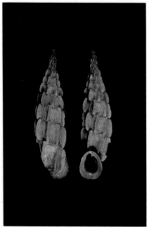

Striking Door Snail (0.7") 2 cm
Albinaria praeclara (Pfeiffer, 1853). Mirabellou, Crete. Photo by R. Goldberg.

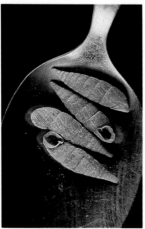

Biplicate Door Snail (0.8") 2 cm
Balea (*Alinda*) *biplicata* (Montagu, 1803). Low Countries to the Balkans. Woodlands.

Superfamily **PARTULOIDEA**
(Partulacea)

Family **PARTULIDAE**
A large group of small snails isolated on small high islands from the Marianas and Palaus to the Society and Marquesas Islands of Polynesia. Most species are arboreal, living in trees and the underside of large-leaved plants. There are about 110 species. All are ovoviviparous, with one to five eggs or young in each individual. There are 12 subgenera. The shell differs from the Achatinellidae in having a refected lip and spirally striate embryonic whorls.

Partula are colonial and usually each species is isolated within one valley in the mountains. The proportion of sinistral to dextral shells may vary geographically.

Bean Partula (1") 2.5 cm
Partula faba (Gmelin, 1791). Raiatea Id., Society Ids. Type of the genus. Found by Capt. Cook, 1769. Common. Syn.: *australis* Férussac.

Two-lined Partula (0.8") 2 cm
Partula bilineata Pease, 1866. Faa-apa Valley, Tahaa Id., Society Ids., on wild banana. Abundant.

Calypso Partula (1.2") 3 cm
Partula calypso Semper, 1865. Pelelu, Palau Ids. In subgenus *Palaopartula* Pilsbry.

Port Carteret Partula (0.8") 1.7 cm
Partula carteriensis (Quoy & Gaimard, 1832). New Ireland; Manus Id. Common today.

Citrine Partula (1") 2.5 cm
Partula citrina Pease, 1866. Uparu Valley, Raiatea Id., Society Ids. Rare. Paratypes in Field Mus. Chicago.

Toothed Partula (0.8") 2 cm
Partula dentifera Pfeiffer, 1852. Wairahi Valley, east Raiatea Id., Society Ids. Was abundant.

Fat Guam Partula (0.7") 1.7 cm
Partula gibba Férussac, 1821. Dense forests in hills, Guam Id., Mariannas Ids. Type of subgenus *Marianella* Pilsbry, 1909.

Ponape Partula (1.1") 2.7 cm
Partula guamensis Pfeiffer, 1846. Ponape Id., Caroline Ids. Never found on Guam. Form *brumalis* Reeve, slenderer.

Tahitian Partula (0.7") 2 cm
Partula otaheitana (Bruguière, 1792). Tahiti Id., Society Ids. Many subspecies in various valleys.

Noduled Partula (0.5") 1.3 cm
Partula nodosa Pfeiffer, 1851. Punaavia Valley, Tahiti Id. Sinistral forms very rare. Forma *trilineata* Pease, 1866, 3-banded. Was common.

Radiolate Partula (0.7") 1.8 cm
Partula radiolata (Pfeiffer, 1846). Guam Id., Mariannas. Common. Forma *rushi* Pilsbry, 1910, is dark brown.

Rosy Partula (1") 2.5 cm
Partula rosea Broderip, 1832. West side of Huaheine Id., Society Ids. Over 8 forms described. Common.

Half-way Partula   (1") 2.5 cm
Partula rosea forma *bipartita*
Garrett, 1884. Lower half yellow; lip white. Occurs with typical *rosea*.

Mt. Alifana Partula (0.8") 2.3 cm
Partula salifana Crampton, 1925. Small colony at top of Mt. Alafan, central Saipan Id., Mariannas. R.T. Abbott, coll., 1943.

Simple Partula   (0.7") 1.9 cm
Partula simplaria Morelet, 1853. Rediscovered on Huaheine Id., Society Ids. Rare.

Sutural Partula   (0.7") 1.9 cm
Partula suturalis Pfeiffer, 1855. Several variable subspecies in Moorea Id. valleys, Society Ids. Paratypes of form *vexillum* Pease, 1866.

Variable Partula   (0.6") 1.7 cm
Partula varia Broderip, 1832. Valleys on west coast of Huaheine Id., Society Ids.

Zebra Partula   (0.8") 2 cm
Partula zebrina Gould, 1848. Hills of Tutuila Id., Samoa. Common. R.T. Abbott, coll. 1939 near Leone.

Inflated Partula   (1") 2.3 cm
Partula inflata Reeve, 1842. Taiwata and Hivaoa Ids., Marquesas Ids. At 1,500 ft. In subgenus *Marquesana* Pils.

Canal Partula   (1.3") 3 cm
Partula canalis Mousson, 1865. Upolu Island, Samoa. Uncommon. Type of subgenus *Samoana* Pilsbry, 1909.

Conic Partula   (1") 2.5 cm
Partula conica Gould, 1848. Massacre Bay, Tutuila Id., Samoa. R.T. Abbott, coll., 1939.

Family **CERIONIDAE**
(Ceridae)

The so-called "peanut shells" or *Cerion* are especially abundant in large colonies near the ocean throughout the Bahamas, Florida Keys, Cuba, the Caymans and parts of Puerto Rico. One variable species, *uva*, occurs in the Dutch West Indies (ABC Islands). Over 600 species have been described, but all but about a dozen are merely local subspecies or colonial distincts. Several Bahama forms were introduced to the Florida Keys, but must have hybridized with the native *incanum*. Only one genus.

Cerions are more active during rains or at night. They can aestivate for many months. Colonies migrate very slowly and interbreed readily.

Cerions are confined to the sea coast and prefer seagrapes for protection. Rats and birds are their enemies. Photo by George Raeihle.

Column Cerion (1.8") 4.5 cm
Cerion columna Pilsbry & Vanatta, 1895. Great Inagua Id., Bahamas. In subgenus *Maynardia* Dall.

Rough Cerion (1.3") 3 cm
Cerion asperum (Maynard & Clapp, 1920). Great Guana Cay, Exumas, Bahamas. In subgenus *Umbonis* Maynard, 1896. Paratypes.

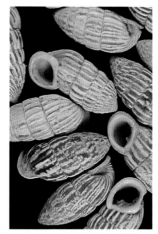

Bland's Cerion (0.8") 2 cm
Cerion (Maynardia) blandi Pilsbry & Vanatta, 1896. Salt Cay, Turks Ids. Paratypes.

Clapp's Cerion (0.7") 1.5 cm
Cerion clappi (Maynard, 1894). Current Settlement, Eleuthera Id., Bahamas. A small form.

Queen Cerion (1.3") 3.4 cm
Cerion regina Pilsbry & Vanatta, 1895. South end of Grand Turk Island.

Exceptional Cerion (0.3") 0.9 cm
Cerion eximium (Maynard, 1894). Cat Island, Bahamas. Topotypes. The color form widespread.

Cat Island Cerion (1.3") 3 cm
Cerion (Umbonis) felis Pilsbry & Vanatta, 1895. Southeastern side of Cat Island, Bahamas. Topotypes.

Greenway's Cerion (1") 2.5 cm
Cerion (Strophiops) greenwayi Clench, 1934. Samana Cay, Acklin Ids., Bahamas. Paratypes.

Fray Cerion (1.2") 3 cm
Cerion incanum (Binney, 1851). Lake Worth to Key West, Florida. Rarely with axial brown streaks (form *fasciatum* Binney, 1854). Abundant.

Abominal Cerion (2") 5 cm
Cerion infandum (Shuttleworth, in Poey, 1858). Matanzas, north coast of Cuba. Form *infandulum* Aguayo & Torre, 1951, is small, heavier ribbed.

Master Cerion (1.5") 4 cm
Cerion mumia form *magister* Pilsbry & Vanatta, 1896. Matanzas, Cuba. Topotypes.

Mayor's Cerion (1") 2.5 cm
Cerion mayori Bartsch, 1922. Middle bight, Andros Id., Bahamas. "Paratypes."

Acorn Cerion   (1") 2.5 cm
Cerion . glans (Küster, 1844). Andros, New Providence and Eleuthera Id., Bahamas.

Governor Cerion   (0.6") 1.5 cm
Cerion gubernatoria (Crosse, 1869). East Point, New Providence Id., Bahamas.

Thin Cerion   (0.5") 1.3 cm
Cerion tenue (Maynard & Clapp, 1915). East End, New Providence Id., Bahamas. Paratypes.

Royal Cerion   (2") 5 cm
Cerion regium (Benson, 1841). Castle Id., Crooked Id. Group, Bahamas.

Bright Cerion   (1.4") 3.2 cm
Cerion niteloides Dall, 1896. Anguila Bay, Cay Sal Banks, Bahamas.

Dwarf Cerion   (0.4") 1.2 cm
Cerion nanum (Maynard, 1889). Salt Rock, Little Cayman Id., Caymans. Paratypes.

Sisal Cerion   (1") 2.5 cm
Cerion sisal Clench & Aguayo, 1952. East side, Boca de Mosquito, Mariel, Cuba. Paratypes.

Chrysalis Cerion   (1.3") 2.6 cm
Cerion chrysalis Beck, 1837. Playa de Marianao, Habana, Cuba.

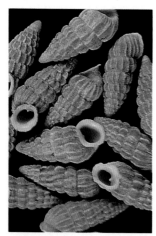

Victor Cerion   (1") 2.5 cm
Cerion victor Torre, 1929. Caleta de Ovando, Oriente Prov., Cuba. Paratypes.

Little Chubby Cerion
    (0.5") 1.1 cm
Cerion crassiusculum Pilsbry & Vanatta, 1898. Cayo Juin, Baracoa, Cuba. Paratypes.

Yuma Cerion   (0.9") 2.2 cm
Cerion yumaensis Pilsbry & Vanatta, 1895. Cabo Engaño, Prov. Altagracia, Dominican Republic.

Puerto Rican Cerion (0.8") 2 cm
Cerion striatellum (Guérin, 1829). Western Puerto Rico (syn.: *crassilabris* Sowerby, 1875, non Parreyss, 1848).

Marbled Cerion (1") 2.5 cm
Cerion marmoratum (Pfeiffer, 1847). Acklin and Crooked Islands, Bahamas. Syn.: *cliffordi* Clench, 1933.

Mona Island Cerion (0.8") 2 cm
Cerion monaense Clench, 1951. Common on Mona Island, between Puerto Rico and Hispaniola. Paratypes.

Mummy Cerion (1") 2.5 cm
Cerion mumia (Bruguière, 1792). Northern coast of Cuba. Forma *gigantea* Sanchez-Roig from Cape Romano is 4.5 cm.

Proteus Cerion (1.2") 3 cm
Cerion proteus (Gundlach, 1860). Gibara, north coast of Cuba. Common near coast.

Shreve's Cerion (1") 2.5 cm
Cerion shrevei Clench & Aguayo, 1952. Little Inagua Id., Bahamas. In subgenus *Umbonis*. Locally common. Paratypes.

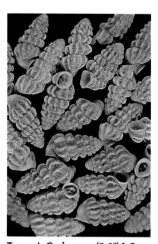

Turner's Cerion (0.6") 1.5 cm
Cerion turnerae Clench and Aguayo, 1952. Lydia Pt., Great Inagua Id., Bahamas. In subgenus *Umbonis*. Paratypes.

Abbott's Cerion (1") 2.5 cm
Cerion utowana subsp. *abbotti* Clench, 1961. Long Id., South Caicos. Paratypes.

Grape Cerion (1") 2.5 cm
Cerion uva (Linn., 1758). Aruba, Curacao and Bonaire, lower Caribbean. Abundant.

Bonaire Cerion (0.7") 1.5 cm
Cerion uva subsp. *bonairensis* H.B. Baker, 1914. Bonaire Id., Dutch West Indies (ABC Islands).

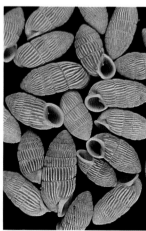

Viola Cerion (0.5") 1.2 cm
Cerion rubicundum Menke, 1829, form *viola* (Maynard, 1890). Great Inagua, Bahamas. Syntypes. Syn.: *inaguense* Clench, 1933.

Cut-offed Cerion (1") 2.5 cm
Cerion dimidiatum (Pfeiffer, 1847). Gibara, Oriente Prov., Cuba.

Fat Albert's Cerion (1") 2.5 cm
Cerion alberti Clench & Aguayo, 1949. Bahia de Banes, Antilla, Oriente Prov., Cuba. Paratypes.

THE SOUTH AMERICAN MEGASNAILS

Superfamily STROPHOCHEILOIDEA

The megasnails are a primitive group of large terrestrial dwellers dominant throughout the tropical and semi-tropical areas of South America. They are the Giant African Achatinas of the new world and consist of six genera and about 68 species and subspecies. Many of these may only be ecological or minor genetic forms. Their identification is difficult, depending upon the size, spacing, shape and extent of the vertical riblets found on the early or nepionic whorls. The best reference for species determination is Bequaert's 1948 monograph. Formerly they were all placed in one family, but José Leme in 1973 separated out the larger, heavier species into the genus *Megalobulimus* and created the family Megalobulimidae based on major anatomical differences. Within this superfamily is the small family Dorcasiidae, limited to southwest Africa.

Best known of the megasnails is the five-inch-long *Megalobulimus oblongus* (Müller, 1774) distributed widely from Colombia to Uruguay and northern Argentina. Evidently it has been introduced by man into the Lesser Antilles and Jamaica. The snail is a ground dweller and nocturnally active. In the morning it burrows into loose earth with only the apex of the shell being exposed. It lays a large, white shelly egg, resembling that of a pigeon or dove. Egglaying takes place at the first rains following a dry spell. About a dozen inch-long eggs are laid at one time during daylight and hatch four or five weeks later. They become sexually mature about three years after birth, and may live for 14 years. Shelly eggs are produced by all species in this family. There are nine named forms of the Oblong Megasnail, including *albus* (Bland and Binney, 1872), a white race dominant on Tobago Island; an elongate form, *perelongatus* Bequaert, 1948, from the Upper Orinoco drainage in Colombia; and a dwarf race, *musculus* Bequaert, 1948, only 5 to 8 cm, from northern Argentina and Paraguay.

The largest species in the genus, and next to the largest living terrestrial snail known, is Popelair's Megasnail from west of the Andes which may reach 16.3 cm (over 6 inches) in shell length. Its extended orange foot exceeds a foot in length. It was once used extensively for food in Ecuador.

A small coprid beetle lives commensally within the folds of the mantle of some species of megasnails and feed upon the mucus produced by the mollusk.

Disturbed from its ground burrow, this Oblong Megasnail from Tobago Island is stretching its foot and head. (Photo by Charlotte Lloyd).

Several species of megasnails lay eggs resembling those of pigeons. This is one of a dozen just laid by an Ovate Megasnail from Brazil.

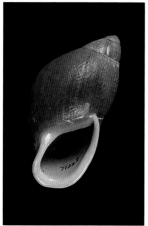

Malleated Megasnail (2.3") 5.5 cm
Mirinaba erythrosoma (Pilsbry, 1895). Sao Paulo, Brazil. Syn.: *porphrostoma* Clench & Archer, 1930. Common. Topotype.

Miller's Megasnail (2.5") 6 cm
Speironepion milleri (Sowerby, 1838). Eastern Brazil. Paratype from Hugh Cuming. Uncommon. Syn.: *kronei* von Ihering, 1901.

Flattened Megasnail (2.5") 6.5 cm
Mirinaba planidens (Michelin, 1831). Sao Paulo to Rio de Janeiro, Brazil. S. *jaussaudi* Morretes is a Parana dwarf.

Popelair's Megasnail (6") 16 cm
Megalobulimus popelairianus (Nyst, 1845). Colombia to Peru. Common. Used as food. Egg 2" (5 cm). Type of genus. Rarely sinistral.

Giant Megasnail (5.5") 15 cm
Megalobulimus maximus (Sowerby, 1825). Bolivia, Peru and western Brazil. Form *vestitus* Pilsbry, 1926, is slenderer.

Attentive Megasnail (3.5") 9 cm
Megalobulimus auritus (Sowerby, 1838). Espirito Santo; Sao Paulo; Rio Prov., Brazil. With dense, minute granulations. Common.

Granulose Megasnail (4") 10 cm
Megalobulimus granulosus (Rang, 1831). Sao Paulo; Matto Grosso; Sta. Catharina, Brazil. Mouth pink; surface granulated.

Bronn's Megasnail (3.5") 9 cm
Megalobulimus bronni (Pfeiffer, 1847). Rio and Sao Paulo Prov., Brazil. Egg 15 mm. Strong riblets on nepionic whorls. Syn.: *browni* H. & A. Adams, 1855.

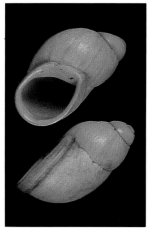

Streaked Megasnail (2.5") 6.5 cm
Megalobulimus capillaceus (Pfeiffer, 1855). Peru and Bolivia at 2,000 m. Nepionic riblets fine, crowded. Mouth rose. Common.

Carriker's Megasnail (3") 7.5 cm
Megalobulimus carrikeri (Pilsbry, 1930). Tarma and Junin Dept., Peru at 6,000 ft. Apex pointed. Whorls malleated.

Lichtenstein's Megasnail (3.4") 8.5 cm
Megalobulimus lichtensteini (Albers, 1854). Dept. Cajamarca, Peru, 1,000 ft. Mouth white. Uncommon.

Half-malleated Megasnail (4") 9 cm
Megalobulimus lichtensteini forma *semimalleatus* (Fulton, 1905). Peru. Rare. Possible syntype.

Modest Megasnail (2") 5 cm
Strophocheilus pudicus (Müller, 1774). Bahia and Parahyba, Brazil. Type of genus. Forma *roseolabris* Bequaert, 1948, has pink mouth.

Ovate Megasnail (6") 14 cm
Megalobulimus ovatus (Müller, 1774). Rio de Janeiro; Sao Paulo; Parana States, Brazil. Common. Syn.: *grandis* von Martens, *chionostoma* Mörch.

Saint Paul's Megasnail
(3.5") 9 cm
Megalobulimus sanctipauli (von Ihering & Pilsbry, 1900). Sao Paulo, Brazil; Paraguay. Like *granulosus*. Holotype.

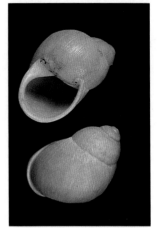

Yellowish Megasnail (1.3") 3 cm
Austroborus lutescens (King & Broderip, 1832). Coastal Uruguay. Eggs 9 mm. In sand and grass. Common. Syn.: *Microborus* Pilsbry, 1926. Type of genus.

Chilean Megasnail (1.6") 3.8 cm
Chiliborus chilensis (Sowerby, 1833). Near Coquimbo, Chile. Uncommon. Syn.: *crenulatus* Pfr., 1845. Type of genus.

Long Angle-mouth Snail
(2.3") 5.4 cm
Gonystomus goniostoma (Férussac, 1821). State of Rio de Janeiro, Brazil. Uncommon. Extinct? Type of genus.

Eminent Angle-mouth Snail
(2") 5 cm
Gonystomus egregius (Pfeiffer, 1845). Organ Mts., Rio, Brazil. Syn.: *hybridus* Gould, 1846. Extinct?

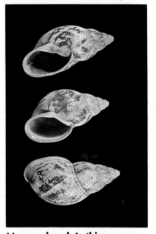

Many-colored Anthinus
(1.2") 3.8 cm
Anthinus multicolor (Rang, 1831). Near Rio de Janeiro, Brazil. Extinct? Type of the genus. Syn.: *A. miersii* Sby.

Turnix Anthinus (2") 5 cm
Anthinus turnix (Gould, 1846). Rio de Janeiro and Alegre, Brazil. Holotype specimen, U.S.N.M. Extinct?

Family DORCASIIDAE

This is a small group of desert snails limited to southwest Africa, but having its nearest, although remote, relatives in South America. Of the three genera, *Dorcasia* with less than 20 species is the best known. The edge of the mantle has small lobes. They have a simple genital system, and lack darts in the penis. The eggs are relatively large.

Alexander's Dorcas Snail
(1.2") 3 cm
Dorcasia alexandri Gray, 1838. Okahanja, Southwest Africa. On low bushes in arid areas. Type of the genus.

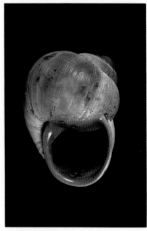

Globular Dorcas (1")
Trigonephrus globulus (Müller, 1774). Cape of Good Hope, South Africa. Type of the genus.

Superfamily
SUCCINOIDEA

Family SUCCINEIDAE
(Amber Snails)

The delicate-shelled amber snails are worldwide in distribution, generally living in very moist areas. The subfamily Catinellinae has two genera, *Catinella* (worldwide) and *Quickia* (Africa and Indian Ocean Islands). The remaining 10 genera are in the subfamily Succineinae. The anatomy is primitive and proper generic placement and species identification are possible in most cases only through dissection of the soft parts.

Decay Amber Snail (0.6") 1.5 cm *Succinea putris* (L., 1758). Widespread throughout western Europe. Animal yellowish tan. Type of the genus.

Refined Amber Snail (0.7") 2 cm *Succinea lauta* Gould, 1859. Hokkaido, northern Japan.

Field Amber Snail (0.6") 1.5 cm *Succinea campestris* Say, 1817. North Carolina to central Florida. Common. Subgenus *Calcisuccinea* Pilsbry.

Hayden's Amber Snail (0.8") 2 cm *Oxyloma haydeni* (Binney, 1858). Nebraska and Colorado.

Silliman's Amber Snail (0.6") 1.5 cm *Oxyloma sillimani* (Bland, 1865). Nevada and California.

Sallé's Amber Snail (0.6") 1.5 cm *Oxyloma salleana* (Pfeiffer, 1849). South central United States. Roots of sedges near water.

Effuse Amber Snail (0.5") 1.4 cm *Oxyloma effusa* (Pfeiffer, 1853). New Jersey to Florida. These are paratypes of Pilsbry's *subeffusa* from Maryland.

Dan Langford's Amber Snail (0.5") 1.3 cm *Succinea kuhnsii* Ancey, 1904. Kaiwiki, Hawaii. Alias Dan Kuhns.

Thaanum's Amber Snail (0.6") 1.5 cm *Succinea thaanumi* Ancey, 1899. Akaka, Honomoii, Hawaii.

Suborder
SIGMURETHRA

The so-called "higher pulmonates" are a diverse assemblage of terrestrial snails, some being shell-less slugs, some semi-slugs, but the majority have large, conspicuous, coiled shells. They are classified into various suborders and families according to the positioning of the kidneys, jaws, and the nature of the foot, whether simple or longitudinally divided along the sides. There are about 10 superfamilies, 39 families and many thousands of species. Most are herbivorous, but a few are carnivorous.

Superfamily
ACHATINOIDEA
(Achatinacea)

This superfamily contains the huge giant African snails, as well as the small, inch-long, turreted *Subulina* and *Rumina*, so well-known in gardens and potted plants. Also here are the Spiraxidae a carnivorous, snail-eating group, including the *Euglandina*. They lay pea-sized eggs in the ground. The tiny, elongate *Caeciliodes* (5 mm) is included in the small family, Ferussaciidae, and is ovoviviparous.

THE GIANT AFRICAN SNAILS

Family **Achatinidae** Pfeiffer, 1878

Members of this family range from the largest known land gastropods, reaching a shell length of about eight inches (20 cm), to the inch-long genera of *Callistoplepa* and *Lignus.* All thirteen genera are endemic to Africa, although a few of the 75 species of the large-sized *Achatina,* or so-called Giant African Snails, have been introduced by man to many tropical countries around the world.

The classification of the family Achatinidae relies on the characters of the nepionic shell formed within the egg, whether smooth, granulose or minutely ribbed. The structure of the columella and the shape of the aperture are also used. A well-illustrated and detail account of this group was made by J.C. Bequaert in 1950 (*Bull. Mus. Comp. Zool.* at Harvard, vol. 105, no. 1, pp. 1-216, 81 pls).

Members of the West African genus *Archachatina* Albers, 1850, have a wide, bulbous or dome-shaped summit to the early granulose nepionic whorls. The shell-covered, yellowish white, oblong eggs may be an inch (2.3 mm) in length and are generally laid in soil on the ground. The shell of the type of the genus, *A. bicarinata* (Bruguière) is always sinistral.

In the smaller *Limicolaria,* of which there are about 70 species, the base of the columella is continuous, not truncated, with the lower lip of the aperture. The large, heavy *Burtoa* from tropical East Africa always lacks the color stripes. Strangest in this family is the very elongate, sinistral *Columna* from the tiny islands in the Gulf of Guinea, West Africa.

The saga of the worldwide spread of the infamous Giant African Snail, *Achatina fulica,* began in 1812 when the French governor of Madagascar had the snail imported from East Africa, purportedly as a source of medicine for his ailing, consumptive wife. Without enemies the large snail multiplied rapidly and spread to vegetable patches. In 1857, the snail was introduced to Bombay, India and from then on there has been a gradual spread of and constant battle against this vegetarian in Asia and the Pacific Islands.

In 1966, a young boy brought this exotic pet from Hawaii to Miami, Florida, where for the next seven years it threatened to spread to the nearby commercial truck farms. Over 18,000 snails were destroyed by Florida State agricultural authorities before the last one (7 inches in length!) was eradicated in 1972 at a cost of over $300,000. (see R.T. Abbott and A.R. Mead, in the bibliography).

Introduced to many tropical areas of southeast Asia and the Pacific Islands, the 6-inch long Giant African Snail, *Achatina fulica* Bowdich, has become a horticultural nuisance and menace to vegetable and fruit growing. The 1966 introductions to southeast Florida were finally eradicated. The cluster of snails will spend the next few nights demolishing these papaya fruits.

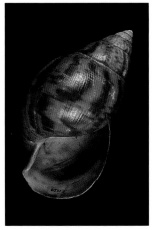

True Achatina (8") 20 cm
Achatina (Achatina) achatina (L., 1758). Northern section of West Africa, Liberia to Nigeria. Usually 15 cm. Eaten by natives. Type of genus.

White-painted Achatina (7") 17 cm
Achatina albopicta (E.A. Smith, 1878). Coast of Kenya and Tanzania. Usually 13 cm. In subgenus *Lissachatina*.

Girdled Achatina (6") 14 cm
Achatina (Achatina) balteata Reeve, 1849. Cameroon to central Angola; also Sierra Leone. Was used as currency.

Stuhlmann's Achatina (4") 10 cm
Achatina stuhlmanni von Martens, 1892. Form of *balteata* ? This is paratype of *rugosa* Putzeys, 1898.

Stuhlmann's Achatina (5") 10 cm
Achatina stuhlmanni von Martens, 1892. Form of *balteata* ? Bwamba, Uganda.

Glutton Achatina (4") 10 cm
Achatina glutinosa Pfeiffer, 1854. Mtimbuka, Nyassaland. Common. Syn.: *petersi* von Martens, 1860.

Giant East African Snail (5")
Achatina fulica (Bowdich, 1822. East Africa, and widely introduced to India, Pacific Islands, Hawaii, etc. Type of subgenus *Lissachatina* Bequaert.

Giant East African Snail (3") 8 cm
Achatina fulica, aberrant "lefthanded," form *sinistrosa* Grateloup, 1840. Rare.

Rodatz's Achatina (5") 13 cm
Achatina fulica Bowdich, forma *rodatzi* Dunker, 1852. Albino race, especially in drier areas. Syn.: *hamillei* Petit, 1859.

Umbilicate Achatina (4") 10 cm
Achatina fulica Bowdich, forma *umbilicata* Nevill, 1879. Rare monstrosity.

Lilac-mouth Achatina (5") 13 cm
Achatina iostoma Pfeiffer, 1852. Cameroon. Surface granular. Aperture bluish. Common.

Panther Achatina (5") 13 cm
Achatina panthera (Férussac, 1832). Rhodesia, Nyasaland, Mauritius. Sculpture coarse, lips pinkish rose. Syn.: *lamarckiana* Pfeiffer, 1846.

Reticulated Achatina (9") 20 cm
Achatina reticulata Pfeiffer, 1845.
Zanzibar. Very coarsely sculptured. Usually 16 cm. Eggs yellow, 9 mm.

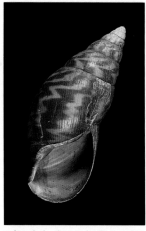

Schweinfurth's Achatina (6")
Achatina schweinfurthi von Martens, 1873. East Africa: Njamnjam-land. Lightning stripes. Syn.: *okapia* Boettger, 1927.

Tavare Achatina (3") 7.5 cm
Achatina tavaresiana (Morelet, 1866). Angola (syn.: *studleyi* Melvill & Ponsonby, 1897; *greyi* DaCosta, 1907).

Tinted Achatina (3") 8 cm
Achatina tincta Reeve, 1842. Angola and Belgium Congo. Apex and rarely columella rose. Subsutural thread.

Varicose Achatina (3.5") 9 cm
Achatina varicosa Pfeiffer, 1861. East London, Cape Province, South Africa. Thin-shelled. Early whorls granulated. Subsutural thread.

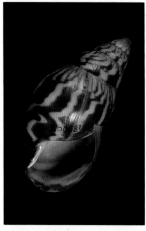

Weyns's Achatina (3.5") 9 cm
Achatina weynsi Dautzenberg, 1891. Belgium Congo. Surface finely shagreened.

Zebra Achatina (5") 13 cm
Achatina zebra (Bruguière, 1792). Cape Province, South Africa. Syn.: *kraussi* Reeve, 1842; *tigrina* Beck, 1837; *zebroides* E.A. Smith, 1878. Common.

Trachea Achatina (1.5") 3 cm
Achatina tracheia Connolly, 1929. Farm Stinie, Kaoko-Veld, S.W. Africa.

Half-sculptured Achatina
(2.2") 6 cm
Achatina semisculpta Pfeiffer, 1845. Lobito, Angola, West Africa. In subgenus *Pintoa* Bourguignat, 1889.

Woodland Achatina (1.5") 4 cm
Achatina sylvatica Putzeys, 1898. Coquilhetville, Belgium Congo. Smooth.

Adeline's Achatina (2")
Archachatina papyracea (Pfeiffer, 1845). Cameroon. Nuclear whorls granulated. This is forma *adelinae* Pilsbry, 1905.

Bicarinate Achatina (5") 15 cm
Archachatina bicarinata (Bruguière, 1792). Islands in the Gulf of Guinea, West Africa. Type of the genus. Syn.: *sinistrorsa* Pfr.

The long, black animal of an *Achatina* may stretch several inches beyond the length of the shell. These vegetarians travel many yards at night for food. Photo by Alice Barlow.

Harmless to the touch, this *Achatina marginata* (Swainson, 1821) from Gabon, West Africa, is eaten by the natives. The cleaned shells were used for adornment in ceremonial headdresses.

Degner's Achatina (4.5") 13 cm
Archachatina degneri Bequaert & Clench, 1936. Near Accra, Gold Coast and Dahomey. Paratype.

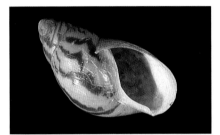

Gaboon Achatina (4.5") 11 cm
Archachatina gaboonensis Pilsbry, 1933. Gabon, West Africa. Holotype specimen, U.S.N. Mus.

Marginate Achatina (6.5") 17 cm
Archachatina marginata (Swainson, 1821). Cameroons to Belgium Congo. Surface microscopically "woven." Several subspecies. Type of subgenus *Calachatina*.

Marginate Achatina (6.5") 17 cm
Archachatina marginata (Swainson, 1821). Lighter specimen from Dahomey, West Africa.

Ventricose Achatina (4.6") 12 cm
Archachatina ventricosa (Gould, 1850). Southeastern Sierre Leone and Liberia. A local food. Holotype specimen at Harvard.

Ventricose Achatina (5") 13 cm
Archachatina ventricosa (Gould, 1850). Liberia. Surface granulose; aperture pink. Forma *spectaculum* Pilsbry, 1933. Sierra Leone.

Krauss's Achatina (4.6") 12 cm
Metachatina kraussi (Pfeiffer, 1846). Natal to Delagoa Bay, South Africa. Common. Surface rough. Type of the genus.

Nile Achatina (4") 10 cm
Burtoa nilotica (Pfeiffer, 1861). Upper Nile region of Sudan. Columella not truncate below. Type of the genus.

Nile Achatina (5") 12.5 cm
Burtoa nilotica (Pfeiffer, 1861). Tambura, Sudan. A Lighter specimen.

Charbonne's Dwarf Achatina (1.2") 3 cm
Limicolaria charbonnieri Bourguignat, 1889. Ituri, Belgium Congo on palm trees. Non-truncate columella.

Distinct Dwarf Achatina
(2") 5 cm
Limicolaria distincta Putzeys, 1898. Stanleyville, Congo, West Africa.

Flamed Dwarf Achatina
(2.5") 6.5 cm
Limicolaria flammea (Müller, 1774). Gold Coast, West Africa.

Flamed Dwarf Achatina
(2.8") 7 cm
Limicolaria flammea (Müller, 1774). Sierra Leone, West Africa. This is subsp. *festiva* von Martens, 1869 from Upper Nile.

Speke's Dwarf Achatina
(2.8") 7 cm
Limicolaria flammea (Müller, 1774). Near Lake Tanganyika in the Sudan. Elongate break. Forma *spekiana* Grandidier, 1881.

Kambeul Dwarf Achatina
(2") 5 cm
Limicolaria kambeul (Bruguière, 1792). Senegal east to the sources of the Nile. Several forma known.

Kambeul Dwarf Achatina
(2") 5 cm
Limicolaria kambeul (Bruguière, 1792) form *turriformis* von Martens, 1895.

Saturated Dwarf Achatina
(2.5") 6.3 cm
Limicolaria saturata E.A. Smith, 1895. Kilimanjaro, Kenya, East Africa.

Martens' Dwarf Achatina
(1.5") 3.2 cm
Limicolaria martensiana E.A. Smith, 1880. Uganda. Upper: white form.

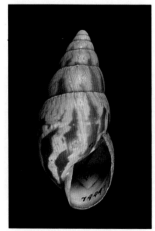

Marten's Dwarf Achatina
(2.2") 5 cm
Limicolaria martensiana E.A. Smith, forma *laikipiaensis* Preston, 1913. Paratype. Kenya.

Müller's Column Snail   9cm
Columna columna (Müller, 1774). Islands in the Gulf of Guinea, West Africa. Was common. Type of the genus.

Lea's Column Snail   (2") 5 cm
Columna leai Tryon, 1866. Prince Island, Gulf of Guinea, West Africa. Smoothish.

Umbilicate Necklace Achatina
(1.5") 4 cm
Perideriopsis umbilicata Putzeys, 1898. Bena Bendi, Belgium Congo. Type of the genus. Worn by natives.

Stanley Falls Necklace Achatina
(1.5") 4 cm
Perideriopsis fallsensis Dupuis & Putzeys, 1900. Forests near Stanley Falls, Congo, West Africa.

Alabaster Lignus Snail   4 cm
Lignus alabaster (Rand, 1831). South end, Prince's Island, Gulf of Guinea, W. Africa. Animal yellow-green.

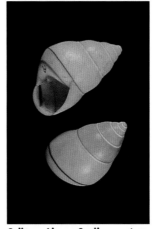

Soliman Lignus Snail   4 cm
Lignus solimanus (Morelet, 1848). Sakbazene and Victoria, Cameroon, W. Africa. Head & tentacles dark green. Columella brown.

Lea's Lignus Snail   (3.5") 9 cm
Lignus leai (Pilsbry, 1933). Liberia, West Africa. Holotype. *Pseudotrochus* is synonym.

Gold-colored Lignus Snail
(3") 8 cm
Lignus auripigmentum (Reeve, 1848). Fernando Po Id., West Africa.

Gold-colored Lignus Snail
(2") 5 cm
Lignus auripigmentum (Reeve, 1848). Prince's Island, Victoria, W. Africa.

Tinted Lignus   (2") 5 cm
Lignus intertinctus (Gould, 1843). Cape Palmas, Liberia. Lectotype in Mus. Comp. Zool.

Graner's Dwarf Achatina
(1.5") 4 cm
Callistopepla graneri Thiele, 1811. Congo region, West Africa. Very thin-shelled.

Strange Achatina   (2.5") 6.5 cm
Atopochochlis exarata (Müller, 1774). San Thomé Id., Gulf of Guinea, West Africa. Type of the genus.

Favanne's False Achatina
(2.5") 6 cm
Leucotaenius favanii (Lamarck, 1822). Madagascar.

Downes's False Achatina   7 cm
Pseudachatina downesii (Sowerby, 1838). Cameroons and Fernando Po Id., W. Africa. Type of the genus.

Dennison's False Achatina
(2.5") 6 cm
Pseudachatina dennisoni (Pfeiffer). Gabon and Cameroons, W. Africa.

Family FERUSSACIIDAE

Shells elongate, less than 10 mm. Mainly tropical, in leaves and earth. Genera *Ferussacia* and *Ceciliodes*.

Family SUBULINIDAE

Shells elongate, apex globular, whorls smooth. Eggs of *Subulina* in shelly cases. Apex lost in semi-tropical *Rumina*. Both have been introduced to United States and *Subulina* occurs in gardens and potted plants.

Tiny Pin Snail 4mm
Ceciliodes acicula (Müller, 1774). Central Europe; British Isles. Introduced to eastern U.S., Bermuda. Type of the genus. In Ferussaciidae.

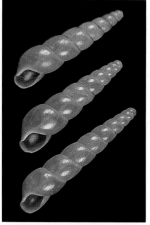

Strebel's Octona Snail
(0.5") 1.3 cm
Subulina octona forma *strebeli* von Martens, 1901. Venezuela and Central America. Similar *octona* widespread tropics.

Terebra Octona Snail (2") 5 cm
Euonyma platyacme Melvill & Ponsonby, 1907. Cape Province, South Africa.

Unsurpassed St. Helena Snail
(2") 5 cm
Chilonopsis aurisvulpinus (Holten, 1802). St. Helena Island, south Atlantic. Now extinct. Syn.: *nonpareil* (Perry, 1811).

Decollate Snail (1.2") 3 cm
Rumina decollata (Linnaeus, 1758). Common pest introduced worldwide to semitropical areas. Loses apex.

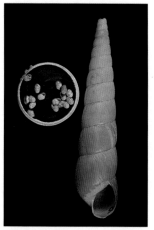

Obelisk Snail (3.5") 9 cm
Obeliscus obeliscus (Moricand, 1833). Bahia and Rio Grande do Sul, Brazil. Ovoviviparous. Uncommon. Type of genus.

Tower Obelisk Snail (5") 11 cm
Neobeliscus calcarius (Born, 1778). Eastern Brazil. Uncommon. Ovoviviparous. Type of genus.

Family STREPTAXIDAE

A variable group of 30 or so genera and about 500 species of tropical, carnivorous snails. Radula long and narrow, with strong, pointed lateral teeth. Eggs usually large and hatch inside oviduct. Foot is undivided holopod type without pedal furrows. Mostly present in Africa, South America and southeast Asia. The genus *Gonaxis* feeds on other large snails, including *Achatina*. *Euglandina* are voracious snail eaters.

Lyonet's Gibbus Snail
(1.5") 3.5 cm
Gibbus lyonetianus (Pallas, 1774). Mauritius. Ground snail; uncommon. Type of the genus.

Costulate Streptaxis (0.3") 7 mm
Odontartemon costulatus (Moellendorff, 1883). Indo-China. Ground snail; uncommon.

Ovoid Edentulina (2") 5 cm
Edentulina ovoidea (Bruguière, 1789). Mayotte Id., Comores; Madagascar. Carnivore.

Four-sided Gonaxis (0.9") 2.1 cm
Eustreptaxis quadrilateralis
(Preston, 1910). Simba Hills,
Kenya. Introduced to Seychelles.

Protracted Gonaxis   5mm
Gonaxis protractus (Gould,
1856). Cape Palmas, Liberia.

Monrovian Gonaxis (1.2") 3 cm
Eustreptaxis monrovius (Rang,
1831). Liberia. (syn.: *nobilis* Gray,
1837; *rimatus* Pfeiffer, 1847).

Kibwezi Gonaxis (0.7") 2 cm
Eustreptaxis kibweziensis (E.A.
Smith, 1894). Coastal Kenya;
introduced unsuccessfully to
Marianas Ids. Carnivore.

Palanga Gonospire (1") 2.5 cm
Gonospira palanga (Férussac,
1821). Mauritius. Type of the
genus. Obliquely striate.

Mashed Gonaxis   (1") 2.2 cm
Streptaxis contusus (Férussac,
1821). Rio de Janeiro, Brazil. Type
of the genus.

Mashed Gonaxis   (1") 2.2 cm
Streptaxis contusus (Férussac,
1821). Brazil Common ground
snail. Photo by J.H. Leal.

Pagoda Gonidomus Snail
               (1.2") 3 cm
Gonidomus pagodus (Férussac,
1821). Mauritius. Ground snail.

Sulcate Gonidomus Snail
               (1.2") 3 cm
Gonidomus sulcatus (Müller,
1774). Mauritius.

Titan Glandina   (4.4") 11 cm
Euglandina titan Thompson,
1987. Near Puerto Santo Tomas,
Guatemala, 800 meters alt.
Holotype illus.

Vanauxem's Glandina (4") 10 cm
Euglandina vanuxemensis (Lea,
1834). High desert plateau of
south-central Mexico. Common.

Singley's Glandina   (2") 5 cm
Euglandina (*Singleya*) *singleyana*
(W.G. Binney, 1892). Western
Texas. Under stones and dead
wood. Uncommon.

Rosy Glandina   (2.4") 6 cm
Euglandina rosea (Férussac, 1821). Southeast
U.S. A common carnivorous species, usually
swollowing small native snails.

Rosy Glandina   (2.4") 6 cm
Euglandina rosea (Férussac, 1821). Southeast
U.S. Young specimens are glistening rosy.
Abundant.

Cuming's Glandina   (1.2") 3 cm
Euglandina cumingii (Beck, 1837). Nicaragua
to Panama. Moderately common.

Gigantic Glandina   (4") 10 cm
Euglandina gigantea Pilsbry 1926. Panama;
Costa Rica, sea-level to 2,600 meters. Syn.:
gabbi Pilsbry, 1926. Apical whorl.

Pilsbry's Glandina   (2.4") 6.3 cm
Euglandina pilsbryi Bartsch, 1909. Bolanos,
Jalisco, Mexico. Holotype illustrated is in the
U.S. Nat. Mus.

Sowerby's Glandina   (4") 10 cm
Euglandina sowerbyana (Pfeiffer, 1846). Vera
Cruz State, Mexico. Apical whorl dome-
shaped. Uncommon.

Rosy Glandina (*Euglandina rosea* (Férussac, 1821) is a voracious snail eater. They
lay about two dozen, white, shelly pea-
sized eggs in the ground. Photo by Alice
Barlow.

Superfamily ACAVOIDEA
(Rhytididacea)

Consists of five families, mostly carnivorous and mostly tropical. Main families are Rhytididae (also called Paryphantidae), Haplotrematidae of the Americas, and the Acavidae.

Family RHYTIDIDAE
(Paryphantidae)

Several genera in New Zealand, Australia, South Africa and New Caledonia. Largest shells are *Paryphanta* from New Zealand with a black, dehiscent peristracum. They feed on earthworms.

Webb's Paryphanta (1") 2.6 cm
Rhytida greenwoodi (Gray, 1850) subspecies *webbi* Powell, 1949. Near Nelson, South Island New Zealand. Holotype illus. Eggs in the family are white and shelly.

Dunni's Paryphanta (1") 2.5 cm
Rhytida dunniae (Gray, 1840). North Island, N.Z. under palm litter. Type of subgenus *Amborhytida* Climo, 1974.

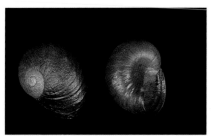

O'Connor's Paryphanta (1.2") 3 cm
Rhytida oconnori Powell, 1946. Pikikiruna Range, South Id., N.Z. Syn.: *hadfieldi* Powell, 1949 (holotype on left).

Cafra Natalina (2.5") 6 cm
Natalina cafra (Férussac, 1821). Cape of Good Hope, South Africa. Type of the genus. Shell fragile. Syn.: *Aerope* Albers, 1860.

Wessel's Natalina (3") 7.5 cm
Natalina wesseliana Kobelt, 1905. Zululand, South Africa.

Paryphanta snails are native to the northern part of New Zealand with some 40 species and subspecies living in high altitude forests and some offshore islands. Most are protected by conservation laws.

Paryphanta's have a relatively thin shell, but are covered by a leathery epidermis which breaks and shatters under dry conditions. They feed on earthworms.

Eggs laid by this Busby's Paryphanta have a 12 mm shelly white casing. Found in soil in Hokianga, South Island, N.Z. Type of the genus.

Busby's Paryphanta (3") 7.5 cm
Paryphanta busbyi (Gray, 1840). Northland Peninsula, New Zealand. Near extinction in and near forests. P. *watti* Powell, 1946, is smaller, flatter.

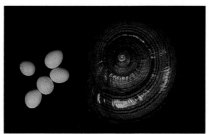

Gillies' Paryphanta (2") 5 cm
Paryphanta gilliesi E.A. Smith, 1880. South Island, N.Z. Granulated parietal callus. In subgenus *Powelliphanta*. Forma *brunnea* Powell, 1938.

Gillies' Brownish Paryphanta (1.6") 4.5 cm
Paryphanta gilliesi forma *subfusca* Powell, 1930. Coastal scrub near Nelson, South Island, N.Z.

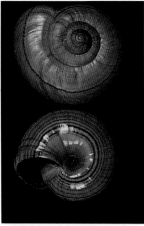

Hochstetter's Paryphanta 7 cm
Paryphanta hochstetteri (Pfeiffer, 1862). Pikikiruna Range, Nelson, South Island, N.Z. 2,500 ft. alt. Common. Upper surface with wavy striae.

Hochstetter's Paryphanta 7 cm
P. hochstetteri (Pfr.) at right: forma *bicolor* Powell, 1930, from Marlborough area. Left: *obscura* (Beutler, 1901), D'Urville Id., N.Z.

Obscure Paryphanta (3") 7 cm
P. hochstetteri (Pfr.) forma *obscura* (Beutler, 1901). Elmslie Bay, South Island, N.Z. Base solid black.

Bicolor Paryphanta (2.5") 6 cm
Paryphanta hochstetteri forma *bicolor* Powell, 1930. Queen Charlotte Sounds area. 3,000 ft. alt. One at right shattered when dried.

Anatoki Paryphanta (3") 7 cm
Paryphanta hochstetteri forma *anatokiensis* Powell, 1938. Western Tasman Mountains, South Id., N.Z. Uncommon.

Glass-eye Paryphanta (2") 5.5 cm
Paryphanta lignaria Hutton, 1888, forma *lusca* Powell, 1949. Glass-eye Creek to Corbyvale, South Id., N.Z. Reddish brown with wide streaks.

Even-colored Paryphanta
(1.7") 5 cm
P. lignaria forma *unicolorata* Powell, 1930. Seddonville Flat, South Id., N.Z. Under flax clumps. Variable striping.

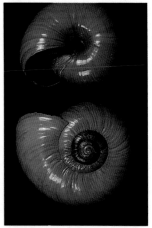

Superb Paryphanta (3.2") 8 cm
Paryphanta superba Powell, 1930, forma *prouseorum* Powell, 1946. West Nelson, N.Z. 2,000 ft. alt. Paratypes.

Travers' Paryphanta (2") 5 cm
Paryphanta traversi Powell, 1930. Levin, Horowhenna coastal plain, North Island, N.Z. Several forms.

Side-zoned Paryphanta (2") 5 cm
Paryphanta traversi forma *latizona* Powell, 1949. Many spiral lines on periphery. Levin, N.Z. Holotype on right.

Shield Paryphanta (0.8") 2 cm
Schizoglossa novoseelandica (Pfeiffer, 1862). Wanganui and Taihape, North Id., N.Z. Uncommon. Eggs shelly white.

Little Jug Paryphanta (1") 2.5 cm
Wainuia urnula (Pfeiffer, 1855). Near Wellington and Kapiti Id., New Zealand. Very thin-shelled.

Family HAPLOTREMATIDAE

One American genus with about 20 rapacious, carnivorous species, with glossy, umbilicate, low, tubular shells. Foot is holopod with no pedal furrows. Lays eggs or may be ovoviviparous, bearing live young. Several large species occur in moist areas of the Pacific west coast. A few small species of the subgenus *Zophos* occur in the West Indies.

Vancouver Haplotreme (1") 2.5 cm
Haplotrema vancouverense (Lea, 1839). N.W. Calif. to Idaho and Alaska. Moist woods. Type of subgenus *Ancomena* H.B. Baker.

Concave Haplotreme (0.7") 1.5 cm
Haplotrema concavum (Say, 1821). Eastern Canada and United States in moist ground leaves. Common. Carnivorous.

Family ACAVIDAE

Widespread tropical family of usually large shells. Foot lacks a side furrow. Shelly eggs are often very large, but *Stylodon* from the Seychelles is ovoviviparous. The Acavinae include the 4-inch *Helicophanta* from Madagascar and the colorful *Acavus* ground snail from Sri Lanka. The Caryodinae contain *Hedleyella* and the flat *Pedinogyra* both from Australia. The turreted Clavatorinae from Madagascar reach 6 inches.

Falconer's Hedleysnail (4") 10 cm
Hedleyella falconeri (Gray, 1834) [syn.: *falconari* Reeve, 1842]. So. Queensland and New South Wales, Australia. Type of genus.

Falconer's Hedleysnail (4") 10 cm
Hedleyella falconeri (Gray, 1834). Largest of the Australia Helix-shaped snails. Uncommon in scrub beneath fig trees.

Uncut Hedleysnail (2.5") 5 cm
Pygmipanda atomata (Gray, 1834). New South Wales, Australia. 3,000 ft., alt. Uncommon Type of the genus.

Larrey's Braziersnail (1") 2.5 cm
Brazieresta larreyi Brazier, 1871. Northern New South Wales, Australia. Type of the genus.

Hay's Flat-whorled Snail (3") 7 cm
Pedinogyra hayii (Griffith & Pidgeon, 1833). These snails burrow in earth and old turkey nests. Lay large eggs. Photo by R.T. Abbott.

Hay's Flat-whorled Snail 7 cm
Pedinogyra hayii (Griffith & Pidgeon, 1833). Southern Queensland. *Helix cunninghami* G.& P., 1834, is an absolute synonym. Common.

Hay's Flat-whorled Snail (3") 7 cm
Pedinogyra hayii (Griffith & Pidgeon, 1833). Ventral view. Named after R.W. Hay, after whom Hay's Peak near Brisbane was named.

Hay's Flat-whorled Snail 7 cm
Pedinogyra hayii (Griffith & Pidgeon, 1833) forma *allani* Iredale, 1937. Outer lip white; brown band dark. Gladstone, Queensland.

Dwarf Flat-whorled Snail
(2") 5 cm
Pedinogyra nanna Iredale, 1937. Gladstone, Queensland in deep litter. Locally common.

Rotary Flat-whorled Snail
(2.5") 6 cm
Pedinogyra rotabilis (Reeve, 1852). Tweeds Head, N.S.W. and southern Queensland. Syn.: *muhlfeldtiana* Reeve.

Launceston Snail   (1.3") 3 cm
Anoglypta launcestonensis (Reeve, 1853). Area of Launceston, northern Tasmania Id., Australia. Uncommon.

Launceston Snail   (1.3") 3 cm
Anoglypta launcestonensis (Reeve, 1853). Northern Tasmania. Top beaded; bottom smooth. Faded color.

Dufresn's Walnut Snail
(1.5") 3 cm
Caryodes dufresnii (Leach, 1815). Tasmania. Syn.: *superior* and *extra* Iredale, 1937.

Macrowhorled Snail
(2.5") 6.5 cm
Macrocyclis laxata (Férussac, 1820). "Chile"; Nahuel Huapi National Park, Argentina. Syn.: *peruviana.*

Macrowhorled Snail (3") 7.5 cm
Macrocyclis laxata (Férussac, 1820), forma *banksii* "Cuming" Küster. A larger form from the Chile-Argentine area.

Polished Ampelita (1.5") 3.5 cm
Ampelita xystera (Valenciennes in Beck, 1837). Madagascar. Type of the genus. Subfamily Acavinae.

Gaudens Ampelita   (2.5") 6 cm
Ampelita gaudens Mabille, 1888. Nossé Be, Madagascar.

Hova Ampelita   (1.5") 3.5 cm
Ampelita hova (Angas, 1877). Madagascar. 3 dark bands. Narrow umbilicus.

Sepulcral Ampelita   (2") 4.8 cm
Ampelita sepulchralis (Férussac, 1820). Madagascar. Sometimes without bands.

Robillard's Ampelita
(1.5") 3.5 cm
Ampelita robillardi (Argas, 1876). Southwest Madagascar.

Magnificent Helicophanta
(3") 7.5 cm
Helicophanta magnifica (Férussac, 1821). Mandraka rainforests Madagascar. Type of the genus.

Farafanga Helicophanta
(3") 7.5 cm
Helicophanta farafanga (H. Adams, 1875). Near Farafanga River, S.E. Madagascar. Thin outer lip.

Souverbie's Helicophanta
(3") 7.5 cm
Helicophanta souverbiana Fischer, 1860. Eastern Madagascar. Outer lip thickened.

Greenish False Ampelita
(1.5") 3.5 cm
Eurystyla viridis (Deshayes, 1832). Madagascar. Formerly in genus *Poecilostylus* Pilsbry, 1890.

Exceptional Clavator (4") 10 cm
Clavator eximius (Shuttleworth, 1852), forma *balstoni* (Angas, 1877). Ekongo, Madagascar. Typical form is 5" long.

Grandidier's Clavator (3.5") 9 cm
Clavator grandidieri (Crosse & Fischer, 1868). Near Ft. Dauphin, Madagascar. Also fossil.

Obtuse Clavator (3.5") 9 cm
Clavator obtusatus (Gmelin, 1791). Andrahomana, Madagascar. Early whorls elongate, smooth.

Studer's Stylodont (2.5") 6 cm
Stylodonta studeriana (Férussac, 1821). Vallé de Mai, Praslin Island, Seychelles. Uncommon on bushes. R.T. Abbott, coll. 1985.

Studer's Stylodont (2.5") 6 cm
Stylodonta studeriana (Férussac, 1821). Feed on green leaves; ovoviviparous. Slow moving.

Studer's Stylodont (2.5") 6 cm
Stylodonta studeriana (Férussac, 1821). Faded museum specimen. Early whorls minutely granulated.

One-toothed Stylodont (2") 5 cm
Stylodonta unidentata (Holten, 1802). Mahé and Silhouette Ids., Seychelle Ids. Uncommon. Chemnitz's name is no good.

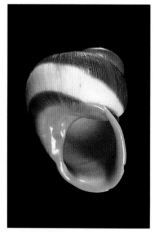

Red-mouthed Acavus (2")
Acavus haemastoma (Linnaeus, 1758). Sri Lanka (Ceylon). Common on ground and a nuisance in gardens.

Red-mouthed Acavus (2") 4.5 cm
Acavus haemastoma (Linnaeus, 1758). Greenish, fuzzy periostracum covers bright outer shell.

Red-mouthed Acavus (2") 4.5 cm
Acavus haemastoma (Linnaeus, 1758). Typical form has red or pink peristome. Sri Lanka.

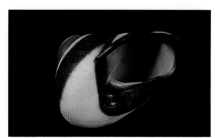

Black-mouthed Acavus (2") 4.5 cm
Acavus haemastoma (L.), forma *melanotragus* (Born, 1778). An uncommon color form from Sri Lanka.

Red-mouthed Acavus (2") 4.5 cm
Acavus haemastoma (Linnaeus, 1758). Group of cleaned Sri Lanka specimens showing banding variations.

Phoenix Acavus (2.5") 6 cm
Acavus phoenix Pfeiffer, 1854. Sri Lanka. Larger, lower, no bands, dull exterior. Uncommon.

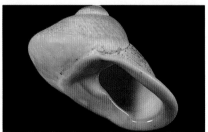

Superb Acavus (2.4") 6 cm
Acavus superba Pfeiffer, 1850. Sri Lanka (Ceylon). Angular edge. This is form *roseolabiata* Nevill, 1888. Rare.

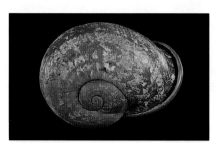

Walton's Acavus (2") 5 cm
Oligospira valtoni (Reeve, 1842). Pusilawe, Sri Lanka. Uncommon. Periostracum hydrophanous. Also spelled *waltoni*.

Walton's Acavus (2") 5 cm
Oligospira valtoni (Reeve, 1842). Sri Lanka. Underside may become eroded with age.

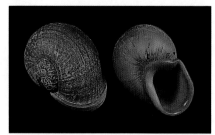

Skinner's Acavus (1.2") 3 cm
Oligospira skinneri (Reeve, 1854). Sri Lanka. Rare. Lip very thick, violet. Periostracum golden-flecked.

Superfamily BULIMULOIDEA
(Bulimulacea)

Consists of 5 major families, Bulimulidae (South America-Australasia) Odontostomidae (South America), Orthalicidae (tropical Americas), Amphibulimidae (mainly West Indies) and the small, elongate Urocoptidae (tropical Americas).

Family BULIMULIDAE

Large, elongate to ovate, ground-dwelling shells. Eggs small, round. Mostly tropical Americas. *Drymaeus* is smaller, arboreal. *Placostylus* larger, Melanesian.

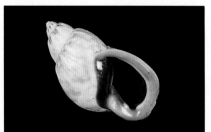

Black-mouthed Auris (2") 5 cm
Auris melastoma (Swainson, 1820). Bahia Prov., Brazil. Mouth black within. Notch at columnella base. Uncommon. [not *melanostoma*].

Ilheos Auris (2.3") 6 cm
Auris illheocola (Moricand, 1836). Ilheos, Bahia Prov., Brazil. Uncommon. Syn.: *melanostoma* Reeve.

Double-lipped Auris (2") 5 cm
Auris bilabiata (Broderip & Sowerby, 1829). Bahia Prov., Brazil. Ground snail, locally common. Lip white.

Double-lipped Auris (2") 5 cm
Auris bilabiata (Broderip & Sowerby, 1829), forma *nigrilabris* Pilsbry, 1896. Black-lipped. Alias *melanostoma* Moricand, 1836.

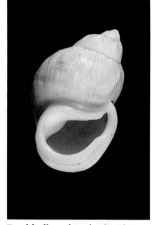

Double-lipped Auris (1.5") 3 cm
Auris bilabiata forma or subspecies *egregia* Jay, 1836. Espiritu Santo and Ilheos Brazil. Ribs weak. Sometimes pinkish.

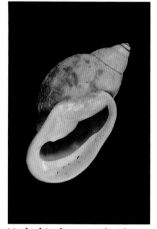

Marked Auris (1.5") 4 cm
Otostomus signatus (Spix, 1827) Bahia Prov., Brazil. Type of genus. Syn.: *vittatus* Spix has axial streaks.

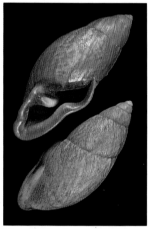

Distorted Auris (2.5") 6 cm
Eudolichotis distorta (Bruguière, 1789). Colombia to Venezuela, on bananas. Sculpture of diamond-shaped granules. Type of genus.

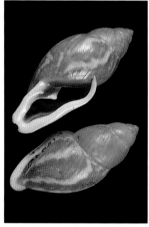

Squirrel-ear Auris (2") 4 cm
Eudolichotis aurissciuri (Guppy, 1866). Trinidad and British Guiana, on trees. Syn.: *aegotis* Pfeiffer.

Squirrel-ear Auris (2") 4 cm
Eudolichotis aurissciuri (Guppy, 1866). Dutch Guiana. A variable species, perhaps forms of *glabra* Gmelin, 1791).

Broad-navel Auris (1.5") 3 cm
Eudolichotis euryomphala (Jonas, 1844). Vicinity of Caracas, Venezuela. Extinct?

Sinuate Auris (2") 5 cm
Eudolichotis sinuata (Albers, 1854). Puerto Cabello area, Venezuela. Notch at base of lip. Extinct?

Moritz's Dryptus Snail
(3.5") 9 cm
Dryptus moritzianus (Pfeiffer, 1847). Venezuela and Colombia. Zigzag streaks rare. Type of genus.

Funck's Dryptus Snail
(3") 8 cm
Dryptus funcki (Nyst, 1843). Prov. of Cumana, Venezuela, in mountains. Uncommon. Syn.: *superbus* Jonas, 1844.

Guerin's Dryptus Snail
(3.5") 9 cm
Dryptus guerini (Pfeiffer, 1846). Colombia. May be form of *moritzianus* says Pilsbry.

Jubilant Dryptus Snail
(4.5") 11 cm
Dryptus guerini subspecies *jubens* (Preston, 1908). Mt. La-paz, Venezuela. Uncommon.

Eared Pleko Snail   (2") 5 cm
Plekocheilus aurissileni (Born, 1778). St. Vincent Id., Lesser Antilles. Zebra stripes of brown. Type of the genus.

St. Lucia Pleko Snail   (1.2") 4 cm
Plekocheilus aulacostyla (Pfeif-fer, 1852). St. Lucia Id., Lesser Antilles. Furrow at top of co-lumella.

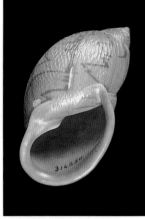

Blainville's Pleko Snail
(2.5") 6 cm
Plekocheilus blainvilleanus (Pfeiffer, 1847.) Venezuela and Colombia. Surface finely wrinkled. Uncommon.

Colored Pleko Snail
(2.2") 5.5 cm
Plekocheilus coloratus (Nyst, 1845). Colombia and near Quito, Ecuador. In subgenus *Eurytus* Albers, 1850.

Wooly Pleko Snail   (2.5") 6 cm
Plekocheilus floccosus (Spix, 1827). Nachiyaca, Ecuador. Fresh, young specimen.

Wooly Pleko Snail   (2.5") 6 cm
Plekocheilus floccosus (Spix, 1827). Napo, Ecuador. Old, thick-ened, eroded specimen.

Flamed Pleko Snail (2.2") 5.5 cm
Plekocheilus fulminans (Nyst, 1843). Cumana Prov., Venezuela and Colombia. Syn.: *bellulus* Jonas, 1844.

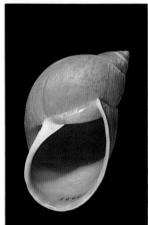

Humped Pleko Snail   (4") 10 cm
Plekocheilus gibbonius (Lea, 1836). Quenden Mts., Colom-bia. Misspelling: *gibboreus* Pfr.

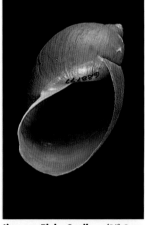

Jimenez Pleko Snail   (3") 8 cm
Plekocheilus jimenezi (Hidalgo, 1870). San José, Ecuador. Nar-row columella; large aperture.

Peppered Pleko Snail
(2.5") 6.5 cm
Plekocheilus piperatus (Sowerby, 1838). Huallaga, Peru. Uncom-mon.

Flea-specked Pleko Snail   4 cm
Plekocheilus pulicarius (Reeve, 1848). Near Bogota, Colombia. Extinct? In subgenus *Eurytus* Albers, 1850.

Four-colored Pleko Snail
(1.3") 3.1 cm
Plekocheilus quadricolor (Pfeiffer, 1847). Merida Prov., Colombia. Yellow blotches and brown zigzags.

Succinoid Pleko Snail
(1.5") 3.5 cm
Plekocheilus succinoides (Petit, 1840). Near Bogota, Colombia. Extinct? Finely granulated.

Tate's Pleko Snail   (2.5") 4 cm
Plekocheilus tatei Haas, 1955. Mt. Diuba, Venezuela. Holotype illus. (in. Amer. Mus. Nat. Hist.).

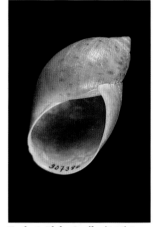

Taylor's Pleko Snail (2.2") 6 cm
Plekocheilus taylorianus (Reeve, 1848). Pinchincha Prov., Ecuador. Syn.: *taylorioides* Miller.

Tetens' Pleko Snail   (2") 5 cm
Plekocheilus tetensii (Dunker, 1875). Sierra Nevada di Santa Marta, Colombia. Indian food.

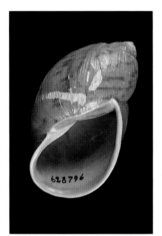

Tricolor Pleko Snail   (2") 5 cm
Plekocheilus tricolor (Pfeiffer, 1852). El Oriente and Gualea, Ecuador.

Twig Pleko Snail   (1.5") 4 cm
Plekocheilus virgatus (Pilsbry, 1935). La Calera, Bogota, Colombia.

Dwarf Pleko Snail   (1") 2.5 cm
Plekocheilus veranyi (Pfeiffer, 1847). Chachopo, Merida Prov., Colombia.

Largilliert's Marvel Snail   6 cm
Thaumastus largillierti (Pfeiffer, 1847). Santa Catarina, Brazil. Syn.: *achilles* Pfeiffer; *consimilis* Reeve.

Purplish Marvel Snail (2.5") 6 cm
Thaumastus porphyreus (Pfeiffer, 1846). Andahuaylas and near Lima, Peru.

Taunais Marvel Snail   (3") 8 cm
Thaumastus taunaisii (Férussac, 1821). Rio de Janeiro and Macahé, Brazil. Syn.: *magnificus* Grateloupe, 1839.

Thompson's Marvel Snail   6 cm
Thaumastus thompsoni (Pfeiffer, 1845). Near Quito, Ecuador. Axially striped. Type of subgenus *Kara* Strebel, 1910.

Granulated Marvel Snail
(3") 8 cm
Thaumastus melanocheilus
(Nyst, 1845). Peru, in high mountains.

Strange Marvel Snail (3") 8 cm
Thaumastus insolitus (Preston,
1909). Rio Tarma, Peru. 2,300
meters, alt. Uncommon.

Two-banded Marvel Snail 6 cm
Thaumastus bitaeniatus (Nyst,
1845). Huacapistrana, Peru.
1,800 meters. Type of subgenus
Scholvienia Strebel, 1910.

Jelski's Marvel Snail (1.5") 4 cm
Thaumastus (Scholvienia) jelskii
(Lubomirski, 1879). East of Oroya,
Peru.

Weyrauch's Marvel Snail
(1.5") 4 cm
Thaumastus (Scholvienia)
weyrauchi Pilsbry, 1944. Carpa-
pata, Rio Tarma, Peru. 2,300
meters. Paratypes.

Derelict Bostryx   (1") 2.5 cm
Bostryx derelictus Broderip,
1832, forma *ascendens* Pilsbry,
1944. (paratype). Ayacucho,
Peru. In subgenus *Lissoacme*
Pilsbry, 1896.

Vilchez's Bostryx   (0.5") 8 mm
Bostryx (Bostryx) vilchezi
Weyrauch, 1960. Cuteroo
Socato, northern Peru. Paratypes.

Swollen Bostryx   (1") 2.3 cm
Bostryx (Lissoacme) tumidulus
(Pfeiffer, 1842). Ambo, Huenco,
Peru. Syn.: *inflatus* Broderip,
1836, non Lamarck).

Weyrauch's Bostryx (0.7") 2 cm
Bostryx (Platybostryx) weyrauchi
Pilsbry, 1944. Ninabamba,
Ayacucho, Peru. Paratypes. Syn.:
Pampasinus Weyrauch.

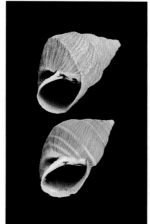

Hennah's Bostryx   (1.3") 3 cm
Bostryx (Platybostryx) hennahi
(Gray, 1830). Arica, Peru on cacti
in sandy places.

Reents' Bostryx   (1") 2.5 cm
Bostryx reentsi (Philippi, 1851).
Chala, Peru. Aperture rose within.
On sandy hills. Topotypes.

Flattest Bostryx   (0.7") 2 cm
Bostryx (Discobostryx) planis-
simus Pilsbry & Olsson, 1949.
Peru mountains. Holotype above.
Type of genus.

Oblique Bostryx (0.8") 2 cm
Bostryx (Bostryx) obliquiportus
Weyrauch, 1960. Quichao, Peru;
in desert conditions. Topotypes.

Bermudez's Bostryx (0.7") 2 cm
Bostryx bermudezi Weyrauch,
1958. Quichao, Peru. Topotypes.
Type of subgenus *Pseudo-
peronaeus* Weyrauch.

Javelin Bostryx (1") 2.5 cm
Bostryx (Geoceras) veruculum
(Morelet, 1860). Ayacueho, Peru.
High in Andes.

Baron's Bostryx (1.2") 3 cm
Xenothauma baroni Fulton, 1896.
Rio Yonan, near Tembladera,
Peru. Limestone cliffs. Type of
genus.

Peruvian Bulimulus (2.5") 6 cm
Plectostylus peruvianus (Bruguière, 1789). Southern Chile and
northern Peru. Type of the genus.

Broderip's Bulimulus (2.5") 6 cm
Plectostylus broderipi (Sowerby,
1832). Southern Chile and northern Peru.

Chilean Bulimulus (1.5") 4 cm
Plectostylus chilensis (Lesson,
1826). Near Valparaiso, Chile.
Rarely banded.

Coquimbo Bulimulus (2") 5 cm
Plectostylus coquimbensis (Brod-
erip, 1832). Near Coquimbo,
Chile.

Quail Bulimulus (1.2") 3 cm
Plectostylus coturnix (Sowerby,
1832). Huasco, Chile. Among
rocks.

Changeable Bulimulus 4 cm
Scutalus proteus (Broderip, 1832).
Peru and Chile, among stones.
Syn.: *granulatissimus* Weyrauch,
1960.

Bolivian Bulimulus (2.6") 6.1 cm
Scutalus bolivianus (Marshall,
1932). Tamanani, 95 mi. N.E. of
Oruro, Bolivia. Holotype illus.

Tupac Bulimulus (2") 5 cm
Scutalus tupacii (Orbigny, 1835).
Bolivian Andes. Salta, Jujuy and
Tucumán Distr., Argentina.

West Indian Bulimulus 1.2 cm
Bulimulus guadalupensis (Bruguière, 1789). Lesser and Greater Antilles; Jamaica. Abundant near habitation. Syn.: *exilis* Gmelin, 1791. Type of genus.

Bristle Bulimulus (1.6") 4 cm
Bulimulus heterotrichus (Moricand, 1836). Eastern coastal Brazil. Type of subgenus *Rhinus* Albers. Bristles wear off usually.

Glassy Drymaeus (1.5") 4 cm
Drymaeus hyrohylaeus (Orbigny, 1835). Bolivia and Argentina, on trees. Common. Type of the genus.

Velvety Bulimulus (0.5") 1.6 cm
Bulimulus (Rhinus) pubescens (Moricand, 1846). Fernando de Noronha, Brazil.

Whitened Bulimulus
(0.6") 1.7 cm
Rabdotus dealbatus (Say, 1821). S.E. United States to New Mexico. Formerly in *Bulimulus*. Several subspecies recognized.

Alternate Bulimulus (1") 2.5 cm
Rabdotus alternatus (Say, 1830). Northern Mexico. Subspecies *mariae* (Albers, 1850) is from Texas. Abundant. Alias *Rhabdotus* von Martens.

Montezuma Bulimulus
(2") 5 cm
Naesiotus montezuma (Dall, 1893). Baja California, Mexico, Granulose. Paratype. Type of *Puritanina* Jacobson, 1958.

Upper Peru Bulimulus (2") 5 cm
Neopetraeus altoperuvianus (Reeve, 1849). Northeast Peru, 1,800 meters.

Atahualpa Bulimulus (2") 5 cm
Neopetraeus atahualpa (Dohrn, 1863). Huaras, Peru. May be form of *tessellatus* (Shuttleworth, 1852).

Cliff-dwelling Bulimulus
(1.5") 4 cm
Neopetraeus cremnobates Pilsbry, 1949. Rio Santa, Peru. Paratypes.

Flat-mouthed Bulimulus
(1.5") 4 cm
Neopetraeus platystomus (Pfeiffer, 1858). Patas Prov., Peru.

Tasmanian Snail (1") 2.5 cm
Tasmanembryon tasmanicus (Pfeiffer, 1851). Tasmania, Australia. Arboreal. Fossil species is *gunni* (Sowerby).

Manatee Snail (1.5") 4 cm
Drymaeus dormani (Binney, 1857). North half of Florida in citrus groves. Paratypes. Forma *albidus* Wright, 1890 is whitish.

Flaring Drymaeus (2") 5 cm
Drymaeus expansus (Pfeiffer, 1848). Eastern Peru and Ecuador. Syn.: *pulchellus* Sowerby, 1835, non Brod., 1832.

Glaucus Drymaeus (1.5") 4 cm
Drymaeus glaucostomus (Albers, 1852). 1,000 ft., Valencia, Venezuela on palms.

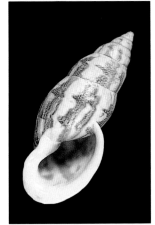

Large Colombian Drymaeus (2") 5 cm
Drymaeus flexuosus (Pfeiffer, 1852) subsp. *megas* Pilsbry, 1944. Upper Magdalena Valley, Colombia. Holotype illus.

Chanchamay Drymaeus (1.5") 4 cm
Drymaeus chanchamayensis (Hidalgo, 1870). Chanchamayo, Peru.

Dombey Drymaeus (2.3") 6 cm
Drymaeus dombeyanus (Pfeiffer, 1846). Central and West Mexico.

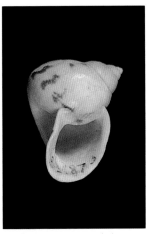

Bartlett's Drymaeus (1") 2.5 cm
Drymaeus bartletti (H. Adams, 1866). Eastern Peru.

Lamas Drymaeus (1.2") 3.3 cm
Drymaeus lamas (Higgins, 1868). Jouctabamba, Oxapampa, Peru.

St. Vincent Drymaeus (1.1") 3 cm
Drymaeus vincentinus (Pfeiffer, 1846). Trinidad; Tobago; St. Vincent.

Broad-mouth Drymaeus (1") 2.5 cm
Drymaeus eurystomus (Philippi, 1867). Chanchamayo, Peru.

Zilch's Drymaeus (1") 2.5 cm
Drymaeus zilchi Haas, 1955. Negritos, Peru. 3,000 ft., alt.

Many-lined Drymaeus (0.8") 2 cm
Drymaeus multilineatus (Say, 1825). South Florida; Venezuela; Curacao; Colombia. Common.

Many-lined Drymaeus
(1.5") 4 cm
Drymaeus multilineatus (Say, 1825). S.E. Florida. Circular epiphragm on twig was former resting place.

Broad-banded Drymaeus
(1.5") 4 cm
Drymaeus multilineatus (Say, 1825), forma *latizonatus* Pilsbry, 1936. Matecumbe and Lignum Vitae Key, Florida.

Branching Drymaeus (1") 2.5 cm
Drymaeus virgulatorum (Morelet, 1863). Eastern slope of the Cordillera, Peru. 3,500 meters, alt.

Twig Drymaeus (1.2") 2.6 cm
Drymaeus virgulatus (Férussac, 1822). Curacao and Aruba form. Common in grass & bushes.

Twig Drymaeus (1.3") 3 cm
Drymaeus virgulatus (Férussac, 1822). Lesser and Greater Antilles. Syn.: *elongatus* Röding, 1798, non Razoumowsky, 1789.

Elegant Drymaeus (1") 2.5 cm
Drymaeus scitulus (Reeve, 1849). Chachapoyas, Peru. Variable color patterns.

Farris' Drymaeus (2") 5 cm
Drymaeus farrisi (Pfeiffer, 1858). Patas Prov.; Chagual, Peru. 5,000 ft., alt.

Rabbit-ear Cochlorina 4 cm
Cochlorina aurisleporis (Bruguière, 1789). Bahia, Rio de Janeiro and Espirito Santo States, Brazil. Variable in color-pattern. Type of genus.

Rabbit-ear Cochlorina
(1.5") 4 cm
C. aurisleporis (Brug.), forma *intensior* Pilsbry, 1898. Santo Domingo, Rio, Brazil. Holotype.

Mouse-ear Cochlorina
(1.2") 3 cm
Cochlorina aurismuris (Moricand, 1837). Bahia Province, Brazil.

Heavenly Cochlorina (1.2") 3 cm
Cochlorina uranops Pilsbry, 1898. Brazil. Base convex and malleated. Freak? Brazil.

Boat Cochlorina (2") 5 cm
Cochlorina navicula (Wagner, in Spix, 1827). Bahia Province, Brazil.

Boat Cochlina (2") 5 cm
Cochlorina navicula (Wagner, in Spix 1827). Bahia, Brazil.

Brick Cochlina (2") 5 cm
Cochlorina navicula (Wagner, in Spix 1827), forma *lateritius* Pilsbry, 1898. Without bands. Bahia, Brazil. Rare.

Crichton's Newboldius (3") 7.5 cm
Newboldius crichtoni (Broderip, 1836). Near Huanuco, Peru. 1,800 meters. Type of genus. Syn.: *illustris* Rolle.

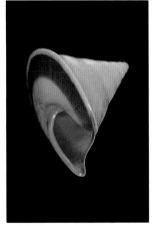

Curran's Pyramid Snail (1") 2.2 cm
Oxychona pyramidella (Wagner, in Spix, 1827) subsp. *currani* Bartsch, 1916. Rio Grungugy, Bahia, Brazil. Holotype.

Two-banded Pyramid Snail (0.8") 2 cm
Oxychona bifasciata (Burrow, 1815). Bahia, Brazil. Rare. Syn.: *bosciana* (Férussac, 1821). Type of genus.

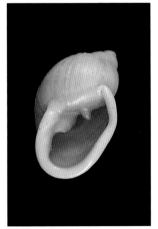

Layard's Placostyle (1") 2.2 cm
Diplomorpha layardi (Ancey, 1884). Vate Island, New Hebrides. Rare. Type of the genus. Subfamily Placostylinae.

Lautour's Placostyle (0.7") 2 cm
Diplomorpha delatouri (Hartman, 1886). Aore and Espiritu Santo Ids., New Hebrides.

Alexander's Placostyle (5") 12 cm
Placostylus alexander (Crosse, 1855). Kanala and Ougap, New Caledonia. Many forms.

Almiranta Placostyle (3") 7 cm
Placostylus almiranta Clench, 1941. Malaita Id., Solomons. 1,500 ft., alt. Holotype.

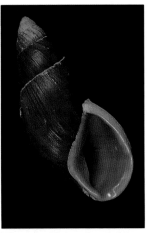

Digressive Placostyle (3") 7 cm
Placostylus (Maoristylus) ambagiosus (Suter, 1906), subsp. *annectens* Powell, 1938 (holotype of syn.: *hancoxi* Powell, 1951). N.Z.

Keen's Digressive Placostyle (3") 7.5 cm
P. ambagiosus subsp. *keenorum* Powell, 1947. Spirits Bay, New Zealand. Photo by N. Douglas.

Pandora Digressive Placostyle (2.8") 7 cm
P. ambagiosus subsp. *pandora* Powell, 1951. Pandora, Spirits Bay, N.Z. Holotype illus.

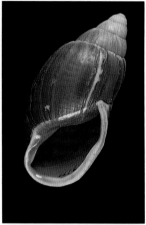

Bivaricose Placostyle (2.3") 6 cm
Placostylus bivaricosus (Gaskoin, 1854). Lord Howe Island. Formerly abundant.

Bollons' Placostyle (4") 10 cm
Placostylus (*Basileostylus*) *bollonsi* Suter, 1908. Three Kings Islands, N.Z. Type of Haas' subgenus.

Wrinkled Placostyle (3.7") 9 cm
P. bollonsi subsp. *caperatus* Powell, 1948. Three Kings Island, N.Z. Holotype. Taller spire.

Threaded Placostyle (3") 7.5 cm
Placostylus bovinus (Bruguière, 1789). Isle of Pines, New Caledonia. Many synonyms; *fibratus* Martyn. Mouth orange.

New Caledonian Placostyle
                            (3") 7.5 cm
Placostylus caledonicus (Petit, 1845). Ile Art, New Caledonia. Ground dweller.

Clery's Placostyle (4") 10 cm
Placostylus (*Eumecostylus*) *cleryi* (Petit, 1850). San Cristobal Id., Solomons. Type of subgenus.

Founak Placostyle (2.6") 7 cm
Placostylus (*Placocharis*) *founaki* (Hombon & Jacquinot, 1854). Santa Isabel Id., Solomons. Common.

Rev. Fox's Placostyle (4") 10 cm
Placostylus foxi Clench, 1950. San Cristobal Id., Solomons.

Sooty Placostyle (2") 5 cm
Placostylus (*Santacharis*) *fuligineus* (Pfeiffer, 1852). Aneiteum, New Hebrides. Ground dweller.

Alien Placostyle (2") 5 cm
Placostylus (*S.*) *fuligineus* forma *alienus* Pilsbry, 1900. New Hebrides.

Gallego Placostyle (2.8") 6 cm
Placostylus gallegoi Clench, 1950. San Cristobal Id., Solomons. Holotype illus.

Thin Fijian Placostyle (2") 5 cm
Placostylus (*Callistocharis*) *gracilis* (Broderip, 1840). Vanua Levu and Ovalau Ids., Fiji. Uncommon.

Thin Fijian Placostyle (2") 5 cm
Placostylus (Callistocharis) gracilis (Broderip, 1840). Ovalau Id., Fiji. This is holotype of syn.: *fulguratus* Jay, 1842.

Guppy's Placostyle (3.2") 8 cm
Placostylus guppyi E.A. Smith, 1891. Solomon Islands.

Hargraves' Placostyle (3") 7.5 cm
Placostylus (Proaspastus) hargravesi (Cox, 1871). Treasury Id.; Malaita, Solomons.

Hong's Placostyle (3") 7.5 cm
Placostylus (Maoristylus) hongii (Lesson, 1830). Northland and off islands, New Zealand. (*P. shongii* was error). Type of subgenus. Rarely sinistral.

Kirakira Placostyle (3.1") 8 cm
Placostylus (Proaspastus) kirakiraensis (Rensch and Rensch, 1934), Kira Kira, San Cristobal Id., Solomons.

Koro Placostyle (2.3") 6 cm
Placostylus koroensis (Garrett, 1872). Kora Kora, Vanua Levu, Fiji. Syntypes. Extinct?

Kreft's Placostyle (2") 5 cm
Placostylus (Callistocharis) kreftii (Cox, 1872). Solomon Islands. Syntype.

Malleated Placostyle (2.5") 6 cm
Placostylus (Callistocharis) malleatus (Jay, 1842). Viti Levu, Fiji. Arboreal.

Macgillivray's Placostyle (2") 5 cm
Placostylus (Placocharis) macgillivrayi (Pfeiffer, 1855). Guadacanal Id., Solomons. Left: syntype from Cuming.

Billy Mann's Placostyle (3") 7.5 cm
Placostylus manni Clapp, 1923. Auki, Malaita, Solomon Islands. Holotype.

Red-lipped Placostyle (2") 5 cm
Placostylus (Aspastus) miltocheilus (Reeve, 1848). San Cristobal Id., Solomons. Common.

Manuga Placostyle (3") 7.5 cm
Placostylus miltocheilus forma *manugiensis* Rensch & Rensch, 1934. Manuga, San Cristobal Id., Solomons. Paratypes.

Marie's Placostyle   (2.7") 7 cm
Placostylus mariei (Crosse & Fischer, 1867). West coast of New Caledonia.

Morose Placostyle   (2") 5 cm
Placostylus morosus (Gould, 1846). Vanua Levu and Viti Levu, Fiji. Arboreal.

Ophir Placostyle   (3") 7.5 cm
Placostylus ophir Clench, 1941. Su'u, Malaita Id., Solomons. Holotype.

Palm Placostyle   (2.3") 6 cm
Placostylus palmarum (Mousson, 1869). Makito, San Cristobal Id., Solomons. On palm trees.

Rossiter's Placostyle (3") 7.5 cm
Placostylus rossiteri (Brazier, 1881). Nehone Bay and Canala, New Caledonia. Type of subgenus *Poecilocharis* Kobelt.

San Cristobal Placostyle
(3") 7.5 cm
Placostylus (*Proaspastus*) *sanchristovalensis* Cox, 1870. San Cristobal Id., Solomons. Type of subgenus.

Salomonis Placostyle (2.5") 6 cm
Placostylus (*Santacharis*) *salomonis* (Pfeiffer, 1852). Erromanga, New Hebrides. Not from Solomons.

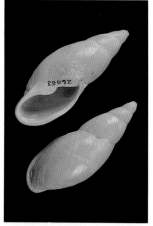

Sellers' Placostyle   (2") 5 cm
Placostylus (*Aspastus*) *sellersi* (Cox, 1871). Guadacanal Id., Solomons. Syntypes.

Seeman's Placostyle (2.5") 6 cm
Placostylus (*Euplacostylus*) *seemani* (Dohrn, 1861). Kandavu Id., Fiji. Type of the subgenus.

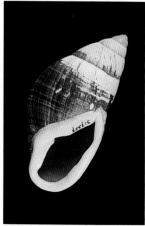

Beetle Placostyle   (3") 7.5 cm
Placostylus scarabus (Albers, 1854). Baaba and Nenemas Ids., New Caledonia.

Strange's Placostyle   (2") 5 cm
Placostylus strangei (Pfeiffer, 1855). Eddystone Id. and New Georgia, Solomons.

False Marie's Placostyle   6 cm
Placostylus submariei (Sowerby, 1869). Kono and Bondé, New Caledonia. Common.

Family
ODONTOSTOMIDAE

Tooth-mouthed Snails

Sometimes considered as only a subfamily (Odontostominae), this group of 10 genera is limited to South America, mostly to the east of the Andes and south of the Amazon to Argentina. Most species have strong teeth and lamellae surrounding the aperture which presumably protect these ground dwellers from beetles and small rodents. The earliest described species was *Anostoma ringens* Linnaeus, 1758, brought back by early explorers of Brazil.

Pilsbry's Choke-mouth Snail (0.8") 2 cm
Anctus laminiferus (Ancey, 1888). Northern Bahia province, Brazil. Syn.: *pilsbryi* Ford, 1891.

Angulate Moricand Snail (1")
Cyclodontina (Moricandia) angulata (Wagner, 1827). Western and southern Brazil; Minas Gerais. Common. Syn.: *C. puro* Spix, 1827).

Eroded Tooth-mouthed Snail (1.5") 3.8 cm
Cyclodontina exesus (Spix, 1827). Bahia Province, Brazil. Shriveled surface. Rarely banded.

Inflated Tooth-mouthed Snail (0.8") 2.4 cm
Cyclodontina inflata (Wagner, 1827). Bahia Province, Brazil; Paraguay. Type of genus.

Burrington's Tooth-mouthed Snail (2.5") 6.5 cm
Cyclodontina labrosa (Menke, 1828). Bahia Prov., Brazil. Syn.: *pantagruelina* (Moricand, 1833). Subgenus *Burringtonia*.

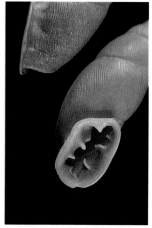

Brazilian Tooth-mouthed Snail (1.5") 3.8 cm
Odontostomus odontostomus Sowerby, 1824. Bahia, Brazil. Syn.: *gargantua* Férussac, 1831. (not 1821).

Banded Tooth-mouthed Snail (1.5") 4 cm
Odontostomus fasciatus (Pfeiffer, 1869). Santa Catharina, Brazil. Syn.: *tenuisculptus* Parodiz, 1962.

Stelzner's Tooth-mouthed Snail (0.5") 1.2 cm
Clessinia cordovana (Pfeiffer, 1855), form *stelzneri* Döring, 1874. Cordova Prov., Argentina. Type of genus; syn.: *Scalarinella*.

Striate Spix Snail (1.3") 3 cm
Clessinia striata (Spix, 1827). Sao Paulo, Brazil. Syn.: *Scalarinella spixii* Orbigny. Type of subgenus *Spixia* Pilsbry & Vanatta, 1898.

Brazilian Closed-mouthed Snail (0.5") 1.2 cm
Tomigerus clausus Spix, 1827. Ilheos District, Bahia Prov., Brazil. Uncommon. Type of genus.

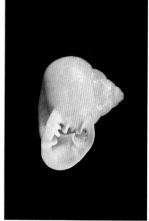

Turbinate Closed-mouth (0.5") 1.2 cm
Tomigerus turbinatus (Pfeiffer, 1845). Bahia Province, Brazil. In subgenus *Digerus* Haas, 1937. Uncommon.

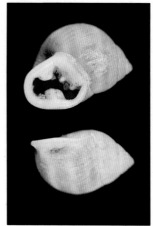

Bonnani's Snail   (1") 2.5 cm
Hyperaulax (Bonnanius) ramagei
(E.A. Smith, 1890). Fernando de
Noronha Id., off Brazil. Type of
subgenus. Syn.: *bouvieri*
Jousseaume, 1900. Nucleus
smooth.

Family ORTHALICIDAE

Sultana and Liguus Tree Snails

Large, elongate, usually tree-
dwelling tropical American
snails; holopod (without foot-
furrow) 7 genera, hundreds of
species and color forms; rarely
sinistral. Eggs elliptical, surface granular. Vegetarians;
colonial. Main genera are *Sultana, Corona, Hemibulimus*
from South America; *Liguus,*
and *Orthalicus* S.E. U.S.,
central America. Sometimes
considered subfamily of Bulimulidae.

Brazilian Up-mouth Snail   (1")
Anostoma octodentatus Fischer,
1807. Eastern Brazil. 8 to 6 weak
teeth (form *depressum* Lamarck,
1822). Syn.: *verreauxianum*
Hupé, 1857. Type of genus.

Ringed Up-mouth Snail
                    (0.7") 2 cm
Anostoma ringens (Linnaeus,
1758). Western Bahia, Brazil.
Tiny spout upper end of lip. Type
of subgenus *Ringicella* Gray.

Ringed Up-Mouth Snail
                    (0.8") 2.4 cm
Anostoma ringens (Linnaeus,
1758). Western Bahia, Brazil.
Rarely carinate (form *carinatum*
Pfeiffer, 1853).

True Sultana Snail   (2.7") 7 cm
Sultana sultana (Dillwyn, 1817).
Northeast South America; Bo-
livia; Peru. Syn.: *gallinasultana*
Lam., 1822; *bolivianus* Spix. Type
of genus.

Adamson's Sultana Snail
                    (3.5") 9 cm
Sultana adamsoni (Gray, 1833).
Near Tolima and Guaduas, Colombia. In subgenus *Melani-
orthalicus* Strebel, 1900.

Blackened Sultana Snail   (2.5")
Sultana atramentaria (Pfeiffer,
1855). Pamplona, Colombia;
Ecuador. Mouth purple tinted
within. Type of subgenus *Melan-
iorthalicus.*

Fraser's Sultana Snail   (3") 8 cm
Sultana fraseri (Pfeiffer, 1858),
forma *augusta* (Jousseaume,
1887). East Ecuador. 4,900 ft.,
alt. Early whorls pitted. Subgenus *Trachyorthalicus.*

Kellett's Sultana Snail (2.4") 6 cm
Sultana kellettii (Reeve, 1850).
Southern Ecuador. Syn.:
jungairinoi (Hidalgo, 1867).
Subgenus *Metorthalicus* Pilsbry,
1899).

Mrs. de Burgh's Sultana
                    (2.8") 7 cm
Sultana deburghiae (Reeve,
1859). High areas of Ecuador.
Syn.: *gloriosa* (Pfeiffer, 1861).
Strong columnellarfold.

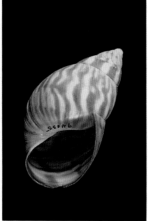

Wavy Orthalicus   (2.5") 6.5 cm
Orthalicus undatus (Bruguière,
1789). Lower West Indies; introduced to Bahamas, Jamaica.
Common. *Oxystylus* is synonym.

Florida Orthalicus (2.4") 6 cm
Orthalicus floridensis (Pilsbry, 1891). Southern third of Florida and Lower Keys. Common. Freezes kill it in winter.

Wavy Orthalicus (2.5") 5 cm
Orthalicus undatus (Bruguière, 1789). Lesser Antilles; introduced to Jamaica and Bahamas. Common. Photo: R. Goldberg.

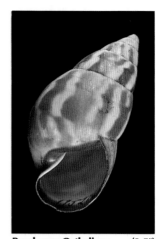

Ponderous Orthalicus (2.5")
Orthalicus ponderosus Strebel and Pfeiffer, 1882. Acapulco, west Mexico.

Buckley's Cupola Snail (3.5") 9 cm
Tholus buckleyi (Higgins, 1872). Ecuador. Nuclear whorls granulose. Type of genus.

Queen Corona Snail (3.5") 9 cm
Corona regina (Férussac, 1821). Peru and upper Amazon on trees. Apex pink. Dextral usually. Type of genus.

Sinistral Corona Snail (3") 7.8 cm
Corona perversa (Swainson, 1821), forma *regalis* (Hupé, 1857). Peru and Ecuador. Rarely dextral. White within.

Pfeiffer's Sultana Snail (2.3") 6 cm
Corona pfeifferi (Hidalgo, 1869). Rio Napo, Ecuador. Axial streaks usually more prominent.

Violet-mouthed Sultana Snail (0.3") 6 cm
Porphyrobaphe iostoma (Sowerby, 1824). Northwest Peru; Andean region and Amazonian drainage. Type of genus.

Approximate Sultana Snail (2.3") 6 cm
Porphyrobaphe approximata Fulton, 1896). Near Bogota, Colombia.

Iris Sultana Snail (2.3") 6 cm
Porphyrobaphe iris (Pfeiffer, 1852). Mountains of Colombia. Syn.: *wallisianus* Mousson, 1873. In subgenus. *Oxyorthalicus* Strebel, 1909.

Granulated Sultana Snail (2.7") 7 cm
Porphyrobaphe irrorata (Reeve, 1849). Central Ecuador. Type of subgenus *Oxyorthalicus* Strebel, 1909.

Dennison's Sultana Snail (3") 8 cm
Hemibulimus dennisoni (Reeve, 1848). Colombia near Bogota. Type of subgenus *Myiorthalicus* Strebel, 1909.

LIGUUS TREE SNAILS

The Florida Tree Snail, *Liguus fasciatus* (Müller, 1774) is limited to southern Florida and is now protected by conservation laws. They feed on algae and lichens adhering to tree limbs.

At one time southern Florida, Cuba and the island of Hispaniola abounded with the two-inch long, colorful tree snails of the genus *Liguus.* Early European explorers and naturalists brought many specimens back to Europe, but it was not until the fifteen hundreds that they appeared in illustrated works on conchology. Linnaeus named the first species, *virgineus,* in 1767. Two hundred years later 160 scientific names had been applied to this very variable and complex group of species. Today, most experts agree that there are fewer than five or six species and that the remaining names apply to either subspecies or mere genetic or ecological color forms.

As is the case with many terrestrial snails, *Liguus* numbers have been drastically reduced by the removal of their protective trees and the radical upheaval of their natural environment. *Liguus virgineus,* the Maiden Liguus, of Haiti and Santo Domingo, has probably suffered the most, mainly because the cutting down of trees for firewood and the excessive collecting of shells for export to the tourist shell trade in Florida.

In Florida, the Liguus Tree Snails prefer to be associated with the Jamaica Dogwood and the wild tamarind tree, *Lysiloma.* The heavy growths of algae, fungi and lichens, usually on the northeast side of the branches and trunks, serve as their main source of food. The trees live in soil rich in limestone in glades in slightly elevated areas known as "hammocks"—a Seminole Indian word referring to a drier, sometimes rocky, spot good for camping.

In areas where lichen growths are heavy the snails may reach a large size; as much as 7 cm in length. Changes in weather and food-supply can cause abrupt changes in the color patterns and intensity of the colors. Because the snails are hermaphroditic, with functioning male and female organs in each individual, the genetics of the color-producing genes is quite complex, most forms mixing and being modified from one generation to another. There is some temporary degree of stability in certain isolated populations, but thousands of years of hurricanes and centuries of Indian and recent shell-collecting visitors has largely eliminated any semblance of separate subspecies.

Sinistral specimens, probably caused by early embryonic aberrations, are known from only a few dozen examples.

These snails are more active at night or during protracted rainy seasons. Freezing weather kills them, and during the colder winter months they aestivate by adhering with the aid of a parchment-like seal, or epiphragm, to the sides of tree branches. Mating is more frequent in the summer and fall when the adults descend from the trees and lay their dozen-or-so, whitish, pea-sized eggs a few inches below the soft, leafy humus soil. In early spring the almost colorless, tiny shelled snails emerge and begin ascending bushes and trees.

Birds, rats and racoons, and sometimes land crabs feed upon tree snails while they are on the ground or crawling in full view on higher branches.

Today, one has to obtain a permit for collecting Florida Liguus and then only for scientific research purposes. However, the building of roads, dumps and new housing are the main causes for the disappearance of these snails. Fortunately a large section of Liguus territory is preserved as part of the Florida Everglades National Park where it is illegal to collect anything.

This specimen of the False Painted Liguus, *Liguus fasciatus* (Müller, 1774) color form *pseudopictus* Simpson, 1920, was raised on an orange tree in the back yard of the famous liguus collector, Ralph Humes. Many rare forms have been raised and preserved in our Everglades National Park.

These three-year-old specimens of *pseudopictus* represent a race extinct in their natural habitat on Lower Matecumbe Key, but now thriving in the Everglades National Park. Most shells of this race lack the broad green band at the base of the shell. Photo: Ralph Humes.

Considered a subspecies by some experts, the Chestnut-banded Liguus displays many color variations. This one is from the Everglades, but those from Key Largo commonly have solid black or brown bands. This snail is foraging near the ground. Next 4 photos: W.J. Weber.

These two *castaneozonatus*, Pilsbry, 1912, or Chestnut-banded, Liguus came from the old Brickell Hammock within the city limits of Miami. One of Florida's first tree snail hunters, Charles Torrey Simpson, found 13 forms or "subspecies" at that locality.

The Rose-tipped Liguus, *Liguus fasciatus* form *roseatus* Pilsbry, 1912, got its name from the fact that its early whorls are rosy-pink. Sometimes the last whorls are banded with yellow and orange. This snail is re-aligning itself on a branch.

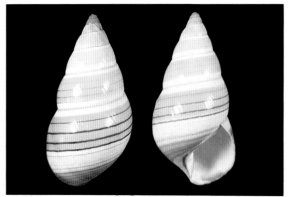

The Rose-tipped Liguus is one of the most widely distributed color forms on the South Florida mainland. Occurring on the Upper Florida Keys as well as in southwest Florida, it was found near Marco Island and the shell mounds of the Ten Thousand Islands.

FLORIDA LIGUUS

The Everglades and Florida Keys were the home of numerous color forms. Subspecies disappeared with the mixing of colonies by hurricanes, pre-Columbian Indians and especially later colonists, including recent shell collectors. Altogether 60 names have been applied to Florida color forms. We present illustrations, some of type specimens, of most of these forms but without associating them with any so-called subspecies.

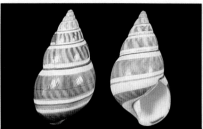

Alternate Liguus (1.3") 4.5 cm
Liguus fasciatus (Müller, 1774) form *alternatus* Simpson, 1920. Timm's Hammock, north of Homestead. Apex and columella pink. Close to *castaneozonatus* and *walkeri*.

Golden Liguus (2") 5 cm
Liguus f. form *aurantius* Clench, 1929. Hammock no. 5, Pinecrest, north Central Everglades. Related to *lossmanicus* and *luteus*.

Barbour's Liguus (2") 5 cm
Liguus f. form *barbouri* Clench, 1929. Hammock no. 21, Pinecrest Everglades. Apex white; base dark. Close to *marmoratus*, *testudineus* and *nebulosus*. Topotypes.

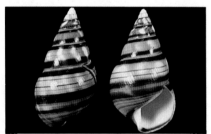

Barbour's Blue Liguus (2") 5 cm
Liguus f. form *barbouri* Clench, 1929. Hammock no. 21, Pinecrest Everglades. Base bluish instead of dark-brown.

Beard's Liguus (2.2") 5.4 cm
Liguus f. form *beardi* Jones, 1979. Hammock of the southern Everglades. First whorl pink, rest whitish brown. Named for Dan Beard, ranger. Paratypes.

Cape Sable Liguus (2.4") 5.8 cm
Liguus f. form *capensis* Simpson, 1920. Cape Sable and central Everglades. Mixed with *eburneus*, *cingulatus* and *elliottenis*. Elongate, apex white, columnella straight.

Chestnut-banded Liguus (2.5") 6.4 cm
Liguus f. form *castaneozonatus* Pilsbry, 1912. Upper Keys and mainland Everglades. Common. Variable patterns. See *walkeri*, *deckerti*.

Chestnut Liguus (1.5") 4 cm
Liguus f. form *castaneus* Simpson, 1920. Cox Hammock near Goulds, Dade Co. Yellowish form close to form *testudineus*.

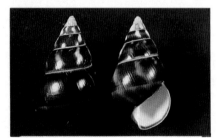

Chestnut Liguus (1.5") 4 cm
Liguus f. form *castaneus* Simpson, 1920. Cox Hammock, near Goulds, Dade Co. Melanistic extreme of *testudineus*.

Ringed Liguus (2") 5 cm
Liguus f. form *cingulatus* Simpson, 1920. Formerly from south central Everglades to Ft. Lauderdale. These are from Brickel Hammock, Miami. Uncommon. Near *elliottensis*.

Clench's Liguus (2") 5 cm
Liguus f. form *clenchi* Frampton, 1932. Hammock 46, Pinecrest Everglades. First nuclear whorl pink, rest white. Near *testudineus* and *fuscoflamellus*.

White Crass Liguus (2") 5 cm
Liguus f. form *crassus* Simpson, 1920. Watson's Hammock, Lower Florida Keys. An albino near *graphicus* and *solidus*. Seldom found.

Deckert's Liguus (2.3") 6 cm
Liguus f. form *deckerti* Clench, 1935. Hammock no. 55, central Everglades. A form of *castaneozonatus* with the loss of all pink.

Delicate Liguus (2") 5 cm
Liguus f. form *delicatus* Simpson, 1920. Matecumbe Keys, upper Florida Keys. Near *graphicus* and *lignumvitae*. Green lines.

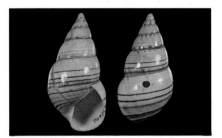

Doherty's Liguus (2.2") 5.5 cm
Liguus f. form *dohertyi* Pflueger, 1934. Lower Matecumbe Key. Near *lignumvitae* and *pseudopictus*. Evidently extinct.

Dryas Liguus (2.2") 5.5 cm
Liguus f. form *dryas* Pilsbry, 1932. No Name and Little Pine Key, Lower Florida Keys. Near *graphicus*.

Dryas Liguus (2.2") 5.5 cm
Liguus f. form *dryas* Pilsbry, 1932. A live specimen from a limited type locality in the Middle Florida Key. Moderately common. Photo by William J. Weber.

Ivory Liguus (2") 5 cm
Liguus f. form *eburneus* Simpson, 1920. Timm's Hammock, north of Homestead and formerly to Miami. Another albino form close to *capensis*.

Elegant Liguus (2") 5 cm
Liguus f. form *elegans* Simpson, 1920. Atoll Hammock, south central Everglades. Pink apex, some green lines. Near *castaneozonatus* and *alternatus*.

Elliott Key Liguus (2.4") 6 cm
Liguus f. form *elliottensis* Pilsbry, 1912. Elliott's Key and other Atlantic ridge Everglade hammocks. See also *capensis* and *cingulatus*.

Everglades Liguus (2") 5 cm
Liguus f. form *evergladesensis* Jones, 1979. Northern central Everglades. Apex and columella pink. Similar to *castaneus* otherwise. Holotype illustrated.

Everglades Liguus (2") 5 cm
Liguus f. form *evergladesensis* Jones, 1979. Paratypes. Breeds true; considered form of subspecies *testudineus* of Collier County.

Farnum's Liguus (2") 5 cm
Liguus f. form *farnumi* Clench, 1929. Hammock no. 7. central Everglades. Near *testudineus* and *marmoratus*. Reportedly extinct.

Florida Liggus   (2") 5 cm
Liguus f. form *floridanus* Clench, 1929. Hammock no. 8, Pinecrest Everglades. Uncommon. Holotype on right. A *testudineus-marmoratus* variety.

Frampton's Liguus   (1.7") 4.7 cm
Liguus f. framptoni Jones, 1979. Southern central Everglades. Allied to *castaneozonatus* variations and *humesi*. Paratypes.

Dark-flammed Liguus   (1.6") 4.5 cm
Liguus f. form *fuscoflammellus* Frampton, 1932. Timm's Hammock, near Naranja, Everglades. Near *testudineus* and *castaneus*.

Dark-flammed Liguus   (1.5") 4 cm
Liguus f. form *fuscoflammellus* Frampton, 1932. Timm's Hammock. Holotype specimen. Rare color form.

Glory-of-the Woods Liguus   (2") 5 cm
Liguus f. form *gloriasylvaticus* Doe, 1937. Pinecrest hammock no. 91, Everglades. A *marmoratus*-like variation. Topotypes.

Graphic Liguus   (2.7") 7 cm
Liguus f. form *graphicus* Pilsbry, 1912. No Name Key and other lower Florida Keys. Near *lignumvitae*, *osmenti* and *dryas*. Topotypes.

Humes' Liguus   (2") 5.5 cm
Liguus f. form *humesi* Jones, 1979. Everglades National Park. Like *castaneus*, but with white columella. Paratypes.

Humes' Liguus   (2") 5.5 cm
Liguus f. form *humesi* Jones, 1979. Near *castaneozonatus* in same hammocks. Named for Ralph Humes.

No Name Liguus   (2") 5 cm
Liguus f. form *innominatus* Pilsbry, 1930. No Name Key, Lower Keys. Like *lignumvitae* but no green lines. Apex pink. Topotypes.

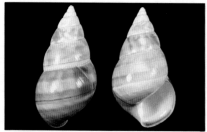

Kenneth's Liguus   (2.3") 6 cm
Liguus f. form *kennethi* Jones, 1979. Everglades National Park. Resembles *framptoni*. Paratypes. Named for Jones' son.

Kenneth's Liguus   (2.3") 6.2 cm
Liguus f. form *kennethi* Jones, 1979. A constant hybrid introduced to Everglades National Park. Holotype. Uncommon.

Lignumvitae Liguus   (2") 5 cm
Liguus f. form *lignumvitae* Pilsbry, 1912. Lignumvitae Key, (topotypes) and Lower Matecumbe Key. A *graphicus*-like form.

Green-threaded Liguus
Liguus f. form *lineolatus* Simpson, 1920. Totten's Key (topotypes) and Upper Florida Keys. Close to form *roseatus* and *livingstoni.*

Livingston's Liguus (1.8") 4.5 cm
Liguus f. form *livingstoni* Simpson, 1920. Originally found in Brickell Hammock, Miami. These are topotypes.

Livingston's Liguus (2") 5 cm
Liguus f. form *livingstoni* Simpson, 1920. Resembling some *roseatus*, these forms also occur in Pinecrest colonies.

Lossman's Liguus (2.3") 5.5 cm
Liguus f. form *lossmanicus* Pilsbry, 1912. Lossman's Key, S.W. Florida to Ft. Lauderdale. Form *mosieri* and *vacaensis* similar. Topotypes.

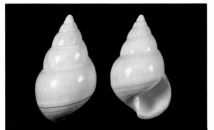

Luteus Liguus (2.0") 5 cm
Liguus f. form *luteus* Simpson, 1920. Key Vaca, Middle Florida Keys. Related to *lossmanicus*, but yellower. Topotypes.

Margaret's Liguus (2.3") 5.5 cm
Liguus f. form *margaretae* Jones, 1979. Introduced hybrid to Southern National Everglades Park. Apex white. Paratypes. Named after Margaret, Mrs. Archie Jones.

Margaret's Liguus (2.3") 5.5 cm
Liguus f. form *margaretae* Jones, 1979. A genetic combination of *lucidovarius* Doe, 1937 and *clenchi* Frampton, 1932. Holotype.

Marbled Liguus (2.3") 5.5 cm
Liguus f. form *marmoratus* Pilsbry, 1912. Key Vaca, Middle Florida Keys, and central Everglades. Allied forms: *barbouri*, *farnumi* and *testudineus.*

Matecumbe Key Liguus (2") 5 cm
Liguus f. form *matecumbensis* Pilsbry, 1912. Upper Matecumbe Key and the mainland. See also *subcrenatus*. Suture border yellow.

Miami Liguus (2.3") 5.5 cm
Liguus f. form *miamiensis* Simpson, 1920. Originally from Brickell Hammock, Miami, but also Everglades. Allied to *castaneozonatus.*

Miami Liguus (2.3") 5.5 cm
Liguus f. form *miamiensis* Simpson, 1920. Everglades National Park. A live specimen about to lay eggs in the soil. Common. Photo by William J. Weber.

Mosier Liguus
Liguus f. form *mosieri* Simpson, 1920. Formerly from Brickell Hammock (topotypes here); also Everglades. See *lossmanicus* and *vacaensis.*

Nebulose Liguus (2") 5 cm
Liguus f. form *nebulosus* Doe, 1937. Hammock no. 10, western Everglades. Near *marmoratus* and *floridanus*.

Ornate Liguus (2") 5 cm
Liguus f. form *ornatus* Simpson, 1920. Paradise Key, Royal Palm State Park. Also Key Largo to Miami. Allied to *testudineus* and *versicolor*.

Ornate Liguus (2") 5 cm
Liguus f. form *ornatus* Simpson, 1920. Southeastern Florida. Common. Live specimen photographed by William J. Weber.

Osment's Liguus (2.7") 6 cm
Liguus f. form *osmenti* Clench, 1942. Howe Key, near Big Pine Key. A *graphicus* without yellow. Holotype on right; paratype left.

Painted Liguus (2") 5 cm
Liguus f. form *pictus* (Reeve, 1842). Big Pine Key, Lower Florida Keys. Allied to *solidus* and *graphicus*. White apex.

Painted Liguus (2") 5 cm
Liguus f. form *pictus* (Reeve, 1842). Big Pine Key. In dry weather, snails aestivate against tree trunks. Photo: W.J. Weber.

False Painted Liguus (2.7") 6 cm
Liguus f. form *pseudopictus* Simpson, 1920. Upper Florida Keys. Pink apex. Allied to *pictus* and *splendidus*.

Rose-tipped Liguus (2.3") 5.5 cm
Liguus f. form *roseatus* Pilsbry, 1912. Goodland Pt., Marco Island, West Florida. Also upper Florida Keys. Allied to *castaneozonatus* and *lineolatus*.

Northern Florida Liguus (2.5") 5 cm
Liguus f. form *septentrionalis* Pilsbry, 1912. Broward and Palm Beach Counties. Glossy; no pink. Fine green lines.

Simpson's Liguus (2.5") 5.7 cm
Liguus f. form *simpsoni* Pilsbry, 1921. Lignumvitae Key and other Upper Florida Keys. Allied to *lignumvitae*. This is *lineatus* Simpson, non Valenciennes, 1833.

Simpson's Liguus (2.5") 5.7 cm
Liguus f. form *simpsoni* Pilsbry, 1921. Upper Florida Keys. Live specimen photographed by William J. Weber. Uncommon.

Hard Liguus (2.3") 5.5 cm
Liguus f. form *solidulus* Pilsbry, 1912. Formerly near Key West on Jamaica dogwood. Yellow band below suture. Allied to *solidus* Say.

Solid Liguus (2.3") 5.5 cm
Liguus f. form *solidus* (Say, 1825). Formerly the southern Lower Florida Keys. Solid, polished, pale-yellow. White line at suture.

Sunset Liguus (2.3") 5.5 cm
Liguus f. form *solisoccasus* de Boe, 1933. Hammock no. 6, western Florida. Like *clenchi* but more streaked. Paratypes.

Splendid Liguus (2") 5 cm
Liguus f. form *splendidus* Frampton, 1932. Lower Matecumbe Key; occurs with *pseudo-pictus*. Stripes darker.

Splendid Liguus (2") 5 cm
Liguus f. form *splendidus* Frampton, 1932. Now extinct in the Keys, transplanted colonies survive in the Everglades park. Photo: W.J. Weber.

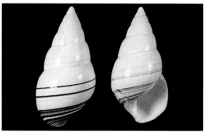

False Crenate Liguus (2.4") 6 cm
Liguus f. form *subcrenatus* Pilsbry, 1912. Lower Matecumbe Key. Allied to *matecumbensis*.

Tortoise Liguus (2") 5 cm
Liguus f. form *testudineus* Pilsbry, 1912. Southeast Florida. Apex usually pink. Allied variations: *versicolor*, *clenchi*, *ornatus*, and *marmoratus*.

Key Vaca Liguus (2.3") 5.5 cm
Liguus f. form *vacaensis* Simpson, 1920. Key Vaca Key, Middle Florida Keys. Allied to *elliottensis*. Solid, porcellanous; elongate.

Violet-smoked Liguus (2") 5 cm
Liguus f. forma *violafumosus* Doe, 1937. Hammock no. 28, Pinecrest Everglades. Allied to *marmoratus* and *floridanus*.

Von Paulsen's Liguus
Liguus f. form *vonpaulseni* F.N. Young, 1960. Little Torch Key, Lower Florida Keys. Resembling *graphicus* and *osmenti*. Paratypes, Florida Museum of Natural History, Gainesville.

Walker's Liguus (1.8") 4.5 cm
Liguus f. form *walkeri* Clench, 1933. Central Everglades. Left: rare sinistral form. Near *castaneozonatus*.

Walker's Liguus (2") 5 cm
Liguus f. form *walkeri* Clench, 1933. Topotypes from Hammock no. 9, Pinecrest Everglades. Apex and columella pink.

Winte's Liguus (2") 5 cm
Liguus f. form *wintei* Humes, 1954. Long Pine Key, central Everglades. Paratypes. Resembles *kennethi*. Named for Erwin C. Winte.

HISPANIOLA ISLAND LIGUUS

The sole species of *Liguus* found in Haiti and Santo Domingo is the Virgin Liguus, *L. virgineus* (Linnaeus, 1767), an abundant, solid-shelled species with variable coloring of narrow, spiral bands. Rarely, there are sinistral coiling specimens. The species is being over-collected and its habitats being destroyed in Haiti. An estimated million specimens were shipped to the United States each year in the early 1980's.

Virgin Liguus (2") 5 cm
Liguus virgineus (L., 1767). Hispaniola Id. Type of genus *Liguus* Montfort, 1810. Synonyms: *puellaris* Röding, 1798; *sinistralis* Crosse, 1891 (left-handed).

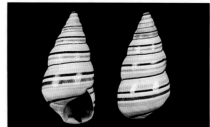

Virgin Liguus (2") 5 cm
Liguus virgineus (Linnaeus, 1767). These two specimens were introduced into southern Florida in 1966. One green band is form *emarginatus* (Swainson, 1822).

CUBAN LIGUUS

Cuba is much richer than Florida in *Liguus*, and probably gave rise to the mainland forms in the geologic past. Unique is the Ribbon Liguus, belonging to the subgenus *Liguellus* Clench, 1946. The remaining two species and 102 Cuban color forms belong to the subgenus *Oxystrombus* Mörch, 1852, with its type being *fasciatus* Müller, 1774.

Ribbon Liguus (1.3") 3.5 cm
Liguus (*Liguellus*) *vittatus* (Swainson, 1822). Oriente Province, Cuba. Locally common. Syn.: *poeyanus* Pfeiffer, 1857.

Blain's Liguus (1.2") 3 cm
Liguus (*Oxystrombus*) *blainianus* (Poey, 1851). Pinar del Rio Prov., Cuba. Right is a paratype.

Howell's Liguus (1.2") 3 cm
Liguus blainianus albino form *howelli* Clench, 1951. 10 mi. west of Mariel, Pinar del Rio. Holotype on right.

Pilsbry's Liguus (1.2") 3 cm
Liguus blainianus form *pilsbryi* Clench, 1935. Sierra de Rangel, Pinar del Rio. Holotype on right. At higher altitudes.

Agate Liguus (1.5") 4 cm
Liguus f. form *achatinus* Clench, 1934. Holguin, Oriente Prov., Cuba. Paratype specimens.

Aguayo's Liguus (2") 5 cm
Liguus f. form *aguayoi* Clench, 1934. Punta Roja, Holgiun, Cuba. Holotype on right.

Angela's Cuba Liguus (1.5") 4 cm
Liguus f. form *angelae* Clench & Aguayo, 1934. Punta Roja, Holguin, Cuba. Paratype specimens.

Archer's Cuban Liguus
Liguus f. form *archeri* Clench, 1934. Mogote de Ramon, Millo, Vinales, Cuba. Named for Allan Archer, a Clench student. Holotype on right. Syn.: *vignalensis* Platt, 1949.

Austin's Cuban Liguus (2.5") 6.4 cm
Liguus f. form *austinianus* Guitart, 1945. Sancti Spiritus, Cuba. Named for Austin College, Texas. Holotype.

Austin's Cuban Liguus (2.7") 7 cm
Liguus f. form *austinianus* Guitart, 1945. Paratypes; Camino del Caney, Sancti Spiritus, Cuba.

Barro's Cuban Liguus (2.4") 6 cm
Liguus f. form *barroi* Jaume, 1952. East of Rio Almendares, Habana Prov., Cuba. Paratypes. Circulares, p. 505.

Bermudez's Liguus (2.5") 6.4 cm
Liguus f. form *bermudezi* Clench, 1934. Mogote la Gueca, Vinales Valley, Cuba. Holotype on right.

Charcoal Liguus (2.7") 6 cm
Liguus f. form *carbonarius* Clench, 1934. Mogote de Pita, Vinales Cuba. Near *flammellus* Clench. Holotype on right.

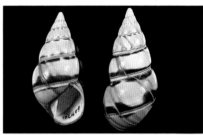

Caribbean Liguus (2.5") 6.4 cm
Liguus f. form *caribaeus* Clench, 1935. Santa Lucia, Pinar del Rio, Cuba. Holotype on right. Syn.: *laureani* Platt, 1949.

Carol's Liguus (2.7") 6 cm
Liguus f. form *caroli* Bartsch, 1937. Isla Turiguano, Camaguey Prov., Cuba. Holotype. Close to *crenatus*.

Deer Liguus (2.7") 6 cm
Liguus f. form *cervus* Clench, 1934. Mogote de Vigil, Vinales, Cuba. Close to *flammellus*. Holotype on right.

Crenate Liguus (2.7") 6 cm
Liguus crenatus Swainson, 1821. Pinar del Rio, Cuba. Lip finely crenate. See *luteolozonatus* and *caroli*.

Clench's Cuban Liguus (2.7") 6 cm
Liguus f. form *cubensis* Clench, 1934. Vinales Valley, Pinar del Rio, Cuba. Close to *flammellus*. Holotype at right.

Fairchild's Cuban Liguus (2.2") 5 cm
Liguus f. form *fairchildi* Clench, 1934. Near Santiago de las Vegas, Cuba. Holotype on right.

Falcon Liguus (2.5") 6.3 cm
Liguus f. form *falconi* Jaume, 1952. Gavilan, Cienfuegos, Santa Clara Prov., Cuba. Circulares, p. 509. Paratypes. Near *viridis*.

Josefa's Liguus   (2.3") 5.9 cm
Liguus fasciatus form *josefae* Guitart, 1945. Sierra de Cantu, Sancti Spiritus. Holotype specimen.

Yellow-banded Liguus   (2.4") 6 cm
Liguus crenatus luteolozonatus Guitart, 1945. Lomas de Banao, Sancti Spiritus. Paratypes.

McGinty's Liguus   (1.5") 4 cm
Liguus fasciatus form *macgintyi* Clench, 1934. Mariel, Pinar del Rio, Cuba. Holotype on right.

Noble Liguus   (1.5") 4 cm
Liguus f. form *nobilis* Clench & Aguayo, 1932. Near Cabanes Bay, Pinar del Rio. Holotype on right.

Organ Liguus   (2") 5 cm
Liguus f. form *organensis* Clench, 1934. El Queque, Vinales Valley, Pinar del Rio. Holotype on right.

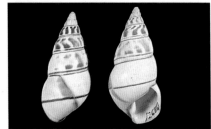

Pallid Liguus   (1.8") 5 cm
Liguus f. form *pallidus* (Swainson, 1821). Cayo Magueyal, Pinar del Rio, Cuba. Common on trees.

Isle of Pines Liguus   (1.5") 4 cm
Liguus f. form *pinarensis* Clench, 1934. Punta del Este, Isle of Pines, Cuba. Holotype on right.

Holy Spirit Liguus   (1.7") 4.7 cm
Liguus f. form *sanctispiritensis* Guitart, 1945. Tuinucu, Sancti Spiritus, Cuba. Holotype on right.

Cut-lip Liguus   (2.5") 6.5 cm
Liguus f. form *sissilabre* Nodal, 1947. Nuevitas, Camaguey. Upper end of lip notched. Rare.

de la Torre's Liguus   (2.5") 6.5 cm
Liguus f. form *torrei* Clench, 1934. Punta del Este, Isle of Pines, Cuba. Holotype on right.

Green Cuban Liguus   (2.5") 6.5 cm
Liguus f. form *viridis* Clench, 1934. Central Soledad, Cienfuegos, Cuba. Holotype on right in Mus. Comp. Zool.

Golden Cuban Liguus   (2.5") 6.5 cm
Liguus fasciatus form *xanthus* Clench, 1934. San Nicholas, Havana Prov., Cuba. Holotype on right.

True Fasciate Liguus (2.5") 6 cm
Liguus fasciatus fasciatus (Müller, 1774). Pinar del Rio to Camaguey, Cuba. A very variable species with many named forms.

Feria's Cuban Liguus (2.2") 5 cm
Liguus f. form *feriai* Clench, 1934. La Sierra, Holguin, Cuba. Holotype on right.

Flammed Cuban Liguus (2.5") 6 cm
Liguus f. form *flammellus* Clench, 1934. Viñales Valley, Cuba. Considered a subspecies by some. Holotype on right.

Russell's Cuban Liguus (2.5") 6 cm
Liguus f. form *russelli* Clench, 1935. Viñales Valley, Pinar del Rio, Cuba. Holotype on right. Near *flammellus*.

Goodrich's Cuban Luguus (2.5") 6 cm
Liguus f. form *goodrichi* Clench, 1934. Castello de Jagua, Cienfuegos, Cuba. Holotype on right.

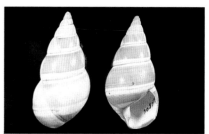

Guitart's Liguus (1.7") 4.5 cm
Liguus f. form *guitarti* Jaume, 1952. Monte Cagueiras, Santa Clara Prov., Cuba. Paratypes. Circulares, p. 511.

Helianthus Liguus (2.5") 6.4 cm
Liguus f. form *helianthus* Clench, 1934. Mogote del Palmarito, Viñales, Cuba. Holotype on right.

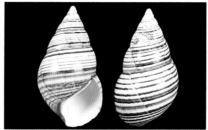

Judas Mountain Liguus (2.7") 7 cm
Liguus f. form *judasense* Jaume, 1952. Sierra de Judas, northern Santa Clara Prov., Cuba. Paratypes.

Maria's Cuban Liguus (2.2") 6 cm
Liguus f. form *mariae* Clench, 1935. Near "Cayo" Magueyal, Pinar del Rio. Holotype on right. Named for Maria Pequeno of Cuba.

LITERATURE ON *LIGUUS*

To the four or five valid species of *Liguus* approximately 163 names have been proposed. Most of them are merely color forms but some do represent isolated, incipient subspecies. References to all of these names may be found in the five first works listed below:

Bayer, F.M., 1948. Charles T. Simpson's Types in the Molluscan genus *Liguus*. Smithsonian Misc. Collections, vol. 107, no. 16, no. 3910: 1-8, 1 color pl.

Clench, W.J., 1946. A Catalogue of the Genus *Liguus* with a Description of a New Subgenus. Occ. Papers on Mollusks (Harvard), vol. 1, no. 10, pp. 117-128. Supplement, *ibid.*, no. 18, pp. 442-444.

Jaume, Miguel L., 1952. Nuevas Formas de *Liguus* de Cuba [and] Catalogo de los Moluscos del Genero *Liguus*. Circulares del Museo y Biblioteca de Malacol. Habana, pp. 503-527.

Jones, Archie L., 1979. Descriptions of Six New Forms of Florida Tree Snails, *Liguus fasciatus*. The Nautilus, vol. 93, no. 4, pp. 153-159, 1 color plate.

Pilsbry, Henry A., 1946. Land Mollusca of North America, Monograph 3, Acad. Nat. Sci. Philadelphia, vol. 2, pt. 1, *Liguus* on pp. 37-102.

Five additional accounts some with colored photographs of some of the forms have been published:

Close, Henry T., 1978. Lure of the *Liguus*—a Beginner's Guide. Of Sea and Shore, vol. 9, no. 1, pp. 3-11. (3 color pls.).

Humes, Ralph, 1965. A Short History of *Liguus* Collecting. Tequesta, the Journal of the Historical Assoc. Southern Florida, vol. 25.

Platt, Rutherford, 1949. Shells Take You Over World Horizons. National Geographic Magazine, vol. 96, no. 1, colored plates.

Parkinson, B., Jens Hemmen and K. Groh, 1987. Tropical Landshells of the World (Weisbaden), 279 pp. (colored pls. 1-7).

Roth, Barry and Arthur E. Bogan, 1984. Shell color and banding parameters of the *Liguus fasciatus* phenotype. Amer. Malacological Bull., vol. 3 (1): 1-10.

Young, Frank N., 1951. Vanishing and Extinct Colonies of Tree Snails, *Liguus fasciatus*, in the Vicinity of Miami, Florida.

——, 1960. Color pattern variation among snails of the genus *Liguus* on the Florida Keys. Bull. Florida State Museum, Biol. series, vol. 5, pp. 259-266, 2 figs.

ADDITIONAL *LIGUUS* SPECIES

Because Jaume's 1952 publication was mimeographed and very limited in circulation, we are listing the new names that he proposed. The number following each species name refers to the page in the Circulares del Museo y Biblioteca de Malacologia de la Habana published on March 10, 1952. We also add two forms described later by Humes and by F.N. Young.

arangoi, Liguus fasciatus, Jaume, 1952, p. 510. Ridge facing Playa de Guanabo, Habana Prov., Cuba. Coll. Luis Arango. Arango's Liguus.

barroi, Liguus fasciatus, Jaume, 1952, p. 505. Loma al Este del Rio Almendares, Bosque de la Habana, Cuba. Barro's Liguus.

falconi, Liguus fasciatus, Jaume, 1952, p. 509. Mountains between Gavilan and the coast, Cienfuegos, Cuba. Falcon Liguus.

guitarti, Liguus fasciatus, Jaume, 1952, p. 511. Cagueiras Mountain, Sancti Spiritus, Santa Clara Prov., (Las Villas), Cuba. Guitart's Liguus.

judasense Liguus fasciatus, Jaume, 1952, p. 504. Sierra de Judas, Norte de la Provincia de Las Vilas [Santa Clara], Cuba. Colectado por Sr. Pompeyo Prida. Judas Mountain Liguus.

leptus, Liguus fasciatus, Jaume, 1952, p. 508. Carretera Central between Artemisa and Mangas, Pinar del Rio, Cuba. Delicate Cuban Liguus.

mayariense, Liguus fasciatus, Jaume, 1952, p. 510. Mayari, Oriente, Cuba. Mayari Liguus.

mirabilis, Liguus fasciatus, Jaume, 1952, p. 512. Carretera Central, near Mangas, Pinar del Rio, Cuba. Miracle Liguus.

porphyreus, Liguus vittatus, Jaume, 1952, p. 514. Ensenada de Mora, Oriente, Cuba. Purple-banded Liguus.

primitivoi, Liguus fasciatus, Jaume, 1952, p. 504. Guanal, south coast of Pinar del Rio, Cuba. Coll. P. Borro. Primitivo's Liguus.

ramosi, Liguus fasciatus, Jaume, 1952, p. 506. Procede de las lomas de Soroa, Candelaria, Pinar del Rio, Cuba. Ramos' Liguus.

romanoense, Liguus fasciatus, Jaume, 1952, p. 508. Cayo Romano, Santa Clara Prov., Cuba. Cayo Romano Liguus.

tabioi, Liguus fasciatus, Jaume, 1952, p. 507. Lado oeste de la Bahia del Mariel, Pinar del Rio, Cuba. Coll. Ernesto Tabio Palma. Tabio's Liguus.

thapsinus, Liguus vittatus, Jaume, 1952, p. 514. Ensenada de Mora, Oriente, Cuba. Yellow-banded Liguus.

trinidadense, Liguus fasciatus, Jaume, 1952, p. 503. Procede del Tio del Inglés, Término Municipal dé Trinidad, Prov. de Las Villas [Santa Clara], Cuba. Colectado por el Sr. Ramón Goenaga. Trinidad Cuban Liguus.

vazquezi, Liguus vittatus, Jaume, 1952, p. 513. Ensenada de Mora, Oriente, Cuba. Coll. Juan Vazquez Orozco. Vazquez's Liguus.

vonpaulseni, Liguus fasciatus, F.N. Young, 1960. Bull. Florida State Museum, Biol. series, vol. 5, p. 261, figs. 1, 2. Little Torch Key, Monroe County. Von Paulsen's Liguus.

wintei, Liguus fasciatus, Humes, 1954. Gastropodia, vol. 1, no. 2, p. 10. Long Pine Key, Florida. Winte's Liguus.

zayasi, Liguus fasciatus, Jaume, 1952, p. 507. 1 km north of Laguna Mala Habitacion, Cabanas, Pinar del Rio, Cuba. Coll. Fernando de Zayas. Zayas' Liguus.

Family AMPHIBULIMULIDAE

A small family of sluglike snails, usually about an inch in size and bearing a small, delicate, ear-shaped shell. There are five genera and about 25 species, all coming from South America or the West Indian islands. They are arboreal, either in trees or among broad-leaved plants. The mantle usually covers most of the shell. Some animals are brownish yellow, others bright green. The genus *Simpulopsis* from Brazil has *Succinea*-like shells and is placed now in the family Bulimulidae (van Mol, 1971).

Puerto Rican Green Ear-snail (1") 2.5 cm
Gaeotis nigrolineata Shuttleworth, 1854. Western Puerto Rico on bananas. Uncommon. Type of genus. (Photo: Charlotte Lloyd).

Broad Ear-snail (1") 2.5 cm
Amphibulima patula (Bruguière, 1789). Lesser Antilles; on bananas. Type of the genus. Subspecies *dominicensis* Pilsbry, 1899, illus., from Laudat.

Family UROCOPTIDAE
The Urocops

A large family of rather small, elongate, many-whorled shells, mostly from the West Indies, although there are many species from southern U.S., Mexico and Central America. Many lose their spires. The nature of the internal columellar axis is used in identification of genera. One genus, *Hendersoniella*, from Mexico, is flat and discoidal.

The foot is small and simple. Most lay small, elliptical, hard, rough, white shells. The family has about 80 genera and subgenera, and perhaps 2,000 species.

Haitian Archicop (1") 2.5 cm
Archegocoptis haitiensis Clench, 1936. Miragoane, S.W. Haiti, 1,000 meters. Paratypes.

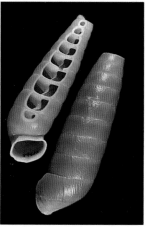

Decollate Calodium Snail (3")
Eucalodium decollatum (Nyst, 1841). Tabasco, S.E. Mexico. In moist ground. Type of the genus. Shell opened to show columellar folds.

Bland's Calodium Snail (3") 7.5 cm
Eucalodium blandianum Crosse & Fischer, 1870. Eastern Mexico, near Jalapa and Orixota. Left: syntype.

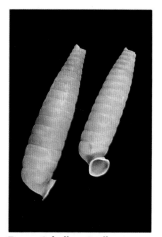

Tower Calodium Snail (2.7") 7 cm
Coelocentrum turris (Pfeiffer, 1856). Chiapas, S.E. Mexico. Type of the genus.

Taylor's Berendtia Snail (1")
Berendtia taylori (Pfeiffer, 1861). Table-lands above Muleje, Baja California. Type of genus.

Hamilton's Holospire (1")
Holospira (*Liostemma*) *hamiltoni* Dall, 1897. Rio Grande Mts., Brewster Co., Texas. Paratypes.

Perplexing Holospire (0.4") 5 mm
Holospira perplexa Thompson, 1967. Oaxaca, Mexico. 6,200 ft., alt.

Palmer's Henderson Snail (0.5") 1.4 cm
Hendersoniella palmeri (Dall, 1905). Alvarez Mtrs., San Luis Potosi, Mexico. Paratypes.

Splendid Anoma Snail
(0.6") 1.3 cm
Anoma splendens (Menke, in Pfeiffer, 1841). Manchester, Jamaica.

Smooth Anoma Snail
(0.7") 1.4 cm
Anoma levis (C.B. Adams, 1851) subspecies *concinna* (C.B. Adams, 1851). Upper Clarendon, Jamaica.

Flag Macroceramus (0.8") 1.5 cm
Macroceramus signatus (Guilding, 1828). Virgin Ids. and this subsp. *salleanus* Pilsbry, 1903, from Santo Domingo.

Fine-ribbed Macroceramus
(0.5") 1 cm
Macroceramus costulatus (Pfeiffer, 1859). Guantanamo, Cuba. R.T. Abbott, legit, 1942.

Festive Macroceramus
(0.5") 1 cm
Macroceramus festus (Pfeiffer, 1859). Side of Guantanamo Bay. (Radio Hill), Cuba. R.T. Abbott, legit, 1942.

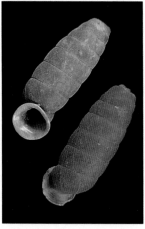

Cylinder Urocop (1") 2.5 cm
Urocoptis cylindrus (Dillwyn, 1817). Interior western Jamaica. Type of the genus.

Sanguin Urocop (1") 2.5 cm
Urocoptis (Spirocoptis) sanguinea (Pfeiffer, 1845). Portland and St. Andrew, Jamaica.

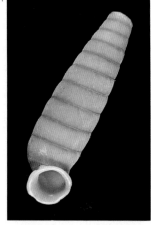

Baqui Urocop (1.4") 3.6 cm
Urocoptis (Urocoptis) baquieana (Chitty, 1855). S.E. Trelawny, Jamaica. Syn.: *adamsiana* Chitty, 1853, non Pfr. 1851.

Nobel Urocop (1.3") 3 cm
Urocoptis (U.) nobilior (C.B. Adams, 1845). Bogwalk, Jamaica. Mouth appressed.

Vignale Urocop (1") 2.5 cm
Urocoptis vignalensis (Wright, in Pfeiffer, 1864). Viñales Valley, Pinar del Rio, Cuba.

Guigou Urocop (1") 2.5 cm
Autocoptis (Urocoptola) guigouana (Petit, 1859). La Gonave Id., Haiti

Gruner's Urocop (1") 2.5 cm
Autocoptis (Urocoptola) gruneri (Dunker, 1844). St. Mark and La Gonave, Haiti.

Vesper Urocop (0.6") 1.5 cm
Tetrentodon vesperalis (Jaume & Torre, 1972). Km 55, Havana to Artemisa, Cuba. Paratypes.

Pallid Urocop (0.6") 1.5 cm
Torrecoptis pallidula (Torre, 1912). Mogote de las Jumaguas, Las Villas, Cuba.

Emil's Urocop (0.6") 1.5 cm
Tetrentodon emilii Torre & Jaume, 1972. Valle del Yumuri, Matansas Prov. Paratypes.

Finely-striate Urocop (1") 2.5 cm
Tetrentodon tenuistriata Aguayo, 1932. Finca El Ingles, Havana Prov., Cuba. Paratypes.

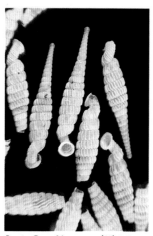

Santa Cruz Urocop (1") 2.5 cm
Tetrentodon santacruzensis Jaume & Torre, 1972. Minas, Camaguey, Cuba. Paratypes.

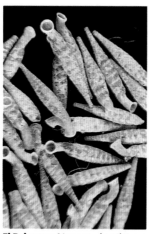

El Palenque Urocop (0.4") 1 cm
Tetrentodon palenquensis (Jaume & Torre, 1972). El Palenque, Matanzas, Cuba. Paratypes.

Very Plicate Urocop (1") 2.5 cm
Pleurostemma perplicata (Beck, 1837) subsp. *maisiensis* Jaume & Torre, 1976. Maisi, Oriente Prov. Paratypes.

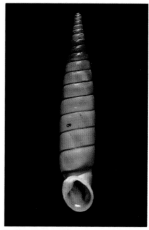

Painted Urocop (1") 2.5 cm
Gongylostoma colorata (Arango, 1882). San Andris, Pinar del Rio, Cuba.

Humboldt's Urocop (1.2") 3 cm
Pycnoptychia humboldtii (Pfeiffer, 1840), subsp. *celsa* Jaume & Torre, 1976. Loma Camoa, Havana, Cuba. Paratypes.

Allen's Urocop 5mm
Tetrentodon (Anafecoptis) alleni Torre, 1929. Guanajay, Pinar del Rio, Cuba. Paratypes.

Half-naked Urocop 8mm
Brachypodella seminuda (C.B. Adams, 1845). St. Mary's Parish, Jamaica.

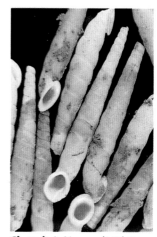

Chemnitz's Urocop (1.3") 3 cm
Apoma chemnitzianum (Férussac, 1821). St. Ann Parish, Jamaica. Type of the genus.

Barbed Urocop (1") 2.5 cm
Idiostemma uncata (Pfeiffer, 1859). Yateras, Guantanamo, Cuba. Type of the genus.

Frosty Urocop (1") 2.5 cm
Gongylostoma (Nesocoptis) pruinosa (Morelet, 1849). Isle of Pines; mountains. Type of subgenus.

Bishop Elliott's Urocop (1") 2.5 cm
Gongylostoma (Callonia) elliotti (Poey, 1858). Sierra de Guane, Pinar del Rio, Cuba. Type of subgenus.

Dautzenberg's Urocop (1") 2.6 cm
Gongylostoma (Callonia) dautzenbergiana (Crosse, 1890). Paso-Real de Guane, Cuba.

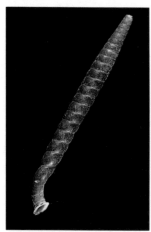

Thin Urocop (1") 2.5 cm
Gongylostoma ischna (Pilsbry, 1903). Cerra del Grillo, Habana Prov., Cuba.

Philippi's Urocop (0.5") 1.2 cm
Gongylostoma (Tetrentodon) philippiana (Pfeiffer, 1845). Habana Prov., Cuba.

Poey's Urocop (0.5") 1.3 cm
Cochlodinella poeyana (Orbigny, 1841). Western Cuba; Key West to Miami. Common. Type of genus.

Chemnitz's Urocop (1.5") 4 cm
Apoma chemnitzanum (Férussac, 1821). St. Catherine and St. Andrews Parishes, Jamaica. Type of the genus. See also p. 123.

Suborder AULACOPODA

Includes many slugs, endodontids, glassy zonitids and large *Ryssota* snails. Foot has one or two grooves on sides. Several families, including Limacidae, Arionidae, Helicarionidae and Charopidae.

Superfamily ARIONOIDEA

Family HELICODISCIDAE

Small disk-shaped shells, mostly from the Americas. Includes genera *Radiodiscus*, *Helicodiscus* and the rare *Polygyriscus* of Virginia.

Virginia Discus (0.2") 4.5 mm
Polygyriscus virginianus (P.R. Burch, 1947). Pulaski Co., Virginia. Limestone rocks. Rare. Photo: Robert E. Batie.

Family ENDODONTIDAE

A large, worldwide family, many limited to tropical islands. The shells are radially ribbed, usually flammuled, small, and disk-shaped. Radulae with square basal plates, tricuspid central teeth and 5 to 8 bicuspid laterals.

Family DISCIDAE

The Americas abound in common *Discus*, *Anguispira* and tiny *Punctum* snails. In the Pacific Islands there are 24 genera (*Aaadonta* to *Zyzzyxdonta*!) and 185 species.

Stevenson's Foxidont Snail (0.5") 1.2 cm
Foxidonta stevensoni Clench, 1950. Fiu, north Malaita Id., Solomons. Rare. Holotype illus..

Netted Disk Snail (1.5") 3 cm
Pararhytida dictyodes (Pfeiffer, 1847). New Caledonia. Type of the genus.

Broad Disk Snail (0.3") 9 mm
Discus patula (Deshayes, 1830). Eastern United States. Common on ground.

Alternate Disk Snail 2 cm
Anguispira alternata (Say, 1816). Eastern U.S. and Canada. Common in dead wood. Rarely sinistral. Many subspecies. Type of genus.

Cumberland Disk Snail (0.6") 1.8 cm
Anguispira cumberlandiana (Lea, 1840). Tennessee and Alabama. In limestone crevices. Edge serrated.

Koch's Disk Snail (1") 2.5 cm
Anguispira kochi (Pfeiffer, 1845). Central U.S. Under logs. Syn.: *solitaria* Say, 1821, not Poiret, 1800. Type of subgenus *Zonodiscus* Pilsbry.

Western Disk Snail (1") 2.5 cm
Anguispira kochi subspecies *occidentalis* (von Martens, 1882). British Columbia to Montana. Syn.: *eyerdami* Clench & Banks, 1939.

Family ZONITIDAE

Large worldwide family of small, glossy shells, usually low-spired and umbilicate. Outer lip sharp. Contains over 100 genera in at least 7 subfamilies. The *Trochomorpha* are common in the South Pacific Islands, while *Zonites*, *Oxychilus* and *Retinella* abound in the northern hemisphere. Some species are the intermediate hosts of lungworms and tapeworms. Most lay eggs, but some (*Vitrea*) give birth to live young.

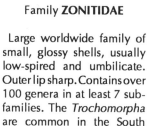

Transparent Vitrine Snail (0.3") 6 mm
Vitrina limpida Gould, 1850. Eastern Canada to Alberta and to central U.S. Very fragile shell; animal twice as long. Common.

Minuscule Vitrine Snail 2 mm
Hawaiia minuscula (Binney, 1840). Canada to northern Mexico, especially common in eastern U.S. In leaf mould. Type of the genus. Only species.

Copper Omphaline (1") 2.6 cm
Mesomphix cupreus (Rafinesque, 1831). Ontario and New England to Arkansas. Syn.: *fulginosus* Binney, 1840.

Unadorned Omphaline 2 cm
Mesomphix inornatus (Say, 1821). Quebec to Kentucky. On wooded hills under logs. Common.

Cellar Glass Snail (0.5") 1.2 cm
Oxychilus cellarius (Müller, 1774). Europe, Asia Minor and North America. In greenhouse, cellars and open lots. Common.

Latissimus Snail (0.6") 1.7 cm
Vitrinizonites latissimus (Lewis, 1875). Humid high mountains of the south Blue Ridge system in North Carolina and Tennessee. Uncommon.

Latissimus Snail (0.6") 1.7 cm
Vitrinizonites latissimus (Lewis, 1875). Tennessee. Shell is thin, with little calcium. Type of the genus; endemic to area.

Gullet Glass Snail (1/4") 8 mm
Ventridens gularis (Say, 1822). Pennsylvania to Alabama. Two long lamellae in aperture. Common; woods.

Belly-tooth Glass Snail
(1/4") 7 mm
Gastrodonta interna (Say, 1822). Indiana to Alabama. Two short teeth bottom of aperture.

Black Glass Snail (1/4") 6 mm
Zonitoides nitidus (Müller, 1774). Europe; N.E. U.S. to Illinois. Animal black. In marsh lands.

Orchard Glass Snail (0.3") 5 mm
Zonitoides (Zonitellus) arboreus (Say, 1816). Canada to Mexico; West Indies. Common nuisance to root crops. Animal grayish.

Bermuda Zonitid (1") 2.5 cm
Poecilozonites bermudensis (Pfeiffer, 1845). Endemic to the Bermuda islands. Type of the genus.

Subfamily
TROCHOMORPHINAE
The Trochus-shaped Snails Solid, flat, umbilicate. This is a live *Trochomorpha* from the Solomons.

Typical Trochus-shaped Snail
(1") 2.5 cm
Trochomorpha typus H.B. Baker, 1938. Tahiti and Moorea. Type of the genus. Syn.: *trochiformis* Fér.

Doherty's Trochus-shaped Snail
(0.8") 1.7 cm
Trochomorpha dohertyi Aldrich, 1898. Marang, Sumatra. Locally uncommon. Syntypes.

Black Trochus-shaped Snail
(0.5") 1.2 cm
Trochomorpha (Nigritella) nigritella (Pfeiffer, 1845). Ponape, Caroline Ids., S.W. Pacific. Type of subgenus.

Macgregor's Coxia Snail
(1.3") 3 cm
Coxia macgregori Cox, 1870. Solomon Island. Uncommon; on ground.

Asterisk Kondo-snail (1/3") 9 mm
Kondoa asteriscus H.B. Baker, 1941. Moen Id., Truk Id., S.W. Pacific. Type of the genus.

Truk Island Brazier Snail
(0.5") 1.2 cm
Brazieria (Probraziera) lutaria H.B. Baker, 1941. Truk Id., Carolines. Type of subgenus.

Gould's Videna Snail (1/2") 1 cm
Videna gouldiana (Pilsbry, 1901). Oshima, Japan. Paratypes. Type of subgenus *Videnvida* Habe, 1955.

Plowshare Videna Snail
(1") 2.5 cm
Videna cultvata (Pilsbry & Hirase, 1904). Tokunoshima, Osumi, Japan.

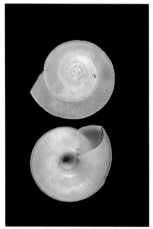

Sibuyan Videna Snail (1") 2.4 cm
Videna sibuyanica Hidalgo, 1887. Sibuyan Id., Philippines.

Panda Videna (0.5") 1.2 cm
Videna repanda (Pfeiffer, 1861). Middle Luzon Id., Philippines. Uncommon.

Lacerated Videna (0.8") 1 cm
Liravidena lacerata (Semper, 1874). Peleliu and Koror Ids., Palaus. Type of the Solem genus. Uncommon.

Cambodian Bertia (3") 8 cm
Bertia cambodJiensis (Reeve, 1860). Cambodia, S.E. Asia. Extinct? Type of the genus. Normally sinistral.

Brooke's Bertia (3") 8 cm
Bertia (Exrhysota) brookei (Adams & Reeve, 1848). Borneo. Extinct? Normally sinistral.

Superfamily LIMACOIDEA

Family HELICARIONIDAE

A very large and diverse family, containing the small, glassy Euconulinae (*Guphya*) of American tropics and *Microcystis* of the Pacific Ids.; Helicarioninae of Australasia and Africa; and the Ariophantinae (*Ryssota* and *Xesta* of S.E. Asia). Altogether about 150 genera and many hundred species.

The family Limacidae, sluglike with a vestigial shell, contains *Limax*, *Milax* and *Deroceras* slugs.

Crespigny's Macroceras
(1") 2.5 cm
Macroceras crespignyi (Higgins, 1868). Labuan Id., Philippines

Rectangular Diastole Snail
(1/3") 9mm
Diastole rectangular (Pfeiffer, 1846). Nukuhiva, Marquesas Ids., Polynesia.

Ornamental Microcystis (1/3") 9 mm
Microcystis ornatella (Beck, 1837). Rapa Id.,
Australs; Pitcairn Island.

Japanese Alta Snail (0.2") 4 mm
Trochochlamys praealta (Pilsbry, 1902). Omi,
Japan. Photo by M. Azuma.

Semi-silky Glass Snail (0.3") 5 mm
Nipponochlamys semisericata (Pilsbry, 1902).
Kurozu, Kii, Japan. Type of the genus. Photo by
M. Azuma.

Kiyosuma Chloritis (0.8") 2 cm
Nipponochloritis kiyosumiensis Azuma, 1982.
Kanagawa Pref., Japan. Photo by Azuma.

Zoned Geotrochus (0.6") 1.5 cm
Geotrochus zonatus van Hasselt, 1823. Sonka-
boumi, Java. Type of the genus.

Conic Geotrochus (1") 1.6 cm
Geotrochus conicoides (Metcalfe, 1851). Borneo. Type of subgenus *Eurybasis* Gude, 1913.

Labuan Geotrochus (1/4") 9 mm
Geotrochus (Eurybasis) labuanensis (Pfeiffer,
1863). Sutong River, Borneo.

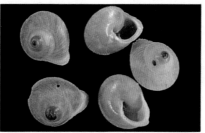

Labillardiere's Tree-trochus (0.5") 1.5 cm
Dendrotrochus labillardierei (E.A. Smith, 1884).
Tong and Wild Ids., Admiralty Islands.

Clery's Tree-trochus (0.5") 1.6 cm
Dendrotrochus helicinoides (Hombron & Jac-
quinot) forma *cleryi* (Récluz, 1851). Admiralty
Islands.

Layard's Tree-trochus (0.5") 1.6 cm
Dendrotrochus layardi (Hartman, 1889). Aoe
Id., Espiritu Santo, New Hebrides. Paratypes.

Blainville's Half-finished Snail (1.5")3 cm
Hemiglypta blainvilleana (Lea, 1840). Lubang
Id., Philippines. Type of the genus.

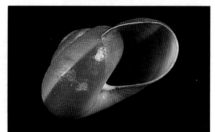

Fouillioy's Half-finished Snail (2") 5 cm
Hemiglyptopsis fouillioyi (Le Guillou, 1845).
Onime, New Guinea.

Globose Half-finished Snail
(1.6") 4 cm
Hemiglypta globosa (Semper, 1870). Mindanao Id., Philippines.

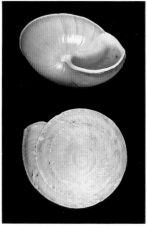

Iloilo Half-finished Snail
(5") 5 cm
Hemiglypta iloilana M. Smith, 1932. Passi, Iloilo, Panay Id., Philippines. Paratypes in Florida Mus. Nat. History.

Panay Half-finished Snail 5 cm
Hemiglypta panayensis (Broderip, 1842), forma *connectens* (Moellendorff, 1898). Morong, Lubang Id., Philippines. Paratypes in Fla. Mus. Nat. Hist.

Libmanan Half-finished Snail (2")
Lepidotrichia (Atrichoconcha) luteofasciata Lea, subsp. *libmanana* Bartsch, 1942. Luzon. Below is *L. (A.) moellendorffi* Bartsch, 1942. Both holotypes.

Tahitian Ryssota   (4") 10 cm
Ryssota otaheitana (Férussac, 1821). Luzon Id., Philippines. Type of the genus. Syn.: *ovum* (Val., 1827).

De Mesa's Ryssota   (4") 10 cm
Ryssota otaheitana subspecies *demesai* Bartsch, 1938. Mount Halcon, Mindoro Id., Philippines. Holotype.

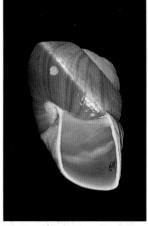

Depressed Ryssota   (3.5") 9 cm
Ryssota otaheitana subspecies *depressa* Moellendorff, 1898. Marinduque Id., Philippines. Paratype.

Samar Ryssota   (4.5") 11 cm
Ryssota otaheitana subspecies *samarensis* Bartsch, 1938. Samar Id., Philippines. Holotype.

Maximum Ryssota   (3.5") 9 cm
Ryssota maxima (Pfeiffer, 1853). Mindanao Id., Philippines. Type of subgenus *Pararyssota* Bartsch, 1938.

Maximum Ryssota   (3.5") 9 cm
Ryssota maxima (Pfeiffer, 1853). Mindanao Id., Philippines. Common. Apical view.

Mearns' Ryssota   (3") 8 cm
Ryssota maxima subspecies *mearnsi* Bartsch, 1938. Philippine Islands. Holotype.

Quadras' Ryssota   (3") 8 cm
Ryssota quadrasi Hidalgo, 1890. Catanduanes Id., Philippines.

Anton's Ryssota   (2.5") 6.5 cm
Ryssota antoni (Semper, 1870).
B'aler Mt., Luzon Id., Philippines.

Baler Ryssota   (3") 8 cm
Ryssota (Lamarckiella) balerana
Bartsch, 1939. Baler, Luzon Id.,
Philippines. Holotype.

Igbaras Ryssota   (2.5") 6.5 cm
Ryssota sauli Bartsch, 1938 *igba-rasana* Bartsch, 1938. Igbaras,
Panay Id., Philippines. Holotype.

Saul's Ryssota   (2.5") 6.5 cm
Ryssota sauli Bartsch, 1938.
Guimara Id., Philippines.
Holotype.

Arrow Ryssota   (2") 5 cm
Ryssota sagittifera (Pfeiffer, 1854).
Mt. Sinait, Luzon Id., Philippines.

Solid Ryssota   (1.5") 3 cm
Ryssota sagittifera subspecies
solida (Moellendorff, 1898,
1898). Dingalan Id., Philippines.

Neptune Ryssota   (3") 7.5 cm
Hemiplecta neptunus (Pfeiffer,
1854). Siam. Extinct?

Lamarck's Ryssota   (2.5") 6 cm
Ryssota lamarckiana (Lea, 1852).
Central Philippines. Type of sub-genus *Lamarckiella*. This is forma
guimarasensis Bartsch, 1938.
Holotype.

Smith's Ryssota   (2") 5 cm
Ryssota oweniana (Pfeiffer, 1853),
subsp. *smithi* Bartsch, 1933.
Iloilo, Panay Id., Syn.: *globosa*
M. Smith, 1932. (holotype illus).

Moellendorff's Ryssota
                 (3") 7.5 cm
Ryssota nigrescens (Moellendorff,
1898), subsp. *moellendorffi*
Bartsch, 1939. Montalban,
Luzon. Holotype illus.

Zeus Ryssota   (2.5") 5 cm
Ryssota (Lamarckiella) zeus Jonas,
1842. Top: holotype of forma
bournsi Bartsch, 1939 (Romblon).
Bottom: holotype of *weberi*
Bartsch, 1939 (Sibuyan).

Bourns' Ryssota   (2.5") 5 cm
Ryssota zeus subsp. *bournsi*
Bartsch, 1939. Romblon, Philip-pines. Holotype.

Mt. Balabac Ryssota
(2.5") 6.5 cm
Ryssota nigrescens (Moellendorff, 1898) subsp. *balabacana* Bartsch, 1939. Mt. Balabac, Luzon Id. Holotype illus.

Sowerby's Ryssota (2") 5 cm
Ryssota sowerbyana (Pfeiffer, 1841). Truk Id., Carolines. Type of the subgenus *Trukrysa* H.B. Baker, 1941.

Sowerby's Ryssota (2") 5 cm
Ryssota (T.) sowerbyana (Pfeiffer, 1841). Truk Id. Syn.: *pachystoma* Hombron & Jacquinot.

Godeffroy's Baby Ryssota
(0.6") 1.5 cm
Orpiella godeffroyana (Garrett, 1872). N.E. Vanua Levu Id., Fiji.

Lord Howe Serrated Snail
Epiglypta howeinsulae (Cox, 1892). Lord Howe Island (north of New Zealand. Type of the genus.

Rugose Arion Helix (1.5") 4 cm
Helixarion rugosa (Fulton, 1910). North Borneo. Syntypes from Fulton. Syn.: *Helicarion*.

Superb Arion Helix
(0.6") 1.5 cm
Helixarion (Fastosarion) superba (Cox, 1871). Mt. Dysander, Queensland, Australia.

Superb Arion Helix
(0.6") 1.5 cm
Helixarion (Fastosarion) superba (Cox, 1871). Queensland, Australia. Type of Iredale's subgenus.

Emperor Arion Helix (2") 5 cm
Helixarion imperator (Gould, 1859). Hong Kong, south China. Largest of the genus.

Brazier's Arion Helix 2.5 cm
Helixarion (Vercularion) brazieri (Cox, 1873). Queensland, Australia. Syn.: *bullaceus* Odhner, 1917. Type of Iredale's subgenus.

Trochoid Asperitas Snail
(1") 2.5 cm
Asperitas trochus (Müller, 1774). Celebes Id., Indonesia.
Family: ARIOPHANTIDAE

Black-striped Asperitas
(1.3") 3.5 cm
Asperitas trochus subsp. *melanoraphe* (E.A. Smith, 1884). South coast of Bali, Indonesia. On bushes.

Penida Asperitas   (1.5") 3 cm
Asperitas inquinata (von der Busch in Pfeiffer, 1842) subsp. *penidae* B. Rensch, 1938. Penida Id., Sunda Ids., Indonesia. Paratypes.

Rarely-spotted Asperitas
            (1.3") 3.5 cm
Asperitas rareguttata (Mousson, 1849). Sunda Islands, Indonesia.

Rarely-spotted Asperitas
            (1.3") 3.5 cm
Asperitas rareguttata (Mousson, 1849) forma *crebiguttata* (von Martens, 1867). Flores and introduced to Bali. Common.

Shield Dyakia Snail   (1.5") 4 cm
Dyakia clypeus (Mousson, 1857). Java Id., Indonesia. Extinct?

Large-nosed Rhino Snail
            (1.3") 3 cm
Rhinocochlis nasuta (Metcalfe, 1851). Sarawak, Borneo. Rare. Type of the genus.

Green Nimble Snail (1.3") 3 cm
Elaphroconcha cochlostyloides forma *viridis* (Schepman, 1892). Mao Marru, Sumba Id., Indonesia.

Nimble Snail   (1.7") 4.5 cm
Elaphroconcha cochlostyloides (Schepman, 1892). Sumba Id., Indonesia.

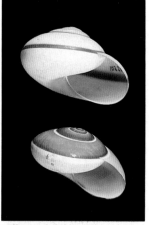

Yellow Naninia Snail
            (1.5") 4 cm
Naninia citrina (Linnaeus, 1758). Widely distributed in Indonesia and Solomons. Syn.: *Xesta*. For varieties, see Jutting, 1964.

Obi Naninia Snail   (1.3") 3 cm
Naninia obiana (Moellendorff, 1902). Obi Id., Moluccas, Indonesia.

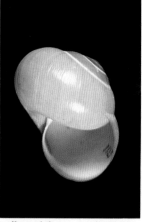

Yolk Naninia   (1.5") 4 cm
Naninia vitellus (Shuttleworth, 1852). Celebes. *Nanina* Gray, 1834, non Risso, 1826, is also synonym.

Clairville Naninia   (2") 5 cm
Naninia clairvillia (Férussac, 1822). Celebes.

Oldham's Naninia   (1.5") 4 cm
Naninia oldhamiana (Iredale, 1941). Orokolo, near Port Moresby, Papua New Guinea. Paratypes.

Dense Hemiplecta (2") 5 cm
Hemiplecta densa (Adams & Reeve, 1850). North Borneo.

Three-banded Ariophanta 2.5 cm *Ariophanta laevipes* (Müller, 1774). Bombay, India. In rock crevices. Type of the genus. Syn.: *trifasciatus* Chemnitz.

Nicobar Ariophanta (1.5") 4 cm *Ariophanta nicobarica* (Deshayes, 1839). Madras Hills, India.

Thyreus Ariophanta (1.5") 4 cm *Ariophanta thyreus* (Benson, 1852). Travancore, south India. Extinct?

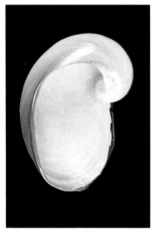

Giant Austen Snail (1.3") 3.5 cm *Austenia gigas* (Benson, 1836). Shillong, Assam Prov., India. Type of genus. Animal much larger.

Giant Austen Snail (1.3") 3.5 cm *Austenia gigas* (Benson, 1836). Shillong, Assam Prov., India. In subfamily Girasiinae.

Wicked Austen Snail (1.2") 3 cm *Megaustenia malefica* (Mabille, 1887). Tonkin, S.E. Asia. In subfamily Macrochlamydinae.

Siam Austen Snail (1") 2.5 cm *Megaustenia siamensis* (Haines, 1858). Thailand forests. Mantle partially covers shell. Photo by Fred Thompson.

Fleming's Austen Snail (1.2") 3 cm *Macrochlamys (Parvatella) flemingi* (Pfeiffer, 1856). West Punjab, N.W. India. Type of subgenus.

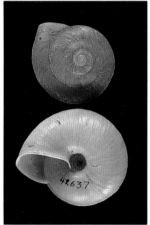

Oxytesta Snail (2.1") 5 cm *Oxytesta oxytes* (Benson, 1831). Khasi Hills, northern India. Type of the genus. Edge sharp.

Lowe's Austen Snail (1.3") 4 cm *Baiaplecta lowi* (de Morgan, 1885). Cameron, Panang, Malaya. Type of the genus.

Dall's Diadema Snail (0.5") 1.4 cm *Syama diadema* (Dall, 1897). Prang, Malay Peninsula. Paratype.

Suborder **HOLOPODA**

Sole of foot usually uniform; no side furrows. No mucus pit at tip end of foot. Do not confuse with suborder Holopodopes.

Superfamily **POLYGYROIDEA** (Polygyracea)

Embraces four families, the well-known Polygyridae of North America; the Corillidae of the Far East and South Africa; the Thysanophoridae of the tropical Americas; and the tiny, discoidal Ammonitellidae mainly of western U.S.A.

Family **POLYGYRIDAE**

Medium-sized, globose shells usually uniformly brown or tan. Lip reflected, sometimes toothed. A North American group of about 260 species, in 14 genera, in two subfamilies: Triodopsinae and Polygyrinae. We follow the 1988 revision by K.C. Emberton. Many so-called species are only hybrid swarms. Most species are ground-dwellers, but *Praticolella* is arboreal.

Some species are the intermediate host for parasites lethal to elk and deer.

Seven-whorled Polygyra 1.4 cm *Polygyra septemvolva* Say, 1818. Georgia, Florida to Texas. No internal lamina in last whorl. Common in grass in acid soils. Type of genus.

Waxy Polygyra (0.5") 1.4 cm *Polygyra cereolus* (Mühlfeld, 1818). Central and southern Florida in calcareous soils. 9 mm form with 5 whorls is *carpenteriana* Bland, 1860.

Flat Polygyra (0.3") 1 cm *Polygyra plana* (Dunker, 1843). Bermuda and western Bahamas. Common.

Eared Polygyra (0.6") 1.5 cm *Polygyra auriculata* Say, 1818. Central Florida. Common. Type of the subgenus *Daedalochila* Beck, 1837.

Palate Polygyra *Polygyra uvulifera* (Shuttleworth, 1852). Southern Florida. Several subspecies. Nearly smooth, dirty gray. Common.

Postell's Polygyra *Polygyra postelliana* (Bland, 1859). North Carolina to northern Florida. Several subspecies exist. Common.

Greedy Polygyra (1/4") 7 mm *Polygyra avara* Say, 1818. St. Johns River valley, Florida. Microscopic hairs. On black soil. Common.

Texas Polygyra (1/3") 9 mm *Polygyra texasiana* (Moricand, 1833). Arkansas and Louisiana to Texas. Weak brown band above periphery. Common.

Moore's Polygyra (1/3") 8 mm *Polygyra mooreana* (W.G. Binney, 1857). Throughout Texas. Common.

Rhoads' Polygyra (1.4") 6 mm *Polygyra rhoadsi* Pilsbry, 1899. Monterrey, northern Mexico.

True Stenotreme (0.4") 1 cm
Stenotrema stenotrema (Pfeiffer, 1842). Arkansas to Virginia; Ohio to Georgia. Microscopic hairs evenly set. Common.

Deceptive Stenotreme
(0.2") 7 mm
Stenotrema deceptum (Clapp, 1905). Alabama and Bledsoe Co., Tennessee. Locally common.

Hirsute Stenotreme (0.3") 8 mm
Stenotrema hirsutum (Say, 1817). Eastern half of U.S.; Ontario. This is forma *barbatum* (Clapp, 1904) from Alabama.

Edgar's Stenotreme (0.4") 9 mm
Stenotrema edgarianum (Lea, 1841). Tennessee. Edge sharp. Alt. 1,500 ft. Uncommon.

Maxillate Stenotreme (0.2") 7 mm
Stenotrema maxillatum (Gould, 1848). Georgia and Alabama. No notch in lower lip. Uncommon.

Carinate Stenotreme
(0.6") 14 mm
Stenotrema spinosum (Lea, 1830). Virginia and Georgia to Tennessee and Alabama. Microscopic hairs. Uncommon.

One-toothed Stenotreme
(0.3") 8.4 mm
Stenotrema monodon (Rackett, 1821). Ontario to Maryland. Type of subgenus *Euchemotrema* Archer. Syn.: *leai* Binney.

Brother Stenotreme
Stenotrema fraternum (Say, 1824). Eastern half of U.S.; Ontario. Common.

Grayish Praticolelle
(0.5") 1.2 cm
Praticolella griseola (Pfeiffer, 1841). East Mexico; S.E. Texas; introduced to Key West and Cuba.

Berlandier's Praticolelle
(0.5") 1.1 cm
Praticolella berlandieriana (Moricand, 1833). Texas and northern Mexico. Common on mesquite and in grass.

Mesodon snails from the Great Smoky Mountains (1.2"). Note opening to lung. About 33 species in this eastern U.S. genus.

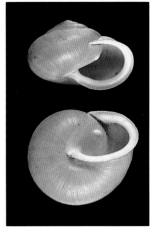

Thyroid Polygyra (1") 2.4 cm
Mesodon thyroidus (Say, 1816). Eastern United States, Ontario to Texas. Type of the genus.

Closed Polygyra   (0.6") 1.5 cm
Mesodon clausus (Say, 1821).
Ohio to Georgia to Alabama.
Small umbilicus always open.
Common.

Dr. Mitchell's Polygyra
                    (0.7") 1.7 cm
Mesodon mitchellianus (Lea,
1839). New York to Ohio and
Kentucky. Umbilicus closed.
Common.

Mrs. Andrews' Polygyra
                    (1") 2.5 cm
Mesodon andrewsae W.G. Binney, 1879. Tennessee to Alabama. High mountains. Holotype
of form *normalis* (Pilsbry, 1900).

Zealous Polygyra   (1.2") 2.8 cm
Mesodon zelatus (A. Binney,
1837). New York to North Carolina to mid-west. Syn.: *exoleta*
(Binney, 1851), holotype illus.

Pennsylvania Polygyra
                    (0.7") 1.9 cm
Mesodon pennsylvanicus (Green,
1827). West Penna. to Missouri.
No umbilicus; aperture irregular.
Common.

Elevated Polygyra   (1") 2.4 cm
Mesodon elevatus (Say, 1821).
New York and Illinois to Mississippi and S. Carolina. Large parietal tooth; high spire. Common.

Pressed Polygyra   (0.6") 1.8 cm
Mesodon appressus (Say, 1821).
Ohio to Virginia to Alabama;
Bermuda. Umbilicus pressed in.
Axial riblets microscopically
papillose. Common.

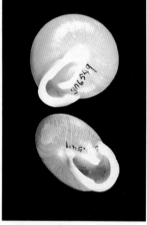

Sargent's Polygyra   (1") 2.5 cm
Mesodon sargentianus (Johnson
& Pilsbry, 1892). Alabama. Periphery angular. Common near
caves.

Inflected Polygyra   (0.5") 1 cm
Mesodon (Inflectarius) inflectus
(Say, 1821). Eastern and southern U.S. Aperture 3-lobed. Finely
striate and with tiny hairs. Common.

White-lipped Polygyra   2.8 cm
Neohelix albolabris (Say, 1816).
Eastern U.S. Several subspecies.
Type of the genus. Subfamily
Triodopsinae (see Emberton,
1988).

Dentiferous Polygyra (1") 2.4 cm
Neohelix dentifera (A. Binney,
1837). Northeast U.S. In humid
dead leaves. Common.

Many-lined Polygyra
                    (1") 2.5 cm
Webbhelix multilineata (Say,
1821). Upper central U.S. Brown-
lined. Type of Emberton's 1988
genus. Common.

Three-toothed Polygyra
(0.5") 1.3 cm
Triodopsis tridentata (Say, 1816).
Upper eastern half of U.S.; Ontario to Georgia. Abundant in hilly limestone. Type of genus.

Fraudulent Polygyra
(0.7") 1.6 cm
Triodopsis fraudulenta (Pilsbry, 1894). Mountains along Virginia and West Virginia borders.

False Polygyra (0.5") 1.1 cm
Triodopsis fallax (Say, 1825). Eastern U.S. from Pennsylvania to Georgia. Tubercle on interior columella. Syn.: *introferens* Bland, 1860. Common.

Hopeton Polygyra (0.6") 1.2 cm
Triodopsis hopetonensis (Shuttleworth, 1852). North Carolina to north Florida and Alabama. Near brackish water; common.

Notable Polygyra (0.9") 2.2 cm
Xolotrema denotata (Férussac, 1821). Upper eastern-central U.S. Surface rough. Syn.: *notata* (Deshayes, 1830). Type of genus.

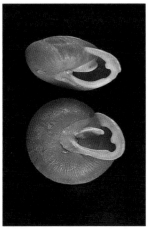

Obstructed Polygyra (1") 2.6 cm
Xolotrema obstricta (Say, 1821). Tennessee and Kentucky. High country; woodland. Uncommon.

Obstructed Polygyra (1") 2.6 cm
Xolotrema obstricta (Say, 1821). Near Nashville, Tenn. Holotype of syn.: *helicoides* (Lea, 1834).

Profound Allogone (1.2") 3 cm
Allogona profunda (Say, 1821). Eastern half of U.S. In deep, upland woods. Common. Subfamily Allogininae.

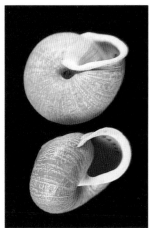

Townsend's Allogone (1") 2.5 cm
Allogona townsendiana (Lea, 1838). Western Oregon and Washington. Minutely streaked in tan.

Idaho Allogone (0.6") 1.9 cm
Allogona ptychophora (A.D. Brown, 1870). S. British Columbia, N.W. U.S., Idaho. Near rock slides. Common.

Columbian Vesperian Snail
(0.5") 1.5 cm
Vespericola columbiana (Lea, 1838). Washington and Oregon. Microscopically pimpled.

Wrinkled Ashmunella
(0.6") 1.6 cm
Ashmunella rhyssa (Dall, 1897) subsp. *miohyssa* (Dall, 1898). Lincoln Co., New Mexico. Under aspen trees. Type of genus.

Toothless Ashmunella
(0.6") 1.6 cm
Ashmunella rhyssa subsp. *edentata* Cockerell, 1900. Cloudcroft, Sacramento Mts., New Mexico, 8,700 ft. Topotypes.

Ferriss' Ashmunella (0.3") 1.1 cm
Ashmunella ferrissi Pilsbry, 1905. Cave Creek Canyon, Chiricahua Mts., Arizona. Topotypes.

Family THYSANOPHORIDAE

Shells usually small, discoidal; mouth without teeth. Five genera in southern U.S., northern South America, Mexico and West Indies. Includes *Microconus, Thysanophora, Microphysula* and the unusual, inch-sized *Macleania* from Puerto Rico. Four Central American *Microconus* are less than 4 mm, turban-shaped and abundant in forests and coffee groves.

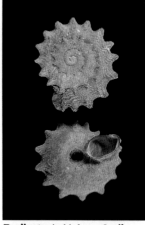

Darlington's McLean Snail
(0.6") 1 cm
Macleania darlingtoni Bequaert & Clench, 1939. Maricao forest, west Puerto Rico, 2,500 ft. Paratypes. Formerly *Mcleania*.

Superfamily OLEACINOIDEA
(Oleacinacea)

Family SAGDIDAE

The bee-hive snails of the tropical Americas are usually less than inch in size, have many glossy whorls, and are generally translucent tan to brown. The genus *Sagda* is well represented in the West Indies, especially Jamaica. The genus *Lacteoluna* occurs in Florida, Bermuda and the West Indies.

Jay's Sagda (1") 2.5 cm
Sagda jayana (C.B. Adams, 1848). John Crow Mts., Jamaica; 1,200 ft. alt. Photo by R.L. Goldberg.

Family OLEACINIDAE

Shells long, narrow, usually with a narrow mouth and glistening; oily surface. Ten genera and numerous species in the tropical Americas. Fast gliders living on the ground. Carnivorous. Eggs shelly and large. *Varicella* and *Oleacina* are the prevalent genera.

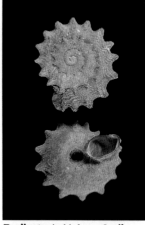

Volute Oily Snail (2.2") 5 cm
Oleacina voluta Gmelin, 1791. Barahona, Santo Domingo. Syn.: *peasi* Pilsbry, holotype illus.

Beach Oily Snail (1.2") 3 cm
Laevaricella (*Boriquena*) *playa* (H.B. Baker, 1940). Coastal Puerto Rico; common.

Deshayes' Oily Snail
(1.7") 4 cm
Laevoleacina oleacea (Deshayes, 1830). Matanzas, Cuba. Syn.: *straminea* (Deshayes, 1851).

Solid Oily Snail (0.3") 1 cm
Laevoleacina solidula (Pfeiffer, 1840). Many parts of Cuba; Nassau, Bahamas.

Arboreal Oily Snail
(0.5") 1.2 cm
Pittieria (*Shuttleworthia*) *arborea* H.B. Baker, 1941. Necaxa, Mexico. 3,120 ft. alt. Paratypes.

Superfamily HELICOIDEA
(Helicacea)

This superfamily is the evolutionary pinnacle of the terrestrial pulmonates, and contains many large, beautiful species. The six worldwide families are the tropical Camaenidae; the North American Oreohelicidae; the abundant New World Xanthonycidae (formerly Helminthoglyptidae), the tree-dwelling Bradybaenidae (Helicostylinae of the Philippines); the small Helicellidae of Europe; and the well-known Helicidae (*Helix* and *Cepaea* of Europe).

Family CAMAENIDAE

A large and colorful family with over 90 genera occurring in the tropics of Australasia, S.E. Asia and the Americas. The genera include the American ground-dwelling Pleurodontinae; the Australian *Thersites*; the tree-dwelling *Amphidromus* of Indonesia; the collectors' items of *Papuina* from Melanesia; and the button-shaped *Obba* from the Philippines. The eggs are small, soft and buried in the soft earth. All are vegetarians.

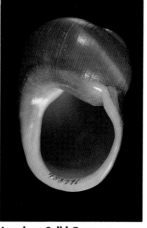

Jamaican Solid Camaena
(2") 5 cm
Eurycratera jamaicensis (Gmelin, 1791). Manchester, Jamaica. Solid shell. Type of the genus.

Saw-tooth Nipple Snail
(2") 5 cm
Thelidomus asper (Férussac, 1821). Mountains of Jamaica. Usually on tree trunks in wet forests. Photo by R.L. Goldberg.

Saw-tooth Nipple Snail
(2") 5 cm
Thelidomus asper (Férussac, 1821). Interior mountain forests of Jamaica. Type of the genus.

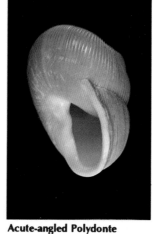

Acute-angled Polydonte
(2") 5 cm
Polydontes (*Parthena*) *acutangula* (Burrows, 1815). El Yunque rain forest, Puerto Rico, 2,500 ft. alt. Photo by R.L. Goldberg.

Acute-angled Polydonte
(2") 5 cm
Polydontes (*Parthena*) *acutangula* (Burrows, 1815). Central mountains of Puerto Rico. Type of the subgenus. Arboreal.

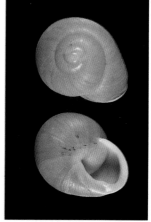

Wavy Nipple Snail (2") 5 cm
Polydontes (*Hispaniolana*) *undulata* (Férussac, 1821). Haiti. Extinct? Type of subgenus.

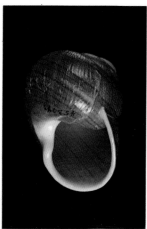

Luquillo Nipple Snail
(1.5") 3.5 cm
Polydontes (*Luquillia*) *luquillensis* (Shuttleworth, 1854). Luquillo Mts., eastern Puerto Rico. Arboreal. Photo by R.L. Goldberg.

Luquillo Nipple Snail 3.5 cm
Polydontes (*Luquillia*) *luquillensis* (Shuttleworth, 1854). El Yunque forest, Puerto Rico. In bracts of bromeliads. Type of the subgenus.

Raspy Nipple Snail (1") 2.5 cm
Polydontes (*Granodomus*) *lima* (Férussac, 1821). Throughout Puerto Rico. Type of the subgenus. Common.

Perplexed Nipple Snail
(1") 2.5 cm
Polydontes perplexa (Férussac, 1821). Grenada and Grenadine Ids., Lesser Antilles. Extinct?

Candelabrum Pleurodont
                    (1.2") 3 cm
Pleurodonte lychnuchus (Müller, 1774). Martinique; Guadeloupe. Surface minutely granular. Rare. Type of genus.

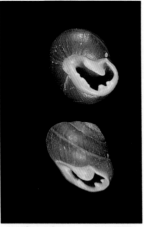

Nut Pleurodont   (0.8") 2 cm
Pleurodonte nux (Holten, 1802). Martinique and Guadeloupe. Rare. Syn.: *nuxdenticulata* Chemnitz.

Imperial Pleurodont (2.4") 6 cm
Polydontes imperator (Montfort, 1810). Baracoa, north coast of Cuba. *Pleurodonta* Beck is synonym.

Orbiculate Pleurodont
                    (1.2") 3 cm
Pleurodonte orbiculata (Férussac, 1821). Martinique, Lesser Antilles. Banding variable.

True Caracolus Snail
                    (2.8") 7 cm
Pleurodonte (*Caracolus*) *caracolla* (Linnaeus, 1758). Throughout wooded Puerto Rico. Common. Type of the subgenus.

Excellent Caracolus Snail
                    (3.5") 8.5 cm
Pleurodonte (*Caracolus*) *excellens* (Pfeiffer, 1852). Santo Domingo and Haiti.

Marginella Caracolus Snail
                    (1.3") 3 cm
Pleurodonte (*C.*) *marginella* (Gmelin, 1791). Puerto Rico; common in trees. Rarely bandless.

Rostrate Caracolus Snail
                    (2") 5 cm
Pleurodonte (*Caracolus*) *rostrata* (Pfeiffer, 1847). Baracoa, Cuba. Form of *marginella*?

Lowe's Caracolus Snail
                    (1.3") 4 cm
Pleurodonte (*C.*) *lowei* Pilsbry, 1929. Cape Maisi, Oriente Prov., Cuba. Named for Herbert N. Lowe.

Apollo Pleurodont   (2.5") 6 cm
Polydontes apollo (Pfeiffer, 1860). Baracoa, eastern Cuba. Voluntarily amputates end of foot.

Carmelite Pleurodont (2") 5 cm
Pleurodonte (*Dentellaria*) *carmelita* (Férussac, 1822). Jamaica. Granulated above; no teeth. Syn.: *Lucerna* Swainson.

Bainbridge's Pleurodont
                    (2.2") 5.5 cm
Pleurodonte (*Dentellaria*) *bainbridgei* (Pfeiffer, 1845). Jamaica. Granulated all over. Teeth on basal lip.

Sinuate Pleurodont (1.1") 2.7 cm
Pleurodonte (Dentellaria) sinuata (Müller, 1774). Jamaica. Type of Schumacher's 1817 subgenus.

Anomalous Pleurodont
(1") 2.5 cm
Pleurodonte (Dentellaria) anomalus (Pfeiffer, 1848). Jamaica. Wooded hills. Uncommon.

Pallid Pleurodont (1") 2.5 cm
Pleurodonte (Dentellaria) pallescens (C.B. Adams, 1851). St. Elizabeth Parish, Jamaica. Paratypes.

Painted Pleurodont (0.9") 2 cm
Pleurodonte (Dentellaria) picturatus (C.B. Adams, 1849). Jamaica. Paratypes.

Acute Pleurodont (1") 2.5 cm
Pleurodonte (Dentellaria) lamarckii (Férussac, 1822). Jamaica. Syn.: *acuta* Lamarck, 1816, non Müller, 1774.

Most Acute Pleurodont
(2") 5 cm
Pleurodonte (D.) peracutissimus (C.B. Adams, 1845). Jamaica. Paratypes.

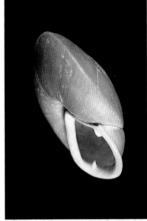

Oreas Labyrinth Snail 6 cm
Lampadion (Isomeria) oreas (Koch, in Philippi, 1844). Colombia. Type of the subgenus. Syn.: *Labyrinthus* Beck (see Rehder, 1967).

Tarapoto Labyrinth Snail
(1.7") 4 cm
Lampadion tarapotomensis (Moricand, 1858). Tarapoto, Peruvian Andes.

Bourcier's Labyrinth Snail
(1.2") 3 cm
Lampadion (Isomeria) bourcieri (Pfeiffer, 1852). Near Quito, Ecuador.

Chiriqui Labyrinth Snail
(1.3") 3 cm
Lampadion chiriquensis (Pilsbry, 1910). Chiriqui, Panama.

Globe Labyrinth Snail
(2:) 5 cm
Lampadion subcastanea (Pfeiffer, 1842). N.W. Ecuador. Syn.: *globosus* Broderip, 1832, non Montagu, 1801.

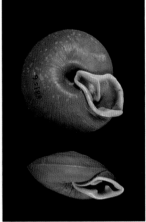

Plicate Labyrinth Snail
(1.5") 4 cm
Lampadion plicatus (Born, 1778). Porto Cabello, Venezuela; Panama.

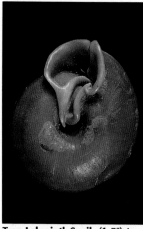

True Labyrinth Snail (1.5") 4 cm
Lampadion otis (Lightfoot, 1786). Panama and Colombia. Syn.: *Labyrinthus labyrinthus* Deshayes. Syntype of *hydiana* Lea, 1838, illus. Type of genus.

Brazilian Gyrating Snail (2") 5 cm
Polygyratia polygyrata (Born, 1778). Brazil. Type of the genus.

Snakeskin Sundial Snail (2") 5 cm
Solaropsis undata (Lightfoot, 1786). Brazil. Syn.: *pellisserpentis* Chemnitz (and Gmelin, 1791).

Brazilian Sundial Snail (1.6") 4 cm
Solaropsis brasiliana (Deshayes, 1832). Rio de Janeiro Province, Brazil. Family *Solaropsidae*.

Gibbon's Sundail Snail (2.9")
Solaropsis gibboni (Pfeiffer, 1846). Near Bogota, Colombia and Ecuador.

Scarred Camaena (1.6") 4 cm
Camaena cicatricosa (Müller, 1774). Southern coast of China; Hong Kong. Common. Type of genus.

Contracted Camaena (1.6") 4 cm
Camaena contractiva Mabille, 1897. Muong-Bo, Tonkin.

Hainan Camaena (1.6") 4 cm
Camaena hainanensis (H. Adams, 1870). Hainan Island, south China.

Traille's Camaena (1.6") 4 cm
Mesanella monochroa (Sowerby, 1841). Palawan Island, Philippines. Paratype of *C. bugsukensis* Bartsch, 1918.

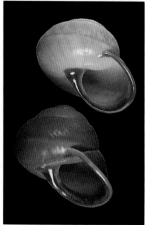

Traille's Camaena (1.6") 4 cm
Mesanella monochroa (Sowerby, 1841). Color variations from Palawan Island, Syn.: *trailli* (Pfeiffer, 1855).

Barney's Camaena (1.3") 3.5 cm
Camaena barneyi (Cox, 1873). Northern Queensland and Barney Islands, Australia.

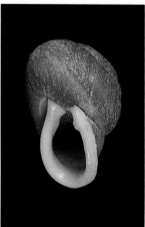

Teat False Obba (1.6") 4 cm
Pseudobba mamilla (Férussac, 1821). Northern Celebes. Uncommon. Type of the genus.

Quoy's False Obba (2.5") 6 cm
Pseudobba quoyi (Deshayes, 1834). Northern Celebes. Deep woods; uncommon.

Flattened Obba (1.3") 3 cm
Obba planulata (Lamarck, 1822). Probably northern Mindanao Id., Philippines. Several Mindoro subsp. Type of genus.

Lister's Obba (1.2") 3 cm
Obba listeri (Gray, 1825). Southern Luzon, and central Philippines. Common. Edge sharp.

Pedro de Mesa Obba (1.2") 3 cm
Obba mesai Bartsch, 1933. Lubang Id., Philippines. Paratypes. Also Mindoro Id. Edge rounded.

Dove Obba (1") 2.5 cm
Obba columbaria (Sowerby, 1841). Polillo Id., Tayabas, Luzon Id., Philippines. Fine ridge behind lip. Uncommon.

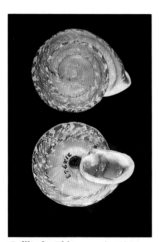

Gallinule Obba (1.2") 3 cm
Obba gallinula (Pfeiffer, 1845). Luzon and central Philippines. These are paratypes of subsp. *majayjayana* Bartsch, 1933, from Laguna Prov., Luzon.

Rota Obba (1.2") 3 cm
Obba rota (Broderip, 1841). Siquijor Id. and Bohol, Philippines. Strong riblets, serrated edge. Common.

Moricand's Obba (1") 2.5 cm
Obba moricandi (Pfeiffer, 1842). (Sowerby's earlier name is invalid). N.E. Mindanao; Bohol. Tiny tooth on lower lip. Uncommon.

Brownish Moricand Obba (1")
Obba moricandi (Pfeiffer, 1842), subsp. *brunnescens* (Moellendorff, 1892). Bislig Id., Philippines. Paratypes. Note tooth on lip.

Marginate Obba (1.2") 2.5 cm
Obba marginata (Müller, 1774). Northern Mindanao Id., Philippines. Common. No tooth on lower lip.

Little Shield Obba (1.7") 4 cm
Obba parmula (Broderip, 1841). Central Philippines. Very flat; bandless. Uncommon.

Raised Shield Obba (1.2") 3 cm
Obba parmula (Broderip, 1841), subsp. *elevata* (Moellendorff, 1892). Cebu Id. Extinct? Paratypes.

Horizontal Obba   (1.6") 4 cm
Obba horizontalis (Pfeiffer,
1845). Romblon and Tablas Ids.,
Philippines. Mouth squarish.
Uncommon.

Bigonia Obba   (1") 2.5 cm
Obba bigonia (Férussac, 1821).
Samar and Leyte, Philippines.
Syn.: *bizonia* Adams; *samarensis*
Pfr., 1842.

Trench Obba   (1") 2.5 cm
Obba scrobiculata (Pfeiffer,
1842), forma *conoidalis* Moellendorff, 1892). Timobo, Leyte; Bislig Id.: Cebu (?) Paratypes. Striate.

Nipple Obba   (1") 2.5 cm
Obba papilla (Müller, 1774).
Northern Celebes. Uncommon.

Bulacan Obba   (1.6") 4 cm
Obba (*Obbiberus*) *bulacanensis*
(Hidalgo, 1888). Bulacan Prov.,
Luzon Id. Type of Haas' subge-
nus. Uncommon.

Liedke's Planispire Snail
                        (1") 2.5 cm
Planispira liedkei Rolle, 1910.
Obi Id., Moluccas, Indonesia.
Paratype. Is *zonaria* L.?

Crow Planispire Snail
                        (1.3") 3 cm
Planispira cornicula (Hombron
& Jacquinot, 1842). Irian, W. New
Guinea.

Blackened Planispire (1.3") 3 cm
Planispira atrofusca (Pfeiffer,
1861). Batjan and Halmahera
Ids., Indonesia.

Crooked-collar Planispire
                        (1") 2.5 cm
Planispira (*Cristigibba*) *torticollis*
(LeGuillon, 1842-1840). Aru and
Sorong Ids.; western New Guinea.
(Syn.: *tortilabia* Philippi, 1845.)

Ribboned Planispire (1") 2.5 cm
Trachia vittata (Müller, 1884). Sri
Lanka and S.E. India.

Trochid Ganesella Snail
                        (1") 2.5 cm
Ganesella (*Coliolus*) *planasi*
(Hidalgo, 1889). Busuanga Id.,
Philippines. Rare.

Canefri's Ganesella (0.9") 2.1 cm
Ganesella (*Coliolus*) *heliodorus*
Jutting, 1965. Dutch New
Guinea. Top is trochid-shaped.
Syn.: *canefriana* Smith, 1895, non
Kobelt.

Perak Ganesella Snail
(0.7") 2 cm
Ganesella perakensis Gude, 1904. Tonkin. Syntype from Fulton.

Adeline's Satsuma (1") 2.5 cm
Satsuma (Luchuhadra) adelinae (Pilsbry, 1901). Osima Osumi, Ryukyu Ids. Paratypes.

Tanegashima's Satsuma
(1") 2.5 cm
Satsuma tanegashimae (Pilsbry, 1901). Osima Osumi, Ryukyu Ids. Paratypes.

Money Satsuma (1.5") 4 cm
Satsuma (Coniglobus) mercatoria (Pfeiffer, 1845). Chinen, Okinawa Id.

Money Satsuma (1.5") 4 cm
Satsuma (Coniglobus) mercatoria (Pfeiffer, 1845). Okinawa Id., Ryukyu Ids.

Fleshy Satsuma (2") 5 cm
Satsuma (Satsuma) myomphala (von Martens, 1865). Hiroshima, Japan.

Batan Satsuma Snail (1.2") 3 cm
Satsuma (Coniglobus) batanica (Adams & Reeve, 1848). Koshun and Batan Id., Taiwan. Syn.: *pancala* Schumacher & Boettger.

Mashed Planispire Snail
(1.3") 3 cm
Stegodera angusticollis (von Martens, 1876). Yangtze Valley, China. Schumacher syntypes.

Talon Chlorite Snail
(1.3") 3.5 cm
Chloritis ungulina (Linnaeus, 1758). Ceram and Amboina, Moluccas, Indonesia. Common. Type of genus.

Favorable Chlorite Snail
(1.3") 3.5 cm
Chloritis fausta Gude, 1906. N. Mecklenburg, New Ireland, New Guinea.

Greatest Chlorite Snail
(2") 5 cm
Chloritis (Discoconcha) majuscula (Pfeiffer, 1856). New Ireland, Admiralty Ids., New Guinea. Syn.: *isis* (Pfeiffer, 1860).

Poling's Chlorite Snail (.05")
Cristigibba (Verdichloritis) polingi (Clench, 1957). Salawati Id., New Guinea. On Waiboe limestone ridge. Common. Upper shell is holotype.

Rohde's Chlorite Snail (2") 5 cm
Chloritis (Sulcobasis) rohdei
Kobelt, 1891. West New Guinea.
Common; widespread.

Smooth Chlorite Snail
             (1.5") 3 cm
Albersia tenuis (Pfeiffer, 1845).
Sekru and Fakfak, New Guinea.
Uncommon.

Waigeu Chlorite Snail (2") 5 cm
Albersia waigiouensis Sykes,
1904. Sorong and Ajamaru, New
Guinea, and Waigeu Id. Topotypes.

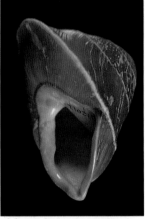

Richmond Thersite Snail
             (2.7") 6.5 cm
Thersites richmondianus (Reeve,
1852). Richmond River, N.S.
Wales, Australia. Type of the
genus. Uncommon.

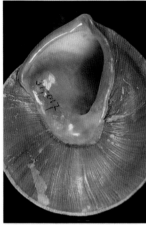

Richmond Thersite Snail
             (2.7") 6.5 cm
Thersites richmondianus (Reeve,
1852). New South Wales, Australia. Genus *Annakelea* Iredale
is synonym.

Two-part Thersite Snail
             (2.7") 6.5 cm
Thersites (Hadra) bipartitus
(Férussac, 1822). Northern
Queensland, Australia. Common.
Type of subgenus.

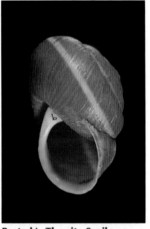

Bartsch's Thersite Snail
             (2.5") 4 cm
Thersites (Hadra) bartschi
Marshall, 1927. Darnley Id.,
Torres Straits, Australia. Syn.: *dalli*
& *waltoni* Marshall, 1927.

Webb's Thersite Snail
             (2.7") 6.5 cm
Thersites (Hadra) webbi Pilsbry,
1900. Cairns, Queensland, Australia. Rare.

Mazee Thersite Snail (2") 5 cm
Thersites (Gnarosophia) mazee
(Brazier, 1878). Mt. Stuart,
Townsville, Queensland, Austra-
lia. Uncommon.

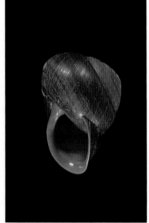

Rawnesley Thersite Snail
             (2") 5 cm
*Thersites (Gnarosophia) rawn-
esleyi* (Cox, 1873). Elliott Range,
Port Denison, Queensland, Australia.

Palm Island Thersite Snail
             (2") 5 cm
*Thersites (Gnarosophia) palmen-
sis* (Brazier, 1876). Palm Id., and
N. Queensland, Australia.

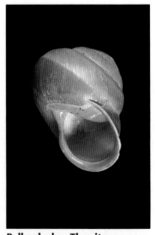

Bellendenker Thersite
             (1.6") 4 cm
*Thersites (Gnar.) bellendenker-
ensis* (Brazier, 1875). Bellendenker Mts., N. Queensland,
Australia.

Northern Thersite Snail
(2.5") 6 cm
Thersites (Mecyntera) septemtrionalis Hedley, 1897. Collingwood Bay, northern New Guinea.

Wharton's Thersite Snail
(2.5") 6 cm
Thersites (Temporena) whartoni (Cox, 1871). Holbourne Island, N. Queensland, Australia. Topotypes.

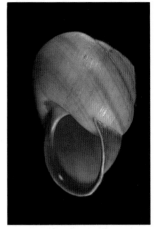

Fraser's Thersite Snail
(1.5") 4 cm
Thersites (Sphaerospira) fraseri (Griffith & Pidgeon, 1833). N.S.W. and south Queensland. Common.

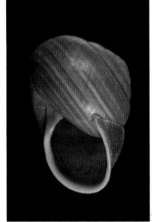

Permuted Thersite Snail
(1.5") 4 cm
Thersites (Sphaerospira) fraseri subsp. *permuta* Iredale, 1937. Clarence River area, Queensland, Australia.

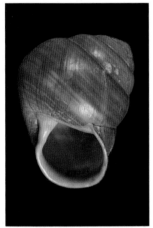

Giant Thersite Snail (3") 7.5 cm
Thersites (Sphaerospira) informis (Mousson, 1869). Mid-Queensland. This is subsp. *dietrichae* Iredale, 1937, from Mt. Dryander, Port Denison.

Etheridge's Thersite Snail
(1.5") 4 cm
Thersites (Bentosites) etheridgei (Brazier, 1877). Mt. Blackwood, Qld., Australia. Uncommon.

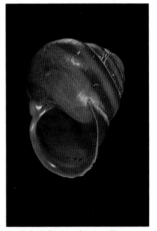

Delightful Thersite Snail
(1.3") 3.5 cm
Thersites (Bentosites) gavisa (Iredale, 1933). Mid-Queensland. Syn.: *gratiosa* Cox, 1871, non Studer, 1820.

Cox's Thersite Snail (1.6") 4 cm
Thersites (Bentosites) coxi (Crosse, 1866). Port Denison district, N.E. Australia.

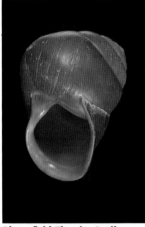

Bloomfield Thersite Snail
(1.6") 4 cm
Thersites (Bentosites) bloomfieldi (Cox, 1864). South Queensland, Australia. Syn.: *warroensis*, Hedley & Musson, 1892.

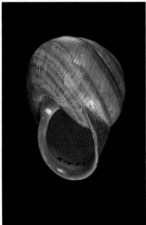

Rockhampton Thersite Snail
(1.6") 4 cm
Thersites (Varohadra) rockhamptonensis (Cox, 1873). Rockhampton district, Queensland, Australia.

O'Connell Thersite Snail
(1.3") 3.5 cm
Thersites (Varohadra) oconnellensis (Cox, 1871). Mid-Queensland. Type of subgenus. Common.

Port Curtis Thersite (1.3") 3.5 cm
Thersites (Varohadra) curtisianus (Pfeiffer, 1864). Port Curtis and Boyne Id., Queensland. Type of subgenus, syn.: *Figuladra* Iredale, 1933.

Additional Thersite Snail
(1.5") 4 cm
Thersites (Varohadra) appendiculatus (Reeve, 1854). Dan Dan scrub, West of Gladestone, Queensland. Common.

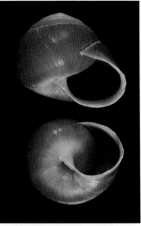

Bernhard's Thersite Snail
(1") 2.5 cm
Thersites (Varohadra) bernhardi (Iredale, 1933). Rockhampton District, Queensland. Uncommon.

Challis Thersite Snail (1.3") 3 cm
Thersites (Varohadra) challisi (Cox, 1873). L Island, mid-Queensland. Also Keppel Id.

Lesson's Thersite Snail
(1.3") 3 cm
Thersites (Varohadra) lessoni (Pfeiffer, 1846). Miriam Vale, S. Queensland.

Dainty Thersite Snail (1") 2.5 cm
Thersites (Varohadra) mattea (Iredale, 1933). Rockhampton, S. Queensland.

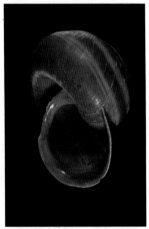

Rainbird Thersite Snail
(2") 5 cm
Thersites (Varohadra) rainbirdi (Cox, 1870). Mt. Dryander, mid-Queensland.

Thorogood Thersite Snail
(2") 5 cm
Thersites (Varohadra) thorogoodi (Iredale, 1937). Prosperine area, Queensland. Rare.

Yeppoon Thersite Snail
(1.6") 4 cm
Thersites (Varohadra) yeppoonensis (Beddome, 1897). Yeppoon area, south Queensland. Locally common.

Yule's Thersite Snail (1.2") 2 cm
Thersites (Varohadra) yulei (Forbes, 1851). Port Molle, mid-Queensland, Australia. Uncommon.

Northern Pumpkin Snail 4 cm
Xanthomelon durvillii (Hombron & Jacquinot, 1841). Northern Territory, Australia. Slightly umbilicate. Syn.: *pomum* (Pfeiffer, 1842). Type of genus.

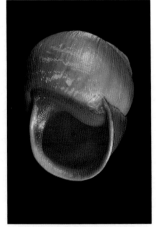

Rosy Pumpkin Snail (1.5") 4 cm
Xanthomelon durvillii (H. & J.) forma *sphaeroideum* (LeGuillon, 1845). Reddish tinged color variant.

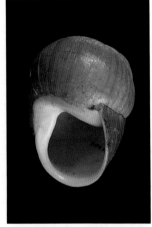

Thick Pumpkin Snail (1.5") 4 cm
Xanthomelon pachystylum (Pfeiffer, 1845). Queensland coast. Common in scrub. Not umbilicate.

PAPUINA TREE SNAILS
(Subfamily Papuininae)

This is a large group of sizable, colorful tree snails of Melanesia, New Guinea and Queensland, Australia. Although somewhat a natural group, and once given the family rank of Papuinidae by Iredale, we follow a more conservative classification as done by van Benthem Jutting (1965), Clench and Turner (1959-1962) and H.B. Baker, particularly in accepting the genus Papuina in a broad sense. 250 known species.

These colorful snails are being endangered by the destruction of their habitats.

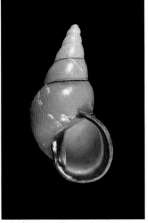

Hinde's Papuina (1.5") 3.5 cm
Papuina (Papustyla) hindei (Cox, 1888). New Ireland and New Britain Ids. Type of subgenus. Syn.: *finschi* von Martens, 1897.

Manus Green Papuina
(1.5") 3.6 cm
Papuina (Papustyla) pulcherrima Rensch, 1931. Central Manus Id., Papua New Guinea. Common in high trees.

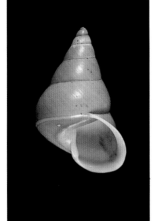

Manus Green Papuina
(1.5") 3.6 cm
Papuina (Papustyla) pulcherrima Rensch, 1931. Sold in Manus markets. On U.S. endangered list. Common.

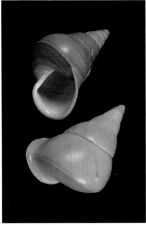

Manus Green Papuina
(1.5") 3.6 cm
Papuina (Papustyla) pulcherrima Rensch, 1931. Partial or almost entirely yellow forms due to dry conditions or tampering.

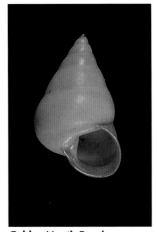

Golden Mouth Papuina
(2") 5 cm
Papuina (Papustyla) xanthochila (Pfeiffer, 1861). Bougainville Id., W. Solomon Ids. Abundant.

New Pommeran Papuina 3 cm
Papuina (Papustyla) novaepom-meraniae Rensch & Rensch, 1929. Matlip, New Britain Id. Paratype. Syn.: *papustyloides* R. & R.

Chance's Papuina (1.3") 3 cm
Papuina (Papustyla) chancei (Cox, 1870). New Britain and New Ireland, Bismarcks. Syn.: *rechingeri* Oberwimmer, 1909; *alba* Leschke, 1912.

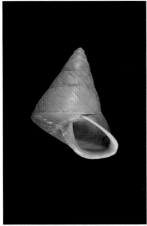

Ferguson's Papuina (1.5") 3.5 cm
Papuina (Papustyla) fergusoni (H. Adams, 1872). New Britain. Syn.: *schneideri* Rensch, 1929 (paratype illus.).

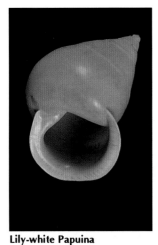

Lily-white Papuina
(1.5") 3.5 cm
Papuina (Papustyla) lilium (Fulton, 1905). Choiseul Id., Solomons. Uncommon.

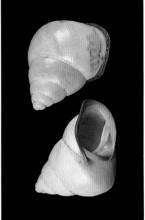

Chapman's Papuina (1.5") 3.5 cm
Papuina (Papustyla) chapmani (Cox, 1870). Russell Id., Louisiade Group, Solomons. Rare.

Adonis Papuina (1.2") 3 cm
Papuina adonis (Angas, 1869). Kupei, Bougainville Id., Solomons.

Acmella Papuina   (1.2") 3 cm
Papuina acmella (Pfeiffer, 1860).
Florida and Isabel Ids., Solomons.
Common.

Splendid Papuina   (1.5") 3.5 cm
Papuina splendescens (Cox,
1865). Maru Sound, Guadalcanal Id., Solomons. Syn.: *brench-
leyi* Brazier.

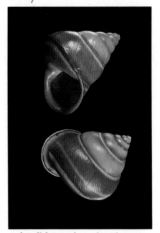

Splendid Papuina   (1.5") 3.5 cm
Papuina splendescens (Cox,
1865). Buin, Guadalcanal Id.,
Solomons. Dark color phase.

Splendid Papuina   (1.5") 3.5 cm
Papuina splendescens (Cox,
1865). Buin, Guadalcanal, Solomons. Narrow-banded form.

Chaffinch Papuina   (1") 2.5 cm
Papuina fringilla (Pfeiffer, 1855).
Monda Id., New Georgia Group,
Solomons. Uncommon.

Miser Papuina   (1.5") 3.5 cm
Papuina miser (Cox, 1873). Flor-
ida Id., Solomons. Syn.: *beatrix*
Angas, 1876.

Aru Cap Papuina   (1.3") 3 cm
Papuina (Papustyla) pileus
(Müller, 1774). Aru Islands, In-
donesia. Common. Type of syn.:
Molmerope Iredale, 1941.

Aru Cap Papuina   (1.3") 3 cm
Papuina (Papustyla) pileus
(Müller, 1774). Aru Islands. Less
banded forms.

Hermione Papuina   (1.3") 3 cm
Papuina (Papustyla) hermione
(Angas, 1869). Bougainville Id.,
W. Solomons.

Milk-splashed Papuina
              (1.5") 4 cm
Papuina (Canefriula) lacteolata
(E.A. Smith, 1887). Owen Stanley
Mts., Papua New Guinea. *P.
lactealota* is misspelling.

Milk-splashed Papuina
              (1.5") 4 cm
Papuina lacteolata (E.A. Smith,
1887). Upau, Owen Stanley Mts.,
Papua New Guinea. Multi-
banded form.

Malanta Papuina   (1.2") 3 cm
Papuina malantanensis (Adams
and Angas, 1876). Malanta Id.,
Solomons.

Conical Papuina (1.3") 3 cm
Papuina meta (Pfeiffer, 1856).
Isabel Id., Solomons.

Hargreaves' Papuina (1.2") 3 cm
Papuina hargreavesi (Angas, 1869). High mountains of Choiseul and Bougainville Ids., Solomons. Syntypes.

Mendana Papuina (1.2") 3 cm
Papuina mendana (Angas, 1867). Bougainville and Shortland Ids., Solomons.

Wanderer Papuina (1.2") 3 cm
Papuina (Glomerata) migratoria (Pfeiffer, 1855). Wanderer Bay, Guadalcanal Id., Solomons. Type of subgenus.

Wanderer Papuina (1.2") 3 cm
Papuina migratoria (Pfeiffer, 1855). North coast of Guadalcanal Id., Solomons. Abbott, photo.

Boivin's Papuina (1.2") 3 cm
Papuina (Solmopina) boivini (Petit, 1841). Fulakora, Florida Id., Solomons. Syn.: *subrepta* Hombon & Jac., 1854.

New Georgia Papuina
(1") 2.5 cm
Papuina (Megalacron) novaegeorgiensis (Cox, 1870). Manus and New Georgia, Admiralty Ids. Type of subgenus.

Chalky Papuina (1") 2.5 cm
Papuina (M.) novaegeorgiensis subsp. *creta* Rensch, 1934. Vitu Id., Bismarcks. Paratypes.

New Guinea Papuina (1") 2.5 cm
Papuina (Megalacron) novoguineensis (Pfeiffer, 1862). Sorong Id., New Guinea.

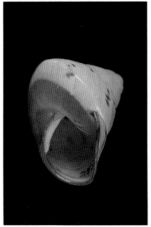

Cox's Papuina (0.8") 2 cm
Papuina (Megalacron) coxiana (Angas, 1867). Isabel Id., Solomons.

Bridal Papuina (0.9") 2.2 cm
Papuina (Megalacron) gamelia (Angas, 1867). St. Stephens Id.; Isabel Id.; Shortland Ids., Solomons.

Guadalcanal Papuina
(1.1") 2.8 cm
Papuina (Megalacron) guadalcanarensis (Cox, 1871). Guadalcanal Id., Solomons. Syntype from Cox.

Macfarlane's Papuina (1") 2.5 cm
Papuina (Megalacron) macfarlanei (Cox, 1873). Buin, Bougainville Id., Solomons.

Nightingale Papuina
(1.3") 3.5 cm
Papuina philomela (Angas, 1872). Ysabel Id., Solomon Islands.

Oblique-mouthed Papuina
(1") 2.5 cm
Papuina plagiostoma (Pfeiffer, 1856). Ysabel Id., Solomons. Syn.: *fulakorensis* Clapp, 1923, its holotype at top.

Bent-mouthed Papuina
(1") 2.5 cm
Papuina (Solmogada) flexilabris (Pfeiffer, 1856). New Georgia Id., Solomon Islands.

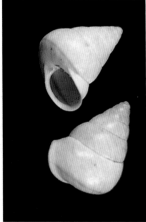

Poiret's Papuina   (0.9") 2.2 cm
Papuina (Noctepuna) poiretiana (Reeve, 1852). Night Island, Queensland, Australia.

Clench's Papuina   (0.9") 2.2 cm
Papuina poiretiana subsp. *clenchi* (McMichael, 1958). Dinner Creek, McIlwrath Range, N. Queensland. Paratypes.

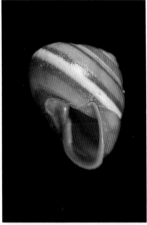

Flag Papuina   (1") 2.5 cm
Papuina (Papuina) vexillaris (Pfeiffer, 1855). Munda, Solomon Islands.

Tower Papuina   (1.7") 4.5 cm
Papuina (Zetemina) pyrgus Sykes, 1903. Waigeu Id., west end New Guinea.

Donna's Papuina   (1") 2.5 cm
Papuina donnaisabella (Angas, 1869). Eddystone Id., Solomons.

Spectacular Papuina
(1.6") 4 cm
Papuina (Papuina) spectrum (Reeve, 1854). N.W. New Guinea and Waigeu Id. (syn.: *waigiouensis* H. Adams, 1865).

Wallace's Papuina   (1.5") 4 cm
Papuina (P.) spectrum forma *wallaceana* Sykes, 1903. Waigeu Id., Indonesia.

Latiaxis Papuina   (1.6") 4 cm
Papuina (Letitia) latiaxis (E.A. Smith, 1883). Cape Rodney, Papua New Guinea. (see *zeno*).

Ernst Mayr Papuina (1") 2.4 cm
Papuina (Megalacron) mayri
(Rensch, 1934). Choiseul Id.,
Solomons. Paratypes.

Sellers' Papuina (1") 2.5 cm
Papuina (Megalacron) sellersi
(Cox, 1872). Temera River,
Guadalcanal Id., Solomons.

Smith's Papuina (1.2") 3 cm
Papuina (Megalacron) smithi
Boettger, 1919. Ulava Id., Solo-
mons.

Ambrosia Papuina (0.8") 2 cm
Papuina (Megalacron) ambrosia
(Angas, 1867). Russell Id.; Isabel
Id., Solomons.

Alfred's Papuina (1") 2.5 cm
Papuina alfredi (Cox, 1871).
Bougainville Id., Solomons.

Lienardi's Papuina (1.2") 3 cm
*Papuina (Megalacron) lienardi-
ana* (Crosse, 1864). Ataa, Malaita Id., Solomons.

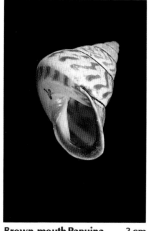

Brown-mouth Papuina 3 cm
*Papuina (Megalacron) phaeo-
stoma* (von Martens, 1877). Bismarck Ids. Paratype of forma
densepicta Rolle, 1902 from New
Meklenburg, P.N.G.

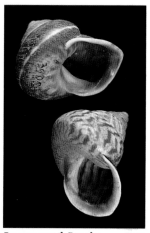

Brown-mouth Papuina 3 cm
Papuina (M.) phaeostoma (von
Martens, 1877). Upper: paratype
of forma *kandanensis* Rensch,
1934. Lower: forma *fulgurata*
Rolle, 1902.

Admiralty Papuina (1.2") 3 cm
Papuina (M.) admiralitatis
(Rensch, 1931). Manus Id.,
Admiralty Ids., P.N.G. Common.

Boyer's Papuina (1.2") 3 cm
Papuina (M.) boyeri (Fischer and
Bernardi, 1857). Woodlark Id.,
New Guinea.

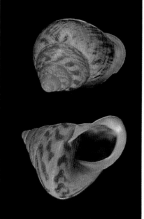

Bequaert's Papuina (1") 2.5 cm
Papuina (M.) bequaerti (Clench
& Turner, 1964). New Ireland
Id., Bismarcks. Syn.: *trochoides*
(Deshayes, 1838, non Poiret,
1789.

Dense-ribbed Papuina
(1") 2.5 cm
*Papuina (Megalacron) densestri-
ata* Fulton, 1902. New Ireland,
Bismarcks. Paratypes.

Lombe's Papuina (1") 2.5 cm
Papuina (M.) lambei (Pfeiffer, 1856). New Britain and New Ireland Ids., Bismarcks. Syntypes. Syn.: *lombei* of authors.

New Ireland Papuina (1") 2.5 cm
Papuina (M.) lambei subsp. *novohibernica* M. Smith, 1946. Kavieng, New Ireland. Paratypes.

Mahur Papuina (1") 2.5 cm
Papuina (M.) lambei forma *mahurensis* Rensch, 1934. Mahur Id., Papua New Guinea.

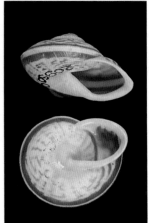

Lihir Papuina (1") 2.5 cm
Papuina (M.) lambei forma *lihirensis* Rensch, 1934. Mashet Id., Lahir Group, Bismarcks.

Purplish Papuina (1.3") 3 cm
Papuina (M.) rufopurpurea (E.A. Smith, 1887). Muswar Id., west New Guinea.

Tabar Papuina (1") 2.5 cm
Papuina (M.) tabarensis Rensch, 1933. Tabar Id., Bismarcks.

Warren's Papuina (1") 2.5 cm
Papuina (M.) tabarensis forma *warreni* Clench & Turner, 1964. Tanga Ids., Bismarcks. Paratypes.

Taumant Papuina (1.5") 4 cm
Papuina (Canefriula) taumantias (Tapparone-Canefri, 1883). Fly River area, S.W. New Guinea.

Frosty Papuina (1") 2.5 cm
Papuina (Papuina) gelata (Cox, 1873). Near Eddystone Id., Solomons. Syn.: *maddocksi* (Brazier, 1881).

Pileola Papuina (1") 2.5 cm
Papuina (Papuina) pileolus (Férussac, 1821). Batjan Id., Moluccas, Indonesia. Syn.: *parabolica* Jutting, 1959.

False Arrow Papuina
(1.2") 3 cm
Papuina (Papuina) pseudolanceolata Dautzenberg, 1903. Obi Id., Moluccas. Syn.: *callosa* Sykes, 1903.

Lufu Papuina (0.5") 1.2 cm
Papuina (Megalacron) lufensis Thiele, 1928. Hermit and Maty Ids., Bismarcks. Syn.: *lufuensis* authors.

Clearwater Papuina (1") 2.5 cm
Papuina (Megalacron) klaarwateri Rensch, 1931. Manus and Bundralis, Admiralty Ids. Common.

Chestnut Papuina (1.2") 3 cm
Papuina (Megalacron) spadicea Fulton, 1902. New Ireland, Bismarcks.

Banded Chestnut Papuina (1.2") 3 cm
Papuina (M.) spadicea subsp. *dunckeri* Leschke, 1912. Mussan Id., Bismarcks.

Exultant Papuina (1") 2.5 cm
Papuina (Papuina) exsultans (Tapparone-Canefri, 1883). Klagerik, Sorong, N.W. New Guinea. Photo by R.L. Goldberg.

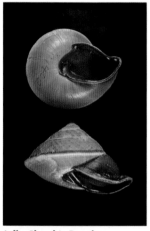

Julia Clench's Papuina (1.4") 3.3 cm
Papuina (Wahgia) juliae (Clench & Turner, 1959). Mt. Hagen Range, New Guinea. 5,000 ft. alt. Paratypes.

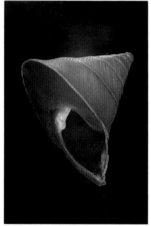

Hedley's Papuina (1.5") 4 cm
Papuina (Papuina) steursiana (Pfeiffer, 1853). Fak-Fak, West New Guinea. Syn.: *hedleyi* (E.A. Smith, 1892).

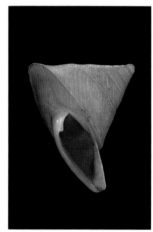

Hedley's Pale Papuina (1.5") 4 cm
Papuina (P.) steursiana forma *concolor* (E.A. Smith, 1897). Kapaur, S.W. New Guinea.

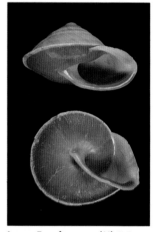

Lance Papuina (1") 2.5 cm
Papuina (Papuina) lanceolata (Pfeiffer, 1862). Ternate, Moluccas; Halmahera Id., Indonesia. Syn.: *pulchrizona* Sykes, 1904.

Subcostate Papuina (1") 2.5 cm
Papuina (Papuina) subcostata Fulton, 1916. Biak Id., West New Guinea.

Eddystone Papuina (0.7") 2 cm
Papuina (Smeatonia) eddystonensis (Reeve, 1854). Eddystone and Simbo Ids., Solomons. Type of subgenus. Syn.: *motacilla* E.A. Smith, 1885.

Goldie's Papuina (1.2") 3 cm
Papuina (Meliobba) goldiei (Brazier, 1881). Near Port Moresby, Papua New Guinea. Syn.: *oxystoma* (E.A. Smith, 1883).

Schaffery's Papuina (2.5") 6 cm
Papuina (Meliobba) schafferyi Iredale, 1940. Mt. Alexander Mossman, Qld., Australia. Paratypes. Type of subgenus.

Bühler's Papuina (1") 2.5 cm
Papuina (Forcartia) buehleri (Rensch, 1933). Manus and New Britain Ids., Admiralty Ids. Type of the subgenus. Common.

Brumer Island Papuina 3 cm
Papuina (Letitia) brumeriensis (Forbes, 1852). Brumer Id., Huon Gulf. Type of subgenus. Syn.: *comriei* Adams & Angas, 1876; *moturina* Iredale.

Zeno Papuina (1.6") 4 cm
Papuina (Letitia) zeno (Brazier, 1876). South half of Papua New Guinea. Syn.: *subglobosa* Fulton, 1902; *zeus* is misspelling.

Secans Papuina (1.6") 4 cm
Papuina (Letitia) secans Hedley, 1894. Collingswood Bay, Papua New Guinea.

Taylor's Papuina (1.3") 3.3 cm
Papuina (Rhynchotrochus) tayloriana (Adams & Reeve, 1850). Widespread in New Guinea. 16 forms or subspecies. Type of subgenus.

Taylor's Papuina (1.3") 3.3 cm
Papuina (Rhynch.) tayloriana (Adams & Reeve, 1850). New Guinea. Many color forms, Syn.: *dampierensis* Fulton, 1920; *monticolus* Iredale, 1941.

Taylor's Papuina (1.3") 3.3 cm
Papuina (Rhynch.) tayloriana (Adams & Reeve, 1850). Syntypes of *strabo* Brazier, 1876 from Gulf Division, Papua New Guinea.

White-keeled Papuina 2.5 cm
Papuina (Rhynch.) albocarinata (E.A. Smith, 1887). D'Entrecasteaux and Trobriand Ids. Syn.: *mysticus* Iredale, 1941; *trobriandensis* Hedley, 1891.

Pleasing Papuina (1") 2.5 cm
Papuina (Rhynch.) grata (Michelin, 1831). Port Dorey and Sorong Id., Papua New Guinea.

Shanty Papuina (1.2") 3 cm
Papuina (Rhynch.) gurgustii (Cox, 1879). Russell Id., Louisiade Ids.

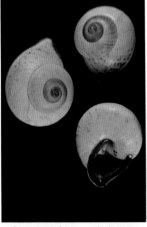

Kubary Papuina (1") 2.5 cm
Papuina (Rhynch.) kubaryi Moellendorff, 1895. Astrolabe Bay, Papua New Guinea (paratypes). Also Hollandia.

Kubary Papuina (1") 2.5 cm
Papuina (Rhynch.) kubaryi Moellendorff, 1895. Medang, Papua New Guinea. Syn.: *albina* Mlldff., 1895; *albida* Ancey, 1895; *albolabiata* Schepman, 1918.

Little Thomas Papuina
(1.5") 4 cm
Papuina (Canefriula) tomasinella (Tapparone-Canefri, 1883). S.W. Papua New Guinea.

Popondetta Papuina
(1.3") 3.5 cm
Papuina (Meliobba) popondetta (Clench & Turner, 1962). Buna-Popondetta region, N. New Guinea. Paratypes.

Ferussac's Cap Papuina
(1") 2.5 cm
Papuina (P.) pileolus (Férussac, 1821). Batjan Id., Moluccas, Indonesia.

Louisiades Papuina (1") 2.5 cm
Papuina (Rynch.) louisiadensis (Forbes, 1852). Sudest Id., Louisiade Ids., Coral Sea.

Cynthia's Papuina (1.1") 3 cm
Papuina (Canefriula) cynthia (Fulton, 1902). West New Guinea. Paratypes.

Hero Papuina (1.5") 4 cm
Papuina (Ryncho.) hero (E.A. Smith, 1891). Biak Id., Admiralty Ids.

Lintsch's Papuina (1.6") 4 cm
Papuina (Meliobba) lintschuana (Kobelt, 1894). Hollandia and Djamna Ids., north New Guinea.

Lance Papuina (1.3") 3.2 cm
Papuina (Papuina) lanceolata (Pfeiffer, 1862). North Moluccan islands. See again, p. 155.

Melanesian Papuina (1") 2.5 cm
Papuina (Megalacron) melanesia (Clench & Turner, 1964). Lorengau, Manus Id., Admiralty Ids. Paratypes.

Melanesian Papuina (1") 2.5 cm
Papuina (M.) melanesia (Clench & Turner, 1964). Manus Id., Admiralty Ids.

Yule Papuina (1") 2.5 cm
Papuina (Rynch.) tayloriana subsp. *yulensis* (Brazier, 1876). Yule Id., New Guinea.

Ogeramu Papuina (1") 2.4 cm
Papuina (Papuanella) ogeramuensis (Kobelt, 1914). Highlands of New Guinea. Type of Clench & Turner subgenus.

Pleasant Papuina (0.8") 2 cm
Papuina (Rhynchotrochus) jucunda Fulton, 1902. Papua New Guinea. Syn.: *caputserpentis* Kobelt, 1914.

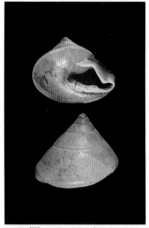

Macgillivray's Papuina (1") 2.5 cm
Papuina (Rhynch.) macgillivrayi (Forbes, 1852). North Queensland coast and Atherton, Australia.

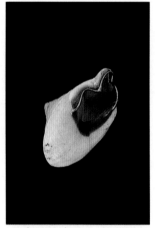

Meek's Pupuina (1.3") 3 cm
Papuina (Rhynch.) meekiana E.A. Smith, 1905. Owgarra, Owen Stanley Range, P.N.G., 8,000 ft. alt.

Misima Island Papuina (1") 2.6 cm
Papuina (Rhynch.) misima (Iredale, 1941). Misima Id., Louisiade Ids. Syn.: *thomsoni* E.A. Smith, 1889, paratypes.

Naso Papuina (1.3") 3.3 cm
Papuina (Rhynch.) naso (von Martens, 1883). Port Moresby area and Mt. Astrolabe, Papua New Guinea. Type of Iredale's name, *Pompalabia*.

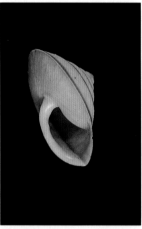

Pratt's Papuina (1") 2.5 cm
Papuina (Rhynch.) pratti Fulton, 1910. Muswar Id., West New Guinea. Syn.: *grata* Bavay, 1908.

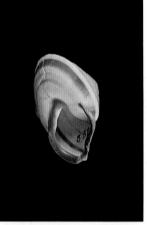

Snout Papuina (1") 2.5 cm
Papuina (Rhynch.) rhynchotus (Boettger, 1918). Wide Bay, New Britain. Syn.: *septentrionalis* Rensch & Rensch, 1929, paratype.

Rolls' Papuina (1.3") 3.3 cm
Papuina (Rhynch.) rollsiana (E.A. Smith, 1887). Ferguson Id., d'Entrecasteaux Ids. Syn.: *bartletti* Cotton, 1941.

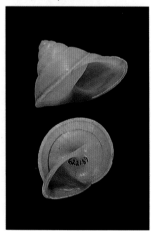

Trochus-shaped Papuina (1") 2.5 cm
Papuina (Rhynch.) trochiformis Preston, 1902. Biak Id., Schouten Ids. and Nunfoor Id., west New Guinea.

Wiegmann's Papuina (1") 2.5 cm
Papuina (Rhynch.) wiegmanni (von Martens, 1894). Umboi Id., and Siassi Ids., New Britain; Finschhafen, P.N.G. Syn.: *tuomensis* Ancey, 1895.

Williams' Papuina (1") 2.6 cm
Papuina (Rhynch.) williamsi Clench & Archer, 1936. Kiriwina Id., Trobriand Ids. Paratypes. Syn.: *atalanta* Clench, 1936, paratypes, banded.

Woodlark Papuina (0.8") 2 cm
Papuina (Rhynch.) woodlarkiana (Souverbie, 1863). Woodlark and Laughlan Ids., Woodlarks. Syn.: *deliciosus* Iredale, 1941.

Lands End Papuina (1") 2.2 cm
Papuina (Papuanella) finisterrensis (Kobelt, 1914). Gemeheng, Hubi, Huon Peninsula, P.N.G. 4,000 ft. alt.

Confirmed Papuina (0.6") 1.6 cm
Papuina (Rhytidoconcha) confirmata Rensch, 1933. Drabui and Lorengau, Manus Id., Admiralty Ids.

Aphrodite Crystal Snail
(1.2") 3 cm
Crystallopsis aphrodite (Pfeiffer, 1859). Ugi Id., Solomon Ids.

Rennell Crystal Snail
(1.2") 3 cm
Crystallopsis rennellensis Clench, 1958. Rennell Island, Solomon Ids. Paratypes.

Tricolor Crystal Snail
(1.2") 3 cm
Crystallopsis tricolor (Pfeiffer, 1850). Ugi Id., Solomon Ids. Syn.: *santaannae* Rensch, 1934.

Painted Crystal Snail
(1.2") 3 cm
Crystallopsis tricolor subsp. *picta* (E.A. Smith, 1885). San Cristoval Id., Solomons.

Fulakor Crystal Snail (1.2") 3 cm
Crystallopsis fulakarensis Clapp, 1923. Ysabel Id., Solomons. Top: holotype.

Hunter's Crystal Snail
(1") 2.5 cm
Crystallopsis hunteri (Cox, 1872). Guadalcanal Id., Solomons. Paratypes. Syn.:

Clench's Crystal Snail
(1") 2.5 cm
Crystallopsis crystallina Clench, 1958. Rennell Id., Solomons. Paratypes.

Paravicini Crystal Snail
(1") 2.5 cm
Crystallopsis purchasi (Pfeiffer, 1858) subsp. *paravicinii* Rensch, 1933. Auki, Malaita Id., Solomons. Paratypes.

Woodford's Crystal Snail
(0.8") 2 cm
Crystallopsis woodfordi (Sowerby, 1889). Russell and Guadalcanal Ids., Solomons.

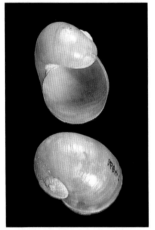

Pilsbry's Chloritis (1.4") 3 cm
Cryptaegis pilsbryi Clapp, 1923. San Cristoval Id., Solomons. Upper: holotype. Type of the genus.

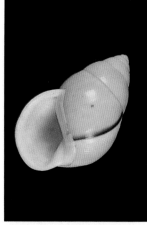

Perverse Amphidromus
(2") 5 cm
Amphidromus perversus (Linnaeus, 1758). Sumatra east to Bali, Indonesia. A dozen named color forms. Common.

Perverse Amphidromus
(2") 5 cm
Amphidromus perversus forma *interruptus* (Müller, 1774). Java. Purplish base; striped.

Perverse Amphidromus
(2") 5 cm
Amphidromus perversus subsp. *emaciatus* (von Martens, 1867). Java and Bali, Indonesia. May coil either direction.

Black-callus Amphidromus (2")
Amphidromus atricallosus (Gould, 1843). Malaya, Burma, south Thailand. Upper: forma *leucoxanthus* (von Martens, 1864).

Black-callus Amphidromus
(2") 5 cm
Amphidromus atricallosus forma (upper) *tener* von Martens, 1867; (lower) *perakensis* Fulton, 1901. Perak.

Laidlaw's Amphidromus
(2") 5 cm
Amphidromus atricallosus subsp. *laidlawi* Solem, 1965. Nong Yang, Thailand. Holotype below.

Cambodian Amphidromus
(3") 7 cm
Amphidromus cambojiensis (Reeve, 1860). North of Saigon, Viet Nam. (or Cambodia?) Lost species.

Dohrn's Amphidromus
(2") 5 cm
Amphidromus dohrni (Pfeiffer, 1863). Poulo-Condor off Viet Nam. Extinct? may be *perversus*.

Dyed Amphidromus (2") 5 cm
Amphidromus entobaptus (Dohrn, 1889). Palawan and Culion Ids., Philippines. Holotype of forma *culionensis* Bartsch, 1917.

Dyed Amphidromus (2") 5 cm
Amphidromus entobaptus (Dohrn, 1889). Culion Id., Philippines. Paratypes of *culionensis* Bartsch, 1917.

Annam Amphidromus (2") 5 cm
Amphidromus inversus (Müller, 1774). Cambodia; Thailand, Sumatra, Celebes. Forma *annamiticus* (Crosse & Fischer, 1863) from Cambodia.

Viet Nam Amphidromus
(1.5") 4 cm
Amphidromus metabletus Moellendorff, 1900. Bai Min Id. and Nha Trang, Viet Nam. Extinct?

Maculated Amphidromus 7 cm
Amphidromus maculiferus
(Sowerby, 1838). Mindanao;
Bohol; Basilan. Forma *multicolor*
Mlldff., 1893 from Leyte, Philippines.

Maculated Amphidromus
(3") 7 cm
Amphidromus maculiferus
(Sowerby, 1838). Over a dozen
named forms. This is paratype of
cotabatoensis Bartsch, 1917.

Schomburgk's Amphidromus
(1.5") 4 cm
Amphidromus schomburgki
(Pfeiffer, 1860). Thailand. Fairly
common.

Webb's Amphidromus (2") 5 cm
Amphidromus webbi Fulton,
1907. Nias Id. and Mentawi
Chain off Sumatra Id., Indonesia.
Syn.: *babiensis* Laidlaw, 1954.

Contrary Amphidromus 3 cm
Amphidromus (Syndromus) contrarius (Müller, 1774). Timor,
Rotti and Saman Ids., Indonesia.
Syn.: *hanieli* and *nikiensis*
Rensch, 1931.

Adam's Amphidromus
(1.3") 3 cm
Amphidromus (Synd.) adamsii
(Reeve, 1848). Borneo; Labuan
Ids., Indonesia. Syn.: *rubiginosus*
Fulton, 1896.

Columella Amphidromus
(1.2") 3 cm
Amphidromus (Synd.) columellaris Moellendorff, 1892. Seirah
Id. (paratypes) and Tenimber Id.,
Indonesia.

Flores Amphidromus
(1.2") 3 cm
Amphidromus (Synd.) floresianus
Fulton, 1897. South Flores and
Sumba Ids., Indonesia.

Gray-mouthed Amphidromus
(1.2") 3 cm
Amphidromus glaucolarynx
(Dohrn, 1861). Thailand and
Cambodia. Extinct? Syn.: *fasciatus* (von Martens, 1867) and
perrieri Rochebrune, 1882.

Painted Amphidromus
(1.2") 3 cm
Amphidromus (Synd.) pictus
Fulton, 1896. Mt. Kinabalu area,
N. Borneo.

Varicolored Amphidromus
(1.2") 3 cm
Amphidromus (Synd.) poecilochrous Fulton, 1896. Sumbawa
Id. and west Flores, Indonesia.
Syn.: *jaeckeli* Laidlaw, 1954.

Quadras' Amphidromus
(1.2") 3 cm
Amphidromus (Synd.) quadrasi
Hidalgo, 1887. Balabac, Palawan. Numerous color forms
described.

Everett's Amphidromus   3 cm
Amphidromus (Synd.) quadrasi
Hidalgo, 1887, subsp. *everetti*
Fulton, 1896. Palawan Id., Phil-
ippines. Syn.: *monticolus* Bartsch,
1918.

Versicolor Amphidromus
          (1.5") 3.6 cm
Amphidromus (Synd.) quadrasi
forma *versicolor* Fulton, 1896.
Balabac Id., Philippines.

Chinese Amphidromus
          (1.3") 3 cm
Amphidromus (Synd.) sinensis
(Benson, 1851). Chittagong,
Pakistan; Pegu, Burma. Extinct?

Umbilicate Amphidromus
          (1.3") 3 cm
Amphidromus (Synd.) sinistralis
(Reeve, 1849). Northern penin-
sula of Celebes Id., Indonesia.
Syn.: *decolor* Tap.-Can., 1884.

Sumatran Amphidromus
          (1.3") 3 cm
*Amphidromus (Synd.) suma-
tranus* von Martens, 1864. Nias,
Sumatra, Indonesia. Lined form
is *sowerbyi* Fulton, 1907.

Ventrose Amphidromus
          (1.2") 3 cm
*Amphidromus (Synd.) ventro-
sulus* Moellendorff, 1900. Phuc-
son, Viet Nam. Topotypes.

Xieng Amphidromus (1.2") 3 cm
*Amphidromus (Synd.) xiengen-
sis* Morelet, 1891. Laos, Cambodia and N. Thailand. Syn.: *clausus* Pilsbry, 1900 (paratypes).

Engano Amphidromus
          (1.3") 3.5 cm
Amphidromus enganoensis Fulton, 1896 forma *fruhstorferi* Laidlaw, 1954. (Syn.: *gracilior* Fruhst;
non Fulton). Dua Id., Indonesia.

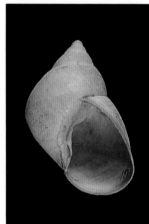

Crystalline Cup Snail (2") 5 cm
Calycia crystallina (Reeve, 1848).
Widespread in New Guinea and
Waigeu Id. Type of the genus.
Syn.: *nigrescens* Fulton, 1910, is
brown with white lines.

Family **XANTHONYCIDAE**
(Helminthoglyptidae)

This New World diverse
group of small- to medium-
sized snails have no teeth in
the shell aperture, and are
generally globose to de-
pressed. There are 8 subfamilies, such as the Cepolinae
(*Hemitrochus*) and the colorful Cuban *Polymita* (Helminthoglyptinae) and the
Sonorellinae of Western North
America.

Variable Cepolis   (0.5") 1.2 cm
Hemitrochus varians (Menke,
1829). Bahamas and Florida Keys.
Abundant on shrubs near shore.
Photo by R. Robertson.

Variable Cepolis   (0.5") 1.2 cm
Hemitrochus varians (Menke,
1829). Bahamas and Florida Keys.
Type of the genus.

Best known is the typical inch-long Painted Polymita, *Polymita picta* (Born, 1778). It is the largest and most fragile of the Oriente species. Professor de la Torre described this quite common form as *iofasciata*. Note the dark, wide border around the base of the columella.

In the flat, high plains to the northeast of Santiago de Cuba one can find this bright yellow and red striped species, *Polymita venusta* (Gmelin, 1791). They live 10-25 feet above ground, and are more active at night. An all-russet-red form occurs in the Sierra Maestra.

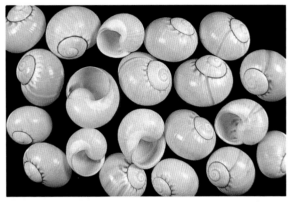

The smaller and thicker-shelled Sulfur Polymita, *Polymita sulphurosa* (Morelet, 1849), exhibits many color variations within the same colony. The original form was completely yellow. These are color types of the color form *flammulata* Torre, 1950. All natural size.

The hills along the southern coast of Oriente Province are the home of the Sulphur Polymita. These delicately-hued Lilac Polymitas are paratypes from the original lot described in 1950 by Dr. de la Torre as *violacea*. Note the oblique "flames" of color in this species.

The Fly-specked Polymita is characterized by a pinkish base and minute blackish fly-specks scattered over the outside of the shell. Although *muscarum* Lea, 1834, is the usual name applied to this species from Banes, Cuba, the earlier name *globulosa* (Férussac, 1821) should probably be used.

Brochero's Polymita from the Cape Maisi region of Oriente was named *brocheri* after General Gregorio Brochero by Pfeiffer in 1864. These are paratypes of Torre's color form *cuestana* which has a pink columella. Arango in 1878 amended the name to *brocheroi*.

Painted Polymita   (1") 2.5 cm
Polymita picta (Born, 1778) color
form *fuscolimbata* Torre, 1950.
Columella and subsutural band
brown. Baracoa region of Oriente, Cuba. Paratypes.

Painted Polymita   (1") 2.5 cm
Polymita picta (Born, 1778) color
muscata Torre, 1950. Jauco, near
Baracoa, Oriente. Note scattered
black dots. Uncommon. See also
subspecies *muscarum*. Paratypes.

Painted Polymita   (1") 2.5 cm
Polymita picta (Born, 1778) color
form *dimidiata* Torre, 1950.
Northern Oriente Province.
Upper part dark, lower part light.
Paratypes.

Painted Polymita   (1") 2.5 cm
Polymita picta (Born, 1778) color
form *obscurata* Torre, 1950.
Northern Oriente. Black all over
with white spiral bands. Paratypes.

Painted Polymita   (1") 2.5 cm
Polymita picta (Born, 1778) color
form *multifasciata* Torre, 1950.
Playa Blanca, Oriente. Narrow
spiral bands. Paratypes.

Painted Polymita   (1") 2.5 cm
Polymita picta (Born, 1778) color
form *iolimbata* Torre, 1950. Cape
Maisi to Baracoa. Aperture interior purplish. Tan forms are rare.

Painted Polymita   (1") 2.5 cm
Polymita picta (Born, 1778).
Northeast coast of Oriente Province. This is the typical form of
picta. The black growth line may
be present or absent.

Painted Polymita   (1") 2.5 cm
Polymita picta (Born, 1778). N.E.
coast of Oriente Province. Paratypes of *nigrofasciata* Torre, 1950.
Background is light yellow. Black
growth stoppages absent.

Painted Polymita   (1") 2.5 cm
Polymita picta (Born, 1778) color
form *nigrofasciata* Torre, 1950.
Background orange-yellow, with
one or two black bands, with
white between.

Painted Polymita   (1") 2.5 cm
Polymita picta (Born, 1778) color
form *roseolimbata* Torre, 1950.
N.E. Oriente. Upper left, typical;
upper center, *albolimbata* Torre;
upper right, form *minor* Torre.

Painted Polymita   (1") 2.5 cm
Polymita venusta (Gmelin, 1791).
Holguin and Mayari, Oriente.
Color form *olivacea* Torre, 1950.
Note reddish subsutural band.
Growth break white or red.

Varicolored Polymita
                    (0.8") 2 cm
Polymita versicolor (Born, 1778).
Southeast Oriente, Cuba. Com-
mon on low bushes.

Sulfur Polymita (0.8") 2 cm
Polymita sulphurosa (Morelet, 1849) forma flammulata Torre, 1950. Northeast Oriente Prov., Cuba. Subform *rubra* Torre, 1950.

Violet Polymita (0.8") 2 cm
Polymita sulphurosa (Morelet, 1849) forma *viridis* Torre, 1950. Oriente Prov., Cuba. Paratypes.

Alabaster Polymita (0.8") 2 cm
Polymita sulphurosa (Morelet, 1849) forma *albida* Torre, 1950. Oriente Prov., Cuba. Paratypes.

Ovando's Polymita (0.9") 2 cm
Polymita (Oligomita) brocheroi (Pfeiffer, 1864) forma *ovandoi* Torre, 1950. Mesa de Ovando, Oriente Prov., Cuba. Paratypes.

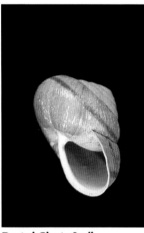

Dented Glypta Snail
(1.5") 3.5 cm
Helminthoglypta arrosa (W.G. Binney, 1855). West coast of California north of Santa Cruz. About 9 subspecies recognized.

Cypress Glypta Snail (1.2") 3 cm
Helminthoglypta dupetithouarsi (Deshayes, 1840). Monterey Co., Calif. Beneath cypress logs.

Trask's Glypta Snail (1") 2.6 cm
Helminthoglypta (Charodotes) traskii (Newcomb, 1861). Ventura, Kern and Santa Barbara Co., Calif. 9 minor subspecies.

Umbilicate Glypta Snail
(1") 2.6 cm
Helminthoglypta umbilicata (Pilsbry, 1897). Monterey, San Luis Obispo, Santa Barbara Co., Calif. Near ocean. Common.

Closed Fragmopha Snail
(1.3") 3 cm
Epiphragmophora (Pilsbrya) clausomphalos (Deville & Hupé, 1850). Tarma, Peru Andes. 3,000 meters alt.

Punta Fragmopha Snail
(1.2") 2.5 cm
Epiphragmophora puntana (Homberg, 1912). Cordoba, San Luis Distr., Argentina.

Three-haired Fragmopha
(1.2") 2.5 cm
Epiphragmophora trigammephora (Orbigny, 1835). S. Bolivia and Salta, N.W. Argentina.

Santa Rita Sonorelle
(0.9") 2.3 cm
Sonorella santaritana Pilsbry & Ferris, 1910. Canyons of Santa Rita Mts., Arizona. 6,000 ft. alt. Many species in Southwest.

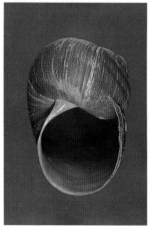

Buffon's Humboldt Snail
(1.3") 3.5 cm
Humboldtiana nuevoleonis
Pilsbry, 1927. Monterey, Nuevo
Leon, Mexico. Syn.: *buffoniana*
(Pfeiffer, 1845).

Granulated Humboldt Snail
(1.6") 4 cm
Humboldtiana pergranulosa
Solem, 1955. San José Range,
Durango, Mexico. Holotype.

Montezuma Humboldt Snail
(2.5") 6 cm
Humboldtiana montezuma
Pilsbry, 1940. Top of El Infer-
nillo, 10,000 ft., Nuevo Leon,
Mexico. Holotype.

Faithful Monadenia Snail
(1.5") 3.6 cm
Monadenia fidelis (Gray, 1834).
British Columbia to northern
Calif. Common; sometimes ar-
boreal. Type of genus.

Smoked Monadenia (1.5") 4 cm
Monadenia infumata (Gould,
1855). Arboreal; Humboldt to
Marin Co., California.

Kellett's Arionta Snail
(1.2") 3 cm
Micrarionta (Xerarionta) kelletti
(Forbes, 1850). Santa Catalina
Id., and Los Angeles Co., Calif.
Common.

Family BRADYBAENIDAE

This is a widely dispersed
family of ground and tree
snails, mainly confined to the
tropics and warmer temperate regions. There are over 80
genera and subgenera con-
tained in two subfamilies, the
most famous being the large,
colorful tree snails of the Philippines (Helicostylinae). The
Bradybaeninae of Europe and
east Asia are smaller and less
colorful. Most lay eggs, but a
few, such as *Euhadra* are ovoviviparous. Some, like
Bradybaena similaris are agricultural pests.

Common Bush Snail (0.7") 2 cm
Bradybaena similaris (Férussac,
1821). Worldwide tropics; pest
in coffee plantations and in trash
areas. 16 synonyms known.

Fruticose Bush Snail
(0.7") 2 cm
Bradybaena fruticum (Müller,
1774). Central Europe. Damp
edges of woods. Common. Horticultural nuisance.

Sought-after False Hadra
(1.5") 3.5 cm
Euhadra quaesita (Deshayes,
1851). Honshu Id., Japan.

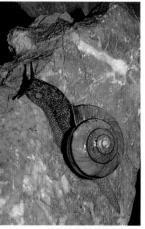

Sought-after False Hadra
(1.5") 3.5 cm
Euhadra quaesita (Deshayes,
1851). Honshu Id., Japan. Photo
by Sadao Azuma.

Perry's False Hadra
(1.5") 3.5 cm
Euhadra quaesita (Deshayes,
1851) forma *perryi* Jay, 1856.
Yedo, Japan. Holotype on left,
Amer. Mus. Nat. Hist.

Subfamily
HELICOSTYLINAE

There are about 290 species of these large, colorful tree snails of the Philippines, many of which have become extinct because of the destruction of thousands of square miles of forests. We illustrate 260 species and named forms. Of the 600 names proposed, the valid ones belong to the genera *Chloraea* (51), *Calocochlia* (72), *Helicostyla* (128), *Chrysallis* (22), *Phoenicobius* (11), *Canistrum* (5), *Steatodryas* (1), *Mesanella* (2) and *Phengus* (2). Some lay eggs in the earth, others enwrap them in leaves in the trees.

Siren Chlorea (1") 2.5 cm
Chloraea sirena (Pfeiffer, 1845). Guimaras, Panay, and Romblon and Mindanao Ids. Syntypes from Hugh Cuming.

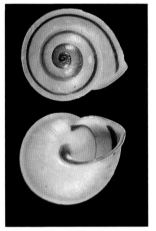

Woodpecker Chlorea (1.2") 3 cm
Chloraea dryope (Broderip, 1841). Romblon, Luzon, Tablas and Sibuyan Ids., Philippines.

Buckle Chlorea (0.7") 2 cm
Chloraea fibula (Reeve, 1842). Ronda, Cebu Id.; Lubang; Marinduque Ids., Philippines.

Paradox Chlorea (1") 2.3 cm
Chloraea paradoxa (Pfeiffer, 1845). Sorsogon area, Luzon, Philippines. Syntypes from H. Cuming.

Audacious Chlorea (1.3") 3 cm
Chloraea thersites (Broderip, 1841). Calapan, Mindoro Id. Upper right: holotype of *vigoensis* Clench & Archer, 1933.

Papery Corasia (1") 2.5 cm
Chloraea (Corasia) papyracea (Broderip, 1841). Mayabig, Mindoro Id., Philippines.

Regal Corasia (1") 2.6 cm
Chloraea smaragdina (Grateloup, 1840). Virac, Catanduanes; N.E. Luzon, Philippines. Rare. Syn.: *reginae* (Broderip, 1841); *caerula* (Mlldff.).

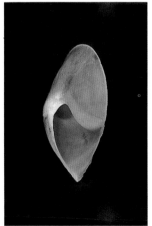

Regal Corasia (1") 2.5 cm
Chloraea (Corasia) smaragdina (Grateloup, 1840). Catanduanes; Luzon, Philippines. May be extinct.

Regal Corasia (1") 2.5 cm
Chloraea (Corasia) smaragdina (Grateloup, 1840). Morong, Luzon Id., Philippines. Syntype of *caerula* (Moellendorff, 1890).

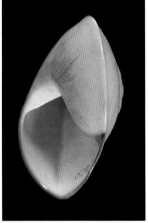

Virgin Corasia (1.5") 4 cm
Chloraea (Corasia) virgo (Broderip, 1841). Negros and Cebu Ids., Philippines.

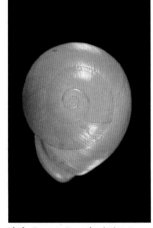

Little Parrot Corasia (1") 2.5 cm
Chloraea (Corasia) psittacina (Deshayes, 1861). Cagayan Prov., N. Luzon, Philippines.

Little Parrot Corasia (1") 2.5 cm
Chloraea (Corasia) psittacina
(Deshayes, 1861). Luzon, Philippines. Syn.: *laurae* Gude, 1896.

Girl Chlorea   (1") 2.5 cm
Chloraea (Corasia) puella (Broderip, 1841). Karakelong Id., Talaud Group, Moluccas Ids. Syn.: *subpuella* (Pilsbry, 1891).

Fragile Chlorea   (1.5") 3.8 cm
Chloraea (Leytia) fragilis (Sowerby, 1841). Leyte Id. Extinct?
Syn.: *leytensis* (Pfeiffer, 1846).

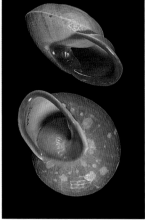

Fire-mouth Tree Snail (3") 7 cm
Calocochlia (Pyrochilus) pyrostoma (Férussac, 1821). Halmahera and Moluccas, Indonesia. Type of subgenus. *Calocochlea* is misspelling.

Cebu Anixa Snail   (1.5") 3.8 cm
Calocochlia (Anixa) zebuensis
(Broderip, 1841). Western Cebu Id. Type of subgenus. Extinct?

Striated Anixa Snail (1.3") 3 cm
Calocochlia (Anixa) zebuensis
(Broderip, 1841) subspecies *striatissima* Pilsbry, 1892 from Cebu. Extinct?

Garibaldi's Anixa Snail
                       (3") 7.5 cm
Calocochlia (Anixa) garibaldiana
(Dohrn & Semper, 1862). Northern Luzon Id., Philippines.

Siquijor Anixa Snail (1.7") 4 cm
Calocochlia (Anixa) siquijorensis (Broderip, 1841). Siquijor Id., Philippines. Syntypes from Hugh Cuming.

Charcoal Anixa Snail (1.3") 3 cm
Calocochlia (Anixa) carbonaria
(Sowerby, 1842). Cebu Id., Philippines. Syntypes from H. Cuming. Extinct?

Cuming's Anixa Snail
                       (1.5") 3.5 cm
Calocochlia (Anixa) cumingii
(Pfeiffer, 1842). Dalaguete, west Cebu, Philippines. Extinct? Syntypes.

Pfeiffer's Anixa Snail
                         (1.3") 3 cm
Calocochlia (Anixa) cumingii
forma *pfeifferi* Semper, 1877. Rhonda, Cebu, Philippines. Extinct?

Master Anixa Snail   (2") 5 cm
Calocochlia (Anixa) magistra
(Pfeiffer, 1852). Cebu, Philippines. Forma *gloynei* Sowerby, 1889.

Gloyne's Anixa Snail   (2") 5 cm
Calocochlia (Anixa) magistra forma *gloynei* (Sowerby, 1889). Cebu Id., Philippines.

Schadenberg's Anixa Snail
            (2.4") 6 cm
Calocochlia (Anixa) schadenbergi (Moellendorff, 1890). Makabenga, Luzon Id. Holotype of syn.: *ilongata* (Bartsch, 1919).

Schadenberg's Anixa Snail
            (2.4") 6 cm
Calocochlia (Anixa) schadenbergi (Moellendorff, 1890). Ventral view of Bartsch's holotype of *ilongata*.

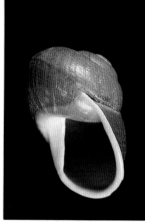

Cryptic Calocochlia (2.5") 6 cm
Calocochlia (Trachystyla) cryptica (Broderip, 1841). Calbayoc, Samar Id. Type of Pilslbry's subgenus.

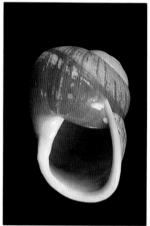

Similar Calocochlia (2.5") 6 cm
Calocochlia (T.) cryptica forma *cretata* (Broderip, 1841). Leyte and Mindanao Ids., Philippines.

Ashy Calocochlia   (2.5") 6 cm
Calocochlia (T.) cryptica forma *cineracea* (Semper, 1877). Mt. Davao, Mindanao Id., Philippines.

Propitious Anixa Snail
            (1.4") 3.3 cm
Calocochlia (Anixa) propitia (Fulton, 1907). Cebu Id., Philippines. Extinct?

Bruguiere's Anixa Snail
            (1.5") 3.5 cm
Calocochlia (Anixa) bruguieriana (Pfeiffer, 1845). Tablas Id., Philippines.

Most Beautiful Calocochlia
            (2") 5 cm
Calocochlia pulcherrima (Sowerby, 1841). Cagayan Prov., N. Luzon Id. Type of the genus. Syn.: *Calocochlea*.

Most Beautiful Calocochlia
            (2") 5 cm
Calocochlia pulcherrima (Sowerby, 1841). forma *luzonica* (Sowerby, 1842). Cagayan Prov., N. Luzon Id., Philippines.

Albay Calocochlia (1.5") 3.8 cm
Calocochlia albaiensis (Sowerby, 1841). Albay Prov., S. Luzon Id., Philippines.

Cailliaud's Calocochlia
            (1.8") 4.5 cm
Calocochlia cailliaudi (Deshayes, 1839). Camaruan, Luzon Id., Philippines. Extinct?

Persimilis Calocochlia   4 cm
Calocochlia persimilis Férussac,
1850. Luzon Id. Upper: forma
callipepla Bartsch, 1930. Lower:
callimorpha Bartsch, 1930.
Holotypes.

Bohol Calocochlia (2.3") 5.5 cm
Calocochlia chlorochroa (Sowerby, 1841). Bohol Id., Philippines. Extinct?

Golden Calocochlia
             (1.8") 4 cm
Calocochlia chrysocheila (Sowerby, 1841). Northern Luzon Id.,
Philippines. Sometimes greenish
yellow.

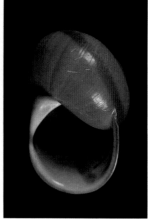

Scarlet-banded Calocochlia
             (2") 5 cm
Calocochlia coccomelos (Sow-
erby, 1841). Tablas and Sibuyan
Ids., Philippines.

Coronado Calocochlia
             (1.4") 3 cm
Calocochlia coronadoi (Hidalgo,
1868). Leyte Id., Philippines. Also
Catanduanes?

Coronado Calocochlia (2") 5 cm
Calocochlia coronadoi (Hidalgo,
1868). Catanduanes Id. form.

Datta Calocochlia (1.7") 4.5 cm
Calocochlia dattaensis (Semper,
1866). Mount Datta, Luzon Id.,
Philippines.

Festive Calocochlia   (2") 5 cm
Calocochlia festiva (Donovan,
1825). Cagayan Prov., Luzon,
Philippines. Syn.: *annae* Semper,
1862.

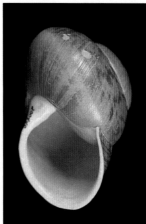

Harford's Calocochlia
             (3.3") 8 cm
Calocochlia harfordi (Broderip,
1841). Negros Id. Possible
syntype from John Jay collection,
AMNH.

Twisted Calocochlia (1") 2.5 cm
Calocochlia intorta (Sowerby,
1841). Negros, Tablas, Panay,
Cebu Ids. Syn.: *difficilis* Pfeiffer,
1853.

Majayjay Calocochlia   4 cm
Calocochlia submirabilis (Mlldff.,
1897) forma *majayjay* Bartsch,
1930. Below: forma *daranga*
Bartsch, 1930. Both holotypes.
Luzon Id.

Matrix Calocochlia (1.4") 3.3 cm
Calocochlia matruelis (Sowerby,
1841). Mindanao Id., Philippines.

Brown-mouthed Calocochlia
(1.6") 4 cm
Calocochlia melanocheila (Valenciennes in Grateloup, 1840). Calapan, Mindoro Id., Philippines.

Mindanao Calocochlia
(1.2") 3 cm
Calocochlia mindanaensis (Sowerby, 1842). Mindanao Id., Philippines.

Norris' Calocochlia (2.1") 5 cm
Calocochlia norrisii Sowerby, 1842 (also Pfeiffer, 1842). Catanduanes Id., Philippines.

Pan Calocochlia (2") 5 cm
Calocochlia pan (Broderip, 1841). Bohol Id., Philippines.

Very Pallid Calocochlia
(2.3") 6 cm
Calocochlia perpallida Bartsch, 1932. Tubukala, Mindoro Id. Holotype.

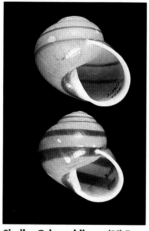

Similar Calocochlia (2") 5 cm
Calocochlia persimilis forma *podagra* Bartsch, 1930. Below: forma *boacana* Bartsch, 1930. Holotypes (syn.: *crassa* Mlldff.). Luzon.

Roissy's Calocochlia
(1.5") 3.8 cm
Calocochlia roissyana (Férussac, 1821). Mindoro Id. Syn.: *cavitala, laymansa, manlaysa* Bartsch, 1932.

Bartsch's Calocochlia
(1.5") 3.8 cm
Calocochlia roissyana (Férussac, 1821) forma *bartschi* Clench & Archer, in Bartsch, 1932. Paratype.

Cavitala Calocochlia 4.5 cm
Calocochlia roissyana forma *cavitala* Bartsch, 1932. Holotype. Below: *fulgens* Sowerby, 1841, forma *sapolana* Bartsch, 1932. Holotype. Mindoro Id.

Sarangan Calocochlia
(1") 2.5 cm
Calocochlia saranganica Hidalgo, 1887. Sarangani and Balut Ids., southern Philippines.

Dautzenberg's Calocochlia
(1.7") 4.5 cm
Calocochlia semperi (Moellendorff, 1893) forma *dautzenbergi* Hidalgo, 1901. Luzon and Palawan.

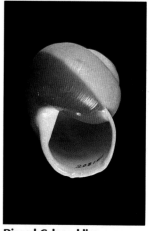

Dipped Calocochlia
(1.5") 3.5 cm
Calocochlia sphaerion (Sowerby, 1841). Leyte Id. Syn.: forma *meridionalis* Mlldff., 1893.

Antimonan Calocochlia
(2.2") 5 cm
Calocochlia submirabilis(Mlldff., 1897) forma *antimonana* Bartsch, 1930. Tayabas Prov., Luzon. Holotype.

Tukan Calocochlia (1.5") 3.8 cm
Calocochlia tukanensis (Pfeiffer, 1871). Tular Id., Talaud Ids. Moluccas, Indonesia.

Tukan Calocochlia (1.5") 3.8 cm
Calocochlia tukanensis (Pfeiffer, 1871). Karakelong Id., Celebes, Indonesia. With periostracum.

Valenciennes' Calocochlia
(1.5") 3.8 cm
Calocochlia valenciennesii (Eydoux, 1838). Northern Mindanao Id., Philippines. Syn.: *crymodes* (Pfeiffer, 1842).

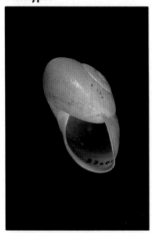

Weber's Calocochlia
(1.4") 3.7 cm
Calocochlia weberi Bartsch, 1919. Candaraman Id., Palawan, Philippines. Holotype.

Zoned Calocochlia (1.7") 4 cm
Calocochlia zonifera (Sowerby, 1842). Central Philippines. Syntype from H. Cuming.

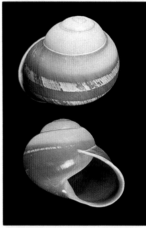

Circe Calocochlia (1.5") 3 cm
Calocochlia zonifera subsp. *circe* (Pfeiffer, 1853). South Samar Id., Philippines.

Nearly-white Calocochlia
(1.4") 3 cm
Calocochlia zonifera forma *paraleuca* (Pilsbry, 1892). Central Philippines. Paratypes.

Globose Calocochlia (2") 5 cm
Calocochlia zonifera forma *globosa* (Kobelt, 1910). Parvav, Samar, Philippines. Paratypes.

Livid-sutured Chlorea
(1") 2.5 cm
Chloraea (Chromatosphaera) lividocincta (Semper, 1877). Tayabas, Luzon Id., Philippines

Mountain Helicostyla 2 cm
Helicostyla (Orustia) monticula (Sowerby, 1841). Cagayan, N. Luzon Id., Philippines. Type of the subgenus.

Butler's Helicostyla
(1") 2.5 cm
Helicostyla (Orustia) butleri (Pfeiffer, 1842). Trinidad, N. Luzon Id., Philippines.

Gravid Helicostyla (1") 2.5 cm
Helicostyla (Orustia) butleri subspecies *gravida* (Kobelt, 1910). Mt. Tirac, Tiagen, Luzon Id., Philippines. Topotypes.

Short Helicostyla (1.2") 3 cm
Helicostyla curta (Sowerby, 1841). La Union, Luzon, Philippines. *Cochlostyla* Férussac, 1821, is syn. of *Helicostyla* Férussac, 1821.

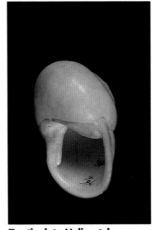

Denticulate Helicostyla
(1.3") 3 cm
Helicostyla denticulata (Jay, 1839). Philippines. Holotype from Amer. Mus. Nat. His., N.Y.

Two-part Helicostyla
(1.2") 3 cm
Helicostyla (Orustia) dimera (Jonas, 1846). Tablas and Luzon Ids., Philippines.

Spherical Helicostyla (1") 2.5 cm
Helicostyla (Pachysphaera) sphaerica (Sowerby, 1841). Ilocos Sur Prov., Luzon Id. Type of subgenus.

Annulated Helicostyla 2.5 cm
Helicostyla (Pachy.) annulata (Sowerby, 1841). Ilocos Norte Prov., Luzon Id. Syn.: *fugensis* Bartsch, 1909, paratypes from Fuga Id.

Girdled Helicostyla (1") 2.5 cm
Helicostyla (Pachy.) balteata (Sowerby, 1841). Ilocos Sur, Luzon Id., Philippines.

Fenestrate Helicostyla
(0.9") 2 cm
Helicostyla (Pachy.) fenestrata (Sowerby, 1841). Morong District, Luzon Id., Philippines. Considered an *Orustia* by some.

Ilocos Helicostyla (1") 2.5 cm
Helicostyla (Pachy.) iloconensis (Sowerby, 1841). Ilocos Sur Prov., Luzon Id., Philippines.

Dusky Helicostyla (1.5") 4 cm
Helicostyla (Orustia) leucophaea (Sowerby, 1841). Bataan, Luzon, Philippines.

Dusky Helicostyla (2.5") 5 cm
Helicostyla (O.) leucophaea forma *subfenestrata* Mlldff., 1898. Syntype from Tiagen, Luzon.

Miraculous Helicostyla 4 cm
Helicostyla (H.) mirabilis (Férussac, 1821). Albay Prov., Luzon Id. Type of the genus. Syn.: *donsalana* Bartsch, 1918.

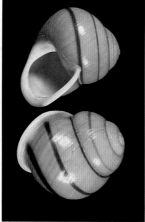

Donsalan Helicostyla (1.5") 4 cm
Helicostyla (H.) mirabilis (Férussac, 1821) forma *donsalana* (Bartsch, 1918). Sorsogon, Luzon Id. Paratypes.

Damahoy's Calocochlia (2.1") 5 cm
Calocochlia damahoyi (Pfeiffer, 1856). Philippines. May be form of *zonifera* (Sowerby).

Dubious Helicostyla (1.2") 3 cm
Helicostyla (H.) dubiosa (Pfeiffer, 1846). Tayabas Prov., Luzon Id. Syn.: *batanica* Reeve, 1851.

Capul Helicostyla (1.5") 3.5 cm
Helicostyla dubiosa subsp. *capulensis* Bartsch, 1930. Capul, Luzon Id. Holotype illus.

Dubious Helicostyla (1.2") 3 cm
Helicostyla dubiosa (Pfeiffer, 1846). Tayabas Prov., Luzon Id. Syn.: *speciosa* Jay, 1839 (holotype), non Ziegler, 1838.

Shining Helicostyla (1.2") 3 cm
Helicostyla (H.) fulgens (Broderip, 1841). Calapan, Mindoro Id., Philippines.

Leopard Helicostyla (2.5") 6 cm
Helicostyla (H.) leopardus (Pfeiffer, 1845). Camarines Prov., Luzon Id.

Leopard Helicostyla (2") 5 cm
Helicostyla (H.) leopardus (Pfeiffer, 1845). Below: forma *meladryas* T. McGinty, 1934, paratypes; above: forma *codenensis* Hidalgo, 1888.

Leopard Helicostyla (2") 5 cm
Helicostyla (H.) leopardus (Pfeiffer, 1845). Catanduanes Id. Paratypes of form *meladryas* T. McGinty, 1934.

Polillo Helicostyla (2") 5 cm
Helicostyla (H.) polillensis (Pfeiffer, 1861). Polillo Island east side of Luzon. Considered a *Calocochlia* by some workers.

Green-streaked Helicostyla (2") 5 cm
Helicostyla (Cochlodryas) viridostriata (Lea, 1840). Burias Id., Philippines. Type of the subgenus.

Many-colored Helicostyla 5 cm
Helicostyla (C.) viridostriata forma *polychroa* (Sowerby, 1841). Temple Id., Philippines. Syntypes from H. Cuming.

Flowery Helicostyla
(1.5") 3.8 cm
Helicostyla (Cochlodryas) florida
(Sowerby, 1841). Mindoro Id.
Syntypes from H. Cuming.

Flowery Helicostyla
(1.5") 3.8 cm
Helicostyla (Cochlodryas) florida
(Sowerby, 1841). White-lipped.
Mindoro Id., Philippines. (Syn.:
helicoides Pfr. 1849).

Flowery Helicostyla 3.8 cm
Helicostyla (C.) florida (Sowerby,
1841). Upper: forma *aureola*
Bartsch, 1932; lower: forma *signa*
Bartsch, 1932. Holotypes. Min-
doro.

Sibolon Helicostyla
(1.2") 3 cm
Helicostyla (C.) mateoi (Bartsch,
1932). Mindoro. Forma
sibolonensis Bartsch, 1932.
Holotype.

Mateo Helicostyla (1.2") 3 cm
Helicostyla (Cochlodryas) mateoi
(Bartsch, 1932). Caluga Id.,
Mindoro. Paratypes. Syn.: *tenera*
Sow., non Gmelin.

Little Wheel Helicostyla
(1") 2.5 cm
*Helicostyla (Cochlodryas) orbit-
ula* (Sowerby, 1841). Mindoro
Id., Philippines.

Effusive Helicostyla
(1.5") 3.8 cm
Helicostyla (Opalliostyla) effusa
(Pfeiffer, 1842). Sibuyan Id. Syn.:
buschi Pfeiffer (syntype below);
leai Pfr., 1846.

Effusive Helicostyla
(1.5") 3.8 cm
Helicostyla (O.) effusa (Pfeiffer,
1842). Batanes Id., Philippines.
Syn.: *buschi* & *leai* Pfeiffer, 1846.

Sickly Helicostyla (2") 5 cm
Helicostyla (Opall.) aegle (Brod-
erip, 1841). Mindanao Id.
Syntypes.

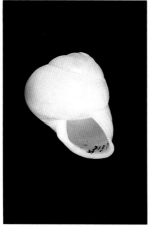

Canonizado's Helicostyla
(1.1") 2.7 cm
Helicostyla canonizadoi (Bartsch,
1932). Polillo Id., Philippines.
Holotype.

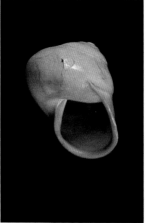

Sea-green Helicostyla
(1.5") 3.8 cm
Helicostyla (O.) halichlora
(Semper, 1866). Calayan, Luzon
Id. Paratype from Semper.

Ignoble Helicostyla
(1.5") 3.8 cm
Helicostyla (Opall.) ignobilis
Sowerby, 1841. Cuyo Id., Palawan, Philippines.

Lacerated Helicostyla 4.3 cm
Helicostyla (Opall.) lacerata
(Semper, 1877). Kapalong,
Davao, Mindanao Id., Philippines. Syn.: *paradoxa* Semper,
1877.

Brown-striped Helicostyla
(1.3") 3.4 cm
Helicostyla (Opall.) phaeostyla
(Pfeiffer, 1856). Philippines.

Simple Helicostyla (1") 2.5 cm
Helicostyla (Opall.) simplex
(Jonas, 1843). Romblon Id.
Syntype from H. Cuming. Syn.:
cossmanniana Crosse, 1886
(chocolate form).

Quadras' Simple Helicostyla
(1") 2.5 cm
Helicostyla (Opall.) simplex
(Jonas, 1843) subsp. *quadrasi*
(Hidalgo, 1886). Torrijos Mt.,
Marinduque Id.

Emerald Helicostyla (2.5") 6 cm
Helicostyla (Opall.) smaragdina
(Reeve, 1842). Lianga, eastern
Mindanao Id. Syntypes.

Yellow Helicostyla (2.5") 6 cm
Helicostyla (Opall.) smaragdina
subspecies *lutea* Semper, 1877.
Agusan, Mindanao Id. Paratype.

Blackened Helicostyla
(2.5") 6 cm
Helicostyla (Opalliostyla) smaragdina forma *nigrescens* (Semper, 1877). Mindanao Id., Philippines. Paratype.

Fleshy Helicostyla (3.5") 8.5 cm
*Helicostyla (Helicobulina)
sarcinosa* (Férussac, 1821). Masbate Id. Type of subgenus (syn.:
Helicobulimus).

Turgid Helicostyla (3") 7.4 cm
Helicostyla (Helicob.) sarcinosa
subsp. *turgens* (Deshayes, 1850).
Guimaras Id., Panay Id., Philippines.

Negros Helicostyla (3.2") 8 cm
Helicostyla sarcinosa subsp.
negrosa Bartsch, 1919. Tayasan,
Negros Id. Holotype.

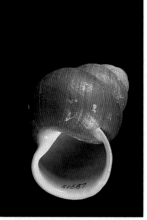

Walnut Helicostyla (3") 7.5 cm
Helicostyla (Helicob.) juglans
(Pfeiffer, 1842). Morong District,
Luzon Id., Philippines.

Wooden Helicostyla (3") 7.5 cm
Helicostyla (Helicob.) lignaria
(Pfeiffer, 1842). Cagayan Prov.,
Luzon Id., Philippines.

Wooden Helicostyla (3") 7.5 cm
Helicostyla (Helicob.) lignaria
(Pfeiffer, 1842) forma *aguinaldoi*
(Bartsch, 1919). Bayombong,
Luzon Id. Holotype illus.

Carola Helicostyla (3") 7.5 cm
Helicostyla (Helicob.) lignaria
(Pfeiffer, 1842) forma *carola*
(Deshayes, 1861). Northern
Tayabas Prov., Luzon Id., Philip-
pines.

Grand Helicostyla (2.5") 6 cm
Helicostyla (Helicob.) grandis
(Pfeiffer, 1845). Nueva Ecija
Prov., Luzon Id., Philippines.

Depressed Helicostyla
(2.7") 6.5 cm
Helicostyla (Helicob.) grandis
forma *depressa* (Moellendorff,
1898). Ilocos Norte, Luzon Id.,
Philippines. Syntype.

Kobelt's Depressed Heliostyla
(3") 7.5 cm
Helicostyla (Helicob.) grandis
forma *depressa* Kobelt, 1913.
Isabela Prov., Luzon Id., Philippines.

Large-mouthed Helicostyla
(2.6") 6.5 cm
*Helicostyla (Helicob.) macros-
toma* (Pfeiffer, 1843). Tarlac,
Luzon Id., Philippines.

Slender Helicostyla (2.5") 6 cm
*Helicostyla (Helicobulina) mac-
rostoma* forma *gracilis* (Moellendorff, 1898). Tarlac, Luzon Id.
Paratypes.

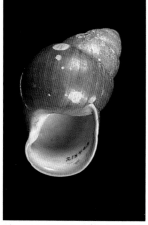

Vizcayan Helicostyla
(3") 7.5 cm
Helicostyla (Helico.) macrostoma
forma *vizcayana* Bartsch, 1919.
Makabenga, Luzon Id. Holotype.

Marinduque Helicostyla
(3") 7.5 cm
*Helicostyla (Helicobulina) mar-
induquensis* (Hidalgo, 1887).
Marinduque Id., Philippines.

Porte's Helicostyla (3") 7.5 cm
Helicostyla (Helicob.) woodiana
(Lea, 1840), forma *portei* (Pfeif-
fer, 1861). Polillo Id. Syntype from
Hugh Cuming.

Red-bottom Helicostyla
(3") 7.5 cm
Helicostyla (Helicob.) rufogaster
(Lesson, 1831) [not *rufogastra*,
1833]. Tarlac, Luzon Id., Philippines.

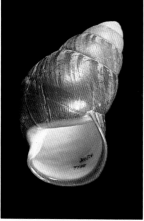

Topping's Helicostyla
(4.2") 10 cm
Helicostyla (Helicob.) rufogaster
forma *toppingi* Bartsch, 1932. Mt.
Maquiling, Luzon Id. Holotype.

Red-bottom Helicostyla
(3") 7.5 cm
Helicostyla (Helicob.) rufogaster forma *manilana* Bartsch, 1932. Manila area, Luzon. Paratype. Extinct.

Banahao Helicostyla (3.5") 9 cm
Helicostyla (Helicob.) rufogaster forma *banahaoana* (Bartsch, 1932). Majayjay, Luzon Id. Holotype.

Turban Helicostyla (2.5") 6 cm
Helicostyla (Helicob.) turbinoides (Broderip, 1841). Albay and Camarines Prov., Luzon Id. Syntype from H. Cuming.

Sula Mountain Helicostyla
(3") 7.4 cm
Helicostyla (Helicob.) turbinoides subsp. *sulana* M. Smith, 1932. Sula Mountain, Catanduanes Id., Philippines. Holotype.

Sula Mountain Helicostyla
(3") 7.4 cm
Helicostyla (Helicob.) turbinoides subspecies *sulana* M. Smith, 1932. Sula Mountain, Catanduanes Id. Paratypes.

Wood's Helicostyla (3.5") 9 cm
Helicostyla (Helicob.) woodiana (Lea, 1840). Polillo Id., east Luzon Id., Philippines.

Paracale Helicostyla
(3.5") 9 cm
Helicostyla (Helicob.) woodiana forma *paracaleana* Bartsch, 1918. Paracale, Luzon Id. Holotype.

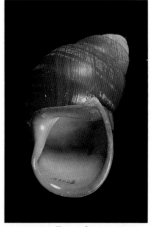

Reeve's Helicostyla
(3.5") 8.5 cm
Helicostyla (Helicob.) woodiana (Lea, 1840), forma *reevei* (Broderip, 1841). In trees, Luzon. Syntype from H. Cuming.

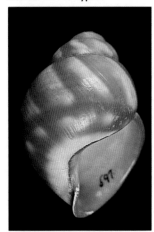

"Doctored Helicostyla"
(3.5") 8.5 cm
A *Helicostyla woodiana* (Lea, 1840) treated with a hot iron by the dealer Balestier in 1898.

Wood's Helicostyla (3.2") 8 cm
Helicostyla (Helicob.) woodiana (Lea, 1840). Polillo Id., east Luzon Id. Manuscript name was applied to this Webb form by Clench & Archer.

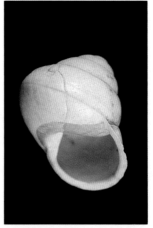

Wasp Helicostyla (2") 5 cm
Helicostyla (Helicob.) bembicodes (Pfeiffer, 1851). Romblon Id., Philippines.

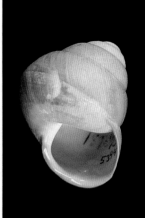

Turbo Helicostyla (2") 5 cm
Helicostyla (Helicob.) turbo (Pfeiffer, 1845). Tablas Id., Philippines.

Changing Helicostyla (2") 5 cm
Helicostyla (Dryocochlias) metaformis (Férussac, 1821). Tayabas Prov., Luzon Id. Type of subgenus.

Changing Helicostyla (2") 5 cm
Helicostyla (Dryoc.) metaformis forma *ovularis* (Menke, 1828). Luzon Id., Philippines.

Hydrophanous Helicostyla
(2") 5 cm
Helicostyla (Dryoc.) hydrophana Sowerby, 1841). Mindoro Id., Philippines. Periostracum absent.

Diana Helicostyla (2") 5 cm
Helicostyla (Dryoc.) diana (Broderip, 1841) forma *calista* Broderip, 1841. Antique Id., Philippines.

Lightning Helicostyla (3") 7 cm
Helicostyla (Dryoc.) fulgetrum (Broderip, 1841). Negros Island Philippines.

Tayasan Helicostyla (2.6") 6 cm
Helicostyla (Dryoc.) fulgetrum forma *tayasana* (Bartsch, 1919). Negros Id. Holotype.

Giant Lightning Helicostyla
(3.2") 8 cm
Helicostyla (Dryoc.) fulgetrum (Broderip, 1841) forma *gigantea* M. Smith, 1932. Panay Id., Philippines . Holotype.

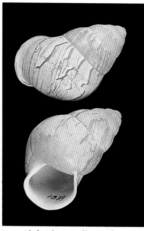

Jaro Lightning Helicostyla
(2") 5 cm
Helicostyla (Dryoc.) fulgetrum (Broderip, 1841) forma *jaroensis* M. Smith, 1932. Jaro, Panay Id. Upper: paratype.

Cloudy Helicostyla (2.5") 6 cm
Helicostyla (Dryoc.) nimbosa (Broderip, 1841). Negros Id. Syntype from H. Cuming.

Antique Helicostyla (3") 7.5 cm
Helicostyla (Dryoc.) nimbosa forma *antiqua* (Bartsch, 1919). Pandan, Panay Id. Holotype illus.

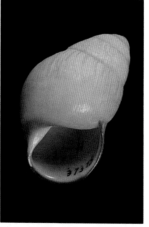

Pictor Helicostyla (1.3") 3 cm
Helicostyla (Dryoc.) pictor (Broderip, 1841). Silay, Negros Id., Philippines.

Satyr Helicostyla (2.5") 6 cm
Helicostyla (Dryoc.) satyrus (Broderip, 1841). Palawan Id. Syn.: *graellsi* Hidalgo, 1886; *librosa* (Pfeiffer); *tagbayugana* Bartsch, 1919.

Tidepole Helicostyla (1.8") 4 cm
Helicostyla satyrus (Broderip, 1841) forma *tidepolensis* (Bartsch, 1919). Tidepole Id., Palawan Id. Holotype illus.

Higgins' Helicostyla (1.8") 4 cm
Helicostyla (Dryoc.) satyrus forma *higginsi* Bartsch, 1919. Bessie Id., Palawan. Holotype illus. (syn. of *satyra* is *palavanensis* Pfr., 1856).

Mantangule Helicostyla
(2") 5 cm
Helicostyla (Dryoc.) satyrus form *mantangulensis* (Bartsch, 1919). Mantangule Id., Palawan. Holotype.

One Way Helicostyla
(2.5") 6 cm
Helicostyla (Dryoc.) solivaga (Reeve, 1849). Palawan Id., Philippines.

Decorated Helicostyla
(2.5") 6 cm
Helicostyla (Dryoc.) ventricosa (Bruguière, 1792). Guimaras Id., Philippines. Syn.: *decorata* (Férussac, 1821).

Decorated Helicostyla
(2.5") 6 cm
Helicostyla (Dryoc.) ventricosa (Bruguière, 1792) forma *guimarasensis* (Broderip, 1841). Guimaras Id.

Nobel Helicostyla (2.5") 6 cm
Helicostyla (Dryoc.) ventricosa (Bruguière, 1792) forma *nobilis* (Reeve, 1848). Igbaras, Panay Id., Philippines.

Nobel Helicostyla (2.5") 6 cm
Helicostyla (Dryoc.) ventricosa (Bruguière, 1792) forma *nobilis* (Reeve, 1848). Iloilo, Panay Id.

Noble Helicostyla (2.5") 6 cm
Helicostyla (Dryoc.) ventricosa forma *nobilis* (Reeve, 1848). Antique Id., Panay. (syn.: *contracta* Mlldff., 1898).

Worcester's Helicostyla
(2") 5 cm
Helicostyla worcesteri Bartsch, 1909. Bantayan Id., Philippines. Holotype illus.

Pitho Helicostyla (3") 7.5 cm
Type of the subgenus *Cochlostyla* Férussac, 1821. Upper shell dry, showing hydrophaneous periostracum. Lower: moistened by rain.

Pitho Helicostyla (2.5") 6 cm
Helicostyla (Cochlostyla) pithogaster (Férussac, 1821). Albay Prov., Luzon Id., Philippines. Common.

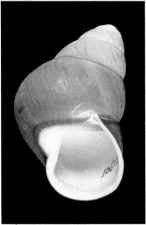

Pitho Helicostyla (3") 7 cm
Helicostyla (Cochlo.) pithogaster (Férussac, 1821), forma *batoana* M. Smith, 1932. Virac, Catanduanes Id. Paratype.

Pitho Helicostyla (3") 7 cm
Helicostyla (Cochlo.) pithogaster (Férussac, 1821), forma *philippinensis* (Pfeiffer, 1846). Luzon (and Marinduque?), Philippines.

Two-colored Helicostyla
(3") 7 cm
Helicostyla (Cochlo.) bicolorata (Lea, 1840), form *melanacme* (Moellendorff, 1898). Legaspi, Luzon Id., Philippines.

Two-colored Helicostyla
(3") 7 cm
Helicostyla (Cochlo.) bicolorata (Lea, 1840), form *subflammulata* Moellendorff, 1897. Mt. Isarog, Luzon Id., Philippines.

Emperor Helicostyla (3") 7.5 cm
Helicostyla (Cochlo.) imperator (Pfeiffer, 1848). Camarines Prov., Luzon Id., Philippines.

Daphne Helicostyla (3") 7.5 cm
Helicostyla (Cochlo.) daphnis (Broderip, 1841). Barili, Cebu Id., Philippines. Extinct?

Gilva Helicostyla (2.5") 6 cm
Helicostyla (Cochlo.) gilva (Pfeiffer, 1845). Bohol Id., Philippines. From Hugh Cuming. Syntype?

Fauna Helicostyla (1.2") 3 cm
Helicostyla (Cochlo.) faunus (Broderip, 1841). Samar Id., Philippines.

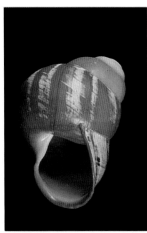

Ticao Helicostyla (2.7") 7 cm
Helicostyla (Cochlo.) ticaonica (Broderip, 1841). Masbate Id. Syntype from H. Cuming. Pronounced: "tick-ow."

Ticao Helicostyla (2.7") 7 cm
Helicostyla (Cochlo.) ticaonica (Broderip, 1841). Ticao; Masbate; Panay Ids. Syn.: *lutea* Pilsbry, 1892; *subglobosa* Lea, 1841.

Modest Ticao Helicostyla 6 cm
Helicostyla (Cochlo.) ticaonica (Broderip, 1841) forma *modesta* Moellendorff, 1898. Naro, Masbate Id.

Ilo Ilo Helicostyla (2.5") 6 cm
Helicostyla (Cochlo.) ticaonica (Broderip, 1841), forma *iloilona* M. Smith, 1932. Passi, Iloilo, Panay Id. Holotype.

Romblon Helicostyla (2") 5 cm
Helicostyla (Hypselostyla) concinna Sowerby, 1841. Romblon Id. Syn.: *romblonensis & subcarinata* (Pfeiffer, 1842); *fuscescens* (Mlldff.)

Archer's Helicostyla (2") 5 cm
Helicostyla (Hypsel.) concinna (Sowerby, 1841) forma *archeri* (Clench, 1936). Top: holotype. Tres Reyes Ids., Marinduque Id., Philippines.

Elegant-formed Helicostyla (1.7") 4 cm
Helicostyla cincinniformis (Sowerby, 1841). Lubang Id., Philippines. Syntypes from Hugh Cuming.

Pedro's Elegant Helicostyla (1.7") 4 cm
Helicostyla cincinniformis (Sowerby, 1841) subsp. *demesana* Clench & Archer, 1931. Lubang Id. Paratypes.

Ultimate Elegant Helicostyla (1.7") 4 cm
Helicostyla cincinniformis (Sowerby, 1841) forma *ultima* Clench & Archer, 1931. Lubang Id. Paratypes.

Elegant-formed Helicostyla 4 cm
Helicostyla (Hypsel.) cincinniformis (Sowerby, 1841). Upper: forma *menagei*. Lower: forma *guntingana* both Bartsch, 1932, holotypes. Lubang Id.

Opal Helicostyla (1.4") 3.5 cm
Helicostyla (Phengus) opalina (Sowerby, 1841). Luzon Id. Possible syntype from C.B. Adams.

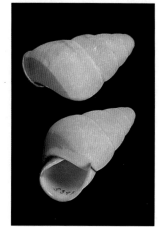

Evanescent Helicostyla (2") 5 cm
Helicostyla (Hypsel.) evanescens (Broderip, 1841). Tarlac, Luzon, Philippines. Rare.

Carinate Helicostyla (2.5") 6 cm
Helicostyla (Hypselostyla) dactylus (Broderip, 1841). Tayabas Prov., Luzon. Type of subgenus. Syn.: *carinata* Lea, 1840, non Perry, 1811.

Carinate Helicostyla (2.5") 6 cm
Helicostyla (Hypsel.) dactylus (Broderip, 1841) forma *rugata* (Hidalgo, 1896). Virac, Catanduanes Id. *H. dactyla*: misspelling.

Carinate Helicostyla (2.5") 6 cm
Helicostyla (Hypsel.) dactylus (Broderip, 1841), forma *lunai* (Bartsch, 1919). Ilocos Norte, Luzon Id.

Carinate Helicostyla (2.5") 6 cm
Helicostyla (Hypsel.) dactylus (Broderip, 1841) forma *nympha* (Pfeiffer, 1842). Camarines Prov., Luzon Id.

Elegant Helicostyla (1.5") 4 cm
Helicostyla concinna (Sowerby, 1841). Romblon Id., Philippines. Freckled form

Elegant Helicostyla (1.5") 4 cm
Helicostyla concinna (Sowerby, 1841) forma *virens* (Pfeiffer, 1842). Southen Burias Id., Philippines.

Camel Helicostyla (2.7") 7 cm
Helicostyla (Hypsel.) camelopardalis (Broderip, 1841). Cebu Id., Philippines. Extinct? Syn.: *boholensis* (Brod., 1841).

Chrysalis Helicostyla
(3") 7.5 cm
Chrysallis chrysalidiformis (Sowerby, 1833). Mansalay, Mindoro. Type of the genus.

Swarthy Helicostyla (3") 7.5 cm
Chrysallis chrysalidiformis forma *fuscata* Bartsch, 1932. Mindoro Id. Holotype illus.

Jay's Helicostyla (3") 7.5 cm
Chrysallis chrysalidiformis subsp. *jayi* Bartsch, 1932. Samar Id. (syn.: *ustulatus* Jay, 1839, non Sowerby, 1833).

Jay's Helicostyla (3") 7.5 cm
Chrysallis chrysalidiformis subsp. *jayi* Bartsch, 1932. Mindoro Id. Holotype illus.

Camoronga Helicostyla
(3") 7.5 cm
Chrysallis chrysalidiformis forma *camorongana* Bartsch, 1932. Abra de Ilog, N. Mindoro Id. Holotype.

White-lipped Helicostyla
(3") 7.5 cm
Chrysallis albolabris (Bartsch, 1932). Mindoro Id. Philippines. Holotype illus.

Anton's Helicostyla (3") 7.5 cm
Chrysallis antonii (Semper, 1880). Western Mindoro Id., Philippines.

Meager Helicostyla (2.5") 6 cm
Chrysallis antonii forma *macilenta* (Bartsch, 1932). Mangarin, S.W. Mindoro. Holotype.

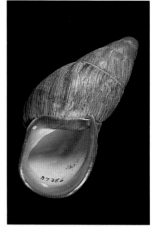

Difficult Helicostyla
(3") 7.5 cm
Chrysallis (C.) aspersa (Grateloup, 1839). Mindoro Id. Syntype of syn.: *mindorvensis* (Broderip, 1841). Syn.: *aspera* Zilch, 1982.

Ilogana Helicostyla (3") 7.5 cm
Chrysallis (C.) aspersa (Grateloup, 1839) forma *ilogana* (Bartsch, 1932). Tara Mangyan, Mindoro. Paratypes.

Yellow-skinned Helicostyla
(3") 7.5 cm
Chrysallis (C.) aspersa (Grateloup, 1839), forma *flavipellis* Clench & Archer, 1933. Mindoro Id. Paratypes.

Luna Helicostyla (3") 7.5 cm
Chrysallis (C.) aspersa (Grateloup, 1839), forma *lunai* Bartsch, 1932. Mamburao, Mindoro Id. Holotype illus.

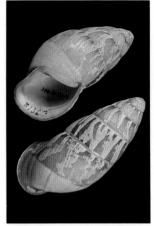

Difficult Helicostyla (2.5") 6 cm
Chrysallis (C.) aspersa (Grateloup, 1840), subsp. *orotis* Clench & Archer, 1933. Mindoro Id. Upper: holotype; lower: paratype.

Bran Helicostyla (3") 7.5 cm
Chrysallis caniceps caniceps Bartsch, 1932. Lake Naujan, Mindoro Id. Holotype illus.

Conic Bran Helicostyla
(3.5") 8 cm
Chrysallis caniceps forma *conica* Bartsch, 1932. S.W. Mindoro Id. Holotype illus.

DeMesa's Bran Helicostyla
(3") 7.5 cm
Chrysallis (C.) caniceps subsp. *demesai* (Bartsch, 1932). Calamintao, Mindoro Id., Philippines. Paratypes.

Contra Costa Helicostyla
(2.8") 7 cm
Chrysallis (C.) caniceps forma *contracostana* Bartsch, 1932. Contra Costa, Mindoro Id. Holotype.

Electric Helicostyla (2.8") 7 cm
Chrysallis electrica (Reeve, 1848) forma *bulalacaoana* Bartsch, 1932. Bulalacao, S.E. Mindoro. Holotype illus.

Electric Helicostyla 6.8 cm
Chrysallis electrica (Reeve, 1848) forma *mangarina* Bartsch, 1932. Mangarina, S.W. Mindoro. Holotype illus.

McGinty's Helicostyla
(2.5") 6 cm
Chrysallis (C.) palliobasis (Bartsch, 1932). Mindoro Id., Philippines. Holotype.

McGinty's Helicostyla 6 cm
Chrysallis palliobasis (Bartsch, 1932). Holotype of synonym, *macgintyi* M. Smith, 1932. Amatang, Mindoro Id.

Troubled Helicostyla
(2.8") 7 cm
Chrysallis perturbator (Bartsch, 1932). Abra de Ilog, N. Mindoro Id. Holotype illus.

Rosy Lipped Helicostyla
(2.8") 7 cm
Chrysallis roseolabra (Bartsch, 1932). Calawagan, N.W. Mindoro Id. Holotype illus.

Calawaga Helicostyla
(2.7") 7 cm
Chrysallis (Dolich.) roseolabra (Bartsch, 1932). Calawagan, Mindoro Id. Paratypes of syn.: *calawaganensis*(M. Smith, 1932).

Rolle's Helicostyla (3.5") 9 cm
Chrysallis (C.) rollei (Moellendorff, 1898). Mt. Halcon, Mindoro Id., Philippines.

Rolle's Black Helicostyla
(3.1") 7.6 cm
Chrysallis rollei forma *nigra* Bartsch, 1932 (1938). Baco, Mindoro Id. Holotype illus.

Vexatious Helicostyla
(3") 7.5 cm
Chrysallis rollei forma *vexator* Bartsch, 1932. Mindoro Id., Philippines. Holotype illus.

Striped Helicostyla (1.4") 3.5 cm
Chrysallis (Dolichostyla) virgata (Jay, 1839). Mindoro Id., Philippines. Holotype. Type of subgenus.

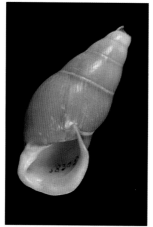

Striped Helicostyla (1.4") 3.5 cm
Chrysallis (Dolich.) virgata (Jay, 1839). Holotype of synonym *porracea* (Jay, 1839). Mindoro Id.

Maxwell Smith Helicostyla 5 cm
Chrysallis (Dolich.) virgata (Jay, 1839) forma *maxwellsmithi* McGinty, 1932. Naujan, Mindoro Id. Holotype in Fla. Mus. Nat. Hist.

Calamianes Helicostyla
(2.5") 6 cm
Chrysallis (Dolich.) calamianica (Quadras & Moellendorff, 1894). Calamianes Archipelago, Philippines.

Well-dyed Helicostyla
(2") 5 cm
Chrysallis (Dolichostyla) calobapta (Jonas, 1843). Tablas Id., Philippines. Syntypes from Hugh Cuming.

Well-dyed Helicostyla
(2") 5 cm
Chrysallis (Dolich.) calobapta (Jonas, 1843), form *tablasensis* (Kobelt, 1916). Tablas Id., Philippines.

Striped Helicostyla (2") 5 cm
Chrysallis (Dolich.) virgata (Jay, 1839) subsp. *dryas* (Broderip, 1841). Mt. Yagaw, Mindoro Id.

Partula Helicostyla (2") 5 cm
Chrysallis (Dolich.) virgata (Jay, 1839) forma *partuloides* (Broderip, 1841). Mindoro Id. (is form *porracea* Jay?).

Partula Helicostyla (2") 5 cm
Chrysallis (Dolich.) virgata (Jay, 1839) forma *partuloides* (Broderip, 1841). Bulalacoa, Mindoro Id. Lip flares.

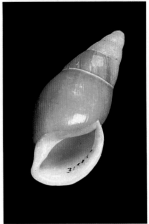

Waxy Helicostyla (2") 5 cm
Chrysallis (Dolich.) virgata subsp. *cerina* Bartsch, 1932. Bulalacao S.E. Mindoro Id. Holotype illus.

Fischer's Helicostyla (2") 5 cm
Chrysallis (Dolichostyla) fischeri (Hidalgo, 1889). Coron Id., Calamianes Ids., Philippines.

Fisher's Helicostyla (1.3") 3 cm
Chrysallis (Dolich.) fischeri (Hidalgo, 1889), forma *semistrigata* (Kobelt, 1916). Calamianes Ids., Palawan, Philippines. Paratypes.

Clay Helicostyla (1.7") 4.5 cm
Chrysallis (Dolich.) fictilis (Broderip, 1841). Mindoro Id., Philippines.

Marbled Helicostyla (1.3") 3 cm
Chrysallis (Dolich.) fictilis forma *marmorosa* (Bartsch, 1932). Ilin Id., S.W. Mindoro Id. Holotype illus.

Furrowed Helicostyla
(1.5") 3.5 cm
Phoenicobius aratus (Sowerby, 1841). San Jose, Mindoro Id., Philippines. Type of the genus.

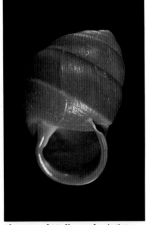

Shortened Helicostyla (2") 5 cm
Phoenicobius brachydon (Sowerby, 1841). Mindoro Id. (smooth form of *aratus* Sowerby?).

Tanned Helicostyla (2.5") 6 cm
Phoenicobius adustus (Sowerby, 1841). Mindoro Id., Philippines.

Little Bell Helicostyla
(1") 2.5 cm
Phoenicobius campanulus (Pfeiffer, 1845), forma *bintuanensis* (Hidalgo, 1889). Sangal Id., Calamianes Ids., Philippines.

Egg-shaped Helicostyla
(1.2") 3 cm
Phoenicobius oomorphus (Sowerby, 1841). Mindoro Id., Philippines.

Amatang Helicostyla (1") 2.5 cm
Phoenicobius oomorphus forma *amatangana* (M. Smith, 1932). Amatang, Mindoro Id. Paratypes.

Ovoid Helicostyla (2") 5 cm
Canistrum ovoideum (Bruguière, 1789). Masbate Id., Philippines. Type of the genus.

Ovoid Helicostyla (2") 5 cm
Canistrum ovoideum forma *euryzonum* (Pfeiffer, 1847). Masbate Id., Philippines.

Ovoid Helicostyla (2") 5 cm
Canistrum ovoideum forma *luzonicum* Sowerby, 1833. Masbate Id., Philippines.

Balanoid Helicostyla (2") 5 cm
Canistrum balanoides (Jonas, 1894). Ilocos, Luzon Id., Philippines.

Stable Helicostyla (1.3") 3 cm
Canistrum stabile (Sowerby, 1841). Temple and Burias Ids., Philippines.

Stable Helicostyla (1.3") 3 cm
Canistrum stabile (Sowerby, 1841). Masbate Id. Periostracum removed in cleaning.

Cepoid Helicostyla (2.5") 6 cm
Steatodryas cepoides (Lea, 1841). Lubang Id., Mindoro Prov., Philippines. Type of genus and sole species.

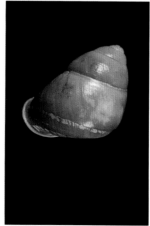

Mearns' Helicostyla (1.5") 4 cm
Helicostyla mearnsi Bartsch, 1905. Atop Mt. Apo, Mindanao, Philippines. Holotype illus.

Nicely Conic Helicostyla
(1.5") 4 cm
Helicostyla euconica (Bartsch, 1932). Calapan, Mindoro, Philippines. Holotype illus.

Lillian's Helicostyla
(1.3") 3.5 cm
Calocochia lillianae (Bartsch, 1932). Mt. Halcon, Mindoro Id. Holotype illus.

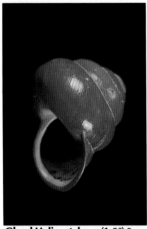

Glued Helicostyla (1.2") 3 cm *Helicostyla (H.) collodes* (Sowerby, 1841). Cebu Id., Philippines. Rarely yellowish. Extinct.

Lost or Dubious Species

The following ten Philippine species are lost or perhaps synonyms of other species. These paintings are from Moellendorff and Kobelt's 1905 to 1916 monograph on the Helicostylinae published in Semper's *Reisen im Archipel. der Philippinen* (Weisbaden, Germany), vol. 10, parts 1-12, 82 pls. Many of these may be extinct. Most figures are of Zilch lectotypes.

General Helicostyla (2.5") *Calocochlia generalis* (Pfeiffer, 1854). Philippines. Kobelt, pl. 28, fig. 6. Differs from Pilsbry's illustrations.

Elera's Calocochlia (2") 5 cm *Calocochlia elerae* (Moellendorff, 1896). Casiguran, Luzon Id. Kobelt, pl. 43, fig. 1. May be *C. melanorhaphe* Quadras & Mlldff.

Bark-colored Helicostyla (2.5") 6.2 cm *Helicostyla (Orustia) corticolor* (Kobelt, 1911). Abra Id., Philippines. May be *montana* (Semper, 1877).

Concealed Helicostyla (2") 5 cm *Helicostyla (Dryocochlias) velata* (Broderip, 1841). Medellin, Cebu Id. Kobelt, pl. 49, fig. 2. Extinct?

Kobelt's Anixa Snail (2") 5 cm *Calocochia (Anixa) kobelti* (Moellendorff, 1890). Morong District, Luzon Id. Kobelt, pl. 37, fig. 4.

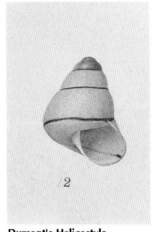

Dumont's Helicostyla (1.5") 4 cm *Helicostyla (Phengus) dumonti* (Pfeiffer, 1846). Catanduanes Ids., Philippines. Kobelt, pl. 53, fig. 2.

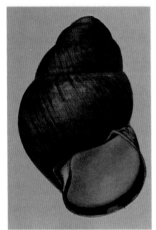

Intermediate Helicostyla (3") 7.5 cm *Helicostyla intermedia* (Moellendorff, 1896, in Q. and Mlldff.) San Jose, Luzon Id. Kobelt, pl. 62, fig. 6.

Solid Helicostyla (3") 7.5 cm *Helicostyla (Dryocochlias) solida* (Pfeiffer, 1842) [not his 1851]. Cagayan Prov., Luzon Id. Kobelt, pl. 62, fig. 3.

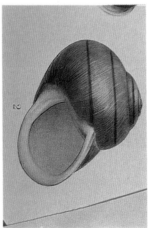

Yellowish White Calocochlia (2.3") 6 cm *Calocochlia leucauchen* (Moellendorff, 1895). Camarines Prov., Luzon. Kobelt, pl. 28, fig. 2.

Vidal's Helicostyla (3") 7.5 cm *Helicostyla (Helicobulina) vidali* (Hidalgo, 1887). Benguet District, Luzon Id. Kobelt, pl. 61, fig. 6.

Family **HELICIDAE**

Numerous worldwide species; includes edible escargot snails. Aperture without teeth. One or two dart sacs. Six semitropical or temperate subfamilies, with about 80 genera and several thousand species. Uses calcareous copulatory "love darts." Yolky shelled eggs buried in soft ground hatch within 3 weeks.

Subfamily **HELICELLINAE**

A western palearctic group of about 30 genera. Ground and bush dwellers; many introduced to U. S., Australia. Live in arid areas. Considered a family by some.

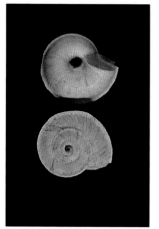

Plain Helicella (.6") 1.2 cm *Cernuella explanata* (Müller, 1774). Mediterranean coasts. Syn.: *Helicella* and *Leucochroa albella* Drap. Common on grasses.

Wrinkled Helicella (.5") 1.3 cm *Candidula intersecta* (Poiret, 1801). Gt. Britain, France to Denmark. In tall grass. Syn.: *Helicella caperata* (Montagu). Uncommon.

Striped Helicella (.7") 20 cm *Cernuella virgata* (da Costa,1778). Gt. Britain, France. Introduced to Eastern U.S. Dry, open dunes with grass. Common. Type of genus.

Maritime Helicella (0.8") 2 cm *Cernuella virgata* subsp. *maritima* Draparnaud 1805. North African coast. Syn.: *lineata* Olivi, 1792.

Obvious Helicella (0.7") 1.8 cm *Helicella obvia* (Menke, 1828). Central Europe, up to 2,000 meters. Common.

Home Helicella (0.3)" 1 cm *Helicella vestalis* Parreyss, in Pfeiffer, 1841. Asia Minor; Egypt. Syn.: *palmarum* Hartman.

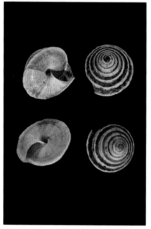

Elegant Land Trochus (0.4") 1 cm *Trochoidea elegans* (Gmelin, 1791). France. Dry, exposed rubble. A handsome common species. Type of the genus.

Elegant Land Trochus (0.3") 1 cm *Trochoidea elegans* (Gmelin, 1791). From a colony in Charleston, South Carolina, U.S.A.,introduced.

Cretian Land Trochus (0.5") 1.2 cm *Trochoidea cretica* (Férussac, 1822). Grecian Islands, Isle of Rhodes.

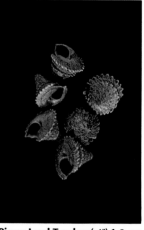

Pigmy Land Trochus (.4") 1.0 cm *Trochoidea pumilio* (Dillwyn, 1817). Northern Morocco. Syn.: *Obelus pumilio* Chemnitz. Subspecies *cyclodon* Orbigny, 1839, occurs in the Canaries.

Turkey Helicella (0.6") 1.5 cm *Helicopsis (Xeroleuca) turcica* (Holten, 1802). Mogador, Morocco, North Africa. Type of the subgenus.

Pointed Helicella (.8") 2 cm
Cochlicella acuta (Müller, 1774).
Western shores of Gt. Britain,
France. In grasses near sand
dunes. Type of the genus. Light-
weight, common.

Bordered Hygromia
(0.6") 1.5 cm
Hygromia limbata (Draparnaud,
1805). South England; western
Europe. Family Hygromiidae.

Hairy Hygromia (0.4") 1 cm
Trichia hispida (Linnaeus, 1758).
Western Europe. Moist woods.
Common, widespread. Intro-
duced to Maine.

Flat-spired Arianta
(1.1") 2.8 cm
*Chilostoma (Campylaea) plano-
spirum* (Lamarck, 1822). Southern central Europe; Austria.

Lucky Arianta (0.7") 1.6 cm
Chilostoma (Faustina) faustinum
Rossmässler, 1835. Eastern Eu-
rope.

Pouzolz's Arianta (2") 5 cm
Chilostoma pouzolzi (Pay-
raudeau, 1826). Dalmatia; Yu-
goslavia; Albania.

Plantation Arianta (1") 2.4 cm
Arianta arbustorum (Linnaeus,
1758). Scandanavia; middle
Europe. Common. Subfamily
Ariantinae. Type of genus.

Stone-loving Arianta
(0.5") 1.2 cm
Helicigona lapicida (Linnaeus,
1758). Western and central Europe. Rocky ground. Common.

Wall Helicella (0.5") 1.2 cm
Marmorana (Murella) muralis
(Müller, 1774). Germany and
France. Stony areas; common.

Pisana Helix (.7") 1.5 cm
Theba pisana (Müller, 1774).
Western coastal France, England.
Common. Near ocean. Subfam-
ily Helicinae. Type of genus.

Pisana Helix (.7") 1.5 cm
Theba pisana (Müller, 1774).
Introduced to Calif. about 1916.
Nuisance in fruit orchards. In U.S.
called White Garden Snail.

Pisana Helix (.7") 1.5 cm
Theba pisana (Müller, 1774).
These are introduced shells living in Brisbane, Australia. Syn.:
rhodostoma Hartmann (red-
mouth).

Spanish Edible Snail (1.2") 3 cm
Otala lactea (Müller, 1774). North Africa; Spain. Introduced to S.E. U.S., Cuba Bermuda, etc. Type of genus.

Freckled Edible Snail
(1.2") 3 cm
Otala punctata (Müller, 1774). Spain and southern France. Common.

Lucas Edible Snail (1") 2.5 cm
Otala lucasii (Deshayes, 1850). Oran, Algiers.

Vermiculate Helix (1.2") 3 cm
Eobania vermiculata (Müller, 1774). Italy; Southern France; northwest Africa. Lip white. Common. Type of the genus.

Gualtieri's Iberus (1.5") 4 cm
Iberus gualtieriana (Linnaeus, 1767). Cadiz and Granada coast of Spain. Common. Type of the genus.

True Alabaster Snail
(0.8") 1.6 cm
Alabastrina alabastrites (Michaud, 1833). Oran, Algiers. Type of the genus.

Minett's Alabaster Snail
(1.5") 4 cm
Alabastrina (Tingitana) minettii (Pallary, 1918). Atlas mountains, Spanish Morocco. Type of subgenus.

Hieroglyphic Alabaster Snail
(1")
Alabastrina (Michaudia) hieroglyphica (Michaud, 1833). Oran, Algiers.

Splendid Helix (.8") 2 cm
Pseudotachea splendida (Draparnaud, 1801). South Europe; Spain to Italy. Near oceanside. Common. Type of genus.

Plicate Helix (0.9") 2.2 cm
Hemicycla plicaria (Lamarck, 1816). Canary Islands. Faintly banded. Riblets. Uncommon. Type of genus. Syn.: *plicatula* Lam.; *chersa* Mabille.

Flesh-mouthed Helix (1") 2.5 cm
Hemicycla sarcostoma Webb & Berthelot, 1832. Fuertaventura and Grand Canary Ids. Wooded areas. Surface microscopically granulated.

Banded Grove Snail (.7") 2 cm
Cepaea nemoralis (Linnaeus, 1758). Western Europe; introduced to U.S. Abundant locally near habitation. Lip dark. Type of genus.

White-lipped Grove Snail
(.7") 2 cm
Cepaea hortensis (Müller, 1774). Western Europe; Northeast U.S. Withstands cold weather. Food of birds. Locally abundant.

Vienna Grove Snail (1") 2.5 cm
Cepaea vindobonensis (Férussac, 1821). Southern Germany, Austria, Poland. In bushes; common.

Nice Helix (1") 2.5 cm
Macularia niciensis (Férussac, 1821). Southern European alpines. Meadows, rocky ledges. Common. Type of the genus.

Raspaili's Helix (1.5") 3.5 cm
Tacheocampylaea raspailii (Payradeau, 1826). Corsica, Mediterranean. On low bushes. Common. Type of genus. Form *pilosa* Kobelt, has fine hairs.

Codrington Helix (2") 5 cm
Codringtonia codringtoni (Gray, 1834). Greece and Aegean Islands. Common edible snail. Variable in colors. Type of genus.

Black-lipped Caucasan Helix
(1.2") 3 cm
Caucasotachea atrolabiata (Krynicki, 1833). Northern Caucasia and Abkhazian, USSR. Common. Type of genus.

French Escargot (1.5") 3.5 cm
Helix pomatia Linnaeus, 1758. Central Europe; introduced to England. Raised in vineyards for food. Common. Type of genus.

French Escargot (1.5") 3.5 cm
Helix pomatia Linnaeus, 1758. Type of the genus. Upper shell is a rare sinistral of "left-handed" specimen (from Poncin, France).

Ligate Helix (2") 5 cm
Helix ligata Müller, 1774. Italy. Common in groves and bushes. Many variable bandings. Aperture white. Common.

Lucorum Helix (2") 5 cm
Helix lucorum Linnaeus, 1758. Central Italy to Asia Minor. Broadly banded; obliquely striate. Common; edible.

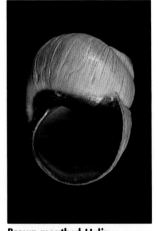

Brown-mouthed Helix
(1") 2.5 cm
Helix melanostoma Draparnaud, 1801. Vineyards and olive groves. Southern France; N. Africa. Common. Sometimes strongly striate.

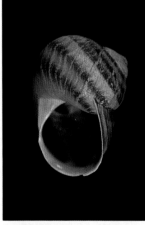

Speckled Escargot (1") 2.5 cm
Helix aspersa Müller, 1774. Gt. Britain; western Europe. Introduced worldwide in warm temperate zones. Also the "Brown Garden Snail."

Speckled Escargot (1") 2.5 cm
Helix aspersa Müller, 1774. Left-handed or sinistral specimens are rare and collector's item. Species is type of subgenus *Cryptomphalus* Charpentier.

Speckled Escargot (1") 2.5 cm
Helix aspersa Müller, 1774. Injury to mantle edge may cause abnormal growth forms. A "scalariform" example.

Speckled Escargot (1") 2.5 cm
Helix aspersa Müller, 1774. In this experiment an *aspersa* animal was placed in an empty *Ennea* shell and became attached.

Mazzull's Helix (1.3") 3 cm
Helix mazzulli Cristofori & Jan, 1834. Sicily. Like *aspersa* but apex pointed; axial riblets. Common.

Green Escargot (1") 2.5 cm
Helix aperta Born, 1778. Southern Europe; north Africa. Introduced to California, Louisiana. Edible snail in markets. Common. Subgenus *Cantareus* Risso, 1826.

Plicate Helix (1.3") 3 cm
Helix subplicata Sowerby, 1825. Madeira Islands, off W. Africa. Common. Axial riblets granular.

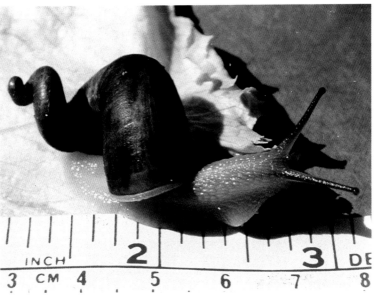

Due to an early injury to the mantle, this odd specimen of *Helix aspersa* from Australia grew with separated whorls, thus forming a "cornucopia like" shell. The snail is normal in other respects.

SOME COMMON FRESHWATER SNAILS

Stagnant Pond Snail   (1.5") 3.5 cm
Lymnaea stagnalis (Linnaeus, 1758). A large family of non-operculate snails, mainly in the cool northern hemisphere.

Stagnant Pond Snail   (1.5") 3.5 cm
Lymnaea stagnalis (Linnaeus, 1758). Common air-breathing snail. Lays jellylike egg globs. Order Basommatophora.

Seminole Ramshorn Snail   (1") 2.5 cm
Planorbella duryi (Wetherby, 1879). The planorbid pond snails have many worldwide genera and and species. No operculum. Family Planorbidae. Lay jelly encased eggs.

Lefthanded Physa   (0.7") 2 cm
Physa heterostropha (Say, 1819). A large family (Physidae) of sinistrally coiling shells, common in ponds. No operculum. Mainly in cool climates; worldwide.

Banded Viviparus   (1") 2.5 cm
Viviparus contectoides Binney, 1865. Live-bearing operculate snails of northern hemisphere lakes. Many species. Aquarium favorite.

Carinate Lanistes   (2") 5 cm
Lanistes boltenianus (Röding, 1798). Nile River, Egypt. Several operculate, left-handed species in African rivers. Viviparidae.

Florida Applesnail   (2.5") 6 cm
Pomacea paludosa (Say, 1829). Several New World tropical species and some Asia and African genera, all operculate. Pilidae.

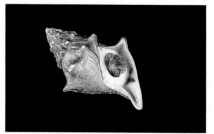

River Io Snail   (1.3") 3 cm
Io fluvialis (Say, 1825). Rivers of Tennessee and Alabama. Becoming extinct due to pollution. One variable species.

Acute Pleurocerid Snail   (1") 2.5 cm
Elimia acuta (Lea, 1831). One of about 200 operculate river snails common in North America. Family Pleuroceridae.

Kangaroo Snails   (1") 2.5 cm
Genera *Thiara*, *Tarebia* and *Melanoides* carry young in head pouch. Common in tropical waters of southeast Asia, India and Africa. Family Thiaridae.

Hydrobid Snails   (0.4") 1 cm
Genera *Bulimus*, *Parastriata*, *Amnicola* and others are small, operculate freshwater snails living among pond and river weeds. Family Hydrobiidae.

Three-ridged Valve Snail   (0.3") 4 mm
Valvata tricarinata (Say, 1817). Operculate, with single, protruding gill plume. Several species common in northern lakes and ponds. Family Valvatidae.

Bibliography

The literature on terrestrial gastropods is very extensive, consisting of many thousands of books, monographs and short research papers. Our bibliography is relatively brief, but such that any newcomer to the study or hobby of land mollusks may be able to delve deeper into any family or seek out checklists for any part of the world.

Our bibliography is divided into three sections:

1. *General introduction* to the study of terrestrial mollusks—their classification, ecology, life histories and economic importance.

2. *Geographical guide* in which are listed some of the books and papers for various continents, countries and states.

3. *Identification guides* and taxonomic reviews of various families, genera and groups of species—arranged in a generally accepted phylogenetic order, with the primitive mollusks listed first and the advanced groups at the end.

Other Bibliographic Sources

Most of the approximate 10,000 articles and research papers on the classification and identification of terrestrial mollusks have been listed by author and by subject matter in the annually published *Zoological Record*, Section 9 on *Mollusca*. Large public and many university libraries subscribe to this invaluable bibliographic source, now published by BIOSIS, 2100 Arch Street, Philadelphia, PA 19103-1399, U.S.A.

We are listing the most recent and most useful works, although many of them are available only at major research centers. More extensive geographical bibliographies may be found in the *Indexes to the Nautilus* (Geographical to vols. 1-90), 238 pp., 1979, American Malacologists, Inc., Melbourne, Florida (about 1500 entries) and some in Parkinson, Hemmen and Groh's *Tropical Landshells of the World*, 1987, pp. 77-108, Wiesbaden, West Germany.

A very useful and recent outline of the classification of "The Living Mollusca" in which all classes, superfamilies, families, genera and subgenera, with their synonyms, are listed in phylogenetic order, has been assembled by Kay Cunningham Vaught of Scottsdale, Arizona. It contains approximately 14,810 names. It was published in 1989 by American Malacologists, Inc., Melbourne, Florida.

Current Journals on Mollusca

(*Journals mainly on marine mollusks)

American Conchologist, Quarterly Bulletin of the Conchologists of America (vol. 17, 1989). (Popular literature), c/o B. Houchin, 2644 Kings Highway, Louisville, Kentucky 40205.

Archiv für Molluskenkunde. (vol. 119, 1988) c/o Natur-

Museum, Senckenberg-Anlage 25, 6000 Frankfurt am Main 1, West Germany.

Basteria. Tijdschrift van de Nederlandse Malacologische Vereniging. (vol. 52, 1988). c/o Zoological Museum, Plantage Middenlaan 53, Amsterdam-C, Netherlands.

Bulletin of the American Malacological Union (1932 to date). c/o Secretary, 3706 Rice Boulevard, Houston, Texas 77005.

*Bulletin of the Institute of Malacology. (vol. 2, 1985). Institute of Malacology, 6-36 Midoricho 3 Chome, Tanashi City, Tokyo 188, Japan.

*Bulletin of Malacology Republic of China. (vol. 12, 1986). Taiwan Museum, No. 2 Siang-Yang Rd., Taipei, Taiwan.

*Club Conchylia. (vol. 20, 1988). "Informationen" subscription: E. Röckel, editor, Neckaranlage 6, 6930 Eberbach, West Germany. Popular literature in German.

*(La) Conchiglia (English edition: The Shell). La Conchiglia, Via C. Federici, 1, 00147 Rome, Italy. Non-technical, popular monthly.

Conchiglie. Notiziario mensile della Unione Malacologica Italiana. (vols. 1-14). Unione Malac. Italiana, Via de Sanctis 73, 20141 Milan, Italy. Continued as Bollettino Malacologico.

*Hawaiian Shell News. (vol 36, new series, 1988). Hawaiian Malacological Society, P.O. Box 10391, Honolulu, Hawaii 96816. Non-technical, popular monthly.

*Johnsonia. (vol. 5, 1974). Monographs of the Marine Mollusca of the Western Atlantic. Museum Comparative Zoology, Cambridge, Massachusetts 02138.

Journal of Conchology. (vol. 31, 1981). Conchological Society of Great Britain and Ireland, c/o Department Geology, Liverpool University, England L69 3BX.

Journal of the Malacological Society of Australia. (vol. 8, 1987). c/o Western Australian Museum, Francis St., Perth, Western Australia 6000, Australia.

Journal of Molluscan Studies (formerly *Proceedings of the Malacological Society of London*). (vol. 54, 1988). Mal. Soc. London, c/o Department of Zoology, Bedford College, Regent's Park, London, England NW1 4NS.

Malacologia. (vol. 28, 1988). c/o Department Malacology, Academy of Natural Sciences of Philadelphia, 19th and The Parkway, Philadelphia, Pennsylvania 19103.

Malakologische Abhandlungen. (vol. 8, 1981). Staatlichen Museum für Tierkunde in Dresden. Augustusstrasse 2, 801 Dresden, East Germany.

Nautilus (The). (vol. 102, 1988). Quarterly. Trophon Corporation, P.O. Box 3430, Silver Spring, Maryland 20901.

Occasional Papers on Mollusks. (no. 59, 1981). Department of Mollusks, Museum of Comparative Zoology, Cambridge, Massachusetts 02138.

Proceedings of the Malacological Society of London, now called *Journal of Molluscan Studies* (see above).

*Texas Conchologist. (vol. 24, 1988). c/o Constance Boone, editor, 3706 Rice Boulevard, Houston, Texas 77005.

*Veliger (The). (vol. 31, 1988). Malacozoological Society of California, Department Zoology, University California, Berkeley, California 94720.

Venus, Japanese Journal of Malacology. (vol. 30, 1988). c/o National Science Museum, 23-1, Hyakunincho-3, Shinjuku-ku, Tokyo 160, Japan.

General Bibliography

Baker, H.B., 1956. Family names in Pulmonata. *The Nautilus*, vol. 69: 128-139; vol. 70: 34. Nomenclatorial technicalities.

Boss, Kenneth J. 1982 [in Parker, S.P., *Synopsis and Classification of Living Organisms*, McGraw-Hill, N.Y. Best English outline of classification of Mollusca down to subfamily level]. Phylum Mollusca, vol. 1, Terrestrial snails, pp. 977-980; 1064-1090.

Ellis, Arthur E., 1926. *British Snails.* Clarendon Press, Oxford. (updated in 1969).

Evans, John G., 1972. *Land Snails in Archaeology.* 436 pp. Seminar Press, N.Y. Excellent. Good bibliography. Iden-.tification of British species.

Fretter, Vera and John Peake, 1975 (editors). *Pulmonates.* Vol. 1. Functional Anatomy and Physiology. 417 pp. Academic Press, N.Y. 12 prominent biologist contributors. Excellent.

Fretter, Vera and John Peake, 1978 (editors). *Pulmonates.* Vol. 2a. Systematics, Evolution and Ecology. 540 pp. Academic Press, N.Y. 15 prominent malacologist contributors. Excellent.

Godan, Dora, 1983. *Pest Slugs and Snails.* 445 pp. Springer, Berlin and N.Y. German edition: 1979, Schadschnecken und ihre Bekämpfung, Stuttgart. Excellent work, with extensive bibliography of about 1,800 entries.

Götting, K.J., 1974. *Malakozoologie.* Grundriss der Weichtierkunde, Stuttgart. 320 pp., 160 figs.

Hyman, Libbie H., 1967. *Mollusca; The Invertebrates,* vol. 6, 792 pp., 249 figs. Pulmonates on pp. 548-650, and its bibliography, pp. 726-769.

Martini and Chemnitz (Küster's edition), 1837-1918. Systematisches Conchylien-Cabinet, Nürnberg. Many parts, many authors, Pfeiffer, Dohrn, Kobelt, Küster. Vol. 1 on *Helix*, part 12, on *Bulimus*, part 13 (1841-1902) (see in Parkinson, Hemmen and Groh, 1987, p. 266 and in Richardson in Tryonia, no. 12, p. 407, 1985 for details). Advanced, but out-of-date, identification source.

Mead, A.R., 1979. *Economic Malacology,* vol. 2B in *Pulmonates,* 150 pp. Academic Press, N.Y.

Nordsieck, H., 1986. The system of the Stylommatophora (Gastropoda), with special regard to the systematic position of the Clausiliidae. II. Importance of the shell and distribution. Archiv. Moll., vol. 117 (1/3): 93-116.

Peake, J.F., 1978. Distribution and ecology of the Stylommatophora. Chapter 10, pp. 430-526, in *Pulmonates,* vol. 2A, Academic Press, London.

Pfeiffer, L., 1852. Monographia Pneumonopomorum Viventium. Cassel, Germany. Vol. 1 (1852), 438 pp.; Supplement 1 (1852), 249 pp.; Supplement 2 (1865), 284 pp.; Supplement 3 (1876), 479 pp. Descriptions and citations of all operculate land shells to 1875, no illus.

Richardson, C. Leonard, 1980 to date. Catalog of Species. Tryonia, Philadelphia, nos. 3, 6, 9, 10, 12, 13, 16. Largest known current catalog of Pulmonate species, subgenera, genera and families with full references and synonymies. Helicidae; Helminthoglyptidae, Bradybaenidae; Oreohe-licidae; Polygyridae, Corillidae and Sagdidae; Streptaxidae (no. 16, 1988).

Russell-Hunter, W.D. (editor), 1983. Ecology [in *The Mollusca,* vol. 6: 1-695. Academic Press, Orlando, N.Y.] Chapt. 10 by W.A. Riddle: Physiological Ecology of Land Snails and Slugs; Chapt. 14 by A.J. Cain: Ecology and Ecogenetics of Terrestrial Molluscan Populations.

Salvini-Plawen, von, L. and R. Tucker Abbott, 1974. *The Mollusks,* in Grzimek's *Animal Life Encyclopedia,* vol. 3, pp. 43-225 (Pulmonates on pp. 127-135). Van Nostrand/Reinhold, N.Y.

Solem, Alan, 1959. Classification of the land Mollusca. In Fretter and Peake's Pulmonata, 2A: 49-97. Academic Press, London.

Solem, G. Alan, 1974. *The Shell Makers*—Introducing Mollusks. 289 pp. John Wiley & Sons, N.Y. Good chapters on land mollusks.

Solem, Alan and A.C. van Bruggen, eds., 1984. World-wide Snails, 289 pp. Symposium papers on biogeographical studies on non-marine Mollusca by Solem, Walden, Gittenberger, Grossu, Verdcourt, van Bruggen, Shikov, et al.

Tompa, A.S. and N.H. Verdonk (editors), 1984 Reproduction. [in *The Mollusca,* vol. 7: 1-486. Academic Press, Orlando, N.Y.]. Chapt. 2 by A.S. Tompa: Land Snails (Stylommatophora).

Trueman, E.R. and M.R. Clarke, 1985. *Evolution,* vol. 10 of *The Mollusca,* 491 pp. Academic Press, N.Y. Contributors: Brian Morton, Alastair Graham, Pojeta, Runnegar, Salvin-Plawen, Solem, Vermeij, et al.

Tryon, G.W., Jr. and H.A. Pilsbry, 1885-1926. Manual of Conchology, Philadelphia. Second series (Pulmonata). Vols. 1-4 by Tryon, 1885-88; vols. 5-28 by Pilsbry, 1888-1935. Best and most comprehensive source, somewhat out-of-date. Found in museum libraries.

Vaught, Kay C., 1989. *A Classification of the Living Mollusca.* 186 pp. American Malacologists, Inc., Melbourne, Florida. All terrestrial supraspecific names listed phylogenetically, with index.

Webb, Walter F., 1948. *Foreign Land and Fresh Water Shells.* 183 pp., 73 pls. Webb Publ., St. Petersburg, Florida. Nomenclature very out-of-date. Classification obsolete.

Wenz, W., 1938-1944. Prosobranchia: Gastropoda. Vol. 1, in Schindewolf's Handbuch der Paläozoologie, vol. 6, pt. 1, 1639 pp. Berlin. See also Zilch, 1959, for Pulmonata, vol. 2.

Wilbur, Karl M. and C.M. Yonge. *Physiology of Mollusca,* 1964, vol. 1: 1-473; 1966, vol. 2: 1-645. 29 contributors. Academic Press, N.Y.

Zilch, A., 1959-1960. Euthyneura; In Vol. 2 of Gastropoda by W. Wenz. In Schindewolf's Handbuch der Paläozoologie, vol. 6, pt. 2: 834 pp., 2515 figs. Berlin. Best illustrated arrangement down to subgenera, recent and fossil.

Geographical Index

Te, G.A., 1976. A summary of pulmonate distribution information contained in Zilch's 1959-1960 Monograph [Wenz's Handbuch der Palaeozool.]. Malacological Review, vol. 9: 39-53.

United States

Burch, John B., 1962. *How to Know the Eastern Land Snails.* 214 pp. W.C. Brown Co., Dubuque, Iowa.

Burch, J.B. and Patterson, C.M., 1966. Key to the genera of land gastropods (snails and slugs) of Michigan. Mus. Zool. Michigan, Circular no. 5, 19 pp., 46 figs.

Hubricht, Leslie, 1985. The distribution of the native land mollusks of the Eastern United States. Fieldiana, Zoology, N.S., no. 24: 1-191, 523 maps.

Miller, W.B., Reeder, Babraksai and Fairbanks, 1984. New, revised taxa in North American terrestrial Mollusca (N. of Mexico) published since 19 March 1948. Tryonia, no. 11: 1-14.

Pilsbry, H.A., 1939-1948. *Land Mollusca of North America* (North of Mexico). Monograph 3, Acad. Nat. Sci. Phila., vol. 1, no. 1 (1939); vol. 1, pt. 2 (1940); vol. 2, pt. 1 (1946); vol. 2, pt. 2 (1948). Most complete coverage of North American land snails.

Foreign Species Introduced to the United States

Abbott, R.T., 1950. Snail Invaders. Natural History Magazine, vol. 59 (2): 80-85.

Alexander, R.C., 1952. Introduced species of land snails in New Jersey. The Nautilus, vol. 65: 132-135.

Introduced around the world to warm climates during the last 300 years, the edible Speckled Escargot, *Helix aspersa*, has arrived in eight of the U.S. states. (Natural size).

Branson, D.L., 1969. Notes on exotic mollusks in Kentucky. The Nautilus, vol. 82: 102-106.

Chichester, L.F. and L.L. Getz, 1969. The zoogeography and ecology of arionid and limacid slugs introduced into northeastern North America. Malacologia, vol. 7: 313-346.

Dees, Lola T., 1970. Edible land snails in the United States. U.S. Dèpt. Interior, Fish and Wildlife Resource Publ. 91: 1-8.

Dundee, D.S., 1974. Catalog of introduced mollusks of eastern North America (north of Mexico). Sterkiana, vol. 55: 1-37.

Hanna, G.D., 1966. Introduced mollusks of western North America. Occ. Papers California Acad. Sci., vol. 48: 1-108, 4 pls.

Mead, A.R., 1971. Helicid land mollusks introduced into North America. The Biologist, vol. 53 (3): 104-111.

Thaanum, D., 1927. Foreign Shells Imported into the Hawaiian Islands. The Nautilus, vol. 40: 133-134.

Townes, G.F., 1957. Introduced species in South Carolina. The Nautilus, vol. 70 (3): 108.

Alabama

Archer, A.F., 1938. Notes on some land mollusks of a palmetto pasture in North-central Alabama. The Nautilus, vol. 51: 106-106.

——, 1941. Land Mollusca of Coosa County, Alabama. The Nautilus, vol. 54: 4-10.

Walker, Bryant, 1928. The terrestrial shell-bearing Mollusca of Alabama. Mich. Univ. Mus. Zool., Misc. Publ. No. 18, 180 pp., 278 figs.

Alaska

Dall, W.H., 1905. Land and fresh-water mollusks. In: Harriman Alaska Exped., vol. 13: 1-171, pls. 1,2.

Tuthill, S.J. and R.L. Johnson, 1969. Non-marine mollusks of the Katalla region, Alaska. The Nautilus, vol. 83: 44-52.

Arizona

Ashmun, E.H., 1899. Collecting in Arizona and New Mexico. The Nautilus, vol. 13 (2): 13-17.

Bequaert, J.C. and W.B. Miller, 1973. *The Mollusks of the Arid Southwest, with an Arizona Check List.* Univ. Arizona Press, Tucson. 271 pp.

Arkansas

Hubricht, L., 1966-1967. Some land snail records from Arkansas and Oklahoma. The Nautilus, vol. 79: 117; vol. 81: 65-67.

California

Edson, H.M. and H. Hannibal, 1911. A census of the land and fresh-water mollusks of southwestern California. Bull. So. Calif. Acad. Sci., vol. 10: 47-64.

Haas, F., 1954. Non-marine mollusks from the Pacific slope of North America. The Nautilus, vol. 67: 94-96.

Ingram, W.M., 1946. A check list of the helicoid snails of California from Henry A. Pilsbry's Monograph. Bull. So. Calif. Acad. Sci., vol. 45 (2): 61-93.

Talmadge, R.R., 1967. Notes on coastal land snails. The Nautilus, vol. 80: 87-89.

Colorado

Ferriss, J.H., 1910. A collecting excursion north of the Grand Canyon of the Colorado. The Nautilus, vol. 23 (9): 109-112.

Henderson, Junius, 1924. Mollusca of Colorado, Montana, Idaho and Wyoming. Univ. Colo. Studies, vol. 13 (2): 1-160.

Connecticut
Jacot, P., 1919. On the land shells of Monroe, Connecticut. The Nautilus, vol. 32: 134-136.

Delaware
Rhodes, N., 1904. A glimpse at the shell fauna of Delaware. The Nautilus, vol. 18: 63-67.

Florida
Auffenberg, K. and L.A. Stange, 1986. Snail-eating Snails. Entomology Circular no. 285, Fla. Dept. Agric., 4 pp., illus.

Ross, L.T., 1964. The land mollusca of Siesta Key, Sarasota County, Florida. The Nautilus, vol. 78: 50-52.

Vanatta, E.G., 1923. Land Shells of Southern Florida. The Nautilus, vol. 33:18; ibid., vol. 34: 93.

Wilson, D., 1960. Land snails from central south Florida. The Nautilus, vol. 73: 137-139.

Georgia
Teskey, M., 1969. The mollusks of Warm Springs, Georgia. The Nautilus, vol. 69: 69-71.

Hawaii
Caum, E.L., 1928. Check List of Hawaiian Land and Freshwater Mollusca. Bull. 56, B.P. Bishop Mus., pp. 1-79.

Chung, Daniel, 1986. Notes on some little known Hawaiian land shells. Hawaiian Shell News, Dec. 1986, vol. 34 (12): 3-4.

Hadfield, M.G., 1986. Extinction in Hawaiian Achatelline snails. Malacologia, vol. 27: 67-81.

Idaho
Baker, H.B., 1932. New land snails from Idaho and Eastern Oregon. The Nautilus, vol. 45: 82-87, pl. 5.

Smith, A.G., 1943. Mollusks of the Clearwater Mountains, Idaho. Proc. Calif. Acad. Sci., ser. 4, vol. 23 (36): 537-554, pl. 48.

Illinois
Baker, Frank C., 1939. Fieldbook of Illinois land snails. Illinois Nat. Hist. Survey, Manual 2, 166 pp., illus.

Hinkley, A.A., 1919. Mollusca found in the vicinity of Dubois, Illinois. The Nautilus, vol. 33: 14-17.

Indiana
Bushey, C.J., 1950. Land snails from Grant County, Indiana. The Nautilus, vol. 63: 119-121.

Call, R.E., 1900. A descriptive catalog of the Mollusca of Indiana. Dept. Geol. Nat. Resources Indiana, vol. 24: 335-535.

Goodrich, C. and H. van der Schalie, 1944. A revision of the Mollusca of Indiana. Amer. Midland Naturalist, vol. 32: 257-320.

Iowa
Shimek, B., 1935. The habitats of Iowa succineas. The Nautilus, vol. 49 (1): 6-10.

Kansas
Leonard, A.B., 1959. Handbook of Gastropods in Kansas, Univ. Kansas, Mus. Nat. Hist., Misc. Publ. no. 20: 1-224, 87 figs., 7 pls.

Kentucky
Hubricht, L., 1969. The land snails of Mammoth Cave National Park, Kentucky. The Nautilus, vol. 82: 24-26.

Kaplan, M.F. and W.L. Minckley, 1960. Land snails from the Doe Run Creek Area, Meade County, Kentucky. The Nautilus, vol. 74: 62-65.

Louisiana
Branson, B.A., 1961. Notes on some gastropods from northern Louisiana. Proc. Louisiana Acad. Sci., vol. 24: 24-30.

Dundee, D.S. and P. Watt, 1961. Louisiana land snails with new records. The Nautilus, vol. 75 (2): 79-83.

Hubricht, L., 1956. Land snails from Louisiana. The Nautilus, vol. 69: 124-126.

Maine
Henderson, J.B., 1913. Land shells from Ellsworth, Maine. The Nautilus, vol. 27 (8): 95-96.

Vanatta, E.G. Land shells of Maine. The Nautilus, vol. 33: 96-99.

Maryland
Grimm, F.W., 1959. Land snails of Carroll County, Maryland. The Nautilus, vol. 72 (4): 122-127.

——, 1961. Land snails from the Upper Patuxent estuar margin (Maryland). Ibid., vol. 74 (3): 106-109.

——, 1961. Land snails from Maryland coastal plain. Ibid., vol. 74 (4): 160-161.

Massachusetts
Clapp, W.F., 1911. A good collecting ground for small shells. The Nautilus, vol. 25: 80.

Clench, W.J., 1930. Additional notes on the colony of Helix nemoralis at Marion, Massachusetts. The Nautilus, vol. 44: 13.

Gould, A.A. and W.G. Binney, 1870. Report on the Invertebrata of Massachusetts, 2nd ed., Boston. 524 pp., 27 pls.

Michigan
Burch, J.B. and Younghun Jung, 1988. Land Snails of the Univ. Mich. Biol. Station Area [northern Michigan]. Walkerana, no. 9: 1-177, 109 figs.

Goodrich, C., 1932. The Mollusca of Michigan. Univ. Michigan Press. 120 pp., 8 pls.

Minnesota
Dawley, C., 1955. Minnesota Land Snails. The Nautilus, vol. 69: 56-62.

Mississippi
Hubricht, L., 1960. Hendersonia occulta fossil in Mississippi (together with other species). The Nautilus, vol. 74: 83.

Missouri
Sampson, F.A., 1912. Shells of southeast Missouri. The Nautilus, vol. 26: 90-95.

——, 1912. *Polygyra albolabris allani* Wetherby, and other Missouri helices. The Nautilus, vol. 25: 130-131.

Montana

Berry, S.S., 1916. Notes on Mollusca of central Montana. The Nautilus, vol. 29: 124-128; 144.

Henderson, Junius, 1933. Mollusca of the Yellowstone Park, Teton Park and Jackson Hole Region. The Nautilus, vol. 47: 1-3.

Nebraska

MacMillan, G.K., 1944. A small collection of land shells from Nebraska. The Nautilus, vol. 57: 130-132.

Walker, B., 1906. A list of shells from Nebraska. The Nautilus, vol. 20: 81-83.

Nevada

Pilsbry, H.A. and J.H. Ferriss, 1918. New land shells from California and Nevada. The Nautilus, vol. 31 (3): 93-95, pl. 7.

New Hampshire

Baker, F.C., 1942. Land and fresh water Mollusca of New Hampshire. Amer. Midland Nat., vol. 27: 74-85.

Getz, L.L., 1962. Localities for New Hampshire Land Mollusks. The Nautilus, vol. 76 (1): 25-28.

New Jersey

Alexander, R.C., 1947. Report on the land mollusks of Cape May, N.J. The Nautilus, vol. 60 (3): 97-100.

——, 1952. Checklist of New Jersey land snails. *Ibid.*, vol. 66 (2): 54-59.

New Mexico

Cockerell, T.D.A., 1896. Land Mollusca from the rejectamenta of the Rio Grande, New Mexico. The Nautilus, vol. 10 (4): 41-43; 1905, ibid., vol. 19 (6): 68-71.

Drake, R.J., 1948-1949. Mollusca of the eastern basin of the Chaco River, New Mexico. The Nautilus, vol. 62 (1): 58; *ibid.*, vol. 62 (3): 94-97.

Ferriss, J.H., 1917. A shell hunt in the Black Range with description of a new *Oreohelix*. The Nautilus, vol. 30: 99-103.

New York

Jacobson, M.K. and W.K. Emerson, 1961. Shells of the New York City Area. Argonaut Books, N.Y. 142 pp.

Muchmore, W.B., 1959. Land snails of E.N. Huyck Preserve, New York. The Nautilus, vol. 72 (3): 85-89.

Robertson, I.C.S. and C.L. Blakeslee, 1948. The Mollusca of the Niagara Frontier Region. Buffalo Soc. Nat. Hist., Bull. 19: 191 pp., 14 pls.

Teator, W.S., 1890. Collecting land shells in eastern New York. The Nautilus, vol. 3: 109-110, 6 figs.; 129-132, 5 figs.

Wheat, S.C., 1907. Land shells from east shore of Cayuga Lake. The Nautilus, Vol. 20: 100-101.

North Carolina

Archer, A.F., 1935. The ecology of the land Mollusca of Asheville, North Carolina. The Nautilus, vol. 48 (3): 77-83.

Beetle, D.E., 1967. Mollusks of the Outer Banks, North Carolina. The Nautilus, vol. 81 (2): 61-65.

Getz, L.L., 1974. Species diversity of terrestrial snails in the Great Smoky Mountains. The Nautilus, vol. 88 (1): 6-9.

North Dakota

Winslow, M.L., 1921. Mollusca of North Dakota. Mich. Univ. Mus. Zool., Occ. Papers, no. 98: 1-18.

Ohio

La Rocque, Aurèle, 1966-1970. Pleistocene Mollusca of Ohio. Ohio Dept. Nat. Resources, Geol., Bull. 62 (parts 1-4), Terrestrial Gastropoda, in part 4, pp. 555-800, pls. 15-18.

Taft, Celeste, 1961. The shell-bearing land snails of Ohio. Ohio Biol. Survey Bull., n.s., vol. 1 (3): 1-108, illus.

Oklahoma

Branson, B.A., 1961. The recent Gastropoda of Oklahoma, III. Proc. Okla. Acad. Sci., vol. 41: 45-69, pls. 1,2.

Dundee, D.S., 1955. Additional localities for land Mollusca in Oklahoma. The Nautilus, vol. 69 (1): 16-18.

Oregon

Haas, F., 1954. Non-marine mollusks from the Pacific Slope of North America (Oregon). The Nautilus, vol. 67 (3): 94-96.

Henderson, Junius, 1929. The non-marine Mollusca of Oregon and Washington. Univ. Colorado Studies, vol. 17: 47-190; 1936, suppl., *ibid.*, vol. 23: 251-280.

Pennsylvania

Heilman, R.A., 1951. The mollusks of Dauphin County, Pennsylvania. The Nautilus, vol. 64: 100-101. Berks County, *ibid.*, vol. 65: 103-104.

Vanatta, E.G., 1920. Land shells from Beaver County, Pennsylvania. The Nautilus, vol. 34 (1): 28.

Rhode Island

Carpenter, H.F., 1887-1907. The shell-bearing Mollusca of Rhode Island. The Nautilus, vols. 1-21.

South Carolina

Mazyck, W.G., 1913. Catalog of the Mollusca of South Carolina. Contrib. Charleston Mus., no. 2. (See review, The Nautilus, vol. 27: 142-143, 1914).

South Dakota

Henderson, Junius, 1927. Some South Dakota Mollusca. The Nautilus, vol. 41 (1): 19-20.

Jones, D.T., 1932. Molluscs in the vicinity of Yankton, South Dakota. The Nautilus, vol. 45 (4): 115-118.

Tennessee

Ferriss, J.H., 1900. The Great Smoky Mountains. The Nautilus, vol. 14: 49-59.

Hubricht, L., 1940. The snails of Ted Cave, Tennessee. The Nautilus, vol. 54 (1): 10-11.

Lutz, L., 1950. A list of the land Mollusca of Claiborne County, Tennessee, with description of a new subspecies of Triodopsis. The Nautilus, vol. 63 (3): 99-105; 121-123.

Texas

Cheatum, E.P., 1935. Gastropods of the Davis Mountains vicinity in West Texas. The Nautilus, vol. 48 (4): 112-116, pl. 5.

Hubricht, L., 1960. Beach drift land snails from southern Texas (exclusive of Polygyridae). The Nautilus, vol. 74 (2): 82-83.

Pilsbry, H.A. and E.P. Cheatum, 1951. Land snails from the Guadalupe Range, Texas. The Nautilus, vol. 64 (1): 87-90, pl. 4.

Utah

Chamberlin, R.V. and D.T. Jones, 1929. Descriptive catalog of the mollusca of Utah. Bull. Univ. Utah, vol. 19 (4): 1-203.

Jones, J.T., 1940. Recent collections of Utah Mollusca, with extralimital records from certain Utah cabinets. Proc. Utah Acad. Sci. Arts Lett., vol. 17: 33-45.

Vermont

Johnson, C.W., 1910. Shells of Mt. Equinox, Vermont. The Nautilus, vol. 24: 72.

Virginia

Beetle, D.E., 1972. A note on land snails associated with Kudzu vine. The Nautilus, vol. 86: 18-19.

Burch, J.B., 1952. A preliminary list of the Mollusca of Hanover County, Virginia. The Nautilus, vol. 66 (2): 60-63. Henrico Co., vol. 68:30-33.

——, 1956. Distribution of land snails in plant associations in Eastern Virginia. The Nautilus, vol. 70: 60-64; 102-105, 1 fig.

Washington

Branson, B.A., 1977. Freshwater and terrestrial Mollusca of the Olympic Peninsula, Washington. Veliger, vol. 19: 310-330.

Eyerdam. W.J., 1934. Land and Freshwater shells from the vicinity of Yakima, Washington. The Nautilus, vol. 48: 46-48.

Henderson, Junius, 1929 and 1936, see under "Oregon" above.

West Virginia

MacMillan, G.K., 1950. The land snails of West Virginia. Ann. Carnegie Mus., vol. 31: 89-238, 15 pls.

Wurtz, C.B., 1948. Some land snails from West Virginia with description of a new species. The Nautilus, vol. 61 (3): 80-95.

Wisconsin

Levi, L.R. and H.W., 1950. New records of land snails from Wisconsin. The Nautilus, vol. 63: 131-138.

Solem, A., 1952. Some mollusks from Door County, Wisconsin. The Nautilus, vol. 65: 127-129.

Wyoming

Beetle, D.E., 1957. The Mollusca of Teton County, Wyoming. The Nautilus, vol. 71: 12-22; 76: 74.

Levi, L.R. and H.W., 1951. A report on land snails from Jackson Hole region, Wyoming. The Nautilus, vol. 65 (2): 60-65.

Canada

Baker, F.C., 1939. Land and freshwater Mollusca from Western Ontario. Canadian Jour. Res., vol. 17, sec. D: 87-102, 1 fig.

Berry, S.S., 1922. Land snails from the Canadian Rockies. Victoria Mem. Mus., Bull. 36: 1-19, 1 pl.

Brooks, S.T., 1936. The land and freshwater Mollusca of Newfoundland. Ann. Carnegie Mus., vol. 25: 83-108.

La Rocque, Aurèle, 1953. Catalogue of the Recent Mollusca of Canada, Nat. Mus. Canada, Bull. 129: 1-406.

MacMillan, G.K., 1954. A preliminary survey of the land and freshwater gastropoda of Cape Breton, Nova Scotia, Canada. Proc. Nova Scotia Inst. Sci., vol. 23: 389-408.

Oughton, J., 1940. Land Molluscs collected at Hebron, Labrador, and Lake Harbour, South Baffin Island. The Nautilus, vol. 53 (4): 127-131.

——, 1948. A zoogeographical study of the land snails of Ontario. Univ. Toronto Studies, Biol. Ser., no. 57: 1-128.

Taylor, G.W., 1889. The land shells of Vancouver Island. Ottawa Naturalist, vol. 3: 84-94.

Vanatta, E.G., 1930. Newfoundland shells (land). The Nautilus, vol. 43: 133-134.

West Indies

Adams, Charles B., 1850. Descriptions of Supposed New Species and Varieties of Terrestrial Shells which Inhabit Jamaica. Contributions to Conchology, vol. 5: 76-84.

Aguayo, C.G. and M.L. Jaume, 1957. Adiciones a la Fauna Malacológica Cubana, I. Mem. Soc. Cubana Nat. Hist., vol. 23 (2): 117-142, 6 pls.: 1958, II, ibid., vol. 24 (1): 91-104, 1 pl.

Baker, H.B., 1924. Land and Freshwater Mollusks of the Dutch Leeward Islands. Occ. Papers. Mus. Zool. Univ. Mich., no. 152: 1-159, 21 pls.

——, 1934. Jamaican Land Snails. The Nautilus, vol. 48: 6-14, pl. 2.

——, 1940. Some Antillean Sagdidae and Polygyridae. The Nautilus, vol. 54: 54-62; for other families, see ibid., vol. 55: 24-30; vol. 56: 81-91; vols. 74, 75, 76 (1941-62).

——, 1962. Puerto Rican land operculates. The Nautilus, vol. 76 (1): 16-22.

Brown, A.D., 1881. Notes on the Land-shells of Dominica. Amer. Naturalist, vol. 15: 56-57.

Brown, L.B., 1903. Notes on the Land and Freshwater Shells of Barbuda. Jour. Conch., vol. 10: 266-273.

Clapp, G.H., 1914. List of Land Shells from Swan Island, with

Descriptions of Five New Species. The Nautilus, vol. 27: 97-101.

Clench, W.J., 1950. Land Shells of Mona Island, Puerto Rico. Jour. de Conchyl., vol. 90: 269-276.

———, 1956. Land Shells of Barbuda Island, Lesser Antilles. The Nautilus, vol. 70: 69-70.

———, 1962. New Species of Land Mollusks from the Republica Dominicana. Breviora Mus. Comp. Zool., vol. 173: 1-5, 1 pl.

———, 1964. Land and Freshwater Mollusca of the Cayman Islands, West Indies. Occ. Papers Moll., Harvard Univ., vol. 2 (31): 345-380, pls. 61-63.

———, 1969. Land Shells of Jost Van Dyke, Virgin Islands. The Nautilus, vol. 82 (4): 144-145.

———, 1970. Land Mollusca of Saba Island, Lesser Antilles. Occ. Papers Moll., Harvard Univ., vol. 3: 53-60.

Coomans, H.E., 1967. The non-marine mollusca of St. Martin (Lesser Antilles). Studies Fauna Curacao, vol. 24: 118-145, 4 figs.

Guppy, R.J.L., 1893. The land and freshwater mollusca of Trinidad. Jour. Conch., vol. 7: 210-231.

Jacobson, M.K., 1968. The Land Mollusca of St. Croix, Virgin Islands. Sterkiana, no. 32: 18-28.

Jacobson, M.K. and K.J. Boss, 1973. The Jamaican Land Shells Described by C.B. Adams, Occ. Papers Moll., Harvard Univ., vol. 3: 305-520, pls. 54-91.

Jacobson, M.K. and W.J. Clench, 1971. On Some *Helicina* from the Dominican Republic. The Nautilus, vol. 84 (3): 101-107.

Pfeiffer, L., 1854-1866. Zur Molluskenfauna von Cuba. Malakozool. Blätter, vols. 1-13.

Pfeiffer, L. and J. Gundlach, 1861. Zur Molluskenfauna der Insel Cuba. Makazool. Blätter, vol. 7: 9-32.

Pilsbry, H.A., 1892. On a Collection of Land Mollusca from the Island of Dominica. Trans. Conn. Acad. Sci., vol. 8: 356-358.

———, 1930. Results of the Pinchot South Sea Expedition. 1. Land Mollusks of the Caribbean Islands, Grand Cayman, Swan, Old Providence and St. Andrew. Proc. Acad. Nat. Sci. Phila., vol. 82: 221-261; 339-354.

———, 1933. Santo Domingan Land Mollusks Collected by Daniel C. Pease, 1932, and by A.A. Olsson, 1916. Proc. Acad. Nat. Sci. Phila., vol. 85: 121-162.

———, 1942. Land Mollusca of the Cayman Islands Collected by the Oxford University Biological Expedition, 1938. The Nautilus, vol. 56: 1-9.

———, 1949. Land Mollusks of Cayman Brac. *Ibid.*, vol. 63: 37-48.

Pilsbry, H.A. and A.P. Brown, 1912. The Land Mollusca of Montego Bay, Jamaica; with Notes on the Land Mollusca of the Kingston Region. Proc. Acad. Nat. Sci. Phila., vol. 64: 572-588, pl. 43.

Pilsbry, H.A. and E.G. Vanatta, 1928. Land Shells of Tortugas Island, Haiti; and a New Haitian *Oleacina*. Proc. Acad. Nat. Sci. Phila., vol. 80: 475-478.

Richards, H.G., 1938. Land Mollusks from the Island of Roatan, Honduras. Proc. Amer. Phila., Soc., vol. 79 (2): 167-178, 3 pls.

Richards, H.G. and P.W. Hummelinck, 1940. Land and Freshwater Mollusks from Margarita Island, Venezuela. Notulae Naturae (Phila.), no. 62: 1-16, figs. 1-4.

Simpson, Chas. T., 1894. Distribution of the Land and Freshwater Mollusks of the West Indian Region, and their Evidence with Regard to Past Changes of Land and Sea. Proc. U.S. Nat. Mus., vol. 17: 423-450.

Smith, E.A., 1896. A List of the Land and Freshwater Molluscs of Trinidad. Jour. Conch., vol. 8: 231-251; vol. 9: 27-29.

———, 1898. On the Land-shells of Curaçao and the Neighboring Islands. Proc. Mal. Soc. London, vol. 3: 113-116.

Thompson, Fred G., 1987. A Review of the Land Snails of Mona Island, West Indies. Bull. Florida State Museum, Biol. Sci., vol. 31, no. 2, pp. 69-106.

Turner, Ruth D., 1960. Land Shells of Navassa Island, West Indies. Bull. Mus. Comp. Zool., vol. 122: 233-244, pls. 1-7.

van der Schalie, H., 1948. The Land and Fresh-water Mollusks of Puerto Rico. Misc. Publ. Mus. Zool. Univ. Mich., vol. 70: 1-134, pls. 1-14.

Vendreys, H., 1899. Systematic Catalogue of Land and Freshwater Shells of Jamaica. Jour. Inst. and Mus. Jamaica, vol. 2: 590-607.

Vernhout, J.H., 1914. The Land and Freshwater Molluscs of the Dutch West Indian Islands. Notes Leyden Mus., vol. 36: 177-189.

Wurtz, Charles, 1950. Land Snails of North Cat Cay (Bahamas), Cayo Largo (Cuba), Grand Cayman, Saint Andrews and Old Providence. Proc. Acad. Nat. Sci., vol. 102: 95-110, pl. 2.

Bahamas

Clapp, G.H., 1913. Land Shells Collected on the Bimini Islands, Gun and Cat Cays, Bahamas. The Nautilus, vol. 27: 63-64.

Clench, W.J., 1937. Shells of Mariguana Island with a review of the Bahama Helicinidae and descriptions of new Bahama species. Proc. New England Zool. Club, vol. 16: 57-70.

———, 1938. Land and freshwater mollusks of Grand Bahama and the Abaco Islands. Mem. Soc. Cubana Hist. Nat., vol. 12: 303-333.

———, 1938. Origin of the land and freshwater mollusk fauna of the Bahamas with a list of the species occurring on Cat and Little San Salvador Islands. Bull. Mus. Comp. Zool., vol. 80: 481-541.

———, 1940. Land and freshwater mollusks of Long Island, Bahama Islands. Mem. Soc. Cubana Hist. Nat., vol. 14: 3-17.

———, 1942. Land shells of the Bimini Islands, Bahama Islands. Proc. New England Zool. Club, vol. 19: 53-67.

———, 1952. Land and freshwater mollusks of Eleuthera Island, Bahama Islands. Revista Soc. Malacologica "Carlos de la Torre," vol. 8: 97-116.

———, 1959. Land and freshwater mollusks of Great and Little Inagua, Bahama Islands. Bull. Mus. Comp. Zool., vol. 121: 29-53.

———, 1961. Land and freshwater mollusks of Caicos, Turks, Ragged Islands and islands on the Cay Sal Bank, Bahamas. Occ. Papers Mollusks, Harvard Univ., vol. 2: 229-260.

——, 1963. Land and Freshwater Mollusks of the Crooked Island Group, Bahamas. Bull. Mus. Comp. Zool., vol. 128 (8): 396-413, 3 pls.

Jacobson, M.K., 1965. On Some Land Snails of Eleuthera, Bahamas. The Nautilus, vol. 78 (4): 120-125.

Pilsbry, H.A., 1930. List of the Land and Freshwater Mollusks. Collected on Andros, Bahamas. Proc. Acad. Nat. Sci. Phila., vol. 82: 297-302, pl. 22.

Bermuda

Haas, F., 1950. On some Bermudian Ellobiidae. Proc. Mal. Soc. London, vol. 28 (4): 197-199.

Peile, A.J., 1926. The Mollusca of Bermuda. Proc. Mal. Soc. London, vol. 17: 71-98.

Pilsbry, H.A., 1900. The air-breathing molluscs of the Bermudas. Trans. Conn. Acad. Sci., vol. 10: 491-512, pl. 62.

Vanatta, E.G., 1911. Bermuda [land] shells. Proc. Acad. Nat. Sci. Phila., vol. 62: 664-672.

——, 1923. Bermuda [land] shells. The Nautilus, vol. 37 (1): 32-33. [additions to 1911].

——, 1924. Land shells of Admiral's Cave, Bermuda. The Nautilus, vol. 38: 6-6.

Central America

Baker, H.B., 1922. The Mollusca Collected by the University of Michigan-Walker Expedition in Southern Vera Cruz, Mexico, Pt. 1, Occ. Papers Mus. Zool. Univ. Mich., vol. 106: 1-94; pt. 2 (1923), vol. 135: 1-6; (1925), pt. 3, vol. 156: 1-56; (1926), pt. 4, vol. 167: 1-49; (1927), pt. 5, vol. 182: 1-36, pls. 1-26.

Basch, P.F., 1959. Land Mollusca of the Tikal National Park in Guatemala. Occ. Papers Mus. Zool. Univ. Mich., no. 612: 1-15.

Bequaert, J. and W.J. Clench, 1936. A Second Contribution to the Molluscan Fauna of Yucatan. Publ. Carnegie Inst. Wash., vol. 457: 61-75; (1938), vol. 491: 257-260.

Branson, B.A. and C.J. McCoy, 1963. Gastropoda of the 1961 University of Colorado Museum Expedition in Mexico. The Nautilus, vol. 76: 101-108.

Breure, A.S.H., 1974. Notes on Land and Freshwater Mollusca from Southern and Central Mexico. Kreukel, vol. 10: 131-148.

Fisher, P. and H. Crosse, 1870-1902. Etudes sur les mollusques terrestres et fluviatiles du Mexique et du Guatemala. In Milne-Edwards Recherches Zoologiques . . . du Mexique. 2 vols., 1 Atlas, pp. 1-731.

Goodrich, C. and H. van der Schalie, 1937. Mollusca of Peten and North Alta Vera Paz, Guatemala. Misc. Publ. Univ. Mich. Mus. Zool., vol. 34: 1-50, pl. 1.

Haas, Fritz and A. Solem, 1960. Non-marine mollusks from British Honduras. The Nautilus, vol. 73 (4): 129-131, figs. 5-7.

Harry, H.W., 1950. Studies of the nonmarine mollusca of Yucatan. Occ. Papers. Mus. Zool. Univ. Mich., no. 524: 1-34.

Hinkley, A.A., 1920. Guatemala Mollusca. The Nautilus, vol. 34: 37-55.

Jacobson, M.K., 1958. Results of the Puritan-American Museum of Natural History Expedition to Western Mexico, 3. The terrestrial mollusks. Amer. Mus. Novitates, no. 1899: 1-14.

——, 1968. On a collection of terrestrial mollusca from Nicaragua. The Nautilus, vol. 81(4): 114-119, 1 fig.

Morrison, J.P.E., 1946. The non-marine mollusks of San José Island, with notes on those of Pedro Gonzales Island, Pearl Islands, Panama. Smiths. Misc. Coll., vol. 106 (6): 1-49, pls. 1-3.

Orbigny, A. d', 1835-1847. Voyage dans l'Amérique Meridionale . . ., vol. 5. Mollusques, 758 pp., 85 pls. Paris/Strasbourg.

Pilsbry, H.A., 1891. Land and freshwater mollusks collected in Yucatan and Mexico. Proc. Acad. Nat. Sci. Phila., vol. 43: 310-328, pls. 14-15.

——, 1926. The land mollusks of the Republic of Panama and the Canal Zone. Ibid., vol. 78: 57-126, pls. 9-10, 40 figs.

——, 1927. Expedition to Guadeloupe Island, Mexico, in 1922. Land and freshwater Mollusks. Proc. Calif. Acad. Sci., ser. 4, vol. 16: 159-203, pls. 6-12, 3 figs.

——, 1953. Inland mollusca of the Northern Mexico. II. Urocoptidae, Pupillidae, Strobilopsidae, Valloniidae and Cionellidae. Proc. Acad. Nat. Sci. Phila., vol. 105: 133-167, pls. 3-10; III, Polygyridae. Ibid., vol. 108: 18-40.

Rehder, H.A., 1942. Some new land shells from Costa Rica and Panama. Jour. Wash. Acad. Sci., vol. 32 (11): 350-352, 19 figs.

——, 1966. The non-marine mollusks of Quintana Roo, Mexico, with the description of a new species of Drymaeus. Proc. Biol. Soc. Wash., vol. 79: 273-296.

Strebel, H., 1873-1882. Beitrag zur kenntnis der Fauna Mexikanischer Land-und Süsswasser-Conchylien. Abhand. Naturw. Ver. Hamburg, vol. 6. (Strebel and G. Pfeffer, 1880-1882), pts. 4 and 5.

Taylor, D.W., 1966. A remarkable snail fauna from Coahuila, Mexico. Veliger, vol. 9 (2): 152-228, pls. 8-19, 24 figs.

Thompson, F.G., 1963. New land snails from El Salvador. Proc. Biol. Soc. Wash., vol. 76: 19-32.

Thompson, Fred G., 1967. The land and freshwater snails of Campeche [Mexico]. Bull. Florida State Mus., vol. 11: 221-256.

van der Schalie, H., 1940. Notes on mollusca from Alta Vera Paz, Guatemala. Occ. Papers Mus. Zool. Mich., no. 413: 1-11.

South America

Altena, C.O. van R., 1975. Land Gastropods of Surinam, with Description of a New Species of Nesopupa. Basteria, vol. 39: 29-50.

Ancey, C.F., 1892. On Some Shells from Eastern Bolivia and Western Brasil. Jour. Conch., vol. 7: 90-97.

——, 1903 and 1904. New Land Snails from South America. The Nautilus, vol. 17: 82-83, 89-90, 102-104.

Baker, Fred, 1913. The Land and Freshwater Mollusks of the Stanford Expedition to Brazil. Proc. Acad. Nat. Sci. Phila., vol. 65: 618-672, pls. 21-27.

Baker, H.B., 1930. The Mollusca Collected by the University of Michigan-Williamson Expedition in Venezuela. Proc.

Acad. Nat. Sci. Phila., vol. 210: 1-94.

Breure, A.S.H., 1977. Notes on Bulimulidae. 5, On some Collections from Colombia. Archiv. Moll., vol. 107 (4/6): 257-270, 25 figs.

Chambers, S.M. and D.W. Steadman, 1986. Holocene terrestrial gastropod faunas from Isla Santa Cruz and Isla Floreana, Galapagos . . .. Trans. San Diego Soc. Nat. Hist., vol. 21 (6): 89-110, illus.

Crawford, G.J., 1939. Report on the terrestrial Mollusca collected by the Percy Sladen Expedition to Lake Titicaca [Peru]. Proc. Mal. Soc. London, vol. 23 (6): 318-332, pls. 20 21.

Dall, W.H. and W.H. Ochsner, 1928. Landshells of the Galapagos Islands. Proc. Calif. Acad. Sci. (4), vol. 17 (5): 141-185, pls. 8-9.

Dautzenberg, P., 1901. Descriptions de coquilles nouvelles rapportées du Péroupar M. Baer. Jour. de Conchyl., vol. 49: 306-313.

Dohrn, H., 1882. Beiträge zur Kenntnis der südamerkanischen Land-conchylien. Jour. Deutch. Malak. Ges., vol. 9: 97-115, pl. 3: 1883, ibid., vol. 10: 346-356.

Haas, Fritz, 1938. Neue Binnen-Mollusken aus Nordost Brasilien. Archiv. Moll., vol. 70: 46-51, 10 figs.; vol. 70: 254-278.

——, 1949. Land and fresh-water mollusks from Peru. Fieldiana Zool., vol. 31 (28): 235-250.

——, 1949. Land-und Süsswassermollusken aus dem Amazonas-Gebiete. Arch. Moll., vol. 78 (4/6): 149-156, pl. 7.

——, 1951. Remarks on and descriptions of South American non-marine mollusks. Fieldiana Zool., vol. 31: 503-545, figs. 97-126; 1953, vol. 34 (9): 107-132.

Haas, F., 1955. On non-marine shells from northeastern Brazil and Peru. Fieldiana, Zool., vol. 37: 303-337.

Haltenorth, Th. and S. Jaeckel, 1940. Über einige am Riv Jary in Nordwesten Brasiliens von der Schultz-Kampf-Henckel-Expedition-1835-37 gemmelte Mollusken (Corona, Zebra, Orthalicus . . .). Archiv. Moll., vol. 72 (4): 97-112, 16 figs.

Jaeckel, A., 1952. Short review of the land-and freshwater molluscs of the North-East states of Brazil, Dusenia, vol. 3 (1): 1-10.

Lubomirski, L., 1879. Notice sur quelques coquilles du Pérou. Proc. Zool. Soc. London, vol. 47: 719-728, pls. 50-51.

Miller, K., 1878. Die Binnenmolusken von Ecuador. Malak. Blätter, vol. 25: 153-199; 1879, ibid., N.F., vol. 1: 117-203, pls. 4-15.

Morretes, Lange de, F., 1949. Ensaio de Catálogo dos moluscos do Brasil. Arqu. Mus. Paranaense, vol. 7 (1): 5-216.

Orbigny, A. d', 1835-1847. Voyage dans l'Amérique Meridionale . . ., vol. 5. Mollusques, 758 pp., 85 pls. Paris/Strasbourg.

Parodiz, J.J., 1944-49. Contribuciones al conocimento de los moluscos terrestres sudamericanos. (nos. 1-6). In Communic. Zool. Mus. Hist. Nat. Montevideo, vol. 1 and 2.

——, 1957. Catalogue of the land Mollusca of Argentina. The Nautilus, vol. 70: 127-135; vol. 71: 22-30, 63-66.

Piaget, J., 1914. Quelques mollusques de Colombie. Mém. Soc. Neuchâteloise Sci. Nat., vol. 5: 253-269.

Solem, Alan, 1956. Non-marine mollusca from Salobra,

Mato Grosso, Brazil and a collection of South Brazilian Artemon. Notula Naturae, no. 287: 1-14.

Tello, J., 1975. Catálogo de la fauna Venezolana. VIII, Mollusca, 599 pp. Caracas.

Thiele, J., 1927. Über einige brasilienische Land-schnecken. Abh. Senckenb. Naturf. Ges., vol. 40 (3): 307-329, pl. 26.

Tillier, S., 1980. Gastéropodes terrestres et fluviatiles de Guyane Française. Mém. Mus. Nat. Hist. Nat. Paris, N.S., ser. A, Zool., vol. 115: 1-189.

van Benthen-Jutting, W.S.S., 1944. Über eine Sammlung Nichtmariner Mollusken aus dem Niederschlagsarmen Gebiet Nordostbrasiliens. Archiv. Hydrobiol., vol. 39: 458-489.

Vernhout, J.H., 1914. The non-marine mollusca of Surinam. Notes Leyden Mus., vol. 36: 1-46.

Weyrauch, W.K., 1956. Neue Landschnecken aus Peru. Arch. Moll., vol. 85 (4/6): 145-164, pl. 11.

——, 1957. Lista de algunos generos, especies y subspecies recien descritos como nuevos para la fauna del Peru. Scientia, Lima, vol. 4 (3): 20-25.

Zilch, A., 1949. Landschnecken aus Peru. Archiv. Moll., vol. 82 (1-3): 49-61, pls. 14-15; 1954, ibid., vol. 83 (1/3): 65-78, pls. 5, 6; 1959, ibid., vol. 88 (1/3): 35-40, pls. 5.

——, 1954. Die Typen und Typoide des Natur-Museums Senckenberg, 12: Clausiliidae. Archiv. Moll., vol. 83: 1-63.

——, 1958. Neue Landschnecken und neue Synonyme aus Südamerika, I. Archiv. Moll., vol. 87: 91-139, pls. 6-9a.

Zischka, R., 1953. Catátogo de las conchas y caracoles Bolivianos. Folia Universitaria, Santa Cruz, vol. 6: 69-85.

Europe

Alzona, C., 1971. Malacofauna Italica, Catalogo e Bibliografia dei Molluschi viventi terrestri e d'acqua dolce. Atti della Soc. Italiana di Sci. Nat. e del Museo Civ. di Storia Nat. di Milano, vol. 111: 1-433. [large bibliography of Italian living land mollusks].

Cameron, R.A.D. and Margaret Redfern, 1976. British Land Snails. Keys and Notes for the Identification of the Species. Synopses of the British Fauna, no. 6, pp. 1-64. Academic Press, London.

Gittenberger, E., W. Backhuys and Th. E.J. Ripken, 1984. De Landslakken van Nederland, 184 pp., 192 figs., 102 maps. Konink, Neder. Natuurhist. Veren., no. 37.

Grossu, A.V., 1955. Mollusca III. Gastropoda Pulmonata. Fauna Republicii Populare Romine, vol. 16: 1-518. Bukarest, Acad. Republ. Pop. Romine; 1956, Gastropoda Prosobranchia si Opisthobranchia, ibid., vol. 17: 1-220. [Pulmonates of Romania].

Kerney, M. P., 1967. Distribution Mapping of Land and Freshwater Mollusca in the British Isles. Jour. Conch., London, vol. 26: 152-160.

Kerney, M.P. and R.A.D. Cameron, 1979. A field guide to the land snails of Britain and North-West Europe. Collins, London, 288 pp., illus.

Kerney, M.P., R.A.D. Cameron and J.H. Jungbluth, 1983. Die Landschnecken Nord-und Mitteleuropas. Paul Parey, Hamburg. 384 pp., 24 pls., 890 figs. Great improvement over 1979 English edition. Good European bibliography.

Klemm, W., 1974. Die Verbreitung der rezenten Land-Gehäuse-Schnecken in Osterreich [Land snails of Austria]. Denkschr. Osterr. Akad. Wissen. Math. Nat. Klasse, vol. 117: 1-503.

Likhachev, I.M. and E.S. Rammel'meier, 1952. Terrestrial Mollusks of the Fauna of the U.S.S.R. [English translation, 1962, 511 pp., 420 figs. Nat. Sci. Foundation, Wash., D.C.; Office of Technical Services, U.S. Dept. of Commerce, Wash., D.C.]

McMillan, Nora F., 1968. British Shells. 196 pp., 80 pls. F. Warne, London. [terrestrials: 116-136; 181-186, 4 pls.]

Taylor, J.W. 1894-1921. Monograph of the land and freshwater Mollusca of the British Isles. 4 vols., 24 parts. Well illustrated. Leeds, Taylor Bros.

van Benthem-Jutting, W.S.S., 1933. Mollusca (I). A. Gastropoda. In Fauna van Nederland, Leiden. [Pulmonata, pp. 155-348].

Wagner, A.J., 1927. Studien zur Molluskenfauna der Balkanhalbinsel mit besonderer Berücksichtigung Bulgariens und Thraziens. . .. Ann. Zool. Mus. Polon. Hist. Nat., vol. 6: 263-399, pls. 10-22.

Asia Minor

Connolly, M., 1941. South Arabian non-marine mollusca. British Mus. Exped. South-West Arabia, 1937-38, vol. 1 (4): 17-41, pl. 3.

Godwin-Austen, H.H., 1882-1920. Land and freshwater mollusca of India, including South Arabia, . . . Afghanistan . . . Burmah . . . Ceylon . . . . Vol. 1: 1-257, 62 pls.; 1884-1914, vol. 2: 1-442, 158 pls.; 1920, vol. 3: 1-65, 7 pls.

Pallary, P., 1924. Faune Malacologique du Sinai. Journ. de Conchyl., vol. 68: 182-217, pls. 10-12.

——, 1929. Première addition à la faune malacologique de la Syrie. Mém. Inst. Egypte, vol. 12: 1-43, pl. 1-3; 1939, ibid., vol. 39: 1-141, pls. 1-7.

Tropical Asia-East Indies

Bavay, A. and P. Dautzenberg, 1899. Description de coquilles nouvelles de l'Indochine. Jour. de Conchyl., vol. 47: 28-55; 1900, ibid., vol. 48: 108-122; 1903, ibid., vol. 51: 201-236; 1909, ibid, vol. 5-6 (4): 229-251 (Tonkin).

Boettger, C.R., 1922. Die Landschneckenfauna der Aru-und Kei-Inseln. Ber. Senckenb. Naturf. Ges., vol. 34 (4): 355-417, pls. 21-23.

Bollinger, C., 1918. Land-Mollusken von Celebes. Rev. Suisse Zool., vol. 26: 309-340, pl. 2.

Bullen, R.A., 1906. On some land and freshwater mollusca from Sumatra. Proc. Mal. Soc. London, vol. 7: 12-17; 126-130.

Dohrn, H., 1889. Beitrag zur Conchylienfauna der Philippinen. Nachr. Bl. Deutsch Malak. Ges., vol. 21: 53-63.

Ehrmann, P., 1912. Die Landmolluskenfauna der Tenimber-Inseln. S.B. Naturf. Ges., Leipzig, vol. 38: 32-71.

Fischer, Paul, 1891. Catalogue et distribution géographique des mollusques terrestres, fluviatiles et marins d 'une partie de l'Indochine (Siam, Laos, Cambodge, Cochinchine, Annam, Tonkin). Bull. Soc. Hist. Nat. d'Autun, vol. 4: 1-193.

Godwin-Austen, H.H., 1895. List and distribution of the landmollusca of the Andaman and Nicobar Islands with descriptions of some supposed new species. Proc. Zool. Soc. London, vol. 63: 438-457.

Gude, G.K., 1903. A classified list of the helicoid land shells of Asia. Jour. Malacol., vol. 10 (2): 45-62, pl. 3.

——, 1914 and 1921. The Fauna of British India, II, 520 pp., 164 figs.; III, 386 pp., pls. 38, 39, 42 figs.

Haas, Fritz, 1952. Some non-marine mollusks from Northwest and Southwest Siam. Bull. Siam Soc. Nat. Hist., vol. 15 (1): 21-25.

Hanley, S. and W. Theobald, 1870-1876. Conchologia Indica: Illustrations of the land and freshwater shells of British India, xviii + 65 pp., 160 pls.

Laidlaw, F.F., 1933. A list of land and freshwater mollusca of the Malay Peninsula. Jour. Royal Asiatic Soc., vol. 11: 211-234.

Niethammer, G., 1937. Zur Landschneckenfauna von Celebes. Arch. Naturgesch., N.F. vol. 6 (3): 389-415, 15 figs.

Paravicini, E., 1935. Beiträge zur Kenntnis der Land-und Süsswassermollusken von Sumatra. Archiv. Moll., vol. 67: 59-63.

Rensch, B., 1932. Die molluskenfauna der kleinen Sundainseln Bali, Lombok, Flores und Sumbawa. Zool. Jahrb., Jena, vol. 63: 1-130.

Rensch, I., 1955. On some Indian land snails. Jour. Bombay Nat. Hist. Soc., vol. 53 (2): 163-176.

Rolle, H., 1908. Zur Fauna von West-Sumatra. Nachr. Bl. Deutsch Malak. Ges., vol. 40: 63-70.

Sarasin, P. and F. Sarasin, 1899. Die Landmollusken von Celebes, Materialien zur Naturgeschichte der Insel Celebes, vol. 2. Weisbaden. 248 pp., 31 pls.

Saul, Mary, 1967. Shell collecting in the limestone caves of Borneo. Sabah Soc. Jour., vol. 3: 105-110, 2 figs.

Smith, E.A., 1895. On a collection of land shells from Sarawak, British North Borneo, Palawan and other neighboring islands. Proc. Zool. Soc. London for 1895: 97 pp., pls. 2-4.

——, 1896. On a collection of landshells from South Celebes. Proc. Mal. Soc. London, vol. 2: 94-103.

——, 1896. A list of the landshells of the islands of Batchian, Ternate and Gilolo. Ibid., vol. 2: 120-122.

——, 1903. The land and fresh-water shells of Sokotra [Id., Indian Ocean]. In the Natural History of Sokotra and Abd-el-Kuri. Liverpool. pp. 111-156, pls. 12, 13.

Solem, Alan, 1964. A collection of non-marine mollusks from Sabah (Malaysia). Sabah Soc. Journ., vol. 2 (1/2): 1-40.

Strubell, B., 1892. Landschnecken aus Halmahera. Nachr. Bl. Deutsch Malak. Ges., vol. 24: 41-50.

Thompson, F.G. and S.P. Dance, 1983. Non-marine mollusks of Borneo. II, Pulmonata. III, Prosobranchia. Bull. Florida State Mus. (Biol. Sci.), vol. 29 (3): 101-130, 75 figs.

Tomlin, R.J. le B., 1929. The landshells of Kaw Tao. Jour. Siam Soc. Nat. Hist., Suppl. 8, pt. 1: 15-17.

Tweedie, M.W.F, 1961. On certain Mollusca of the Malayan limestone hills. Bull. Raffles Mus., Singapore, vol. 26: 49-64, 1 fig.

van Benthem-Jutting, W.S.S., 1928. Non-marine mollusca of Sumba. Treubia, vol. 10: 153-162.

———, 1929. A list of the land and freshwater mollusca from Java. Ibid., vol. 11: 76-88.

———, 1934. Non-marine mollusca from Nias Island. Misc. Zool. Sum., vol. 84/85: 1-17, figs. 1-10; ibid., vol. 89: 1-4.

———, 1935. Land and freshwater mollusca from Poeloe Weh. Ibid., vol. 95: 1-9, 1 fig.

———, 1937. Non-marine mollusca of Enggano Island. Treubia, vol. 16: 47-50, fig. 1.

———, 1941. On a collection of non-marine mollusca from the Talaud Islands and from Morotai. Ibid., vol. 18: 1-27.

———, 1948. Systematic studies on the non-marine mollusca of the Indo-Australian Archipelago. [operculates] Treubia, vol. 19 (3): 539-604, 60 figs.; 1950 [pulmonates], ibid., vol. 20 (3): 381-505, 107 figs.; 1952, ibid., vol. 21 (2): 291-435, 90 figs.

———, 1953. Annotated list of non-marine mollusca of the Moluccan islands Ambon, Haruku, Saparua and Nusa Laut. Treubia, vol. 22 (2): 275-318, 2 figs.

———, 1958. Non-marine mollusca of the island of Misool. Nova Guinea, N.S., vol. 9 (2): 293-338, 18 figs.

———, 1959. Non-marine mollusca of the North Moluccan Islands Halmahera, Ternate, Batjan and Obi. Treubia, vol. 25 (1): 25-87.

———, 1962. Coquilles terrestres nouvelles de quelques collines calcaires du Cambodge et du Sud Vietnam. Jour. de Conchyl., vol. 102 (1): 3-15, 6 figs.

von Martens, E., 1891. Landschnecken des Indischen Archipels. In: Max Weber, Zoologische Ergebnisse einer Reise nach Ostindien, vol. 2: 209-264, pls. 12-14.

Yen, Teng-Chien, 1935. The Non-marine gastropoda of North China. Publ. Mus. Hoangpo Paiho de Tien Tsin, no. 34: 1-57, 3 pls.

Philippines

Clench, W.J. and A.F. Archer, 1933. Land mollusks from the islands Mindoro and Lubang, Philippines. Papers Michigan Acad. Sci., vol. 17: 535-552, pls. 57-58.

Faustino, L.A., 1930. Summary of Philippine Land Shells [checklist]. Philippine Jour. Sci., vol. 42 (1): 85-198.

Hidalgo, J.G., 1890. Obras malacológicas de las Islas Filipinas. Mem. Acad. Cienc. Nat. Madrid, vol. 14: 1-160.

Moellendorff, O.F. von, 1888. Von den Philippinen (Nachträge und Berichtigungen zur Fauna von Cebu.). Malak. Blätt. (NF), vol. 10: 144-164, pl. 4.

———, 1890. Die Landschnecken-Fauna der Insel Cebu. Ber. Senckenb. Naturf. Ges., 1890: 189-292, pls. 7-9.

———, 1891. Beitrag zur Fauna der Philippinen. ix, Die Insel Siquijor. Nachr. Bl. deutch. Malak. Ges., vol. 23: 37-58.

———, 1893. Materialien zur Fauna der Philippinen. xi, Die Insel Leyte. Ber. Senckenb. Naturf. Ges., vol. for 1893: 51-154, pls. 3-5.

———, 1898. Verzeichniss der auf den Philippinen lebenden Landmollusken, Abhand, Naturf. Ges. Görlitz, vol. 22: 26-208.

Quadras, J.F. and O.F. von Moellendorff, 1893-1896. Diagnoses Specierum Novarum ex insulis Philippinis. Nachr.

Bl. Deutch Malak. Ges., vol. 25: 169-184; 1894, vol. 26: 81-104, 113-130; 1895, vol. 27: 105-121; 1896, vol. 28: 1-15, 81-93.

Semper, C., 1870-1885. Reisen in Archipel der Philippinen, 2, pt. 3: Landmollusken: 1-327 (Lfg. 1-7. Wiesbaden).

Smith, Maxwell, 1932. New Philippine Island Land Shells. The Nautilus, vol. 46 (2): 62-65.

Melanesia
(New Guinea-Solomons)

Clench, W.J., 1958. The land and freshwater mollusca of Rennell Island, Solomon Islands. In: The Natural History of Rennell Island, British Solomon Islands, vol. 2: 155-202, pls. 16-19.

Gude, G.K., 1913. The helicoid land shells of the Fiji Islands, with definitions of three new genera . . .. Proc. Mal. Soc. London, vol. 10: 325-330, pl. 14.

Iredale, Tom, 1941. A Basic List of the Land Mollusca of Papua. Australian Zoologist, vol. 10: 51-94, pl. 3.

Rensch, Ilse, 1934. Systematische und Tiergeographische Untersuchungen über die Landschnecken des Bismarck-Archipels. Archiv für Naturgeschichte, N.F., vol. 3, pt. 3, pp. 445-488; 1937, part 2, ibid., vol. 6, pp. 526-644, 54 figs.

———, 1934. Studies on Papuina and Dendrotrochus, Pulmonata Mollusks from the Solomon Islands. Amer. Mus. Novitates, no. 763, pp. 1-26.

———, 1940. Nachträge zur Landschneckenfauna des Bismark-Archipels. Zoologischer Anzeiger, vol. 131, pp. 29-39.

van Benthem-Jutting, W.S.S., 1963. Non-marine Mollusca of West New Guinea, Pt. 2, Operculate Land Shells. Nova Guinea, Zoology, vol. 23, pp. 653-726; 1964, Pt. 3, Pulmonata, pp. 1-74; 1965, Pt. 4, Pulmonata, 2, pp. 205-304, pl. 7-10. (good coverage; large bibliography for New Guinea.)

Polynesia, Micronesia
(for Hawaii, see under United States)

Abbott, R. Tucker, 1949. New Syncerid Mollusks from the Mariana Islands (Synceridae). Occ. Papers B.P. Bishop Mus., vol. 19 (15): 261-274, 9 figs.

Garrett, A., 1884. The terrestrial mollusca inhabiting the Society Islands. Proc. Acad. Nat. Sci. Phila., ser. 2, vol. 9: 1-98.

———, 1887. On the terrestrial mollusks of the Viti [Fiji] Islands, Pt. 1, Proc. Zool. Soc. London, for 1887: 164-189; Pt. 2, ibid., pp. 284-316.

———, 1887. Mollusques terrestres des Iles Marquises. Bull. Soc. Malac. France, vol. 4: 1-48.

———, 1887. The terrestrial mollusca inhabiting the Samoa or Navigator Islands. Proc. Acad. Nat. Sci. Phila., vol. 39: 124-153.

Moellendorff, O. von, 1895. The land shells of the Caroline Islands. Jour. Malacol., vol. 7 (5): 101-126, 3 figs.

Odhner, N.H., 1922. Mollusca from Juan Fernandez and

Easter Island. In C. Skottsberg. Nat. Hist.... Easter Island, vol. 3: 219-254, pls. 8-9.

Pease, W.H., 1871. Catalogue of the land shells inhabiting Polynesia, with remarks on their synonymys, distribution and variation, and descriptions of new genera and species. Proc. Zool. Soc. London, for 1871: 449-477.

Reigle, N.J., 1964. Nonmarine mollusks of Rongelap Atoll, Marshall Islands. Pacific Science, vol. 18: 126-129, 1 fig.

Australia

Burch, J.B., 1976. Outline of classification of Australian terrestrial molluscs (native and introduced). Jour. Malacol. Soc. Australia, vol. 3 (3/4): 127-151.

Cox, J.C., 1868. A monograph of Australian land shells. 111 pp. 20 pls.

Gabriel, C.J., 1929. Report on land shells from Cann River, Victoria. Victoria Naturalist, vol. 46: 130-134.

Iredale, Tom, 1933. Systematic notes on Australian land snails. Record Australian Mus., vol. 19: 37-59.

——, 1937. A basic list of the land mollusca of Australia. Australian Zool., vol. 8 (4): 287-333; vol 9 (1): 1-39, pls. 1-3; 1938, vol. 9 (2): 83-124, pls. 12, 13.

——, 1937. An annotated check list of the land shells of South and Central Australia. South Australian Nat., vol. 18 (1/2): 6-57, pls. 1, 2.

——, 1939. A review of the land mollusca of Western Australia. Jour. Royal Soc. Western Austr., vol. 25 (1): 1-88, pl. 1-5.

——, 1941. Guide to the land shells of New South Wales. Part III. Australian Naturalist, vol. 11 (1): 1-8; Part V, 1943, ibid., vol. 11 (3): 62-69.

——, 1944. The land mollusca of Lord Howe Island. Austr. Zool., vol. 10 (3): 299-334, pls. 17-20.

——, 1945. The land mollusca of Norfolk Island, ibid., vol. 11 (1): 46-71, pls. 2-5.

Smith, B.J. and R.C. Kershaw, 1979. Field Guide to the non-marine Mollusca of South Eastern Australia. (ANV Press, Canberra). 285 pp., illus.

——, 1981. Tasmanian Land & Freshwater Mollusca. Fauna of Tasmania Handbook no. 5 (Univ. Tasmania, Hobart). 148 pp., illus.

New Zealand

Climo, F.M., 1973. The Systematics, Biology and Zoogeography of the Land Snail Fauna of Great Island, Three Kings Group, New Zealand. Jour. Royal Soc. N.Z., vol. 3: 565-628.

——, 1974. Description and Affinities of the Subterranean Molluscan Fauna of New Zealand, N.A. Jour. Zool., vol. 1 (3): 247-284.

Dell, R.K., 1954. The land mollusca of Steward and Solander Islands. Trans. Roy. Soc. N.Z., vol. 82 (1): 137-156, 13 figs.

Powell, A.W.B., 1979. New Zealand Mollusca. 500 pp., 120 text figs., 78 pls. Collins, Auckland. Excellent land shell section, pp. 297-352.

Japan

Azuma, Masao, 1982. Colored Illustrations of the Land Snails of Japan. Hoikusha Publ., Osaka. 333 pp., 513 sp. in color. Shells, anatomy and bibliography of Japanese works.

Okutani, T., 1983. The Mollusks of Japan. Gakken Illustrated Nature Encyclopedia, vol. 2, 294 pp. Pulmonates in color pls. 42-65.

Africa-Madagascar

Adensamer, W., 1929. Beitrag zur Molluskenfauna von Südwestafrika. Ann. Naturhist. Mus. Wien, vol. 43: 387-399, pls. 12, 13.

Bacci, G., 1943. Nuovo contributo alla conoscenza della malacofauna dell' Africa Orientale Italiana. Ann. Mus. Civ. Stor. Nat. Genova, vol. 61: 120-140.

Blume, W., 1952. Beitrag zur Kenntnis der Landschnekken-Fauna SW-Afrikas. Arch. Moll., vol. 81 (4/6): 113-117, 2 figs.

Boettger, O., 1889. Zur Kenntniss der Land-und Süssivasser Mollusken von Nossi-Be [Madagascar]. Nach. Bl. Deutsch Malak. Ges., for 1889 (3/4): 1-13; ibid., for 1890 (5/6): 81-101.

——, 1910. Nachtrag zur Liste der Binnenmollusken von Kamerun [Cameroons]. Nachr. Bl. Deutsch Malak., vol. 42: 79-81.

Connolly, M., 1939. A Monographic Survey of South African Non-marine Mollusca. Annals South African Mus., vol. 33: 1-660, pls. 1-19.

Cooke, A.H., 1893. On the geographical distribution of the land and freshwater mollusca of the Malogasy region. The Conchologist, vol. 6: 131-139.

Crosse, H., 1874. Faune malacologique terrestre et fluviatile de l'île Rodriguez [Indian Ocean]. Jour. de Conchyl., vol. 22: 221-242, pl. 8.

Dautzenberg, P., 1921. Contribution à la faune malacologique du Cameroun. Rev. Zool. Afr., vol. 9: 87-192, pl. 6.

Deshayes, G.P., 1863. Catalogue des mollusques de l'île de La Réunion.

Germaine, L., 1921. Faune malacologique terrestre et fluviatile des îles Mascareignes. 495 pp., 13 pls., 42 figs. Paris.

——, 1934. L'Origine et la composition de la faune terrestre et fluviatile des Iles Seychelles. C.R. Congr. Soc. Sav. Paris, sect. Sciences: 113-133.

Girard, A.A., 1893. Révision de la faune malacologique des Iles St. Thomé et de Prince Id. Jour. Sci. Math., Phys. et Natur., ser. 2, vol. 3: 28-42.

Hidalgo, J.G., 1910. Molluscos de la Guinea Española. Mem. Roy. Soc. Esp. Hist. Nat., vol. 29: 507-524.

Kobelt, W., 1913. Landschecken aus Deutsch-Ostafrika und Uganda. Rev. Suisse Zool., vol. 21 (2): 57-74, pl. 2.

Martens, von, 1898. Land-and Süsswasser-Molluskender Seychelles. I. Conchyliologischer Teil. Mitt. Zool. Samml. Mus. Naturk. Berlin, vol. 1 (1): 1-35, pls. 1 and 2.

Melvill, J.C. and J.H. Ponsbonby, 1898. A contribution towards a check-list of the non-marine molluscan fauna of South Africa. Proc. Mal. Soc. London, vol. 3: 166-184; 1899, Ann. Mag. Nat. Hist., ser. 7, vol. 4: 192-200, pl. 3.

Ortiz de Zarate, A. and J. Alvarez, 1960. Resultados de la expedición Peris-Alvarez a la isla de Annobón (Guinea Expañola. I. Los gastropodos terrestres.) Bol. Real. Soc. Esp. Hist. Nat. (Biol.), vol. 58: 87-103.

Pilsbry, H.A., 1919. A review of the land mollusks of the Belgium Congo chiefly based on the collections of the American Museum Congo Expedition, 1909-1915. Bull. Amer. Mus. Nat. Hist., vol. 40: 1-370, pls. 1-23.

Preston, H.B., 1912. Additions to the land-molluscan fauna of Rhodesia. Ann. Mag. Nat. Hist., series 8, vol. 9: 69-72.

Sykes, E.R., 1909. The land and freshwater mollusca of the Seychelles archipelago. Trans. Linn Soc. London, series 2, Zool., vol. 13: 57-64.

Verdcourt, B., 1972. The zoogeography of the non-marine mollusca of East Africa. Journ. Conch., vol. 27: 291-348.

——, 1978. Notes on East African land and freshwater snails. Basteria, vol. 42: 15-26, p. 77.

van Bruggen, A.C., 1964. On some molluscs from Mount Gorongosa, Portuguese East Africa, with descriptions of two new streptaxids. Rev. Zool. Bot. Africa, vol. 70: 113-122.

——, 1966. Notes on non-marine molluscs from Mozambique and Bechuanaland, with a checklist of Bechuanaland species. Ann. Transvaal Mus., vol. 25: 99-112.

——, 1966. The terrestrial mollusca of the Kuger National Park: a contribution to the malacology of the Eastern Transvaal. Ann. Natal Mus., vol. 18: 315-399.

——, 1969. Studies on the land molluscs of Zululand with notes on the description of land mollusks in Southern Africa. Zool. Verh. Leiden, vol. 103: 1-116.

——, 1970. A contribution to the knowledge of non-marine mollusca of South West Africa. Zool. Meded. Leiden, vol. 45: 43-73.

——, 1981. The African element among the terrestrial molluscs of the island of Madagascar. Proc. Kon. Nederl. Akad. Wet., ser. C, vol. 84: 115-129.

Azores, Canary Islands Saint Helena

Backhuys, W., 1975. Zoogeography and Taxonomy of the Land and Freshwater Molluscs of the Azores. Backhuys and Meesters, Amsterdam, 350 pp., 32 pls.

Germain, L., 1932. L'origine et l'évolution de la faune malacologique de l'île de Saint-Hélène. C.R. Congr. Soc. Savantes en 1926, Sci.: 1-20.

Groh, K., 1985. Landschnecken aus quartaren Wirbeltierfundstellen der Kanarischen Inseln (Gastropoda). Bonner Zool. Beitr., vol. 36 (3/4): 395-415.

Indian Ocean Islands

Connolly, M., 1925. Notes on a Collection of Non-marine Mollusca from the Islands in the Indian Ocean. Jour. Conch., London, vol. 17: 257-266.

Gerlach, Justin, 1987. The Land Snails of Seychelles. 44 pp., 61 spp. Privately publ., Weedon, England.

Lionnet, Guy, 1984. Terrestrial Testaceous Molluscs of the Seychelles. In Biogeography and Ecology of the Seychelles Islands, pp. 239-244.

Mörch, O.A.L., 1876. Révision des Mollusques Terrestres des Iles Nicobar. Jour. de Conchyl., vol. 24: 353-367.

von Martens, E., 1887. List of the shells of Mergui and its archipelago, collected by Dr. John Anderson. Jour. Linn. Soc., vol. 21 (130): 155-222, pls. 14-16.

NEW COUNTRY NAMES

This is a list of new names for some of the old countries cited in malacological literature. The new name is listed first.

AFRICA
Benin: Dahomey
Botswana: (northern South Africa)
Burundi: (Belgium) Buanda
Central African Republic: French Equatorial Africa
Chad: French Equatorial Africa
Congo: French Equatorial Africa
Cote D'Ivoire: Ivory Coast
Equatorial Guinea: Bioko Id., off Rio Muni
Ghana: Gold Coast
Guinea: French West Africa
Guinea-Bissau: formerly Portuguese
Lesotho: in South Africa
Malawi: formerly British East Africa area
Mali: French West Africa
Mauritania: French Sahara
Namibia: South-West Africa

Pakistan: West Pakistan
Rwanda: Ruanda-Urundi
Somalia: formerly Italian and British Somalia
Tanzania: Tanganyika and Zanzibar
Zaire: Belgium Equatorial Africa
Zambia: Northern Rhodesia
Zimbabwe: Southern Rhodesia

TROPICAL AMERICAS
Belize: British Honduras
El Salvador: San Salvador
Guyana: British Guiana
Surinam: Dutch Guiana
Isla de la Juventud (Cuba): Isla de Pinos
Guantanamo, Holguin, Bayamo, Tunas; Santiago de Cuba: formerly Oriente Province

Santa Clara Prov.: Villas Prov.
Ciego de Avila: western Camaguey Prov., Cuba

ASIA
Bangladesh: East Pakistan
Bhutan: China-India
Brunei: British Borneo
Kampuchea: west Cambodia
Laos: west Vietnam
Malaysia: Malay; Sarawak; Sabah
Sri Lanka: Ceylon
Thailand: Siam
Vietnam: Tonkin

OCEANIA
Kiribati: Gilbert Islands
Tuvalu: Ellice Islands
Vanuatu: New Hebrides

Classification of the Landshells
with an Illustrated Bibliography

Phylum MOLLUSCA

For a phylogenetic arrangement and bibliographies of the marine mollusks, see the *Compendium of Seashells* by Abbott and Dance, 1986, American Malacologists, Inc., Melbourne, Florida.

Class GASTROPODA
Subclass PROSOBRANCHIA

Order Archaeogastropoda

Superfamily NERITOIDEA
(syn.: Neritacea)

Family HELICINIDAE

Family HELICINIDAE; subfamily Vianinae. *Viana regina* (Morelet, 1849). Cuba. 2.5 cm. See p. 34.

Baker, H.B., 1940. New Subgenera of Antillean Helicinidae, *Hjalmarsona* and *Striatemoda*. The Nautilus, vol. 54: 70-71.

Bartsch, P., 1918. Classification of the Philippine operculate land shells of the family Helicinidae, with a synopsis of the species and subspecies of the genus *Geophorus*. Jour. Wash. Acad. Sci., vol. 8 (20): 643-657.

Boss, K.J. and M.K. Jacobson, 1973. Monograph of the genus *Alcadia* in Cuba. Bull. Mus. Comp. Zool., vol. 145 (7): 311-358, 6 pls.

——, 1973. Monograph of *Ceratodiscus*. Occ. Papers Moll., Harvard Univ., vol. 3 (45): 253-279, pls. 45-48.

——, 1974. Monograph of the genus *Lucidella* in Cuba (Prosobranchia: Helicinidae). *Ibid.*, vol. 4 (48): 1-27, pls. 1-4.

——, 1975. Proserpine Snails of the Greater Antilles (Prosobranchia: Helicinidae). *Ibid.*, vol. 4 (51): 53-90, pls. 10-13.

Clench, W.J. and M.K. Jacobson, 1968. Monograph of the Cuban genus *Viana* (Mollusca: Archaeogastropoda, Helicinidae). Breviora, no. 298, 25 pp., 4 pls.

——, 1971. Monograph of the Cuban genera *Emoda* and *Glyptemoda*. Bull. Mus. Comp. Zool., vol. 141 (3): 99-130, 7 pls.

——, 1971. A monograph of the genera *Calidviana, Ustronia, Troschelviana* and *Semitrochatella* in Cuba. *Ibid.*, vol. 141 (7): 402-463, 8 pls., 1 fig.

Guppy, R.J.L., 1895. On a land shell of the genus *Helicina* from Grenada and the classification of the Helicinidae. Jour. Conch., vol. 9.

Jacobson, M.K. and W.J. Clench, 1971. On some *Helicina* from the Dominican Republic. The Nautilus, vol. 84 (3): 101-107, 1 fig.

Neal, M.C., 1934. Hawaiian Helicinidae. B.P. Bishop Mus. Bull., vol. 125: 1-102.

Pilsbry, H.A. and C.M. Cooke, 1908. Hawaiian species of *Helicina*. Occ. Papers B.P. Bishop Mus., vol. 3 (2): 199-210, 1 pl.

Wagner, J.A., 1905. Helicinenstudien. Denkschr. Math.-Naturw. Klasse Kaiserlich, Akad. Wiss., Wien. Vol. 77: 1-94, 9 pls.; vol. 78:1-46, pls. 10-14.

Subfamily **Helicininae.** <u>Main genera:</u> *Helicina* Lamarck, 1899; *Alcadia* Gray, 1840; *Ceratopoma* Möllendorff, 1893; *Oligyra* Say, 1818; *Sturanya* Wagner, 1905; *Sulfurina* Möllendorff, 1893.

Subfamily **Hendersoniinae.** <u>Two genera:</u> *Hendersonia* Wagner, 1905; *Waldemaria* Wagner, 1905.

Subfamily **Proserpininae.** <u>Two genera:</u> *Prosperpina* Sowerby, 1839; *Calidviana* H.B. Baker, 1954.

Subfamily **Vianinae.** (syn.: Stoastomatinae). <u>Main genera:</u> *Viana* H. and A. Adams, 1856; *Calybium* Morelet, 1891; *Eutrochatella* Fischer, 1885; *Geophorus* Fischer, 1885; *Heudeia* Crosse, 1885; *Lucidella* Swainson, 1840; *Stoastoma* C.B. Adams, 1849.

Family CERESIDAE

<u>Main genera:</u> *Proserpinella* Bland, 1865; *Ceres* Gray, 1856; *Staffola* Dall, 1905.

Subfamily **Ceratodiscinae.** <u>Two genera:</u> *Ceratodiscus* Simpson and Henderson, 1901; *Fadyenia* Chitty, 1857.

Order Caenogastropoda

Superfamily CYCLOPHOROIDEA

Family CYCLOPHORIDAE

Family CYCLOPHORIDAE. *Cyclophorus siamensis* (Sowerby, 1850). Southeast Asia. 6 cm. See p. 38.

Bartsch, Paul, 1915. The Philippine land shells of the genus *Schistoloma*. Proc. U.S. Nat. Mus., vol. 49 (2104): 195-204, pl. 51.

——, 1919. The Philippine Island landshell of the genus *Platyraphe*. Jour. Wash. Acad. Sci., vol. 9 (24): 649-655.

——, 1932. The Philippine land mollusks of the genus *Opisthoporus*. Bull. 100, U.S.N.M., vol. 6, pt. 6: 323-327, pl. 81, 82.

Chitty, E., 1857. On the Jamaican *Cyclotus*, and the Description of twenty-one Proposed New Species and Eight New Varieties of that Subgenus from Jamaica. Proc. Zool. Soc. London, vol. 25: 142-157.

Cox, J.C., 1907. A list of Cyclophoridae found in Australia, New Guinea and adjacent groups of islands. Sydney. 28 pp.

Kobelt, W., 1902. Cyclophoridae in Das Tierreich, vol. 16, (pts. 1 to 39): 1-662, 110 figs. Berlin.

Robertson, R., et al, 1987. Cyclophoracea, Archaeogastropoda. In Catalog of the Types of Recent Mollusca of the Academy of Natural Sci. Phila. *Tryonia*, no. 15, pt. 5, pp. 1-140.

Solem, Alan, 1956. The helicoid cyclophorid mollusks of Mexico. Proc. Acad. Nat. Sci. Phila., vol. 108: 41-59, pls. 5, 6.

Thompson, F.G., 1963. Systematic notes on the land snail of the genus *Tomocyclus* (Cyclophoridae). Breviora, no. 181: 1-11, 1 pl.

——, 1969. Some Mexican and Central American land snails of the family Cyclophoridae. Zoologica, N.Y., vol. 54 (2): 35-77, 7 pls.

Tielecke, H., 1940. Anatomie, Phylogenie und Tiergeographie der Cyclophoriden. Arch. Natg. N.F., vol. 9: 317-371.

Torre, Carlos, de la, P. Bartsch and J.P.E. Morrison, 1942. The cyclophorid operculate land mollusks of America. Bull. U.S. Nat. Mus., 181: 1-306, 42 pls.

Zilch, A., 1954. Die Typen und Typoide des Natur-Museums Senckenberg. 13: Mollusca, Cyclophoridae, Cyclophorinae. Archiv. Moll., vol. 83 (4/6): 141-157, pl. 13-16; 1955 *ibid.*, vol. 84 (4/6): 183-210, pls. 13-15; *ibid.*, vol. 85 (4/6): 171-196, pls. 12-15.

Subfamily **Cyclophorinae**. Main genera: *Cyclophorus* Montfort, 1810; *Aulopoma* Troschel, 1847; *Craspedotropis* Blanford, 1864; *Crossopoma* van Martens, 1891; *Cyathopoma* Blanford, 1861; *Cyclosurus* Morelet, 1881; *Cyclotus* Swainson, 1840; *Japonia* Gould, 1859; *Leptopoma* Pfeiffer, 1847; *Mychopoma* Blanford, 1869; *Scabrina* Blanford, 1863; *Theobaldius* Nevill, 1878; *Megacyclotus* Bartsch, 1942.

Subfamily **Spirostomatinae**. Sole genus: *Spirostoma* Heude, 1885.

Subfamily **Alycaeinae**. Main genera: *Alycaeus* Gray, 1850; *Chamalycaeus* Kobelt and Möllendorff, 1897.

Zilch, A., 1957. Die Typen und Typoide des Natur-Museums Senckenberg. 20. Alycaeinae. Archiv. Moll., vol. 86 (4/6): 141-150, pls. 5-6.

Subfamily **Pterocyclinae**. Main genera: *Pterocyclos* Benson, 1832; *Pearsonia* Kobelt, 1902; *Platyrhaphe* Möllendorff, 1890; *Rhiostoma* Benson, 1860.

Family MEGALOSTOMATIDAE. *Farcimen procer* (Poey, 1854). Cuba. 3 cm. See p. 44.

Family POTERIIDAE
(syn.: Amphicyclotidae)

Main genera: *Poteria* Gray, 1850; *Amphicyclotus* Crosse and Fischer, 1879; *Buckleyia* Higgins, 1872; *Crocidopoma* Shuttleworth, 1857; *Ostodes* Gould, 1862; *Neocyclotus* Fischer and Crosse, 1886.

Girardi, E-L., 1978. The Samoan land snail genus Ostodes (Mollusca: Prosobranchia: Poteriidae). Veliger, vol. 20 (3): 191-250, 2 pls.

Family MEGALOSTOMATIDAE

Main genera: *Megalomastoma* Swainson, 1840; *Akerostoma* Troschel, 1847; *Cyclojamaica* Bartsch, 1942; *Farcimen* Troschel, 1847; *Tomocyclus* Crosse and Fischer, 1872.

Subfamily **Hainesiinae**. Main genera: *Hainesia* Pfeiffer, 1856; *Acroptychia* Crosse and Fischer, 1877.

Family MAIZANIIDAE

Main genera: *Maizania* Bourguignat, 1889; *Craspedopoma* Pfeiffer, 1847.

van Bruggen, A.C., 1982. A revision of the African operculate land snail genus *Maizaniella* (. . . Maizaniidae), with the description of six new taxa. Proc. Konink. Nederl. Akad. van Weten., ser. C, vol. 85 (2): 179-204, 31 figs.

——, 1986. Further notes on Afrotropical prosobranch land molluscs (. . . Maizaniidae. . .). *Ibid.*, vol. 89 (4): 357-378.

Verdcourt, B., 1964. The genus *Maizania* Bgt. (Gastropoda, Maizaniidae) in eastern Africa. Jour. East Afr.-Nat. Hist. Soc. and Coryndon Mus., vol. 24 (109): 1-22.

Family PUPINIDAE
(syn.: Realiidae)

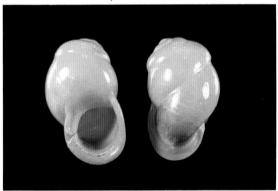

Family PUPINIDAE. *Moulinsia aurantia* (Grateloup, 1840). Philippines. 8 mm. See p. 46.

Main genera: *Pupina* Vignard, 1829; *Hedleya* Cox, 1892; *Moulinsia* Grateloup, 1840.

Subfamily **Pupinellinae**. Main genera: *Pupinella* Gray, 1850; *Raphaulus* Pfeiffer, 1856; *Realia* Gray, 1849 [+ *Liarea* Gray, 1852]; *Schistoloma* Kobelt, 1902; *Tortulosa* Gray, 1847; *Cytora* Kobelt and Möllendorff, 1897.

Climo, F.M., 1970. The systematic positions of *Cytora* Kobelt and Möllendorff, 1853. Trans. Royal Svc. N.Z., Biol. Sci., vol. 12 (19): 213-216.

Powell, A.W.B., 1954. The Molluscan Land Operculate Genus *Liarea* [*Realia*]. Records Auckland Inst. Mus., vol. 4(5): 271-293.

Family DIPLOMMATINIDAE

Berry, A.J., 1962. The growth of *Opisthostoma* (*Plectostoma*) *retrovertens* Tomlin, a minute cyclophorid from a Malayan limestone hill. Proc. Mal. Soc. London, vol. 35 (1): 46-49.

——, 1964. The reproduction of the minute cyclophorid snail *Opisthostoma (Plectostoma) retrovertens* from a Malayan limestone hill. Proc. Zool. Soc. London, vol. 142 (4): 655-663.

Laidlaw, F.F., 1950. A list of the species referred to the genus *Diplommatina* (Mollusca, Prosobranchia, Cyclophoridae). Recorded from Borneo. Bull. Raffles Mus. Singapore, no. 23: 212-229. Also, 1949, *ibid.*, no. 19: 199-215 for Malayan species.

Smith, E.A., 1894. A list of the Bornean species of the genus *Opisthostoma* and descriptions of four new species. Ann. Mag. Nt. Hist., series 6, vol. 14: 269, figs.

Thompson, F.G., 1978. Two new land snails of the genus *Opisthostoma* from Borneo. (. . . Diplommatidae). Proc. Biol. Soc. Wash., vol. 91 (2): 386-391.

Tillier, S., 1981. Clines, convergence and character displacement in New Caledonian diplommatinids (land prosobranchs). Malacologia, vol. 21 (1/2): 177-208, 33 figs.

van Benthem-Jutting, W.S.S., 1952. The Malayan species of *Opisthostoma* (. . . Cyclophoridae), with a catalogue of all the species hitherto described. Bull. Raffles Mus. Singapore, no. 24: 5-62.

Zilch, A., 1953. Die typen und typoid des natur-museum Senckenberg, 9: Cyclophoridae, Diplommatininae. Archiv. für Moll., vol. 82 (1/3): 1-47, 13 pls.

Subfamily **Diplommatininae.** Main genera: *Diplommatina* Benson, 1849; *Nicida* Blanford, 1868; *Opisthostoma* W. & H. Blanford, 1860; *Palaina* Semper, 1865.

Subfamily **Cochlostomatinae.** Sole genus: *Cochlostoma* Jan, 1830; *Pollicaria* Gould, 1856.

Superfamily LITTORINOIDEA

Family POMATIASIDAE

Family POMATIASIDAE. *Tropidophora deliciosa* (Férussac, in Sowerby, 1850). Madagascar. 2.5 cm. See p. 48.

Fischer-Piette, E., 1949. Mollusques terrestres de Madagascar genre *Tropidophora*. Jour. de Cinchyl., vol. 89: 5-149, 5 pls.

Solem, Alan, 1961. A preliminary review of the pomatiasid land snails of Central America. Archiv. Moll., vol. 90 (4/6): 191-213, pls. 10-12.

Subfamily **Pomatiasinae.** Main genera: *Pomatias* Stüder, 1789; *Otopoma* Gray, 1850; (+ *Georgia* Bourguinat, 1882, non Thomson, 1857); *Tropidophora* Troschel, 1847; *Tudorella* Fischer, 1885.

Subfamily **Cyclotopsinae.** Sole genus: *Cyclotropsis* Blanford, 1864.

Family CHONDROPOMATIDAE
(syn.: Licinidae; Annulariidae)

Family CHONDROPOMATIDAE. *Chondropometes vignalense* (Pfeiffer, 1863). Cuba. 1.8 cm See p. 50.

Baker, H.B., 1924. New Land Operculates from the Dutch Leeward Islands. The Nautilus, vol. 37: 1-6.

Bartsch, Paul, 1946. The Operculate Land Mollusks of the Family Annulariidae of the Island of Hispaniola and the Bahamas Archipelago. Bull. 192, U.S. Nat. Mus., pp. 1-264.

Thompson, Fred G., 1978. A New Genus of Operculate Land Snails from Hispaniola with Comments on the Status of Family Annulariidae. The Nautilus, vol. 92 (1): 41-54.

Torre, de la, Carlos and Paul Bartsch, 1938. The Cuban Operculate Land Shells of the Subfamily Chondropominae. Proc. U.S. N. Mus., vol. 85, no. 3039: 193-423, pls. 7-39.

——, 1941. The Cuban Operculate Land Mollusks of the Family Annulariidae, Exclusive of the Subfamily Chondropominae. Proc. U.S. N. Mus., vol. 89, no. 3096: 131-385, pls. 9-57.

Subfamily **Chondropomatinae.** Two genera: *Chondropoma* Pfeiffer, 1847; *Chondrothyra* Henderson and Bartsch, 1920 (subgenera *Chondrothyrium*, *Chondrothyroma*, *Chondrothyretes* all Henderson and Bartsch, 1920).

Subfamily **Adamsiellinae.** Sole genus: *Adamsiella* Pfeiffer, 1851.

Subfamily **Choanopomatinae.** (syn.: Annulariinae). Main Genera: *Choanopoma* Pfeiffer, 1848; *Abbottella* Henderson and Bartsch, 1920; *Blaesospira* Crosse, 1890; *Eutudora* Henderson and Bartsch, 1920; *Tudora* Gray, 1850; *Weinlandipoma* Bartsch, 1946.

Subfamily **Cistulopsinae.** Main Genera: *Cistulops* H.B. Baker, 1924; *Licina* Gray, 1847; *Troschelvindex* H.B. Baker, 1924.

Subfamily **Rhytidopomatinae.** Main genera: *Rhytidopoma* Sykes, 1901; *Opisthosiphon* Dall, 1905; *Parachondria* Dall, 1905 (+ *Clenchipoma* and *Haitipoma* Bartsch, 1946); *Xenopoma* Crosse, 1890.

Superfamily RISSOIDEA

Family ASSIMINEIDAE

Subfamily **Assimineinae.** Main genera: *Assiminea* Fleming, 1828; *Acmella* Blanford, 1869; *Cyclotropis* Tapparone-Canefri, 1883.

Abbott, R. Tucker, 1958. The gastropod genus *Assiminea* in the Philippines. Proc. Acad. Nat. Sci. Phila., vol. 110: 213-278, pls. 15-25.

Subfamily **Omphalotropidinae**. <u>Main genera</u>: *Omphalotropis* Pfeiffer, 1851; *Garretia* Pease, 1873; *Pseudocyclotus* Thiele, 1894; *Quadrasiella* Möllendorff, 1894.

Family ACICULIDAE

<u>Main genus</u>: *Acicula* Hartman, 1821 (+ *Acme* Hartman, 1821). Operculate, less than 3 mm; not treated here.

Family TRUNCATELLIDAE

<u>Main genera</u>: *Truncatella* Risso, 1826; *Geomelania* Pfeiffer, 1845.

Family TRUNCATELLIDAE. *Truncatella pulchella* Pfeiffer, 1839. West Indies. 4 mm. See p. 54

Clench, W.J. and R.D. Turner, 1948. The genus *Truncatella* in the Western Atlantic. Johnsonia, vol. 2 (25): 149-164, pls. 65-73.
de la Torre, Alfredo, 1960. Caribbean species of *Truncatella*. The Nautilus, vol. 73 (3): 79-88.

Order Archeopulmonata

Superfamily ELLOBIOIDEA

Family ELLOBIIDAE
(syn.: Auriculidae)

Family ELLOBIIDAE. *Cassidula rugata* Menke, 1853. South Australia. 2.5 cm. See p.56.

Subfamily **Ellobiinae**. <u>Main genera</u>: *Ellobium* Röding, 1798 (+ *Auricula* Lamarck, 1799); *Cassidula* Férussac, 1821; *Leucophytia* Winckworth, 1949; *Pythia* Röding, 1798 (+ *Scarabus* Montfort, 1810).

Haas, F., 1950. On some Bermudian Ellobiidae. Proc. Mal. Soc. London, vol. 28 (4/5): 197-199, 1 pl.
Harry, H.W., 1951. Growth Changes in the Shell of *Pythia scarabaeus* (Linné). Proc. Calif. Zool. Club, vol. 2 (2): 1-14 pp.
Hubendick, B., 1956. A conchological survey of the genus *Plecotrema* (Gastropoda, Ellobiidae). Proc. Mal. Soc. London, vol. 32: 110-126, pl. 23.
Kobelt, W., 1898-1901. Die Familie Auriculacea, Zweiter Tiel. In Syst. Conchyl.-Cab., Martini-Chemnitz, vol. 1, pt. 16: 77-316, pls. 10-33.
Martins, A.M.F., 1976. Notes on the habitat of five Halophile Ellobiidae in the Azores. Publ. EM, Centen. da Aberturo do Mus. Carlos Machado, Ponta Delgada. 24 pp., 1 pl.
Morrison, J.P.E., 1950. American Ellobiidae. Annual Report Amer. Mal. Union for 1950, p. 8.
Morton, J.E., 1955. The Evolution of the Ellobiidae with a discussion on the Origin of Pulmonata. Proc. Zool. Soc. London, vol. 125 (1): 127-168.
Pfeiffer, L., 1876. Monographia Pneumonopomorum Viventium, 3rd suppl.: Auriculaceorum, pt. secunda. S.T. Fischer, Kassel. 479 pp.

Subfamily **Melampodinae** (syn.: Melampinae). <u>Three genera</u>: *Melampus* Montfort, 1810; *Detracia* Gray, 1840; *Tralia* Gray, 1840.

Subfamily **Pedipedinae**. <u>Main genera</u>: *Pedipes* Bruguière, 1792; *Blauneria* Shuttleworth, 1854; *Laemodonta* Philippi, 1846; *Marinula* King and Broderip, 1832; *Ovatella* Bivona, 1832 [subgenus, *Myosotella* Monterosato, 1906 (+ *Alexia* Leach, 1847)].

Clench, W.J., 1964. The genera *Pedipes* and *Laemodonta* in the Western Atlantic. Johnsonia, vol. 4 (42): 117-127.

Subfamily **Carychiinae**. <u>Two genera</u>: *Carychium* Müller, 1774; *Zospeum* Bourguignat, 1856.

Brooks, S.T. and G.M. Kutchka, 1937. Occurrence of the family Carychiidae in West Virginia. Annals Carnegie Mus., vol. 25: 155-161.

Family OTINIDAE

<u>Single genus</u>: *Otina* Gray, 1847.

Morton, J.E., 1955. The Functional Morphology of *Otina otis*, a Primitive Marine Pulmonate. Jour. Mar. Biol. Assoc. U.K., vol. 34: 113-150.

Order Basommatophora

Family AMPHIBOLIDAE. *Amphibola avellana* (Bruguière, 1789). New Zealand. 1.5 cm. Only operculate pulmonate. See p. 57.

Superfamily **AMPHIBOLOIDEA**

Family **AMPHIBOLIDAE**

Two genera: *Amphibola* Schumacher, 1817; *Salinator* Hedley, 1900.

Farnie, W.C., 1924. The development of *Amphibola crenata* (Martyn). Quart. Journ. Micros. Sci., vol. 68 (3): 453-469.

Hubendick, B., 1945. On the Family Amphibolidae. Proc. Mal. Soc. London, vol. 26: 103-110.

Robertson, R. and K. Oyama, 1958. The family Stenacmidae. Nautilus, vol. 72: 68. Now placed in Epitoniidae (marine).

Watters, P.A., 1964. Distribution of *Amphibola crenata* (Pulmonata) in the Dunedin Area, with Notes on the Probably Origin of the Species. Trans. Royal Soc. N.Z., Zool., vol. 4 (4): 117-134.

Superfamily **CHILINOIDEA**

The family Chilinidae of South America and the Latiidae from New Zealand are freshwater basommatophoras.

Superfamily **SIPHONARIOIDEA**

Family **TRIMUSCULIDAE**

One genus: *Trimusculus* Schmidt, 1818 (+ *Gadinia* Gray, 1824).

Hubendick, B., 1946. Systematic Monograph of the Patelliformia. Kungl. Svensk. Vet. Akad. Handl., ser. 3, vol. 23 (5): 1-93, 6 pls.

Rehder, H.A., 1940. On the molluscan genus *Trimusculus* Schmidt 1818, with notes on some Mediterranean and West African siphonarias. Proc. Biol. Soc. Waash., vol. 53: 67-70.

Schumann, R.W., 1911. Uber die Anatomie und die Systematische Stellu;ng von *Gadinia peruviana* und *garnoti*. Zool. Jahrb., suppl. 13, Fauna Chilensis, vol. 4: 1-88.

Family **SIPHONARIIDAE**

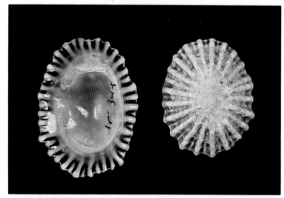

Family SIPHONARIIDAE. *Siphonaria diemenensis* Quoy & Gaimard, 1833. South Australia. 2.5 cm. Note horseshoe scar opens at side. See p. 57.

Main genera: *Siphonaria* Sowerby, 1823 (with subgenera: *Benhamina* Finlay, 1927; *Liriola* Dall, 1870, and others); *Siphonacmea* Habe, 1958; *Williamia* Monterosato, 1884 (conserved name; + *Brondelia* Bourguignat).

Abe, N., 1940. The homing, spawning and other habits of a limpet, *Siphonaria japonica* Donovan. Sci. Reports Tohoku Imperial Univ., ser. 4, Biol., vol. 15 (1): 59-95.

Allanson, B., 1958. Systematics and Distribution of *Siphonaria* in South Africa. Hydrobiologia, vol. 12.

Burch, J.B., 1984. The limpet genus *Brondelia*. Bull. Amer. Mal. Union, vol. 2: 88. [name rejected ICZN 1986; see *Williamia*].

Hubendick, B., 1946. Systematic Monograph of the Patelliforma.

Kungl. Svenska Vet. Handl., ser. 3, vol. 23 (5): 1-93, 6 pls.

——, 1947. On South African Siphonariidae. Annals Natal. Mus., vol. 11 (1): 161-164.

Jenkins, B.W., 1982. Redescriptions and relationship of *Siphonaria zelandica* Quoy and Gaimard to *S. australis* Quoy and Gaimard with a description of *S. propria* sp. nov. (Mollusca: Pulmonata: Siphonariidae). Jour. Mal. Soc. Australia, vol. 6 (1/2): 1-35.

Marshall, B.A., 1981. The genus *Williamia* in the western Pacific (Mollusca: Siphonariidae). New Zealand Jour. Zool., vol. 8: 487-492.

Morrison, J.P.E., 1963. Notes [list] on American *Siphonaria*. Annual Report for 1963 Amer. Mal. Union, pp. 7-9.

——, 1972. Mediterranean *Siphonaria*: West and East, Old and New. Argamon, vol. 3 (1/4): 51-62.

Voss, N.A., 1959. Studies on the Pulmonate gastropod, *Siphonaria pectinata* (Linnaeus) from the southeast coast of Florida. Bull. Marine Sci. Gulf and Caribbean, vol. 9: 84-99.

Freshwater Superfamilies

Not treated in this book are the freshwater basammatophoran superfamilies Acroloxoidea, Lymnoidea, Physoidea and Planorboidea. (for references, see K.J. Boss, 1982, pp. 1061-1064).

Order **Stylommatophora**
Suborder **Orthurethra**

Superfamily **ACHATINELLOIDEA**

Family **ACHATINELLIDAE**

Family ACHATINELLIDAE. *Achatinella dimorpha* Gulick, 1858. Oahu, Hawaii. 1.8 cm. See p. 58.

(see Pilsbry, H.A. and C.M. Cooke, *Manual of Conchology*, series 2, vol. 22. Achatinellidae, pp. 1-369; Geneology and Migrations, by Alpheus Hyatt, pp. 370-399. This vol. has 63 pls., many in color).

Cooke, C.M. Jr., 1941. Hawaiian land shells. Paradise of the Pacific, vol. 53 (12): 20-25.

Gulick, J.T., 1905. Evolution—racial and habitudinal. Carnegie Inst. Wash., pub. no. 25: 1-269.

Hadfield, M.G., 1986. Extinction in Hawaiian Achatinelline snails. Malacologia, vol. 27 (1): 67-81.

Twing, E.W., 1907. Reprint of the original descriptions of the genus *Achatinella* with additional notes by E.W. Twing. Occ. Papers B.P. Bishop Mus., vol. 3 (1): 1-196, 3 pls.

Welch, d'Alte, 1938. Distribution and variation of *Achatinella mustelina* Mighels in the Waianae Mountains, Oahu. Bull. B.P. Bishop Mus., vol. 152: 1-164.

——, 1954. Distribution and variation of the Hawaiian tree snail, *Achatinella bulimoides* Swainson on the leeward and northern slopes of the Koolau Range, Oahu. Proc. Acad. Nat. Sci. Phila., vol. 106: 63-107; 1958, . . . Windward Slope . . ., *ibid.*, vol. 110: 123-212.

Zilch, A., 1960. Typen und Typoide des Natur-Museums Senckenberg. 26. Mollusca: Achatinellacea. Archiv. Moll. vol. 91 (1/3): 77-94, pls. 2-3.

Subfamily **Achatinellinae.** Four genera: *Achatinella* Swainson, 1828; *Newcombia* Pfeiffer, 1854; *Partulina* Pfeiffer, 1854; *Perdicella* Pease, 1869.

Subfamily **Tekoulininae.** Sole genus: *Tekoulina* Solem, 1972.

Subfamily **Pitysinae.** Main genera: *Pitys* Mörch, 1852; *Strobilops* Anton, 1839; *Tubuaia* Cooke and Kondo, 1960.

Subfamily **Lamellideinae.** Main genera: *Lamellidea* Pilsbry, 1910; *Tornatellina* Pfeiffer, 1842.

Subfamily **Tornatellidinae.** Main genera: *Tornatellides* Pilsbry, 1910; *Auriculella* Pfeiffer, 1855; *Gulickia* C.M. Cooke, 1915.

Cooke, C.M., Jr. and Y. Kondo, 1960. Revision of the Tornatellidae and Achatinellidae. B.P. Bishop Mus. Bull. 222: 1-303, 123 figs.

Superfamily **COCHLICOPOIDEA**
(syn.: Cionellacea)
(syn.: Chondrinoidea)

Family **AMASTRIDAE**

Family AMASTRIDAE. *Laminella sanguinea* (Newcomb, 1853). Oahu, Hawaii. 2 cm. See p. 62.

Main genera: *Amastra* H. and A. Adams, 1855; *Carelia* H. and A. Adams, 1855; *Kauaia* Sykes, 1900; *Laminella* Pfeiffer, 1854; *Leptachatina* Gould, 1847. (see Pilsbry, H.A., *Manual of Conchology* series 2, vol. 23, Amastrinae, pp. 1-65; Tornatellininae, pp. 66-270. (1914-1916); and Hyatt and Pilsbry, vol. 21, pp. 1-387, 56 pls., (1910-1911).

Cooke, C.M., Jr. 1910-1911. Genus *Leptachatina* Gould, 1847. In: Tryon-Pilsbry, *Manual of Conchology*, ser. 2, vol. 21 (part 81): 1-64; (part 82, 1911): 65-92.

——, 1917. Some New species of *Amastra*. Occ. Papers. B.P. Bishop Mus., vol. 3 (3): 221-250, pls. 5-7.

——, 1931. The land snail genus *Carelia*. Bull. B.P. Bishop Mus., vol. 85: 1-98, pls. 1-18.

——, 1933. New species of Amastridae. *Ibid.*, vol. 10 (6): 3-27, pls. 1-2.

Family **COCHLICOPIDAE**
(syn.: Cionellidae)

Main genera: *Cochlicopa* Férussac, 1821 (+ *Cionella* Jeffreys, 1829); *Azeca* Leach in Fleming, 1828.

Gittenberger, E., 1983. On Iberian Cochlicopidae and the genus *Cryptazeca* (Gastropoda, Pulmonata). Zool. Mededel., vol. 57 (23): 301-320.

Superfamily **PUPILLOIDEA**

Family **VERTIGINIDAE**

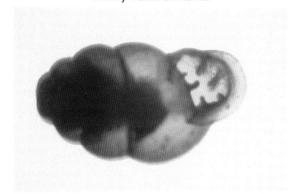

Family VERTIGINIDAE. *Vertigo rugosula* Sterki, 1890. Southeast U.S. 2 mm. See p. 63.

Single genus: *Vertigo* Müller, 1774 (4 subgenera).

(see Pilsbry, H.A. *Manual of Conchology*, series 2, vol. 25, pp. 69-222, 1919); and vol. 26 (1921).

Haas, F., 1960. Caribbean land molluscs: Vertiginidae. Studies on the Fauna of Curaçao and other Caribbean Islands, vol. 10 (41): 1-17.

van Benthem-Jutting, Tera, 1949. The Malayan species of Boysidia, Paraboysidia, Hypselostoma and *Gyliotrachela* (. . . Vertiginidae) with a catalogue of all the species hitherto described. Bull. Raffles Mus. Singapore, vol. 21: 5-47.

Subfamily **Truncatellininae.** Main genera: *Truncatellina* Lowe, 1852; *Columella* Westerlund, 1878; *Negulus* Boettger, 1889.

Subfamily **Gastrocoptinae.** (syn.: Hypselostomatinae). Main genera: *Gastrocopta* Wollaston, 1878; *Boysidia* Ancey, 1881; *Cavipupa* Pilsbry, 1934; *Chaenaxis* Pilsbry and Ferriss, 1906; *Hypselostoma* Benson, 1856; *Ulpia* Scott, 1955; *Gyliotrachela* Tomlin, 1930.

Solem, A., 1981. Small land snails: Northern Australia. I. *Gyliotracheia*. Journ. Mal. Soc. Aust., vol. 5 (1/2): 87-100.

Subfamily **Aulacospirinae.** Two genera: *Aulacospira* Möllendorff, 1890; *Systenostoma* Bavay and Dautzenberg, 1909.

Subfamily **Nesopupinae.** Main genera: *Nesopupa* Pilsbry, 1900; *Lyropupa* Pilsbry, 1900; *Pupisoma* Stoliczka, 1873; *Staurodon* Lowe, 1852; *Sterkia* Pilsbry, 1898.

Family **PLEURODISCIDAE**
(syn.: Pyramidulidae)

Main genera: *Pleurodiscus* Wenz, 1919; *Pyramidula* Fitzinger, 1833.

Family PUPILLIDAE

(see Pilsbry, H.A., *Manual of Conchology*, series 2, vol. 24, pp. 1-380, 49 pls. 1918; and vol. 28, pp. 63-226, maps: vol. 27 (1922-26).

Arias, S., 1955. Los Pupillidae Collectados en Venezuela Septentrional. Mem. Soc. Cienc. Nat. La Salle, vol. 15 (41): 140-169, 7 figs.

Brooks, S.T. and Gordon M. Kutchka, 1938. Occurrence of the family Pupillidae in West Virginia. Annals Carnegie Mus., vol. 27: 63-85.

Gittenberger, E., 1978. Beiträge zur Kenntnis der Pupillacea, VIII. Einiges über Orculidae. Zool. Verhand., Leiden, no. 163: 3-44, 2 pls.

Solem, Alan, 1986. Pupilloid land snails from the south and midwest coasts of Australia. Jour. Mal. Soc. Australia, vol. 7 (3/4): 95-124.

Steenberg, C.M., 1925. Études sur l'anatomie et la systématique des maillots (Fam. Pupillidae s. lat.). Vidensk. Medd. Dansk. naturh. Fur., vol. 80: 1-215.

Subfamily **Pupillinae**. Main genera: *Pupilla* Leach in Fleming, 1828 (+ *Pupa* Draparnaud, 1801) *Pupoides* Pfeiffer, 1854; *Microstele* Boettger, 1886.

Caziot, E. and E. Margier, 1909. Etude historique de la classification des *Pupa* du système européen. Bull. Soc. France, vol. 34: 134-147.

Subfamily **Lauriinae**. Main genera: *Lauria* Gray in Turton, 1840; *Agardhia* Gude, 1911; *Leiostyla* Lowe, 1852.

Family VALLONIIDAE

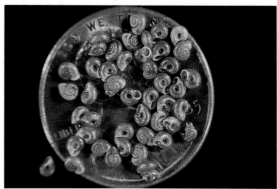

Family VALLONIIDAE. *Vallonia pulchella* (Müller, 1774). Europe. 2.5 mm.See p. 64.

Main genera: *Vallonia* Risso, 1826; *Acanthinula* Beck, 1847; *Planogyra* Morse, 1864; *Spelaeodiscus* Brusina, 1886; *Zoogenetes* Morse, 1864.

Hubendick, B., 1950. The validity of *Vallonia excentrica* Sterki. Proc. Mal. Soc. London, vol. 28 (2/3): 75-78.

Sterki, V., 1893. Observations on *Vallonia*. Proc. Acad. Nat. Sci. Phila., vol. 45: 234.

Family STROBILOPSIDAE

One genus: *Strobilops* Pilsbry, 1893.

(see Pilsbry, H.A., *Manual of Conchology*, ser. 2, vol. 28, pt. 109, pp. 1-62, pl. 1-8, 1935).

Miller, W.B. and C.C. Christensen, 1980. A new *Strobilops* (Mollusca: Pulmonata: Strobilopsidae) from Baja California Sur, Mexico. Proc. Biol. Soc. Wash., vol. 93 (3): 593-596.

Morrison, J.P.E., 1953. Two new American species of *Strobilops*. The Nautilus, vol. 67: 53-55.

Wenz, W., 1916. Zur Kenntnis der Gattung *Strobilops* Pils. Nachr. Deutsch Malak. Ges., vol. 4: 178-192.

Family ORCULIDAE

Main genera: *Orcula* Held, 1837; *Pagodulina* Clessin, 1976; *Schileykula* Gittenberger, 1983; *Speleodentorcula* Gittenberger, 1985.

Gittenberger, E., 1985. *Speleodentorcula* gen. nov.: Griechenland. Zool. Medld. Leiden, vol. 59 (19): 221-228.

Family CHONDRINIDAE

Main genera: *Chondrina* Reichenbach, 1828; *Abida* Leach in Turton, 1831; *Fauxulus* Schaufuss, 1869; *Sandahlia* Westerlund, 1887.

Gittenberger, E., 1984. Vicariantists and dispersalists among the Chondrininae. M. World wide snails. E.J. Brill Co. pp. 56-69.

Superfamily ENOIDEA

Family ENIDAE
(syn.: Buliminidae)

Family ENIDAE. *Chondrus zebra* (Olivier, 1801). Asia Minor. 1.4 cm. See p. 65.

Main genera: *Ena* Leach in Turton, 1831; *Buliminus* Beck, 1837; *Chondrus* Cuvier, 1817; *Draparnaudia* Montrouzier, 1859; *Mirus* Albers, 1850; *Pupinidius* Möllendorff, 1901; *Pupopsis* Gredler, 1898; *Yakuena* Habe, 1955.

Forcart, L., 1935. Monographie der türkischen Enidae. Verh. naturf. Ges. Basel, vol. 51: 106-263, 3 pls.

Gittenberger, E., 1967. Die Enidae (Gastropoda, Pulmonata) Gesammelt von der Nederländischen biologischen Expedition in die Türkei in 1959. Zool. Meded., Leiden, vol. 42 (13): 125-141.

Habe, T., 1955. Anatomical studies on the Japanese land snails (6). The superspecific groups of the family Enidae. Zoological Mag., vol. 65 (7): 262-266.

Heller, J., 1976. Enidae of the Aegean Islands. Jour. Moll. Studies, vol. 42: 371-393.

Hesse, P., 1933. Zur Anatomie und Systematik der Familie Enidae. Archiv. Naturg., N.F., vol. 2 (2): 145-224.

Lindholm, W.A., 1925. Beitrag zur Systematik und Nomenklatur der Familie Enidae (Buliminidae). Archiv. Moll., vol. 57: 23-41.

Mordan, P.B., 1984. Taxonomy and biogeography of southern Arabian Enidae.... In: World Wide Snails, E.J. Brill, Co. pp. 124-133, illus.

———, 1986 A taxonomic revision of the southern Arabian Enidae *sensu lato* (Mollusca: Pulmonata). Bull. Brit. Mus. Nat. Hist. (Zool.), vol. 50 (4): 207-271, illus.

Subfamily **Jaminiinae.** Main genera: *Jaminia* Risso, 1829; *Multidentula* Lindholm, 1925.

Subfamily **Chondrulinae.** Main genera: *Chondrula* Beck, 1837; *Zebrina* Held, 1837.

Subfamily **Spelaeoconchinae.** Single genus: *Spelaeoconcha* Sturany, 1912.

Family CERASTUIDAE
Main genera: *Cerastua* Strand, 1928 (+ *Cerastus* Albers, 1860); *Altenaia* Zilch, 1972; *Conulinus* von Martens, 1895; *Rhachis* Albers, 1850; *Rhachistia* Connolly, 1925; *Zebrinops* Thiele, 1931.

Order **Mesurethra**

Superfamily CLAUSILIOIDEA

Family MEGASPIRIDAE
Two genera: *Megaspira* Jay, 1836; *Callionepion* Pilsbry and Vanatta, 1899.

Family COELOCIIDAE
Two genera: *Coelocion* Pilsbry, 1904; *Perrieria* Tapparone-Canefri, 1878.

Family CLAUSILIIDAE

Family CLAUSILIIDAE. *Isabellaria scalaris* (Pfeiffer, 1849). Malta. 1 cm. (photo by R. Goldberg). See p. 66.

Brandt, R.A., 1956. Zur Clausiliidenfauna der Cyrenaika. Archiv. Moll., vol. 85 (4/6): 121-144, pls. 9, 10.

Cooke, A.H., 1915. The genus *Clausilia*: a study of its geographical distribution. Proc. Mal. Soc. London., vol. 11 (5): 249-269.

Ehrmann, P., 1905. Über einige peruanische Clausiliiden. Nachr. Bl. Deutsch Malak. Ges., vol. 37: 65-72.

Forcart, L., 1975. Palestine Clausiliidae. Proc. Mal. Soc. London, vol. 51: 467-476.

Lindholm, W.A., 1924. A Revised Systematic List of the Genera of the Clausiliidae, Recent and Fossil, with their subdivisions, synonymy, and types. Proc. Mal. Soc. London, vol. 16: 53-80; Supplement, *ibid.*, vol. 16: 261-266.

Loosjes, F.E., 1950. Some new gastropods of the family Clausiliidae from the Philippine Islands and Siam. Proc. U.S. Nat. Mus., vol. 100 (no. 3269): 539-545.

———, 1953. Monograph of the Indo-Australian Clausiliidae, Beaufortia, vol. 31: 1-226, 56 figs.; 1963, Supplement, in Med. Zool. Rijksmus. Nat. Hist., Leiden, vol. 39: 153-169, pl. 5.

Nordsieck, H., 1979. Anatomie und systematic: Clausilien; System die rezenten europaischen Clausilien. Archiv. Moll., vol. 109 (4/6): 249-275.

Peile, A.J., 1925. Note on the Species of *Phaedusa* from the Nicobar Islands. Proc. Mal. Soc. London, vol. 16: 255-256.

Pilsbry, H.A., 1945. Peruvian land mollusca. IV, Clausiliidae. The Nautilus, vol. 58 (3/4): 79-84, pl. 3.

———, 1949. Peruvian land mollusks of the genus *Nenia* (Clausiliidae). Proc. Acad. Nat. Sci. Phila., vol. 101: 215-232, pls. 17-22.

———, 1949. Review of Peruvian species of *Temesa* (Mollusca, Clausiliidae). Notulae Natura, No. 214: 1-8.

Polinski, W., 1921. Neue Clausiliiden aus Peru. Bull. Acad. Polon. Sci.: Lettr., Cl. Sci. Math. Nat., vol. 1921 B: 121-143; *ibid.*, vol. 1924 B: 739-744, pl. 49.

Sykes, E.R., 1893. On the Clausiliae of Sumatra with Descriptions of two New Species and a New Variety. Proc. Mal. Soc. London, vol. 1: 28-30.

———, 1899. Note on the Clausiliae Recorded from Celebes. Jour. Malacol., vol. 3: 48-49.

Szekeres, M.I., 1969. Neue Argaben zur Kenntnis der Clausiliiden Südostasiens. Archiv. Moll., vol. 99 (5/6): 313-317, 12 figs.

Weyrauch, W.K., 1963. Aporte al conocimiento de Temesa, I. (Clausiliidae, Mollusca). Acta Zool. Lilloana, vol. 19: 261-288.

Subfamily **Clausiliinae.** Main genera: *Clausilia* Draparnaud, 1805; *Fusulus* Fitzinger, 1833; *Graciliaria* Bielz, 1867; *Julica* Nordsieck, 1963; *Ruthenica* Lindholm, 1924.

Subfamily **Baleinae.** Main genera: *Balea* Gray, 1824; *Laciniaria* Hartmann, 1844; *Mentissa* H. and A. Adams, 1855; *Mucronaria* Boettger, 1877; *Vestia* Hesse, 1916.

Subfamily **Neniinae.** Main genera: *Nenia* H. and A. Adams, 1855; *Ardinia* Polinski, 1922; *Peruinia* Polinski, 1922; *Steeriana* Jousseaume, 1900; *Zilchiella* Weyrauch, 1957.

Subfamily **Mentissoidinae.** Main genera: *Mentissoidea* Boettger, 1877; *Acrotoma* Boettger, 1881; *Armenica* Boettger, 1877; *Galeata* Boettger, 1877; *Idyla* H. and A. Adams, 1855; *Roseniella* Thiele, 1931.

Subfamily **Alopiinae.** Main genera: *Alopia* H. and A. Adams, 1855; *Albinaria* Vest, 1867; *Charpentieria* Stabile, 1864; *Cochlodina* Ferussac, 1821; *Cristataria* Vest, 1867; *Isabellaria* Vest, 1867; *Medora* H. and A. Adams, 1855; *Sericata* Boettger, 1878; *Triloba* Vest, 1867.

Subfamily **Phaedusinae.** Main genera: *Phaedusa* H. and A. Adams, 1855; *Hemiphaedusa* O. Boettger, 1877; *Stereophaedusa* Boettger, 1877.

Subfamily **Garnieriinae.** Two genera: *Garnieria* Bourguignat, 1877; *Tropidauchenia* Lindholm, 1924.

Subfamily **Serrulininae.** Main genera: *Serrulina* Mousson, 1873; *Laeviphaedusa* Likharev and Steklov, 1965; *Microphaedusa* Nordsieck, 1978.

Subfamily **Megalophaedusinae.** Main genera: *Megalophaedusa* O. Boettger, 1877; *Formosana* O. Boettger, 1877; *Luchuphaedusa* Pilsbry, 1905; *Nesiophaedusa* Pilsbry, 1905; *Pauciphaedusa* Minato and Habe, 1983; *Streptodera* Lindholm, 1925.

Subfamily **Zaptychinae**. <u>Main genera</u>: *Zaptyx* Pilsbry, 1901; *Zaptychopsis* Ehrmann, 1927.

Family **CERIONIDAE**
(syn.: Ceriidae)

Family CERIONIDAE. *Cerion glans* (Küster, 1844). Bahamas. 2.5 cm. See p. 70.

<u>One genus</u>: *Cerion* Röding, 1798 (+ *Pupa* Lamarck, 1801; *Strophia* Albers, 1850).
(see Pilsbry, H.A., *Manual of Conchology*, series 2, vol. 14, pp. 174-281, pl. 27-47, 1902; also see under Bahamas in geographical index).

Clench, W.J., 1957. Catalogue of the Cerionidae (Mollusca, Pulmonata). Bull. Mus. Comp. Zool., vol. 116: 121-169. [also geographical index].

Clench, W.J. and C. G. Aguayo, 1952. The *scalarinum* Species Complex (*Umbonis*) in the Genus *Cerion*. Occ. Papers Moll., Harvard Univ., vol. 1 (17): 413-440, pls. 51-57.

Gould, Stephen Jay, 1988. Prolonged stability in local populations of *Cerion agassizi* (Pleistocene-Recent) on Great Bahama Bank. Paleobiology, vol. 14 (1): 1-18.

Gould, Stephen J. and David S. Woodruff, 1986. Evolution and Systematics of *Cerion* on New Providence Island: a Radical Revision. Bull. Amer. Mus. Nat. Hist., vol. 182, art. 4, pp. 389-490.

Maynard, C.J., 1894-1896. Monograph of the Genus *Strophia* [*Cerion*]. Contributions to Science, Newton, Mass., vol. 2: 107-182; vol. 3: 1-40, pls. 1-7.

Mayr, Ernst and C.B. Rosen, 1956. Geographical Variation and Hybridization in Populations of Bahama Snails (*Cerion*). Bull. Amer. Mus. Nat. Hist., no. 1806: 48 pp., 9 figs.

Superfamily **PARTULOIDEA**

Family **PARTULIDAE**

Family PARTULIDAE. *Partula suturalis* Pfeiffer, 1855. Moorea Id., Society Islands. 1.2 cm. See p. 68.

<u>One genus</u>: *Partula* Ferussac, 1821 (11 subgenera, including *Eua* Pilsbry and Cooke, 1934; *Samoana* Pilsbry, 1909). (see Pilsbry, H.A. *Manual of Conchology*, vol. 20, pp. 155-336, pls. 16-39, 1909-10).

Crampton, H.E., 1916. Studies on the variation, distribution and evolution of the genus *Partula*. The species inhabiting Tahiti. Carnegie Inst. Wash., pub. no. 228; 1925, Guam and Saipan, *ibid.*, pub. no. 228A; 1932, Moorea, *ibid.*, pub. no. 410.

Kondo, Yoshio, 1968. Partulidae: preview of anatomical revision. The Nautilus, vol. 81 (3): 73-77.

———, 1970. Some aspects of Mariana Islands Partulidae. Occ. Papers B.P. Bishop Mus., vol. 24 (5): 73-90.

———, 1973. Samoana of the Society Islands (Pulmonata: Partulidae). Malacological Review, vol. 6: 19-33.

Pilsbry, H.A. and C.M. Cooke, Jr., 1934. Partulidae of Tonga and related forms. Occ. Papers B.P. Bishop Mus., vol. 10 (14): 3-22.

Superfamily **STROPHOCHEILOIDEA**
(see Pilsbry, H.A. *Manual of Conchology*, series 2, vol. 10, pp. 1-37, pls. 1-23, 1895).

Family **STROPHOCHEILIDAE**
<u>Two genera</u>: *Strophocheilus* Spix, 1827; *Gonystomus* Beck, 1837 (+ *Anthinus*).

Lange de Morretes, F., 1952. Novas especies Brasileiras da familia Strophocheilidae. Arquiv. Zool. Dept. Sao Paulo, vol. 8 (4): 109-126, pls. 1-4.

Family **MEGALOBULIMIDAE**

Family MEGALOBULIMIDAE. *Megalobulimus oblongus* (Müller, 1774). Trinidad. 7 cm. (with egg). See p. 74.

<u>One genus</u>: *Megalobulimus* Miller, 1878.

Leme, J.L.M., 1973. Anatomy and Systematics of the Neotropical Strophocheiloidea (Gastropoda, Pulmonata) with the Description of a New Family. Arquivos de Zoologia, São Paulo, vol. 23, fasc. 5: 295-337, 53 figs., 2 pls.

Bequaert, Joseph, 1948. Monograph of the Strophocheilidae, a Neotropical Family of Terrestrial Mollusks. Bull. Mus. Comp. Zool., Harvard, vol. 100, no. 1, 210 pp., 32 pls.

Family **DORCASIIDAE**
<u>Three South African genera</u>: *Dorcasia* Gray, 1838; *Trigonephrus* Pilsbry, 1905; *Tulbaghina* Melvill and Ponsonby, 1898.

Connolly, M., 1915. Notes on South African Mollusca. III. A Monograph of the Dorcasiidae. Ann. So. African Mus., vol. 13, pp. 120-178, pls. 2-5.

Order **Heterurethra**

Superfamily **SUCCINEOIDEA**

Family **SUCCINEIDAE**

Family SUCCINEIDAE. *Oxyloma haydeni* (Binney, 1858). Western U.S. 1.5 cm. See p. 77.

Boettger, C.R., 1939. Bemerkungen über die in Deutschland vorkommenden Bernstein schnecken (Fam. Succineidae). Zool. Anz., vol. 127 (3/4): 49-64.

Franzen, D.S., 1959. Anatomy of *Succinea ovalis* Say. Proc. Mal. Soc. London, vol. 33: 193-199, 7 figs.

——, 1963. Variations in the anatomy of the Succineid gastropod, *Oxyloma refusa*. The Nautilus, vol. 76 (3): 82-95, 4 figs.; also vol. 77: 74-81, vol. 79: 82-95.

Miles, C.D., 1958. The family Succineidae in Kansas. Univ. Kansas Sci. Bull., 38 (2): 1499-1543, 1 pl.

Odhner, N.H., 1950. Succineid studies: genera and species of subfamily Catinellinae *nov*. Proc. Mal. Soc. London, vol. 28: 200-210.

Patterson, C.M., 1971. Taxonomic Studies of the Land Snail Family Succineidae. Malacological Review, vol. 4: 131-202, 140 figs.

Quick, H.E., 1933. The anatomy of British *Succinea*. Proc. Mal. Soc. London, vol. 20: 295-318, pls. 23-25.

Rao, H.S., 1924. Asiatic Succineidae in the Indian Museum. Rec. Indian Mus., vol. 26: 367-408.

Shilejko, A.A. and J.M. Likharev, 1986. [Terrestrial mollusks of the family Sbornik]. Trud. Zool. Muz. MGV, vol. 24: 197-239, illus.

Zilch, A., 1978. Die Typen und Typoide des Natur-Museums Senckenberg: Succineacea. Arch. Moll., vol. 109 (1/3): 109-136.

Subfamily **Succineinae**. Major genera: *Succinea* Draparnaud, 1801; *Camptonyx* Benson, 1858; *Omalonyx* Orbigny, 1841; *Hyalimax* H. and A. Adams, 1855; *Oxyloma* Westerlund, 1885.

Subfamily **Catinellinae**. Major genera: *Catinella* Pease, 1870; *Quickella* C. Boettger, 1939; *Indosuccinea* Rao, 1924; *Neosuccinea* Matekin, 1956; *Quickia* Odhner, 1950 (+ *Burchella* Patterson, 1970).

Superfamily **ATHORACOPHOROIDEA**

Family *ATHORACOPHORIDAE*

Four genera: *Athoracophorus* Gould, 1852; *Aneitea* Gray, 1850; *Aneitella* Cockerell, 1891; *Palliopodex* Burton, 1963.

"Leaf-veined" slugs of New Zealand and Australasia. Five genera: *Athoracophorus, Aneitea, Reflectopallium, Palliopodex* and *Pseudoaneitea*. Not included in this book.

Burch, J.B. and C.M. Patterson, 1969. The Systematic Position of the Athoracophoridae. *Malacologia*, vol. 9: 259-260.

Burton, D.W., 1963. A Revision of the New Zealand and Subantarctic Athoracophoridae. Trans. Royal Soc. N.Z., vol. 3: 47-75.

Powell, A.W.B., 1979. *New Zealand Mollusca*. (20 New Zealand Athoracophoridae, sp. illus.).

Order **Sigmurethra**

Suborder **Holopodopes**
(do not confuse with Holopoda, see below)

Superfamily **ACHATINOIDEA**

Family **ACHATINIDAE**

Family ACHATINIDAE. *Achatina degneri* Bequaert & Clench, 1936. West Africa. 13 cm. See p. 78.

Major genera: *Achatina* Lamarck, 1799; *Archachatina* Albers, 1850; *Burtoa* Bourguignat, 1889; *Callistopepla* Ancey, 1888; *Columna* Perry, 1811; *Lignus* Gray, 1834; *Limicolaria* Schumacher, 1817; *Metachatina* Pilsbry, 1904; *Perideriopsis* Putzeys, 1898; *Pseudachatina* Albers, 1850; [*Leucotaenius* von Martens, see now under Acavidae].

(see Pilsbry, H.A., *Manual of Conchology*, series 2, vol. 17, pp. 1-232, 65 pls., 1904-05; *Limicolaria* and *Burtoa* in vol. 16, pp. 205-329, pl. 1-37, 1904).

Abbott, R.T., 1949. March of the Giant African Snail. Natural History Magazine, vol. 58 (2): 68-71.

Bequaert, J.C., 1950. Studies in the Achatininae, a Group of African Land Snails. Bull. Mus. Comp. Zool., vol. 105 (1): 1-216.

Crowley, T.E. and T. Pain, 1959. A monographic revision of the African land snails of the genus *Burtoa*. Ann. Mus. Royal Congo Belge, (8th ser.), Soc. Zool., vol. 79: 7-35.

——, 1970. A monographic revision of the African land snails of the genus *Limicolaria* Schumacher (Achatinidae). Ann. Mus. Royal Afr. Centr. (8th ser.), vol. 177: 1-61, pls. 1-6.

Mead, A.R., 1961. *The Giant African Snail: A Problem in Economic Malacology.* Univ. Chicago Press.

Zilch, A., 1951. Die Typen und Typoide des Natur-Museums Senckenberg. Achatinacen (1): Achatinidae. Senckenbergiana, vol. 32: 39-47.

Family COELIAXIDAE
Three African genera: *Coeliaxis* Adams and Argas, 1865; *Pyrgina* Greef, 1882; *Cryptelasmus* Pilsbry, 1907 (subfamily *Cryptelasminae* Zilch, 1959).

Family THYROPHORELLIDAE
Sole Genus: *Thyrophorella* Graeff, 1882.

Family FERUSSACIDAE
Main genera: *Ferussacia* Risso, 1826; *Cecilioides* Férussac, 1814.

(see Pilsbry, H.A., *Manual of Conchology*, series 2, vol. 19, pp. 211-338, pls. 38-51, 1908).

Darteville, E. and L. Venmans, 1951. Ferussaciidae du Congo Belge. Basteria, vol. 15 (3/4): 62-68, 2 figs.

Verdcourt, B., 1986. The identity of some species of *Ceciliodes* Férussac, 1814 from a river drift in Kenya (Mollusca: Ferussaciidae). Revue Zool. Afr., vol. 99 (4): 365-368, illus.

Family SUBULINIDAE

Family SUBULINIDAE. *Subulina octona* (Bruguière, 1789). Tropical worldwide. 1.3 cm. See p. 84.

(see Pilsbry, H.A., *Manual of Conchology*, ser. 2, vol. 18, pp. 1-357, pl. 1-51, 1906-07).

Baker, H.B., 1940. Mexican Subulinidae and Spiraxidae with New Species of *Spiraxis*. The Nautilus, vol. 53: 89-94, pl. 11.

van Bruggen, A.C., 1964. On the distribution of the genus *Xerocerastus* (Subulinidae). Zool. Meded. Leiden, vol. 39: 224-234.

Subfamily **Subulininae.** Major genera: *Subulina* Beck, 1837; *Chilonopsis* G. Fischer, 1848; *Glessula* von Martens, 1860; *Lamellaxis* Strebel, 1882 (subgenus *Allopeas* H.B. Baker, 1935); *Leptinaria* Beck, 1837; *Opeas* Albers, 1850; *Subulona* von Martens, 1889.

Subfamily **Rumininae.** Major genera: *Rumina* Risso, 1826; *Xerocerastus* Kobelt and Möllendorff, 1902.

Family SPIRAXIDAE
Baker, H.B., 1939. A Revision of *Spiraxis* C.B. Adams. The Nautilus, vol. 53: 8-16, pls. 3-5; 49-53, pl.9.

Thompson, Fred G., 1987. Giant Carnivorous Land Snails from Mexico and Central America. Bull. Florida State Museum, Biol. Sci., vol. 30 (2): 29-52, 32 figs.

Subfamily **Obeliscinae.** Major genera: *Obeliscus* Beck, 1837; *Cupulella* Aguayo and Jaume, 1948; *Rhodea* H. and A. Adams, 1855; *Synapterpes* Pilsbry, 1896.

Superfamily STREPTAXOIDEA
(Streptaxacea)

Family STREPTAXIDAE
Major genera: *Streptaxis* Gray, 1837; *Edentulina* Pfeiffer, 1878; *Gonaxis* Taylor, 1877; *Indoartemon* Forcart, 1946; *Perrottetia* Kobelt, 1905; *Tayloria* Bourguignat, 1889; *Tonkinia* Mabille, 1887.

Clench, W.J., 1958. New Records of West Indian Streptaxidae. The Nautilus, vol. 72 (1): 19-20.

Dance, S.P., 1970. Non-marine molluscs of Borneo. I. Streptaxacea: Streptaxidae. Jour. Conch., vol. 27 (3): 149-162, pl. 6.

Pilsbry, H.A., 1897. New Brazilian Streptaxidae. Proc. Acad. Nat. Sci. Phila., vol. 49: 477-479.

Richardson, C.L., 1988. Streptaxacea: Catalog of species. Part 1, Streptaxidae. Tryonia, Philadelphia, no. 16: 1-326. (includes all genera and subgenera, as well as species).

Verdcourt, B., 1961. Notes on the snails of North-East Tanganyika. 9. A new species of *Gonaxis* (Streptaxidae) from the Usambara Mountains, with notes on the classification of the genus. Occ. Papers Coryndon Memor. Mus., vol. 8: 1-23, 18 figs.

van Bruggen, A.C., 1967. An introduction to the pulmonate family Streptaxidae. Jour. Conch., vol. 26: 181-188.

——, 1973. Distribution patterns of the genus *Gulella* (Streptaxidae). Malacologia, vol. 14: 419-425.

——, 1980. Size clines and subspecies in the streptaxid genus *Gulella* Pfr. (Pulmonata) in Southern Africa. Zool. Verh. Leiden, vol. 154: 1-44.

Verdcourt, B., 1962. Preliminary keys for the identification of the species of the genus *Gulella* Pfr. occuring in East Africa, Ann. Mus. Royal Afr. Centr. Sci. Zool., vol. 106: 1-39, pls. 1-5.

Subfamily **Enneinae.** (syn.: Ptychotrematinae). Major genera: *Ennea* H. and A. Adams, 1855; *Brüggennea* Dance, 1972; *Gibbus* Montfort, 1810; *Gonidomus* Swainson, 1840; *Gonospira* Swainson, 1840; *Gulella* Pfeiffer, 1856; *Ptychotrema* Pfeiffer, 1853 (with 7 subgenera); *Steptostele* Dohrn, 1866.

Superfamily ACAVOIDEA

Family RHYTIDIDAE
(syn.: Paryphantidae)
Major genera: *Rhytida* Albers, 1860; *Natalina* Pilsbry, 1893; *Ougapia* Crosse, 1894; *Paryphanta* Albers, 1850; *Wainuia* Powell, 1930.

O'Connor, A.C., 1945. Notes on the Eggs of New Zealand Paryphantidae, with Description of a New Subgenus. Trans. Royal Soc. N.Z., vol. 75: 62-64.

Powell, A.W.B., 1930-1949. The Paryphantidae of New Zealand.

Family RHYTIDIDAE. *Paryphanta hochstetteri* (Pfeiffer, 1862). New Zealand. 7 cm. See p. 87.

Family ACAVIDAE. *Acavus haemastomus* (Linnaeus, 1758). Sri Lanka. 5 cm. See p. 89.

Nos. 1-6 in Records Auckland Mst. Mus. 1930, vol. 1: 17-56; 1932, vol. 1 (3): 155-162; 1936, vol..2 (1): 29-41; 1938, vol. 2 (3): 133-150; 1946, vol. 3 (2): 99-136; 1949, vol. 3 (6): 347-367.

——, 1979. *New Zealand Mollusca*. Collins, Auckland. (Excellent illus. account of N.Z. Paryphantidae, pp. 335-349).

van Bruggen, A.C., 1967. An Introduction to the pulmonate family Streptaxidae. Jour. Conch., vol. 26 (3): 181-188.

Watson, H., 1934. *Natalina* and other South African snails. Proc. Mal. Soc. London, vol. 21: 150-198, pls. 19-21.

Family CHLAMYDEPHORIDAE

Sole genus: *Chlamydephorus* W.G. Binney, 1879. Slug with internal shell.

Family SYSTROPHIIDAE

Major genera: *Systrophia* Pfeiffer, 1855; *Happia* Bourguinat, 1889; *Miradiscops* H.B. Baker, 1925; *Tamayoa* H.B. Baker, 1925.

Family HAPLOTREMATIDAE

Two genera: *Haplotrema* Ancey, 1881; *Austroselenites* Kobelt, 1905.

Baker, H.B., 1931. The land snail genus *Haplotrema*. Proc. Acad. Nat. Sci. Phila., vol. 82: 405-425, pls. 33-35.

Family ACAVIDAE

Main genera: *Acavus* Montfort, 1810; *Ampelita* Beck, 1837; *Helicophanta* Férussac, 1821; *Leucotaenius* von Martens, 1860; *Oligospira* Ancey, 1887; *Stylodon* Beck, 1837; *Clavator* von Martens, 1860.

(see Pilsbry, H.A., *Manual of Conchology*, series 2, vol. 13, *Caryodes* pp. 125-126, pl. 5, 1900; vol. 6, *Pedinogyra* pp. 13-16; *Ampelita*, pp. 16-56; *Helicophanta*, pp. 59-74; *Panda* 75-66; *Acavus*, pp. 76-84; *Stylodonta*, pp. 85-89, pls. 1-19, 1890; vol. 5, *Pentellaria* [*Lucerna* in Pilsbry], pp. 97-118; *Caracolus*, pp. 118-127; *Isomeria*, pp. 135-158; *Labyrinthus*, pp. 159-176; *Solaropsis*, pp. 177-196, pls. 21-64, 1889-90).

Germain, L., 1925. La Distribution. Géographique et l'origine des Mollusques de la Famille des Acavides, C.R. Congr. Soc. Savantes 1924, Sci.: 254-268, 1 fig.

Meade, A.R., 1986. Transfer *Leucotaenius*: Achatinidae to Acavidae. Arch. Moll., vol. 116 (4-6): 137-155.

Family CARYODIDAE

Main genera: *Caryodes* Albers, 1850; *Anoglypta* von Martens, 1860; *Hedleyella* Iredate, 1914; *Pedinogyra* Albers, 1850.

Family MACROCYCLIDAE

Sole genus: *Macrocyclis* Beck, 1837 from Chile.

Family CHLAMYDEPHORIDAE

Sole sluglike genus from South Africa: *Chlamydephorus* Binney, 1879.

Superfamily BULIMULOIDEA
(syn.: Orthalicoidea)

Family BULIMULIDAE

Family BULIMULIDAE. *Placostylus miltecheilus* (Reeve, 1848). Solomon Islands. 5 cm. See p. 101.

Main genera: *Bulimulus* Leach, 1914; *Bostryx* Troschel, 1847; *Bothriembryon* Pilsbry, 1894; *Leiostracus* Albers, 1850; *Naesiotus* Albers, 1850; *Rabdotus* Albers, 1850; *Scutalus* Albers, 1850; *Aspastus* Albers, 1850; *Auris* Spix, 1827; *Berendtia* Crosse and Fischer, 1869; *Cochlorina* Jan, 1830; *Diplomorpha* Ancey, 1884; *Drymaeus* Albers, 1850; *Dryptus* Albers, 1860; *Neopetraeus* von

Martens, 1885; *Oxychona* Mörch, 1852; *Placostylus* Beck, 1837; *Plekochilus* Guilding, 1827; *Thaumastus* Albers, 1860.

(see Pilsbry, H.A., *Manual of Conchology*, series 2, vol. 13 (*Bothriembryon*, pp. 1-19; *Placostylus*, pp. 19-120, pls. 6-45, 1900; *Plekocheilus*, vol. 10, pp. 62-92; *Auris*, vol. 10, pp. 95-124, pls. 39-44, 1896; *Bulimulus, Bostryx*, vol. 10, 1896, and vol. 11, 1897-98).

Breure, A.S.H., 1974. Caribbean Land Molluscs: *Bulimulidae* I. Bulimulus. Studies Fauna Curaçao, vol. 45: 1-80, pls. 1-7.

——, 1975. Notes on Bulimulidae, 2. On a Small Collection of *Simulopsis* Beck, 1837, from Southern Brazil, with Descriptions of Three New Species. Basteria, vol. 39: 97-113, 14 figs.

——, 1975. Caribbean Land Molluscs: Bulimulidae II. *Plekocheilus* and *Naesiotus. Ibid.*, vol. 46: 71-93, pls. 6-8.

——, 1979. Systematics, Phylogeny and Zoogeography of Bulimulinae (Mollusca). Zool. Verh. Leiden, vol. 169: 1-215.

Dall, W.H., 1920. On the relations of the sectional groups of *Bulimulus* of the subgenus *Naesiota* Albers. Jour. Wash. Acad. Sci., vol. 10: 117-122.

Hedley, C., 1892. The range of *Placostylus*: a study in ancient geography. Proc. Linn. Soc. N.S. Wales, ser. 2, vol. 7: 335-339.

Family BULIMULIDAE; subfamily Orthalicinae. *Liguus pictus* (Reeve, 1842). Lower Florida Keys. 5 cm. See p. 108.

Kendrick, G.W. and B.R. Wilson, 1975. Nomenclatural notes on the land snail genus *Bothriembryon* Pilsbry, 1894 (Pulmonata: Bulimulidae) with redescription of the type and two other species. Record West. Australian Mus., vol. 3: 295-325.

Kershaw, R.C., 1986. Anatomical notes on the land snail *Bothriembryon* (Bulimulidae) from South Australia and Western Australia. Record South Aust. Mus., vol. 19 (16): 327-337.

Kobelt, W. and O. von Möllendorff, 1903. Catalog der Familie Buliminidae. Nachr. Bl. Deutsch Malak. Ges., vol. 35: 36-60; 65-71.

Odhner, N.H., 1951. Studies on Galapagos Bulimulids. Jour. de Conchyl., vol. 90 (4): 253-268, 2 pls.

Parodiz, J.J., 1962. New and little-known species of South and Central American land snails (Bulimulidae). Proc. U.S. Nat. Mus., vol. 113: 429-456, pls. 1-2.

Pilsbry, H.A. and A.A. Olsson, 1949. The landsnail genus *Xenothauma* and other carinate Bulimulidae of Peru. Notulae Naturae, no. 215: 1-14, figs. 1-19.

Powell, A.W.B., 1947. Distribution of *Placostylus* Land Snails in Northern New Zealand. Records Auckland Inst. Mus., vol. 3 (3): 173-188.

Rehder, H.A., 1940. New mollusks of the genus *Naesiotus* from Ecuador. The Nautilus, vol. 53 (4): 111-118.

Weyrauch, W.K., 1956. Neue Landschnecken aus Peru. Arch. Moll., vol. 85 (4/6): 145-164, pl. 11.

——, 1956. The genus *Naesiotus*, with descriptions of new species

and notes on other Peruvian Bulimulidae. Proc. Acad. Nat. Sci. Phila., vol. 108: 1-17, pl. 1.

——, 1960. Zur Kenntnis von Newboldius (Bulimulidae). Archiv. Moll., vol. 89 (1/3): 49-56, pls. 7, 8.

Zilch, A., 1972. Die Typen und Typoide des Natur-Museums Senckenberg, 48. Mollusca: Bulimulidae (1). Archiv. Moll., vol. 102 (1/3): 133-145.

Subfamily **Orthalicinae.** All genera: *Orthalicus* Beck, 1837; *Chersina* Beck, 1837; *Corona* Albers, 1850; *Hemibulimus* von Martens, 1885; *Lignus* Nevill, 1878; *Liguus* Montfort, 1810; *Porphyrobaphe* Shuttleworth, 1856; *Pseudotrochus* Hermannsen, 1847; *Sultana* Shuttleworth, 1856.

Breure, A.S.H., 1973. Catalogue of Bulimulidae. I. Amphibuliminae. Basteria, vol. 37, pp. 51-56.

Clench, W.J., 1946. A Catalogue of the Genus *Liguus* with a Description of a New Subgenus. Occ. Papers Mus. Comp. Zool., vol. 1 (10): 117-128.

Jones, Archie L., 1979. Descriptions of Six New Forms of Florida Tree Snails, *Liguus fasciatus*. The Nautilus, vol. 94 (4): 153-159, 12 color figs.

Roth, Barry and Arthur E. Bogan, 1984. Shell Color and Banding Parameters of the *Liguus fasciatus* Phenotype. Amer. Malacological Bull., vol. 3 (1): 1-10.

Simpson, Charles T., 1929. The Florida Tree Snails of the Genus *Liguus*. Proc. U.S. Nat. Mus., vol. 73, no. 2741: 1-44, pls. 1-4.

Strebel, H., 1909. Revision der Unterfamilie der Orthalicinen. Jahrb. Wiss. Anst. Hamburg, vol. 26: 1-191, pls. 1-33.

Family **ODONTOSTOMIDAE**

Family ODONTOSTOMIDAE. *Anostoma octodentatum* (G. Fischer, 1807). Brazil. 2.5 cm. See p. 105.

Main genera: *Odontostomus* Beck, 1837; *Anctus* von Martens, 1860; *Anostoma* G. Fischer, 1807; *Cyclodontina* Beck, 1837; *Spixia* Pilsbry and Vanatta, 1898; *Tomigerus* Spix, 1827.

(see Pilsbry, H.A., *Manual of Conchology*, series 2, vol. 14, pp. 24-116, pls. 7-12, 1901).

Breure, A.S.H., 1974. Catalogue of Bulimulidae (Gastropoda Euthyneura), II. Odontostominae. *Basteria*, vol. 38, pp. 109-127.

de Oliveira, Maury Pinto, 1978. *Cyclodontina* (*Moricandia*) *angulata*, (Wagner, 1827). Comunic. Malacol. no. 10, Univ. Fed. de Juiz de Fora, Bull. 23, pp. 3-27 (radula; anatomy).

von Ihering, H., 1905. On the genus *Tomigerus* Spix, with descriptions of new species. Proc. Mal. Soc. London, vol. 6: 197-199.

Family **AMPHIBULIMULIDAE**

Major genera: *Amphibulima* Lamarck, 1805; *Gaeotis* Shuttleworth, 1854; *Simpulopsis* Beck, 1837 (+ *Bulimulopsis* Pilsbry, 1899).

Family **UROCOPTIDAE**

Family UROCOPTIDAE. *Gongylostoma elliotti* (Poey, 1858). Cuba. 2.5 cm. See p. 121.

(see Pilsbry, H.A., *Manual of Conchology*, series 2, vol. 15, pp. 1-328, 1902-03; vol. 16, pp. 1-174, 1903-04; Index to species, pp. 196-204).

Bartsch, Paul, 1926. New Urocoptid Land Shells from Mexico. Proc. U.S. Nat. Mus., vol. 70 (4): 1-13, pl. 1.

——, 1945. New Urocoptid Mollusks from Mexico. Jour. Wash. Acad. Sci., vol. 35 (3): 92-95.

Clench, W.J., 1935. Some new Urocoptidae from Hispaniola. Proc. Boston Soc. Nat. Hist., vol. 41 (1): 1-12, pls. 1, 2.

——, 1966. Notes and Descriptions of New Urocoptidae from Cuba and Hispaniola. Breviora, no. 245: 14 pp., 2 pls.

Jaume, M.L. and Alfredo de la Torre, 1976. Los Urocoptidae de Cuba (Mollusca-Pulmonta). Ciencias Biologicas, serie 4, no. 53, 122 pp. Habana, Cuba. (also 1972, Circular Mus. Bibliot. Zool., Habana, pp. 1526-1649).

Pilsbry, H.A., 1929. Studies on West Indian Mollusks, II: The Locomotion of Urocoptidae and Descriptions of New Forms. Proc. Acad. Nat. Sci. Phila., vol. 81: 443-467.

——, 1953. Inland mollusks of Northern Mexico. II. Urocoptidae, Pupillidae, Strobilopsidae, Valloniidae and Cionellidae. *Ibid.*, vol. 105: 133-167, pls. 3-10.

Thompson, F.G., 1971. Some Mexican land snails of the genera *Coelostemma* and *Metastoma* (Urocoptidae). Bull. Florida State Mus., vol. 15: 267-302.

——, 1976. The genus *Epirobia* in Chiapas, Mexico. The Nautilus, vol. 90 (1): 41-46, 3 figs.

Thompson, F.G. and R. Franz, 1976. Some Urocoptid Land Snails from Hispaniola. Rev. Biol. Trop., vol. 21 (1): 7-33, 9 figs.

Subfamily **Urocoptinae**. All genera: *Urocoptis* Beck, 1837; *Cochlodinella* Pilsbry and Vanatta, 1898; *Levistemma* Jaume and A. de la Torre, 1976; *Tenuistemma* Jaume and A. de la Torre, 1976; *Arangia* Pilsbry and Vanatta, 1898; *Tomelasmus* Pilsbry and Vanatta, 1898; *Gongylostomella* Pilsbry,

1941; *Poecilocoptis* Pilsbry, 1941; *Steatocoptis* Pilsbry, 1941; *Capillacea, Pfeiffericoptis, Centralia, Teneria* all Jaume and A. de la Torre, 1976; *Nesocoptis* Pilsbry, 1941; *Gongylostoma* Albers, 1850; *Uncinicoptis, Geminicoptis, Sagracoptis* all Jaume and A. de la Torre, 1976; *Sectilumen* Pilsbry and Vanatta, 1898; *Callonia* Crosse and Fischer, 1870; *Callocoptis, Acrocoptis, Poeycoptis, Nodulia, Trilamellaxis, Organocoptis, Amphistemma, Planostemma* all Jaume and A. de la Torre, 1976; *Liocallonia* Pilsbry, 1902; *Paracallonia* Pilsbry, 1903; *Badiofaux* Pilsbry, 1941; *Pycnoptychia* Pilsbry and Vanatta, 1898; *Idiostemma* Pilsbry and Vanatta, 1898; *Pleurostemma* Pilsbry, 1941.

Subfamily **Johaniceraminae**. Sole genus: *Johaniceramus* Jaume and A. de la Torre, 1976.

Subfamily **Eucalodiinae**. Main genera: *Eucalodium* Crosse and Fischer, 1868; *Coelocentrum* Crosse and Fischer, 1872; *Epirobia* Strebel and Pfeiffer, 1880; *Hendersoniella* Dall, 1905.

Subfamily **Holospirinae**. Main genera: *Holospira* von Martens, 1860; *Coelostemma* Dall, 1895.

Subfamily **Microceraminae**. Sole genus: *Microceramus* Pilsbry and Vanatta, 1898.

Family **PLECTOPYLIDIDAE**
(syn.: Corillidae)

Three genera: *Plectopylis* Benson, 1860; *Corilla* H. and A. Adams, 1855; *Amphicoelina* Haas, 1933.

Benson, W.H., 1860. Notes on Plectopylis . . . internal plicate epiphragms . . . Annals Mag. Nat. Hist., ser. 3, vol. 5. 5: 243-247.

Family **SCULPTARIIDAE**
Sole South African genus: *Sculptaria* Pfeiffer, 1855.

Superfamily **ENDODONTOIDEA**

Family **ENDODONTIDAE**
(syn.: Punctidae; Flammulidae; Helicodiscidae)

Major genera: *Endodonta* Albers, 1850; *Australdonta* Solem, 1976; *Glyptaulax* Gude, 1914; *Libera* Garrett, 1881; *Thaumatodon; Zyzzyxdonta* Solem, 1976.

Cumber, R.A., 1961. A Revision of the Genus *Phenacohelix* Suter, 1892 (Mollusca: Flammulinidae) with Descriptions of a New Species, and Studies on Variation, Distribution and Ecology. Trans. Royal Soc. N.Z., Zool. vol. 1 (13): 163-196.

Solem, Alan, 1957. Philippine Snails of the Family Endodontidae. *Fieldiana*, Zool. vol. 42: 1-12.

——, 1958. Endodontide Landschnecken von Indonesien und Neu Guinea. Arch. für Moll., vol. 87: 19-26, pl. 3.

——, 1976. Endodontoid Land Snails from Pacific Islands. Part I, pp. 1-508; Part II (1983), p. 336. Field Mus. Nat. Hist., Chicago. (definitive, illustrated work).

——, 1978. Endodontoid land snails: Pacific Islands. II. Punctidae, Charopidae. pp. 1-336. Field Mus. Nat. Hist., Chicago.

Weyrauch, W.K., 1965. Neue und verkannte Endodontiden aus Südamerika. Archiv. Moll., vol. 94 (3/4): 121-134, pl. 7.

Subfamily **Punctinae**. <u>Major genera</u>: *Punctum* Morse, 1864; *Laoma* Gray, 1850.

Family HELICODISCIDAE
<u>Major genera</u>: *Helicodiscus* Morse, 1864; *Polygyriscus* Pilsbry, 1948; *Radiodiscus* Pilsbry and Ferriss, 1906; *Zilchogyra* Weyrauch, 1965.

Family CHAROPIDAE
Mordan, P. and S. Tillier, 1986. New Caledonian charopid land snails. I. Revision of the genus Pararhytida. Malacologia, vol. 27 (2): 203-241, illus.

Solem, A., 1970. The land snail genus *Afrodonta* (Mollusca: Pulmonata: Endodontidae). Ann. Natal Mus., vol. 20: 341-364.

Stanisic, John, 1987. Studies on the Charopidae of tropical and subtropical Australia. I. *Oreokera*: A primitive genus from the high mountains of North Queensland (Charopidae). Jour. Malac. Soc. Aust., vol. 8: 1-21, 2 pls.

Subfamily **Charopininae**. <u>Major genera</u>: *Charopa* Albers, 1860; *Afrodonta* Melvill and Ponsonby, 1908; *Chaureopa* Climo, 1985; *Gerontia* Hutton, 1883; *Lauopa* Solem, 1983; *Pilula* von Martens, 1898; *Ptychodon* Ancey, 1888; *Trachycystis* Pilsbry, 1892.

Subfamily **Trukcharopinae**. <u>Major genera</u>: *Trukcharopa* Solem, 1983; *Jokajdon* Solem, 1983; *Russatus* Solem, 1983.

Subfamily **Semperdoninae**. <u>Major genus</u>: *Semperdon* Solem, 1983.

Subfamily **Amphidoxinae**. <u>Major genera</u>: *Amphidoxa* Albers, 1850; *Flammulina* von Martens, 1873; *Hedleyconcha* Pilsbry, 1893; *Therasia* Hutton, 1883.

Subfamily **Rotadiscinae**. <u>Sole genus</u>: *Rotadiscus* Pilsbry, 1926.

Family OTOCONCHIDAE
<u>Sole New Zealand genus</u>: *Otoconcha* Hutton, 1884.

Family DISCIDAE
<u>Two genera</u>: *Discus* Fitzinger, 1833 (5 subgenera); *Anguispira* Morse, 1864.

Family DISCIDAE. *Anguispira alternata* (Say, 1816). Eastern U.S. 2 cm. See p. 125.

Superfamily LIMACOIDEA

Family LIMACIDAE (slugs)
<u>Major genera</u>: *Limax* Linnaeus, 1758; *Deroceras* Rafinesque, 1820.

Family BOETTGERILLIDAE
<u>Sole genus</u>: *Boettgerilla* Simroth, 1910 (slug with internal shell).

Family AGRIOLIMACIDAE
<u>Sole Genus of slugs</u>: *Agriolimax* Mörch, 1865.

Family TRIGONOCHLAMYDIDAE
<u>Major slug genera</u>: *Trigonochlamys* O. Boettger, 1881; *Parmacellilla* Simroth, 1910.

Superfamily ZONITOIDEA
(syn.: Vitrinoidea)

Family ZONITIDAE

Family ZONITIDAE. *Vitrinizonites latissimus* (Lewis, 1875). Appalachian mountains, U.S. 1.7 cm. See p. 125.

<u>Main genera</u>: *Zonites* Montfort, 1810; *Mesomphix* Rafinesque, 1819; *Omphalina* Rafinesque, 1831; *Oxychilus* Fitzinger, 1833; *Paravitrea* Pilsbry, 1898; *Retinella* Fischer in Shuttleworth, 1877; *Vitrinozonites* W.G. Binney, 1879; *Godwinia* Sykes, 1900.

Baker, H.B., 1928. Minute American Zonitidae. Proc. Acad. Nat. Sci. Phila., vol. 80: 1-44, pls. 1-8.

———, 1930. The North American Retinellae. Proc. Acad. Nat. Sci. Phila., vol. 82: 193-219, pls. 9-14.

Forcart, L., 1957. Taxionomische Revision paläartischer Zonitinae. I. Archiv. Moll., vol. 86 (4/6): 101-136.

Godwin-Austen, H.H., 1912. A review of South African landmollusca belonging to the family Zonitidae. Ann. Mag. Nat. Hist., ser. 8, vol. 9: 122-139, 569-585.

Family VITRINIDAE
<u>Major genera</u>: *Vitrina* Draparnaud, 1801; *Vitrea* Fitzinger, 1833; *Hawaiia* Gude, 1911; *Pristiloma* Ancey, 1887.

Baker, H.B., 1929. Nomenclature in the genus *Vitrina*. The Nautilus, vol. 42 (4): 137-139.

Groh, K. and J. Hemmen, 1986. Vitriniden: Madiera Archipels. Arch. Moll., vol. 116 (4-6): 183-217.

Family DAUDEBARDIIDAE

<u>Main genera</u>: *Daudebardia* Hartmann, 1821; *Deceballia* Grossu, 1969. [*Pseudolibania* is a marine Pleurobranchidae slug].

Forcart, L., 1950. Systématique des mollusques en forme de *Daudebardia* et révision de espèces d'Anatolie et de l'île de Crête. Jour. de Conchyl., vol. 90 (2): 107-117.

Family PARMACELLIDAE

<u>Two genera of slugs with reduced shells</u>: *Parmacella* Cuvier, 1804; *Kandaharia* Godwin-Austen, 1914.

Alonso, M.R., M. Ibanez and J.A. Diaz, 1986. Clave de identificacion del genero *Parmacella* Couvier, 1804. Iberus, vol. 6: 141-147.

Family MILACIDAE

<u>Two genera of slugs with reduced internal shells</u>: *Milax* Gray, 1855; *Aspidophorus* Fitzinger, 1833.

Alonso, M.R., M. Ibanez and M. Bech, 1985. Claves de identificacion de las babosas (pulmonados desnudos de Cataluna [Spain]. Miscellania Zool., vol. 9: 91-107.

Suborder HOLOPODA

Superfamily POLYGYROIDEA

Family POLYGYRIDAE
(syn.: Mesodontidae)

Family POLYGYRIDAE. *Mesodon zaletus* (A. Binney, 1837). Eastern U.S. 2.8 cm. See p. 134.

<u>Major genera</u>: *Polygyra* Say, 1818; *Daedalochila* Beck, 1837; *Mesodon* Rafinesque in Férussac, 1821; *Praticolella* von Martens, 1892; *Stenotrema* Rafinesque, 1819; *Trilobopsis* Pilsbry, 1939.

Archer, A.F., 1948. Land snails of the genus *Stenotrema* in the Alabama region. Geol. Survey Alabama, Mus. Papers, no. 28: 1-85, pls. 1010.

Hubricht, L., 1983. The genus *Praticolella* in Texas (Polygyridae). The Veliger, vol. 25 (3): 244-250, 18 figs.

Richardson, Leonard, 1986. Polygyracea: Catalog of Species. *Tryonia*, no. 13, Philadelphia, pp. 1-139; 1-40; 1-38. Part I, Polygy-

ridae: Ashmunellinae, pp. 2-23; Polygyrinae, pp. 24-72; Thysanophorinae, pp. 73-86; Triodopsinae, pp. 87-104; Part 2, Corillidae, pp. 1-40; Part 3 Sagdidae, pp. 1-38. Large bibliographies, and index by species.

Subfamily **Triodopsinae.** <u>Major genera</u>: *Triodopsis* Rafinesque, 1819; *Neohelix* von Ihering, 1892; *Webbhelix* Emberton, 1988; *Xolotrema* Rafinesque, 1819; *Allogona* Pilsbry, 1939; *Vespericola* Pilsbry 1939; *Ashmunella* Pilsbry and Cockerell, 1899; *Cryptomastix* Pilsbry, 1939.

Emberton, K.C., 1988. The genitalic, allozymic and conchological evolution of the eastern North American Triodopsinae (Gastropoda: Pulmonata: Polygyridae). Malacologia, vol. 28 (1/2): 159-273, 51 figs.

Family THYSANOPHORIDAE

<u>Main genera</u>: *Thysanophora* Strebel and Pfeiffer, 1880; *Mcleania* Bequaert and Clench, 1939.

Thompson, F.G., 1958. The land snail genus *Microconus*. The Nautilus, vol. 72 (1): 5-10, pl. 1.

———, 1977. The Polygyrid genus *Mc Leania* in Hispaniola. The Nautilus, vol. 91 (2): 77-80, 1 fig.

Family AMMONITELLIDAE
(syn.: Megomphicidae)

<u>Three genera</u>: *Ammonitella* Cooper, 1868; *Polygyrella* Cooper, 1863: *Polygyroidea* Pilsbry, 1930.

Superfamily ATHORACOPHOROIDEA

Family ATHORACOPHORIDAE

<u>Major genus</u>: *Athoracophorus* Gould, 1852. Shell-less slugs, not treated in this book.

Burch, J.B. and C.M. Patterson, 1969. The systematic position of the Athoracophoridae. Malacologia, vol. 9 (1): 259-260.

Superfamily SAGDOIDEA

Family SAGDIDAE

Family SAGDIDAE. *Sagda jayana* (C.B. Adams, 1848). Jamaica. 2.5 cm. See p. 138.

Baker, H.B., 1940. Some Antillean Sagdidae or Polygyridae. The Nautilus, vol. 54 (2): 54-62, pls. 4, 5.

Goodfriend, G.A., 1986. Radiation of the land snail genus *Sagda*: Comparative morphology, biogeography and ecology of the species of North-central Jamaica. Jour. Linn. Soc. (Zool.), vol. 87 (4): 367-398, illus.

Subfamily **Sagdinae.** Major genera: *Sagda* Beck, 1837; *Hojeda* H.B. Baker, 1926; *Proserpinula* Albers, in von Martens, 1860; *Stauroglypta* H.B. Baker, 1935.

Subfamily **Aquibaninae.** Major genera: *Aquibana* Pilsbry, 1926; *Suavitas* Pilsbry, 1926.

Superfamily OLEACINOIDEA

Family SPIRAXIDAE
[see after Achatinidae]

Family OLEACINIDAE

Family OLEACINIDAE. *Laevaricella playa* (H.B. Baker, 1940). Puerto Rico. 3 cm. See p. 138.

Auffenberg, K. and L.A. Stange, 1986. Snail-eating Snails of Florida [*Varicella*; *Euglandina*]. Entomology Circular Fla. Dept. Agric. no. 285, 4pp.

Baker, H.B., 1941. Outline of American Oleacininae and new species from Mexico. The Nautilus, vol. 55 (2): 51-61, pl. 5.

——, 1941. Puerto Rican Oleacininae. The Nautilus, vol. 55 (1): 24-30, pls. 1-2.

——, 1943. The mainland genera of American Oleacininae. Proc. Acad. Nat. Sci. Phila., vol. 95: 1-14, pls. 1-3.

Subfamily **Oleacininae.** Major genera: *Oleacina* Röding, 1798; *Rectoleacina* Pilsbry, 1907; *Strebelia* Crosse and Fischer, 1868.

Subfamily **Varicellinae.** Major genera: *Varicella* Pfeiffer, 1856; *Glandinella* Pfeiffer, 1878; *Laevaricella* Pilsbry, 1907; *Sigmataxis* Pilsbry, 1907.

Family TESTACELLIDAE
Sole genus: *Testacella* Couvier, 1800. Slug with internal shell.

Diaz, J.A., M.R. Alonso and M. Ibanez, 1986. Los pulmonados desnudos de las Islas Canarias. I. Superfamilia Testacelloidea Gray 1840 y Zonitoidea Mörch, 1864. Vieraca, vol. 16 (1/2): 81-96.

Superfamily GASTRODONTOIDEA

Family GASTRODONTIDAE
Main genera: *Gastrodonta* Albers, 1850; *Poecilozonites* Boettger, 1884; *Striatura* Morse, 1864; *Ventridens* Binney and Bland, 1869; *Zonitoides* Lehmann, 1862.

Pilsbry, H.A., 1924. Recent and Fossil Bermudan Snails of the Genus *Poecilozonites*. Proc. Acad. Nat. Sci. Phila., vol. 76: 1-9, figs. 1-6.

Superfamily HELICARIONOIDEA

Family EUCONULIDAE
Main genera: *Euconulus* Reinhardt, 1883; *Eurychlamys* Godwin-Austen, 1899; *Guppya* Mörch, 1867; *Habroconulus* Fischer and Crosse, 1872; *Macroceras* Semper, 1870; *Palaua* H.B. Baker, 1941.

Family HELICARIONIDAE
(syn.: Helixarionidae)

Family HELICARIONIDAE. *Helixarion virens* (Pfeiffer, 1849) forma *aquila* (Cox, 1868). Queensland. 3 cm. Queensland Museum photo. See p. 127.

Baker, H.B., 1938. Zonitid snails from Pacific Islands, Part I. Bull. B.P. Bishop Mus., vol. 158: 1-102, pls. 1-20.

——, 1940. Part 2. Hawaiian genera of Microcystinae. *Ibid.*, vol. 165: 105-210, pls. 21-42.

Bartsch, Paul, 1938. A Synopsis of the Philippine Land Mollusks of the subgenus *Ryssota*. Proc. Biol. Soc. Wash., vol. 51: 101-120.

——, 1942. A synopsis of the Philippine land mollusks of the genus *Hemitrichia*. Proc. Biol. Soc. Wash., vol. 55: 27-44.

——, 1942. A Synopsis of the Philippine Land Mollusks of the Genus *Hemitrichia* [now *Hemitrichiella*], ibid., vol. 55: 27-44.

Habe, T., 1943. Reviews of Japanese Helicarionidae. Jap. Jour. Malac., vol. 13: 92-96.

Solem, A., 1981. Small land snails: Northern Australia. II. *Westralcystis*. Jour. Mal. Soc. Aust., vol. 5 (3/4): 175-193.

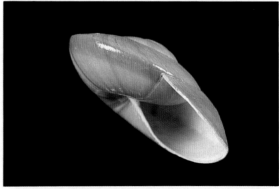

Family HELICARIONIDAE, subfamily Sesarinae. *Ryssota uranus* (Pfeiffer, 1861). Philippines. 5 cm. See p. 129.

Subfamily **Helicarioninae**. <u>Main genera</u>: *Helixarion* Férussac, 1821; *Amphiblema* Gude, 1911; *Epiglypta* Pilsbry, 1893; *Westralcystis* Iredale, 1939.

Subfamily **Sesarinae**. <u>Main genera</u>: *Sesara* Albers, 1860; *Dendrotrochus* Pilsbry, 1894; *Geotrochus* Hasselt, 1823; *Hemiglypta* Möllendorff, 1893; *Kaliella* Blanford, 1863; *Orpiella* Gray, 1855 (+ *Eurypus* Semper, 1870); *Lepidotrichia* Bartsch, 1942 (+ *Hemitrichia* Möllendorff, 1888); *Ryssota* Albers, 1850; *Sivella* Blanford, 1863.

Subfamily **Ereptinae**. <u>Main genera</u>: *Erepta* Albers, 1850; *Dupontia* Godwin-Austen, 1908; *Plegma* Gude, 1911.

Subfamily **Microcystinae**. <u>Main genera</u>: *Microcystis* Beck, 1837; *Cookeana* H.B. Baker, 1938; *Diastole* Gude, 1913; *Lamprocystis* Pfeiffer, 1883; *Liardetta* Gude, 1913; *Pittoconcha* Preston, 1913.

Family **AILLYIDAE**
<u>Sole genus</u>: *Aillya* Odhner, 1927.
van Mol, J.J., 1978. Etude de la Morphologie et des Affinités Systématique de *Ailly camerunensis* Odhner. Rev. Zool. Afr. Tervuren, vol. 92: 1003-1021.

Family **ARIOPHANTIDAE**

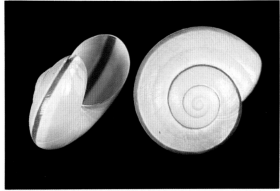

Family ARIOPHANTIDAE. *Naninia aulica* (Pfeiffer, 1852). New Guinea. 5 cm. See pp. 131-133.

<u>Main genera</u>: *Ariophanta* Desmoulins, 1829; *Euplecta* Semper, 1870; *Hemiplecta* Albers, 1850; *Naninia* Sowerby, 1842 (and subgenus *Xesta* Albers, 1850).
Laidlaw, F.F., 1931. On a new subfamily Dyakinae of the Zonitidae. Proc. Mal. Soc. London, vol. 19: 190-201.
——, 1932. Notes on Ariophantidae from the Malay Peninsula, with descriptions of new genera. Proc. Mal. Soc. London, vol. 20 (2): 80-94.

Subfamily **Dyakiinae**. <u>Main genera</u>: *Dyakia* Godwin-Austen, 1891; *Asperitas* Gude, 1911.

Subfamily **Parmarioninae**. <u>Main genera</u>: *Parmarion* P. Fischer, 1855; *Damayantia* Issel, 1874.

Subfamily **Girasiinae**. <u>Main genera</u>: *Girasia* Gray, 1855; *Austenia* Nevill, 1878; *Mariaella* Gray, 1855.

Subfamily **Macrochlamydinae**. <u>Main genera</u>: *Macrochlamys* Benson, 1832; *Baiaplecta* Laidlaw, 1956; *Megaustenia* Cockerell, 1912; *Oxytesta* Zilch, 1956; *Syama* Godwin-Austen, 1908.

Subfamily **Chroninae**. <u>Only genus</u>: *Chronos* Robson, 1914.

Subgenus **Durgellinae**. <u>Main genera</u>: *Durgella* Blanford, 1863; *Sitala* H. Adams, 1865; *Sakiella* Godwin-Austen, 1908.

Family **TROCHOMORPHIDAE**
<u>Main genera</u>: *Trochomorpha* Albers, 1850; *Bertia* Ancey, 1887; *Brazieria* Ancey, 1887; *Coxia* Ancey, 1887; *Kondoa* H.B. Baker, 1941; *Videna* H. and A. Adams, 1855.
Gude, G.K., 1914. The fauna of British India, including Ceylon and Burma. Mollusca. II. (Trochomorphidae-Janellidae). 520 pp., London.

Family **UROCYCLIDAE**

Subfamily **Urocyclinae**. <u>Main genera</u>: *Urocyclus* Gray, 1864; *Acantharion* Binder and Tillier, 1983; *Bukobia* Simroth, 1896; *Verrucarion* van Mol, 1970.
Van Goethem, J.L., 1977. La Systematique des Urocyclinae. Malacologia, vol. 16 (1): 133-138.

Subfamily **Trochozonitinae**. <u>Main genera</u>: *Trochozonites* Pfeiffer, 1883; *Africarion* Godwin-Austen, 1883; *Sheldonia* Ancey, 1887; *Zonitarion* Pfeiffer, 1883.

Family **CYSTOPELTIDAE**
<u>Sole genus</u>: *Cystopelta* Tate, 1881.

Superfamily **HELICOIDEA**

Family **SOLAROPSIDAE**
<u>Two genera</u>: *Solaropsis* Beck, 1837; *Psadara* Miller, 1878.

Family **CAMAENIDAE**

Family CAMAENIDAE. *Mesanella monochroa* (Sowerby, 1841). Philippines. 4 cm. See p. 142.

Subfamily **Camaenidae**. <u>Main genera</u>: *Camaena* Albers, 1850; *Amphidromus* Albers, 1850; *Calycia* H. Adams, 1865; *Caracolus* Montfort, 1810; *Chloritis* Beck, 1837; *Eurycratera* Beck, 1837; *Ganesella* Blanford, 1863; *Hadra* Albers, 1860; *Lampadion* Röding; *Labyrinthus* Beck, 1837;

Mandarina Pilsbry, 1895; *Obba* Beck, 1837; *Planispira* Beck, 1837; *Pleurodonte* G. Fischer, 1807 (+ *Dentellaria* Schumacher, 1817); *Pleurodontes* Montfort, 1810; *Polygyratia* Gray, 1847; *Rhagada* Albers, 1850; *Satsuma* A. Adams, 1868; *Sphaerospira* Mörch, 1867; *Thersites* Pfeiffer, 1855; *Trachia* Albers, 1860; *Varohadra* Iredale, 1933; *Xanthomelon* von Martens, 1860; *Zachrysia* Pilsbry, 1894.

(see Pilsbry, H.A., *Manual of Conchology*, series 2, vol. 6, *Hadra, Camaena, Obba, Chloritis, Planispira*, pp. 125-308, pls. 32-69, 1890-91).

Bartsch, Paul, 1933. The land shells of the genus *Obba* from Mindoro Province, Philippine Islands. Bull. 100, U.S. Nat. Mus., vol. 6, pt. 8: 343-371, pls. 88-93.

Bishop, M.J., 1978. A revision of the genus *Thersites* Pfeiffer (Pulmonata: Camaenidae). Jour. Mal. Soc. Australia, vol. 4 (1/2): 9-21, 16 figs.

Clench, W.J., 1962. New Land Mollusks in the Families Camaenidae and Fruticicolidae from Hispaniola. Rev. Mus. Argention Cienco., vol. 8: 213-227, 2 pls.

Gude, G.K., 1906. Further remarks on the genus *Chloritis*, with descriptions of eleven new species. Proc. Mal. Soc. London, vol. 7: 105-118, pl. 13.

Marshall, W.B., 1927. The Australian Land Shell *Thersites bipartita* and its Allies. Proc. U.S. Nat. Mus., vol. 72, no. 2711, 16 pp., 3 pls.

Pilsbry, H.A., 1928. Studies on West Indian Mollusks. The Genus *Zachrysia*. Proc. Acad. Nat. Sci. Phila., vol. 80: 581-606.

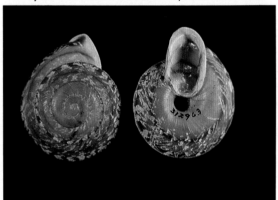

Family CAMAENIDAE. *Obba gallinula* (Pfeiffer, 1845). Philippines. 3 cm. See p. 142.

Richardson, Leonard, 1985. Camaenidae: Catalog of Species. Tryonia no. 12, Acad. Nat. Sci. Philadelphia, pp. 1-479. Best source to all names. Camaeninae, pp. 1-322; Papuininae, pp. 323-392. Bibliography, pp. 393-406. This huge list covers such popular genera as *Amphidromus, Calycia, Camaena, Caracolus, Chloritis, Hadra, Labyrinthus, Obba, Pleurodonte, Solaropsis, Sphaerospira, Thersites, Varohadra, Xanthomelon, Zachrysia* and the various genera of Papuininae: *Crystallopsis, Megalacron, Meliobba, Papuina, Papuanella, Papustyla, Rhynchotrochus, Smeatonia*, etc.

Solem, A., 1979-1985. Camaenids: Western and Central Australia. I. Taxa of Trans-Australian distribution. Rec. West. Australian Mus., Suppl. 10: 1-142; also suppl. 11: 143-320 (1981); pp. 321-425 (1981); suppl. 17: 427-705 (1984); suppl. 20: 707-981 (1985).

———, 1966. The neotropical land snail genera *Labyrinthus* and *Isomeria* (Camaenidae). Fieldiana, Zool., vol. 50: 1-226, figs.

Wurtz, C.B., 1955. The American Camaenidae (Mollusca: Pulmonata). Proc. Acad. Nat. Sci. Phila., vol. 107: 99-143, pls. 1-19.

Zilch, A., 1964. Die Typen und Typoide des Natur-Museums Senckenberg. Camaenidae. Archiv. Moll., vol. 93 (5/6): 243-262, pl. 6.

Genus *Amphidromus*

(see Pilsbry, H.A., *Manual of Conchology*, series 2, vol. 13, pp. 127-234, pls. 46-71, 1900).

Family CAMAENIDAE. *Amphidromus martensi* Boettger, 1894. Northeast Borneo. 5 cm. See p. 160.

Barnett, James L., 1985. Philippine Land Snails of the Genus *Amphidromus*. Carfel Philippine Shell News, vol. 7 (2): 3; 1985, *ibid.*, vol. 7 (3): 4; 1985, *ibid.*, vol. 7 (4): 10.

Bartsch, Paul, 1917. The Philippine Land Shells of the genus *Amphidromus*. Bull. 1, U.S. Nat. Mus.: 1-47, pls. 1-22.

———, 1918. The Landshells of the Genus *Amphidromus* from the Islands of the Palawan Passage. Jour. Wash. Acad., vol. 8: 60-63.

Laidlaw, Frank F. and Alan Solem, 1961. The Land Snail Genus *Amphidromus*--a Synoptic Catalogue, Fieldiana: Zoology, vol. 41, no. 4, pp. 505-677.

Solem, Alan, 1965. Land snails of the genus *Amphidromus* from Thailand. Proc. U.S. Nat. Mus., vol. 117 (3519): 615-628, 2 pls.

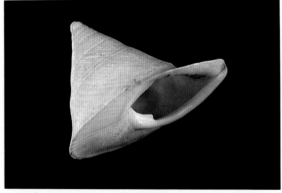

Family CAMAENIDAE. Subfamily Papuininae. *Papuina steursiana* (Pfeiffer, 1853). New Guinea. 4 cm. See p. 149.

Subfamily **Papuininae.** Main genera: *Papuina* von Martens, 1860; *Crystallopsis* Ancey, 1887; *Forcartia* Clench and Turner, 1962; *Megalacron* Rensch, 1934; *Meliobba* Iredale, 1940; *Papuanella* Clench and Turner, 1959; *Papustyla* Pilsbry, 1893; *Rhynchotrochus* Möllendorff, 1895; *Smeatonia* Iredale, 1941; *Solmotella* Iredale, 1941.

(see L. Richardson, 1985, above for list of species and genera with their original references).

(see Pilsbry, H.A., *Manual of Conchology*, series 2, vol. 7, pp. 1-89, pls. 1-15, 1891).

Family **XANTHONYCHIDAE**
(syn.: Helminthoglyptidae; Cepolidae)

Andrews, E., 1932. Some Habits of a Cuban Snail, *Polymita picta* Born. The Nautilus, vol. 46: 22-27.

Baker, H.B., 1961. Puerto Rican Xanthonychidae. The Nautilus, vol. 74 (4): 142-149.

Berry, S.S., 1940. A proposed dichotomy of the snail genus *Monadenia*. Bull. So. Calif. Acad. Sci., vol. 38 (3): 203-204.

Pilsbry, H.A., 1927. The structure and affinities of *Humboldtiana* and related helicid genera of Mexico and Texas. Proc. Acad. Nat. Sci. Phila., vol. 79: 165-192, pls. 11-14.

Richardson, Leonard, 1982. Helminthoglyptidae [is Xanthonycidae]: Catalog of Species. *Tryonia*, no. 6, pp. 1-117. List of thousands of species arranged by genera and the subfamilies Cepolinae, pp. 1-29 (includes *Cepolis* and *Polymita*); Helminthoglyptinae, pp. 30-63; Humboltianinae, pp. 64-67; Sonorellinae, pp. 67-81; Xanthonycinae, pp. 81-86. Large bibliography, pp. 88-95.

Roth, B. and P.H. Pressley, 1986. Observations on the range and natural history of *Monadenia setosa* in the Klamath Mountains, California, and the taxonomy of some related species. Veliger, vol. 29 (2): 169-182, illus.

Torre, de la, Carlos, 1950. El Género *Polymita*. Mem. Soc. Cubana Hist. Nat., vol. 20 (1): 5-10, pls. 1-11.

Subfamily **Xanthonychinae**. <u>Main genera</u>: *Xanthonyx* Crosse and Fischer, 1867; *Bunnya* H.B. Baker, 1941; *Leptarionta* Crosse and Fischer, 1872.

Family XANTHONYCHIDAE. Subfamily Helminthoglyptinae. *Polymita picta* (Born, 1778). 2 cm. p. 162.

Subfamily **Helminthoglyptinae**. <u>Main genera</u>: *Helminthoglypta* Ancey, 1887; *Epiphragmophora* Döring, 1873; *Glyptostoma* Bland and Binney, 1873; *Greggelix* W.B. Miller, 1972; *Humboldtiana* von Ihering, 1892; *Micrarionta* Ancey, 1880; *Monadenia* Pilsbry, 1895; *Polymita* Beck, 1837; *Sonorella* Pilsbry, 1900.

Subfamily **Cepolinae**. <u>Two main genera</u>: *Cepolis* Montfort, 1810 (with subgenera: *Coryda* Albers, 1850; *Hemitrochus* Swainson, 1840; *Plagioptycha* Pfeiffer, 1856); *Dialeuca* Albers, 1850.

Subfamily **Oreohelicidae**. <u>Main genera</u>. *Oreohelix* Pilsbry, 1904; Pilsbry, 1905.

Pilsbry, H.A., 1948. Inland mollusks of northern Mexico. I. The genera *Humboldtiana*, *Sonorella*, *Oreohelix* and *Ashmunella*. Proc. Acad. Nat. Sci. Phila., vol. 100: 185-203, pls. 12-14.

Richardson, Leonard, 1984. Oreohelicidae: Catalog of Species. *Tryonia*, Acad. Nat. Sci. Phila., no. 10: 1-30.

Subfamily **Oopeltinae**. <u>Sole genus</u>: *Oopelta* Mörch, 1867.

Family **BRADYBAENIDAE**

Barnett, James L., 1983. Philippine Landsnails: *Helicostyla* subsections *Chrysallis* and *Prochilus*. Carfel Philippine Shell News, vol. 5 (2): 5-6; also vol. 5 (6): 3-4; vol. 7 (2): 5; vol. 5 (3): 5, 6; vol. 5 (5): 3.

——, 1985. The *Helicostyla* of Batanes. *Ibid.*, vol. 7 (6): 10. Nomenclature obsolete.

Bartsch, Paul, 1932. The Tree Snails of the genus *Cochlostyla* of Mindoro Province, Philippines. Jour. Wash. Acad. Sci., vol. 22 (12): 335-344.

——, 1932. The Philippine Land Mollusks *Cochlostyla rufogaster* and *Obba marmorata* and their Races. Bull. 6 (6), U.S. Nat. Mus.: 329-342, pls. 83-86.

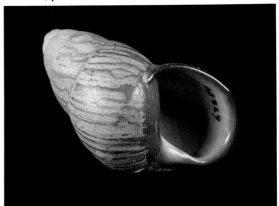

Family BRADYBAENIDAE. Subfamily Helicostylinae. *Helicostyla satyrus* (Broderip, 1841). Philippines. p. 172.

——, 1938. The Tree Snails of the genus Cochlostyla of Mindoro Province, Philippine Islands. Bull. 100 (6), U.S. Nat. Mus.: 373-533, pls. 94-120.

Clench, W.J. and A.F. Archer, 1931. Land Shells from Lubang Island, Philippines. Occ. Papers Boston Soc. Nat. Hist., vol. 5: 333-337, pl. 17.

——, 1933. Land Mollusks from the Islands Mindoro and Lubang, Philippines. Papers Michigan Acad. Sci., vol. 17: 535-552, pl. 57-58.

Hidalgo, J.G., 1890. Obras Malacológicas, Part I. Estudios Preliminares sobre la Fauna Malacológica de las Islas Filipinas. Mem. Acad. Cienc. Nat. Madrid, vol. 14: 1-160; 1901, vol. 5: 161-632 of part I; 593-608 of part 3, 15 pls.

Kobelt, W., 1905-1916. Landmollusken [Helicostylids] in Semper, C., Reisen im Archipel der Philippinen. Wissenschaftliche Resultate 10, vol. 3, 367 pp., 82 pls. (17 parts).

Richardson, Leonard, 1983. Bradybaenidae: Catalog of Species. *Tryonia*, no. 9, pp. 1-253. Acad. Nat. Sci. Phila. [Helicostylinae, pp. 102-192; bibliography, pp. 193-207].

Zilch, A., 1968. Die Typen und Typoide des Natur-Museums

Senckenberg, no. 41, Bradybaeninae. Arch. für Mollusk, vol. 82: 131-140, pls. 21-25.

——, 1982. Die Typen und Typoide des Natur-Museums Senckenberg. Bradybaenidae (2): Helicostylinae. Archiv für Mollusk., vol. 112 (1-6): 49-156, pls. 1-4.

Family BRADYBAENIDAE. Subfamily Helicostylinae. *Calocochlia pulcherrima* (Sowerby, 1841). Philippines. 5 cm. See p. 167.

Subfamily **Bradybaeninae**. Main genera: *Bradybaena* Beck, 1837; *Aegista* Albers, 1850; *Cathaica* Möllendorff, 1884; *Euhadra* Pilsbry, 1890; *Pseudobuliminus* Gredler, 1886.

Subfamily **Helicostylinae**. Main genera: *Helicostyla* Férussac, 1821 (with subgenera *Cochlodryas* von Martens, 1860; *Dryocochlias* Möllendorff, 1898; *Helicobulina* Broderip, 1841 (+ *Chromatocochlias* Agassiz, 1846; *Coenobita* Gistl, 1848); *Hypselostyla* von Martens, 1868; *Opalliostyla* Pilsbry, 1896; *Orustia* Mörch, 1853; *Pachysphaera* Pilsbry, 1892); *Calocochlia* Hartmann, 1840 (subgenera *Anixa* Pilsbry, 1894 (+ *Axina* Albers, 1850); *Pyrochilus* Pilsbry, 1892); *Canistrum* Mörch, 1852; *Chloraea* Albers, 1850 (subgenera: *Chromatosphaera* Pilsbry, 1892; *Leytia* Pilsbry, 1892; *Corasia* Albers, 1850; *Pfeifferia* Gray, 1853); *Chrysallis* Albers, 1850 (subgenus *Dolichostyla* Pilsbry, 1896 (+ *Prochilus* Albers, 1860); *Mesanella* Clench and Turner, 1952; *Phengus* Albers, 1850; *Phoenicobius* Mörch, 1852; *Steatodryas* Pilsbry, 1932.

(see Richardson, L., 1983, above for list of species).

(see Pilsbry, H.A., *Manual of Conchology*, series 2, vol. 7, pp. 89-210, pls. 25-61, 1892; vol. 8, pp. 5-54, pls. 1-15, 1892).

Family HELICELLIDAE

Main genera: *Helicella* Férussac, 1821; *Candidula* Kobelt, 1871; *Cernuella* Schlüter, 1838; *Cochlicella* Férussac, 1820; *Leuchrochroa* Beck, 1837; *Monacha* Fitzinger, 1833; *Trochoidea* Brown, 1827; *Xeropicta* and *Xerosecta* Monterosato, both 1892.

(see Tryon, George W., Jr., *Manual of Conchology*, vol. 4, 1888).

Gude, G.K. and B.B. Woodward, 1921. On *Helicella*; Férussac. Proc. Mal. Soc. London, vol. 14: 174-190.

Hesse, P., 1926. Beiträge zur genaueren Kenntnis der Subfamilie Helicellinae. Archiv für Moll., vol. 58: 113-141.

Family HYGROMIIDAE

Uvalieva, K.K., 1986. [Key to land molluscs of the family Hygromiidae of Kazakhstan and Central Asia]. Izvestiya Akad. Nauk Kazakh. SSR (Biol), 1986 (2): 29-35, illus.

Subfamily **Hygromiinae**. Major genera: *Hygromia* Risso, 1826; *Angiomphala* Shileyko, 1978; *Euomphalia* Westerlund, 1889; *Monachoides* Gude and Woodward, 1921; *Stenomphalia* Lindholm, 1927; *Zenobiella* Gude and Woodward, 1921.

Subfamily **Trichiinae**. Major genera: *Trichia* Hartmann, 1841; *Leucozonella* Lindholm, 1927; *Plicuteria* Shileyko, 1978; *Xerocampylea* Kobelt, 1871.

Subfamily **Halolimnohelicininae**. Single genus: *Halolimnohelix* Germain, 1913.

Family HELICIDAE

Adensamer, W., 1937. *Cylindrus obtusus* (Draparnaud, 1805) seine relikthafte Verbreitung . . . Viriabilität . . . zoogeographisch . . . Archiv Moll., vol. 69: 66-115, 1 pl.

Albers, J.C., 1850. Die Heliceen, nach natürlicher Verwandtschaft systematisch geordnet. 262 pp. Berlin.

Baker, H.B., 1943. Some Antillean Helicidae. The Nautilus, vol. 56: 81-91.

Boettger, C.R. and W. Wenz, 1921. Zur Systematik der zu den Helicidensubfamilien Campylaeinae . . . . Arch. Moll., vol. 53: 6-55.

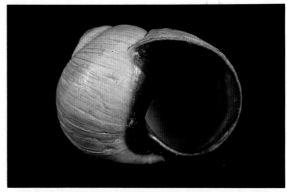

Family HELICIDAE. *Helix melanostoma* Draparnaud, 1801. Southern France. 2.5 cm. See p. 189.

Cesari, Paolo, 1978. Il genere *Helix*. La Malacofauna del Territorio Italiano. Conchiglie, vol. 14 (3-6): 35-90, pls. 1-12. (excellent).

Germain, L., 1929. Les Helicidae de la faune française. Archives Mus. Nat. Lyon, vol. 13: 1-422, pl. 1.

Gittenberger, E., 1979. On *Elona*: Elonidae, Family nov. Malacologia, vol. 18: 139-145.

Gude, G.K., 1903. A classified list of the helicoid land shells of Asia. Jour. of Malacol., vol. 10 (2): 45-62, pl. 3.

Ibañez, M., K. Groh, et al, 1987. Revision of the genus *Hemicycla* Swainson, 1840 on Tenerife: the group of *Hemicycla plicaria* (Lamarck, 1816). Arch. Moll., vol. 118, nos. 1/3, pp. 77-103.

Mandahl-Barth, G., 1950. Systematische Untersuchungen über die Heliciden-Fauna von Madeira. Abh. Senckenb. Naturf. Ges., vol. 469 (1943): 1-93, pls. 1-17.

Richardson, Leonard, 1980. Helicidae: Catalog of Species. *Tryonia*, no. 3, part 1, pp. 1-697 [complete list arranged by subfamilies and genera]: Campylaeinae, pp. 1-60; Geomitrinae, pp. 61-80;

Helicellinae, pp. 80-255; Helicinae, pp. 256-350; in Part 2, pp. 351-422; Helicodontinae, pp. 422-436; Hygromiinae, pp. 437-498; Leptaxinae, pp. 499-505; Sphincterochilinae, pp. 505-506. Lists over 7000 names. Large bibliography, pp. 516-547. Index to names, pp. 548-696.

von Ihering, H., 1919. Analyse der Süd-Amerikanischen Heliceen. Jour. Acad. Nat. Sci. Phila., vol. 15: 475-500.

Family HELICIDAE. *Alabastrina hieroglyphica* (Michaud, 1833). Algiers. 2.5 cm. See p. 191.

Subfamily **Helicinae.** Main genera: *Helix* Linnaeus, 1758; *Alabastrina* Kobelt, 1904; *Cepaea* Held, 1837; *Codringtonia* Kobelt, 1898; *Eobania* Hesse, 1913; *Eremina* Pfeiffer, 1855; *Hemicycla* Swainson, 1840; *Iberus* Montfort, 1810; *Levantina* Kobelt, 1871; *Macularia* Albers, 1850; *Murella* Pfeiffer, 1877; *Otala* Schumacher, 1817; *Theba* Risso, 1826.

Subfamily **Geomitrinae.** Main genera: *Geomitra* Swainson, 1840; *Discula* Lowe, 1852; *Spirorbula* Lowe, 1852; *Tectula* Lowe, 1852.

Subfamily **Helicigoninae.** (syn.: Campylaeinae). Main genera: *Helicigona* Férussac, in Risso, 1826; *Arianta* Leach in Turton, 1831; *Campylaea* Beck, 1837; *Cylindrus* Fitzinger, 1833; *Elona* H. and A. Adams, 1855.

Subfamily **Helicodontinae.** Main genera: *Helicodonta* Férussac in Risso, 1826; *Drepanostoma* Porro, 1836; *Soosia* Hesse, 1918.

Family SPHINCTEROCHILIDAE
Sole genus: *Sphincterochila* Ancey, 1887.
Forcart, L., 1972. Systematische: gattung Sphincterochila. Arch. Moll., vol. 102 (4/6): 147-164.

Superfamily ARIONOIDEA
Sluglike pulmonates, not treated in this book.
Chichester; L.E., 1973. The terrestrial slugs of northeastern North America. Sterkiana, vol. 51: 11-42.
Chichester, L.E. and L.L. Getz, 1969. The zoogeography and ecology of arionid and limacid slugs introduced into northeastern North America. Malacologia, vol. 7: 313-346.
Climo, F.M., 1969-71. Classification of New Zealand Arionacea. Records Dominion Mus., vols. 6, 7.
Cockerell, T.D.A., 1891. On the geographical distribution of slugs. Proc. Zool. Soc. London, 1891: 214-226.

Family ARIONIDAE

Subfamily **Arioninae.** Sluglike genera with reduced or wanting internal shell: *Arion* Férussac, 1819; *Arionculus* Lesson, 1881.

Subfamily **Binneyinae.** Two genera: *Binneya* Cooper, 1863; *Hemphillia* Bland and Binney, 1872.

Subfamily **Ariolimacinae.** Sluglike genera with reduced or wanting internal shell: *Ariolimax* Mörch, 1859; *Hesperarion* Simroth, 1891.

Subfamily **Anadeninae.** Sluglike genera with reduced internal shell: *Aradenus* Heynemann, 1863; *Prophysaon* Bland and Binney, 1873.

Family PHILOMYCIDAE
Sluglike genera, without shells: *Philomycus* Rafinesque, 1820; *Pallifera* Morse, 1864.

Order SYSTELLOMMATOPHORA

Sluglike animals, without shells. Pulmonary cavity posterior. Worldwide. Superfamily Onchidioidea, marine intertidal; superfamily Veronicelloidea with families of slugs, Veronicellidae; the Asian carnivores Rathouisiidae; and the tiny, wormlike, intertidal Rhodopidae. None treated in this book.

Boss, Kenneth J., 1982 (in S.P. Parker, Synopsis and Classification of Living Organisms, vol. 1, pp. 1082-1090. [key references].
Britton, K.M., 1984. Onchidiacea: worldwide review. Jour. Moll. Studies, vol. 50: 179-191.

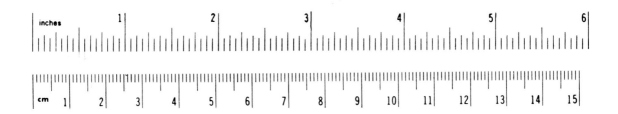

Acknowledgments

Many kind private collectors and professional malacologists from all parts of the world assisted me in assembling this book. I thank them all for their gracious help. Photograph credits, except for those I took, are mentioned alongside of the appropriate illustrations. I especially wish to thank the mollusk curators at several museums where I was granted permission to carry out research: United States National Museum, Smithsonian Institution, in Washington; the Museum of Comparative Zoology at Harvard University; the Academy of Natural Sciences of Philadelphia; the Florida Museum of Natural History, Gainesville; the American Museum of Natural History, New York; the Field Museum of Natural History, Chicago; the British Museum (of Natural History), London; the Australian Museum, Sydney; the Instituto de Ecologia y Sistemática (Poey Museum), Academia de Ciencias de Cuba, Havana; and the private landshell collections of Dr. Harry G. Lee, Jacksonville, Florida; Richard Goldberg, Long Island, New York; Ronald Knight, Manus Island, Papua New Guinea; and Archie Jones of Miami, Florida.

My particular thanks go to those who read and assisted in the preparation of the manuscript: Dr. Fred Thompson; Richard Goldberg; Cecelia Abbott; and Joyce Dance (of TransType, Edisto Island, South Carolina).

About the Author

R. TUCKER ABBOTT is one of the leading conchologists of the world, having served as a research scientist and field collector for forty years at Harvard University, the Smithsonian Institution and the Academy of Natural Sciences of Philadelphia. Dr. Abbott has led numerous expeditions for mollusks to China, the Philippines, Africa, Cuba and other out-of-the-way collecting grounds. He was Editor-in-Chief of *The Nautilus*, one of the oldest and most influential scientific periodicals concerned with malacology, and also the author of numerous popular books including *American Seashells, Kingdom of the Seashell* and the *Compendium of Seashells*. He is now Founding Director of the new Shell Museum on Sanibel Island, Florida.

Florida Conservation News observed, "R. Tucker Abbott is to seashell collectors what John J. Audubon was to birdwatchers, and his books on seashell identification form the backbone of most shell collectors' libraries."

Wending her lonely way across a Jamaican leaf this tiny woodland traveller seeks out a mate. Her operculum is worn like a bonnet upon the back of her foot, and ahead are two outstretched tentacles. *Parachondrops jarvisi* Henderson, 1901. Photo: Richard Goldberg.

INDEX TO SCIENTIFIC NAMES